CUBA AND THE UNITED STATES

CUBA AND THE UNITED STATES
Intervention and Militarism, 1868–1933

José M. Hernández

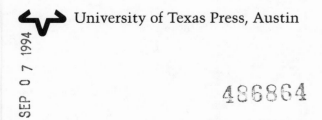 University of Texas Press, Austin

Requests for permission to reproduce material from this work
should be sent to Permissions, University of Texas Press, Box 7819,
Austin, TX 78713-7819.

∞ The paper used in this publication meets the minimum
requirements of American National Standard for Information
Sciences—Permanence of Paper for Printed Library Materials,
ANSI Z39.48-1984.

Library of Congress Cataloging-in-Publication Data

Hernández, José M.
    Cuba and the United States : intervention and militarism,
    1868–1933 / José M. Hernández. — 1st ed.
        p.   cm.
    Includes bibliographical references and index.
    ISBN 0-292-73073-X
        1. United States—Foreign relations—Cuba.   2. Cuba—
    Foreign relations—United States.   I. Title.
    E183.8.C9H47   1993
    327.7307291—dc20   92-21342

To Elena, my wife

Contents

Preface

To set out to reconstruct the past of any nation is never an easy task, and to reconstruct Cuba's past is by no means an exception. This is attributable to a variety of factors. To begin with, there is the vexing problem of Cuban archival collections, whose access has been at best uncertain during the last thirty years and has often hinged on the political credentials (or lack thereof) of the researcher. Then there is the fairly extensive Cuban practice of making available private papers only to sympathetic and trustworthy individuals. Finally, there is the ultimate unreliability of secondary sources, much of which is the work of amateur historians whose approach is generally uncritical and who are frequently impervious to impartiality. There are, to be sure, the usual number of above-average publications that have illuminated some aspects of Cuba's history. But serious scholars would do well not to be overly impressed by the large number of works on certain phases, nor by the alacritous unanimity with which these works subscribe to certain conclusions and accept or deny certain facts.

This caveat is particularly pertinent in regard to the voluminous literature produced by the study of the Cuban wars of independence (1868–1898). That this should be a period about which it has been difficult for Cubans to write with any degree of objectivity is perhaps to be expected, as it is to be assumed that Spaniards have experienced the same sort of difficulty. But it is one thing to narrate the wars from a Cuban point of view and an entirely different thing to obscure reality with the romantic foliage of nationalistic fervor—overstating or embellishing some facts, glossing over others, and even setting aside those that prove too embarrassing or too mystifying to be handled otherwise.

This kind of rhapsodic history, into which so many Cubans have fallen (as well as some foreign authors), has provided the stuff of the Cuban myth of national redemption and has populated the pantheon of glittering heroes and saintly martyrs that is without doubt its most important constituent element. Yet the image of rebel Cuba that emerges from its pages is sometimes anything but real. Apart from a few well-known partial accounts, which are undeniably useful, there is as yet no first-class comprehensive history of the Cuban independence movement. Above all, no one thus far has been able to shake off the intellectual constraints imposed by the myth—to do away with all the fetishes and to look at the period from a new and detached perspective.

On the contrary, the influence of this *independentista* perspective has become so pervasive that it has come to dominate Cuban historiography as a whole. As a consequence, Cuban people and events, especially those of the nineteenth and early twentieth centuries (but also of the sixteenth, unlikely as it may seem!), have been uniformly categorized in a strictly Manichean fashion: on the one hand, the good, the advocates of independence, those who fought and died to achieve it; on the other, the evil or the shortsighted, the apostates who joined hands with the odious metropolis, those who opposed or did not actively pursue emancipation from the Spanish yoke. This polarization of forces perhaps fits a gest or a political manifesto, but is completely alien to historical study and its methods. It has, for one, made it extremely difficult to render a clear presentation of Cuba's problems. For, to cite just the most obvious instance, how are dispassionate historians to undertake the study of the words and deeds of Cuba's liberators if an institutionalized national consciousness insists on regarding them as "prophets, apostles, and Christs," as José Martí (Cuba's foremost hero) was once portrayed? Or, to mention another example closer to the subject matter of this volume, how can we truly assess the impact of immediate postindependence events such as the U.S. interventions of 1898–1902 and 1906–1909 if, in order to do so, we must deal not with the historical consequences of just another protracted war of national liberation but with the legacy of a struggle of nearly epic proportions?

These are precisely the questions that I pose in this book. I have endeavored to sweep away the deadweight of nationalistic excess (and, en passant, the accompanying rhetorical excess) from the history of Cuba's independence movement and have striven instead to regard it as a process of merely human dimensions, a sequence of events that was carried out by some great men and punctuated with some heroic deeds, but one that also laid bare a number of weaknesses and shortcomings and had some unwelcome results. It is only in this light, I believe, that the significance of the early U.S. interferences in Cuban affairs can be fully understood, and for this reason I have devoted many pages to the Cuban struggle against Spain and the vicissitudes that the Cuban liberating army subsequently went through. Eventually, advances in research through the collaborative effort of many historians will further clarify the realities of this period. I can only hope that this book will be considered part of that effort.

I began to realize that I would have to direct my research in that direction when, in the course of my reflections, I began to wonder how far Cuba's evolution after independence had diverged from that of other Latin American republics. Two separate events had to be examined in this connection: the achievement of political emancipation and the U.S. interventions. I set out to go through them as thoroughly as I could. Since then, I have traveled a long and arduous road in an intellectual journey that I could not possibly have completed without the help and encouragement of many friends and colleagues. Among them I must single out for special recognition a number of Georgetown colleagues: in the History department, Jules Davids, Thomas J. Dodd, Jr., and Luis E. Aguilar-León; in the Spanish department, Enrico Mario Santí and Roberto Esquenazi-Mayo. I must mention too Professor Enrique Baloyra, of the University of Miami, and Reverend Manuel Maza, S.J., one of my graduate students, who also read the manuscript and made valuable suggestions. It would have been impossible for me to have access to all the sources I needed without the assistance of the staff of the Hispanic Division of the Library of Congress, most especially that of Georgette Dorn and Dolores Martin. I am deeply indebted to them for their help.

Of course, no one contributed as much to the completion of this book as my wife, Elena, who helped in so many elusive and subtle ways.

Despite all this kind support and advice, however, no one but me should be held responsible for the opinions, interpretations, and conclusions included in the pages that follow. All the errors, misjudgments, and biases must be exclusively recorded on the debit side of my ledger.

Introduction

Militarism is considered in this book to be the domination of the domestic affairs of a given country by its armed forces. After attaining independence from Spain, Latin American countries typically have experienced this condition, which has been associated with the violent making and unmaking of governments, outright or masked dictatorships, and, not infrequently, financial mismanagement. At times, strongmen have been able to perpetuate themselves in power and force themselves upon the people for lengthy intervals of personal rule. But, especially toward the beginning of the national period and most particularly in certain countries, the struggle for spoils and power among soldier-politicians ushered in chaotic political situations where would-be caudillos and petty tyrants rose and fell with amazing rapidity and no one, individual or institution, was able to guarantee life and property. Such was the situation that the United States had to face in the Caribbean and Central America after its emergence as a world power following the Spanish-American War.

The Colossus of the North reacted to what it regarded as threats to its imperial interests by intervening militarily in five countries: Cuba, Haiti, the Dominican Republic, Panama, and Nicaragua. In all five cases the goal of intervention was to restore order and build up an institutional base for stability in the future. This effort invariably included the training of constabularies or a similar type of armed force that would be capable of preserving internal order in behalf of duly elected officials. It seemed obvious that without such responsible, nonpolitical military establishments, democratic governments would lack a fulcrum of power on which to rely in times of crisis.

As though to prove once again that political events unfold according to a perverse logic of their own, the policies so neatly delineated by the United States for the five occupied countries backfired without exception. In Haiti, between 1915 and 1934, the U.S. Marines trained a 3,000-man constabulary. Upon the marines' departure, this force quickly resumed the traditional political activities of the Haitian military and ultimately turned into the mainstay of Colonel Paul Magloire's dictatorship in 1950. The Dominican Republic fared no better after an eight-year occupation (1916–1924). Suffice it to say that the awesome Rafael Leónidas Trujillo, who subsequently ruled the country for thirty-one years, was precisely the man whom the marine officers left at the head of the newly organized Dominican army upon their withdrawal. No such specimen sprang up in Panama, U.S. protectorate for three decades. But the Panamanian national police, created in deference to U.S. wishes and later reformed by the marines, eventually became the preeminent political force in the country. By the 1940s its chief was openly seating and unseating civilian presidents, a practice that lasted until 1952, when the chief himself, Colonel José Antonio Remón, took charge of the government. This is also what General Anastasio Somoza did in Nicaragua in 1936, taking advantage, Trujillo-style, of his position as chief of the U.S.-trained Nicaraguan National Guard. It was thus that a country where U.S. armed intervention had been the rule since 1912 finally was transformed into the private domain of the Somoza family and the Nicaraguan Guard.

No one will venture to affirm that the stability-enforcing policies of the United States proved more successful in the case of Cuba. But the similarities between events in Cuba and what happened in the other countries are more apparent than real. The United States occupied Cuba two times, the first in 1898 and the second in 1906, and on both occasions U.S. authorities concerned themselves with the problem of stable government and building up efficient and responsible armed bodies capable of supporting it adequately. During the first occupation a small rural guard was created for this purpose, and this guard was reorganized, retrained, and expanded during the second. Yet this force did not produce a political leader of any consequence nor did it become the cradle of a new political elite. As part of the army that was subsequently organized by the Cuban governments, the guards did participate in the revolts and attempts at revolt of the republican era and were frequently involved in the fraud and coercion that characterized many Cuban elections. Neither coups nor revolutions, however, broke the rhythm of constitutional life on the island before 1933; and although its first dictator (Gerardo Machado) was a general, his right to that appellation derived from his feats as a freedom fighter during the wars of independence. The armed forces that gave him support had been reorganized several

times after the last U.S. occupation and were only remotely connected with the actions taken by U.S. authorities at that time.

Given the undeniable political role of the Cuban military between
1909 and 1933, how can we then postulate that U.S. policy also
failed to check irresponsible militarism in the case of Cuba? The
key fact that must be noted apropos of this problem is that the ones
who controlled political life in the island throughout this period
were the veterans of the struggle against Spain, the generation of
lesser heroes which, on account of the early demise of the truly great
leaders, was able to establish itself as a dominant political caste. By
this it is not meant solely that its members held high offices, formed
powerful associations to advance their interests, and were thus able
to secure for themselves a substantial share of the national budget.
What is signified more precisely is that these men, while paying lip
service to constitutionalism and affecting to care for orderliness, actually behaved much like the liberators of the Spanish American
mainland four generations before. Like them, the Cuban veterans
made politics their own plaything, transformed democratic processes into a mocking pretense, and monopolized the spoils of office
for their own benefit and that of their followers. Because Cuba was
then also a U.S. protectorate, they could not have recourse to violence as openly, frequently, and successfully as their Spanish American counterparts. But they managed, to a large extent, to control the
mechanisms for the transfer of power and thus subject the nation to
their whims.

In the case of Cuba, therefore, historical analysis must focus not
on the ultimate success or failure of the military reforms carried out
by the two interventions, but on the way in which the United States
reacted to the presence of a largely irregular force of liberators who
had been involved in a long, bloody fight for independence and were
anxious to reap the fruits of their strenuous efforts. Essentially what
happened is that for reasons more directly related to U.S. politics
than to the Cuban situation, the second intervention ran contrary
to the first. In 1898 the chief goal of U.S. policy was to assert U.S.
control over Cuba. Consequently, the Cuban liberating army was
forced to disband and the potential political influence of the veterans was neutralized as much as possible within the framework of
the political system approved for the island. In 1906, however, the
main U.S. preoccupation was to "keep Cuba quiet," as befitted the
political interests of the incumbent administration. As a result,
doors were opened to the former generals and colonels who made up
the leadership of the rebellious Liberal party as well as to the chieftains of the factions that came after them. Provided they would

not indulge in destructive excesses, the United States was willing to tolerate them, even if it meant constantly interfering in the affairs of the country in an attempt to avoid yet another large-scale occupation.

It is the purpose of this work to study the historical process described above. Some facts will be revealed; others will be reconstructed or reinterpreted; still others will simply be put in a new perspective. Hopefully the truth will be served. This is a subject on which there is a dearth of monographic studies, for to a large extent it has been treated as part of more comprehensive surveys or as an introduction to investigative efforts concentrated on more recent developments. Works on the civil-military problem during the Cuban wars of independence are virtually nonexistent, nor is there any account isolating for the purpose of analysis the efforts that some Cubans made at the time to save their country from the ills that plagued the other Latin American republics after political emancipation. Yet all these problems and efforts, regardless of whether they succeeded or failed, are the substance of which the Cuban politico-military tradition is made. Knowledge of this tradition is central to an understanding of the subsequent evolution of Cuba. It is the purpose of this study to trace its origin and explain how it came into being.

CUBA AND THE UNITED STATES

1. The Struggle for Independence

"My most ardent desire is that this war end quickly. It is not only laying waste the country, but also transforming its inhabitants into soldiers. Soldierly habits are not conducive to the reconstruction of a nation like ours that has been under a military dictatorship for so many years."[1] So wrote General Calixto García in the spring of 1898, as he watched the unfolding of the events that eventually culminated in the intervention of the United States in the 1895–1898 Cuban war of independence.

At the time, García was second in command of the Cuban liberating army, a position that represented the high-water mark in an illustrious career as a freedom fighter that spanned over three decades. Born in 1839, he had lived through many of the changes that had shaken both the metropolis and the colony throughout the nineteenth century. No doubt he knew well what he was referring to when he wrote the remarks quoted above.[2]

The Spanish Colonial Rule

In all likelihood what the general meant by "military dictatorship" was the fact that Cuba had remained under the rigors of martial law during much of the time after the liberation of the Spanish mainland colonies (1825–1878). The government of the island had always been of a military character, for Havana lay in a place of commanding importance in the Caribbean, and therefore the Spanish authorities had never thought of entrusting it to a civilian.[3] Before 1825, nevertheless, the so-called Key to the Indies usually had been garrisoned by relatively few regular troops, although there had been also an urban militia and a rural colonial one. The latter especially had been composed almost exclusively of creoles, who had gradually succeeded in penetrating the regular officer corps. Thus by 1808, when Napoleon invaded Spain and the empire began to disintegrate, creoles were in control of both the regulars and the militia. For all intents and purposes they were the masters of their own destiny.[4]

As it happened, Cubans then chose to remain loyal to the Spanish king. But as a new decade opened in 1820, crucial events taking place on both sides of the Atlantic began to change the political outlook. The first of these events was the temporary collapse of absolutism in the Peninsula, the result of yet another manifestation of the militaristic tendencies that had developed in the Spanish army during the struggle against Napoleon.[5] The second was the defeat suffered by the Spanish army at Ayacucho, Peru (1824). This battle for all practical purposes signaled the end of Spanish rule in Central and South America; from then on, the islands of Cuba and Puerto Rico were all that remained of the Spanish empire in the New World. The third event was the emergence within the Cuban creole population of a rather small group that began to consider seriously the prospect of independence.[6] The combined effect of these events was to heighten to an unprecedented degree Spain's traditional reliance on armed force to rule and defend its overseas possessions. As a consequence, the predominance that the military achieved in Spain in the nineteenth century became even more marked in Cuba, and the island was subjected to the most authoritarian regime that any Spanish American colony ever had to endure.[7]

First, however, Cubans had an opportunity that no other Spanish Americans had before 1808[8]—to witness a full-fledged mutiny of Spanish troops, in this particular case the revolt that forced Captain General Juan Manuel Cagigal to restore in the colony the Spanish Constitution of 1812. More than that, Cubans were able to see how the commanders of the rebellious battalion were rewarded with important positions in the colonial government. There was no doubt that the new political ill that was plaguing the Peninsula was rapidly spreading overseas, as was also evidenced by the further disciplinary breakdowns in the ranks of the troops stationed on the island that occurred while the liberal interregnum lasted.[9] These instances of insubordination became precedents for future excesses, but the military unrest had abated somewhat by the time the Spanish monarchy regained its autocratic powers in April 1823.

Several months later the incumbent captain general, Francisco Dionisio Vives, discovered and suppressed the Soles y Rayos de Bolívar conspiracy, a movement advocating independence and the abolition of slavery.[10] Vives owed his appointment to the liberal regime, but he quickly aligned himself with the policies of absolutism and clamped an iron hand on Cuba, thenceforth striving forcefully to keep dissidence in check. Conspiratorial activities (either instigated

by Bolívar or the Mexicans) were almost constant during his administration, however, and he requested extraordinary powers to deal
with them. After some hesitation (and after yet another conspiracy
was crushed in 1824), he was granted authority such as no captain
general before him had ever had. By the decree of May 28, 1825,
he was invested with *facultades omnímodas,* that is, all-embracing
powers similar to those usually given to "governors of besieged
strongholds." Thus Vives could "banish from the island such persons, whether or not they be employed by the government, whatever
their occupation, rank, class, or station in life, whose residence in
its territory may be considered detrimental, or whose public or private behavior may seem suspicious." Indeed, so sweeping were his
powers that in fact he could do much as he pleased: he could confine
to a dungeon for life, ostracize, confiscate the property of, or otherwise punish whomever he chose. Not even the awesome authority
of the monarchy could stand in his way, for he was also granted
the power "to suspend the enforcement of royal commands and
decrees . . . that could be adjudged prejudicial to the King's service"
and to issue instead the provisional orders that he deemed advisable. The instrument for the enforcement of such orders was a
newly established military tribunal called the Permanent Executive
Military Commission, which was empowered to try political crimes
and those committed in uninhabited areas. Since this commission
superseded the civil courts, thenceforward unsuccessful conspirators could not hope that, if captured, their lives would be spared, as
had often happened before.[11]

Vives had also complained to Madrid about the meagerness of his
military resources, and thus some of the troops defeated in the
mainland were redeployed to Cuba. It was at this time that the island assumed the appearance of an armed camp, for at one point it
was garrisoned by more than forty thousand men.[12] Everything was
placed under military surveillance—commerce, travel, social affairs,
even the most personal activities. More often than not it was impossible for a private citizen to entertain a stranger at his house without
prior notice to the local police. The press was strictly censored, and
so were the theater and opera.[13] Public assemblies and meetings
were banned. Mention of independence, public references to political reform, even discussions of the evil of slavery were forbidden.
The entry of foreigners was severely limited, and the importation of
books that attacked the Catholic religion or the rights and prerogatives of the monarchy, or that in any other way advocated the rebellion of vassals or nations, was prohibited. As José Martí said many
years later, Cuba thus became a huge "prison surrounded by wa-

ter"[14] over which the captain general ruled like an oriental despot, assisted by an army and a bureaucratic machinery in which no native Cubans were allowed to serve.[15]

Since the *facultades omnímodas* were also granted to Vives' successors, Spain kept Cuba under this type of government from 1825 onward. As both commanders in chief of the insular army (never less than 25,000 to 30,000 strong during this period[16]) and heads of the civil administration, the captains general held the colony in their hands. But both Vives, who governed until 1832, and his immediate successor sought to cooperate with the wealthy creole oligarchy in everything related to their economic interests.

This state of affairs ended abruptly, however, when General Miguel Tacón was appointed captain general in April 1834. A reactionary who had suffered many defeats in the last campaigns against South American independence, Tacón had been instructed by the government in Madrid, despite its renewed liberal orientation,[17] to use the utmost severity in the governance of Cuba. Since he was naturally suspicious of all Cubans without distinction, he carried out this task admirably, so admirably in fact that he became the first ruler of the island to exploit to the full the unlimited authority granted to his predecessors. He concentrated all the powers of the colonial administration in his hands, even to the point of performing the functions of postmaster general and supervising the penal institutions. Thus his authority hung at all hours over the head of the creoles, with whom he refused to cooperate and whom he often imprisoned or banished without a charge filed or a trial held, much less a record made.[18]

Under Tacón's tyranny, Cubans lost the right to bear arms, the right to vote and send a delegation to the Spanish Cortes, and even the right to learn what was debated in the sessions of that body, for its records too were rigidly censored.[19] Also, since many competent teachers were kept out of the classroom for political reasons, elementary and higher education declined. This is, after all, what could be expected under an administration that devoted three-fourths of the income produced by custom duties, its chief source of revenue, to defray the cost of the army quartered on the island,[20] a fact that illustrates, perhaps better than any other, the sort of military despotism that oppressed Cuba. The regime was so immutable that Madrid itself was unable to alter its authoritarian course. When the central government abolished the Permanent Executive Military Commission, Tacón invoked his *facultades omnímodas* and kept the commission; and when elections were ordered in Spain in 1836 he again made use of his powers and forbade the municipal council of Havana to arrange the voting. This time, General Manuel Lorenzo, the governor of eastern Cuba, chose to defy him, proclaimed the Constitution of 1812 on the island, and called for elections. As events subsequently proved, Lorenzo's action was merely an inconsequential gesture, but Tacón opposed it so fiercely that he was even ready to resort to civil war to put an end to it. Ultimately, of course, he prevailed in Madrid, which made plain once and for all that the liberal cause was dead in Cuba and not even a high colonial official with important connections in the Peninsula like Lorenzo could revive it.[21]

After the departure of Tacón (1838), Cuba was never again the same. During the decade that immediately preceded the first war of independence, the Ten Years' War, conditions improved to some extent under two proconsuls with liberal proclivities, Francisco Serrano and Domingo Dulce. But the tensions that Tacón's policies built into the life of the colony never disappeared. Owing to his tendency to surround himself with *peninsulares*, born in Spain, and either to ignore or harass the creoles, the distinction between the two groups that had begun to develop in the days of Vives grew considerably sharper during his harsh administration; and this distinction, which was essentially one of political identification and loyalty, was solidified as the century progressed. True, there were Cuban-born persons who were pro-Spanish. On the whole, however, and to a larger extent than elsewhere in Spanish America, the upper segment of society was divided along lines determined by the place of birth of its members. At the top stood the natives of Spain, who monopolized all the offices, honors, and emoluments; far below them were the creoles, relegated to a secondary position in their own land. It was an unequal partnership that contained within itself the seeds of its own dissolution. While it lasted, it was forced upon the inferior group manu militari.

Nevertheless, despite its strength the Spanish regular army came to be regarded as insufficient for this purpose. For a number of reasons—corruption, maladministration, and poor hygiene—the soldiers who were available for combat duty were often less numerous than those who were confined to military hospitals by illness. Thus, in order to cope with the increasingly unruly Cubans, Captain General José Gutiérrez de la Concha, by decree of February 12, 1855, created the Voluntarios de la Isla de Cuba, or Volunteer Corps, which consisted of civilian volunteers. The Volunteers, to which some politically acceptable Cubans were admitted, were led by amateur officers recruited from middle- and upper-class Spaniards, usually prominent merchants who took upon themselves the responsibility of arming, equipping, and otherwise financing their own companies. The highest rank among the officers was that of colonel. The corps had its own clubs, such as the Casino Español in Havana, and published its own newspaper. It worked as an adjunct of the Spanish police and a spy network in peacetime. In time of insurrection, it was supposed to maintain the home front in cities and towns, relieving the regular troops of garrison duty so that they could move out to battle. When Concha first appealed to the Spanish elements on the island, the numerical strength of the corps grew rapidly, though only to dwindle during the ensuing years. At the outbreak of the Ten Years' War on October 10, 1868, the Volunteers had been reduced to 10,323 men in all of Cuba. No one considered them capable of defending even the urban areas.[22]

Cubans knew, of course, that the goal of these Spanish efforts was to develop the capability of quelling decisively any possible internal disturbances rather than protecting the island from external aggression. In 1850 and 1851 General Narciso López, a former officer of the Spanish army, had led two filibustering expeditions to Cuba, and since he had been associated with annexationist elements in the United States, it had been possible for Spanish authorities at the time to talk about a defensive buildup. But López had been captured and executed (as a result of the failure of his second attempt), and since then there had been no more attacks by outside enemies. The truth was that the Spanish forces stationed on the island were nothing but an instrument of repression to be used against its population, and this the Cubans bitterly resented. This sentiment was frequently reflected by the writers of the period in novels and short sketches that analyzed the customs and mores of colonial society,[23] and it was also reflected in the manifesto issued by the Cuban insurgents when they finally rose to begin the Ten Years' War. In that document they enumerated the causes of the revolt, and among them they mentioned the fact that Cuba had no enemies and therefore needed neither an army nor a naval force. "Yet," they proclaimed, "the Spanish government forces us to pay for the upkeep of an armed force which has no purpose but to keep our necks under a degrading iron yoke."[24]

The Ten Years' War

As might be expected, the militarization of Cuba reached new heights during the decade spanned by the long conflict.[25] When hostilities began, however, Spain only had on the island 7,000 regulars available for combat duty.[26] Consequently, the local authorities had no choice but to order the mobilization of the Volunteers, who were quickly reorganized and armed with Remington rifles purchased in the United States. By January 1, 1869, they added up to over 20,000 infantry and 13,500 cavalry,[27] and toward the end of the decade, according to unofficial estimates, they were over 85,000 strong.[28]

The Volunteers made only a modest contribution to the Spanish war effort.[29] But when the Cuban insurgents rose the Volunteers found themselves for the moment in the crucial position of being the principal force available for containing the rebellion. Thus they became a pressure group powerful enough to dictate colonial policy, and neither the central government nor the captain general could do anything to restrain them. They proved to be the most powerful force for a reactionary policy toward Cuba; nothing short of the complete extermination of the insurgents and their sympathizers seemed to satisfy them. They killed, took prisoners, pilfered, and ransacked at will. They forced the courts to condemn clearly innocent prisoners to death.[30] They meddled in the affairs of the colonial administration, even in the military sphere. When Captain General Domingo Dulce, acting on instructions from Madrid, launched a program of moderate reform and attempted to end the war by negotiation, they first compelled him to repudiate his own policies and then demanded his resignation, which they obtained (June 1869). The governors of the towns of Matanzas, Cárdenas, and Colón were similarly deposed by the Volunteers; and they even forced a Spanish troop commander of whose military performance they disapproved to take refuge in a ship anchored in the harbor of Havana in order to escape their anger. Their idol was the fat and cruel count of Valmaseda, military commander in eastern Cuba who, disobeying the orders of his superiors, on April 4, 1869, proclaimed war to the death against the rebels operating in his department.[31]

The influence of the Volunteers reached a peak in Cuba during the early phase of the war. Subsequently they continued to pressure the various captains general who came to govern the island but did not openly challenge their authority. This is probably attributable to the fact that when Madrid meekly accepted the expulsion of Dulce (as it did, based on a sober appraisal of Cuban political and economic realities), the Volunteers won their cause, for such an acceptance implied that the short-lived attempt at reform and negotiation had been abandoned and that thenceforward Spain's policy would essentially be that of the Volunteers. It was indeed a great victory for the party of reaction, but it was also a bad precedent and a further cause for alarm for one of the important groups that had joined the fight for Cuban self-determination in the rural areas (or "in the woods," as Cubans used to say).[32]

Cubans declared their independence more than half a century after their Spanish American counterparts, and at the time they did so Francisco Solano López was completing the ruin of Paraguay, the brutish Mariano Melgarejo was oppressing Bolivia, and Ecuador lay inanimate under the iron heel of Gabriel García Moreno. The star of the nimble Antonio Guzmán Blanco was rising in Venezuela. Thus, in addition to the excesses of the Volunteers and the rigors of Spanish military rule, Cubans had been able to witness the adversities experienced by the other Spanish American republics at the hands of the caudillos. Many Cuban revolutionaries, especially the more intellectual ones—the university students and young professionals—tended to look at warriors in general as potential despots. The generalized violence of war, as they saw it, could lead only to military rule and dictatorship. They therefore endeavored to prevent such a denouement in the struggle in which they had involved themselves. They all agreed that only by establishing an insurgent movement closely modeled on those of the United States or revolutionary France would the military be kept in its place.[33]

Such was the position of the group of insurgents that had assembled in the province of Camagüey, where an expedition had brought, in December 1868, more than 50 Havana youths, many of whom were the scions of distinguished colonial families. The most prominent of these insurgents was Ignacio Agramonte, a dashing young lawyer whose radical liberal political creed epitomized that of the group. Agramonte and his idealistic colleagues had begun the struggle under their separate and autonomous Revolutionary Committee, for they refused to accept the leadership of Carlos Manuel de Céspedes, the sugar planter who had raised the banner of rebellion in the neighboring province of Oriente. They disliked the fact that he had precipitated the war in order to put himself at the head of the movement, but what they totally rejected was his conservative outlook and his unipersonal command. Taking advantage of the relative remoteness of the area in which the revolt had started, Céspedes had succeeded in establishing in the interior of Oriente (a handful of towns, hamlets, and farms) a formal if unorthodox Cuban republic that kept so many elements of the colonial order that it seemed a prolongation of the status quo rather than a new enterprise. Céspedes, moreover, had assumed the title of captain general and ruled pretty much as the Spanish governors ruled, concentrating all civil and military functions in his hands.[34] Agramonte's reaction was swift and decisive. "We Camagüeyans," he proclaimed at the outset, "are determined not to depend ever on any dictatorship whatsoever, nor to follow in the footsteps of the first authority of the Eastern department."[35] The Revolutionary Committee, for its part, was equally unequivocal. It stated in its very first resolution that "the military power [in Camagüey] is subordinated to the civil power, and the authority of the latter is limited by the rights of the people."[36]

After some fruitless attempts at negotiation, the vicissitudes of war and the realities of revolutionary politics finally forced Céspedes to come to terms with the Camagüeyans. In January 1869, the count of Valmaseda smashed his republican enclave in Oriente, as a result of which he lost whatever control he previously had over military operations. Then, in March, another group of insurgents who had risen in Las Villas (central Cuba) chose to support the Camagüeyan position. Under the circumstances, it was apparent that in order to salvage at least some of his former prestige and authority, Céspedes had to reach a compromise with the other insurgent groups. This is precisely what he did after some hesitation. By virtue of this compromise, these groups recognized him as the president of the emerging republic; for his part, he relinquished the supreme military command of the liberating army and agreed to exercise his powers in accordance with a constitution. An assembly hastily convened by the Camagüeyans and their allies in the town of Guáimaro drafted, discussed, and approved this constitution in only a day (April 10, 1869). It was a document in which not a single concession was made to Céspedes' ideas and attitudes. Its most salient feature was the unicameral body to which it entrusted the legislative power, an all-powerful House of Representatives empowered to name and rename at its discretion the president of the republic and the general in chief of the army. As Antonio Zambrana, one of the framers of the constitution (the other was Agramonte), put it, the House was the hub of the system; it was "the depository of supreme authority; the true center of public power; the body really entrusted with the task of governing whose supervision and influence would surely reach into all parts of the administration."[37]

As it turned out, however, the Guáimaro Constitution merely provided a new frame of reference for the old disputes. Céspedes never gave up his ambition to regain his former position as sole chief of the revolutionary movement, and the House, which was in reality the bulwark of Camagüeyan liberalism, never had any trust in him.[38] Recurrent political crises, therefore, were to be expected, and they indeed marred the relations between the president and the

House for the next four years. During that period, orders were continually issued from Céspedes' headquarters in the woods as though he were a true generalissimo, despite the fact that he was supposed to act through a central military command. The House, for its part, accused him of all sorts of real and imaginary transgressions: unduly interfering in military plans, promoting an "incendiary torch" policy, hindering the assembly's legislative chores, illegally appointing agents of the revolution abroad, obstructing the legislation on presidential succession (a sensitive subject that the constitution had overlooked). It also appears that Céspedes usually preferred relatives and close friends for vital appointments, and for this too he was disparaged by many, as well as for the rigid formality observed in his camp, his methods, and the hangers-on of his entourage. On December 17, 1869, General Manuel de Quesada (Céspedes' brother-in-law), who had been appointed supreme commander of the liberating army because of his professional background, was accused of being a militarist and summarily dismissed by the House. On more than one occasion in the years that followed, the legislators similarly discussed the convenience of deposing Céspedes. But on many of these occasions Spanish military pressure prevented them from meeting in session and thus further action had to be postponed. Céspedes, after all, enjoyed the prestige of being the initiator of the rebellion. The question of his impeachment had to be fully considered and debated.

Spanish military activity also set in motion another process in rebel Cuba. Between November 1868 and December 1869, Spain sent to the island its best group of army officers and no less than 34,500 veteran soldiers. In addition, it sent a train of artillery equipped with Krupp cannons of the latest model, fourteen warships, and approximately 1,500 marine corpsmen. Counting the forces that were already stationed in Cuba and the thousands in the Volunteer Corps and other auxiliary units, by December 26, 1869, the metropolis had concentrated on the island, according to unofficial estimates, approximately 107,400 men.[39] It was indeed a formidable fighting machine, and when it finally began to roll across Cuban soil scenes similar to Céspedes' defeat in Oriente occurred many times. Faced with greatly inferior numbers and war matériel, Cubans generally avoided large-scale combat. They abandoned the towns and hamlets they had initially occupied and hid in mountain ridges and forests, from which they emerged to destroy communications, burn plantations and estates of pro-Spanish elements, and ambush isolated enemy detachments. Guerrilla warfare thus substituted for conventional military strategy. A new variety of insurgent leader appeared in Cuba: the guerrilla leader.

As Spanish pressure mounted, guerrilla leaders arose in nearly every district, quarter, or even corner of the Cuban countryside. Most led small, highly mobile bands that usually operated in the area where they had grown up and consequently knew best. Their power and army rank varied in proportion to the importance of their resources and the size of the territory under their control. All of them had to be self-sufficient in order to survive, and for this reason (as well as their relative isolation and slow communication) they developed a tendency to work out their own tactics and to exercise an absolute authority over their men and territory. But they were not completely autonomous, for they were normally part of an overall command and organization. Within this organization, which was relatively loose, the lesser local chieftains were subordinated to more powerful leaders and so on, until the hierarchy reached the effective commander or general. This leader's power rested on his superior skill and strength, and he controlled the forces in a certain region or territorial division of the island. Sometimes the general ordered the concentration of these forces in a given district, although only at rare intervals and then for no more than short stretches. Since the men had to live off the land whenever they were away from their bases, it was impossible to concentrate more than 1,500 of them in a district for more than two or three weeks without laying waste the district.[40]

General Calixto García, undisputed chief of the Holguín (Oriente) insurgents, was himself a top regional leader of the type described above, as was General Vicente García (no kin to Calixto), who was something of a rebel feudal lord in the district of Las Tunas, also in Oriente. Even Agramonte, after he became the master of guerrilla strategy in his native Camagüey, fits this description. Despite his ideological preoccupations and his past role as a constitution maker, his command has been characterized by his adjutants as an "outright dictatorship," and the same can be said, mutatis mutandis, of the mode of procedure of most of the Ten Years' War chieftains. They were the ones who laid down the rebel law in their territories, and they were therefore the real wielders of power in the insurrectionists' camp. In this context it is easy to understand why the idealistic language of the Guáimaro Constitution soon began to ring hollow and why the central government it proclaimed came to be a chimeric institution. Geography and the realities of an atrocious war of extermination rendered it unviable.[41]

Céspedes believed in his leadership, but his correspondence reveals that he was aware of the threat posed by the regional commanders.[42] There are indications that the House was cognizant of this fact too. Its members, for instance, having finally decided some time in 1873 to remove the president from office, immediately set out to court the generals in order to gain their support.[43] Agramonte rendered no help (he was killed by a stray Spanish bullet on May 11 of that year), but they struck a responsive chord in Oriente, where Céspedes' constant intervention in military affairs had turned him into an obstacle for the two Garcías, Calixto and Vicente, both of whom wished to be sole commanders of Oriente. In fact, it was the generals who precipitated the crisis by pressing the House into action. The record shows that the president was deposed in October 1873, after the legislators succeeded in resuming their official duties at Bijagual, an insignificant hamlet located in Oriente. They wasted so many days, however, wrangling over constitutional issues that many thought they were resorting to quibbling. Then, on October 14, rebel forces from almost every quarter of the province began to concentrate in Bijagual, and on the twenty-sixth, Calixto García himself arrived at the head of upwards of 2,000 men. Whatever the avowed purpose of García's appearance, the fact is that afterward there was no more hesitation, no more procrastination. Céspedes was deposed on the twenty-seventh. For those watching the general as he reviewed his men arrayed in parade formation shortly after the House adjourned, it must have been difficult to conclude that what had just happened was not a military coup d'etat but rather the upshot of a constitutional procedure.[44]

With Céspedes out of the way, the generals called the shots in free Cuba with increasing frequency. They made no further pretense about being subordinated to a constitutional government. Calixto García became the leading figure of the revolution, and he was appointed to the position that he coveted, sole commander of Oriente, thereby reaping the fruit of his dealings at Bijagual. This action of the new president, the Camagüeyan Salvador Cisneros Betancourt, antagonized many officers in Oriente, but none was more deeply offended than Vicente García, who thenceforward embarked on an implacable campaign against Cisneros Betancourt which he continued even after Calixto García was captured by the Spaniards. In late April 1875, with the backing of pro-Céspedes elements (Céspedes had been killed by the enemy on February 27, 1874), Vicente García staged a revolt at Lagunas de Varona in Las Tunas that resulted in the president being overthrown. By this time, also in violation of the orders of an overcautious government, a rebel column under General Máximo Gómez had successfully invaded Las Villas, going far enough west to threaten the rich sugar triangle Matanzas-Cárdenas-Colón. It was a military feat that became politically the source of unmanageable troubles: it exacerbated the regionalist feelings in the rebel camp, and this in turn intensified the disruptive tendencies that the two Garcías, especially Vicente, had set in motion.[45]

These tendencies eventually proved to be as much the cause as the effect of the setbacks that befell the rebels during 1876. Cuban exiles discontinued their active financial support of the rebellion and consequently military supplies ceased to come through. The western invasion launched by General Gómez was finally stopped by the Spaniards near Cienfuegos (Las Villas) in February. Cubans began to lose the strong grip they had gained on much of the countryside of Oriente and Camagüey after they recovered from the initial Spanish onslaught. The old racist whispering campaign against the daring mulatto general Antonio Maceo, one of the most feared insurgent commanders, resurfaced with a vengeance.[46] In Camagüey, the House prostituted its most cherished principles by consulting Vicente García before appointing a new president, Tomás Estrada Palma (destined to become the first president of the Cuban republic in 1902). In Oriente, a group of insurrectionists turned their arms against their fellow Cubans and proclaimed the mulatto Doroteo, a runaway slave from Las Villas, emperor of the island. Lacking the means to revive the fighting spirit of their men, insurgent commanders, for the first time since the outbreak of the war, began to ponder the possibility of a defeat. Such was the situation when, crowning this long series of misfortunes, Gómez and the group of Camagüeyan officers who had accompanied him to Las Villas had to surrender their commands and leave the area as a result of a regionalist mutiny. Gómez, who was a professional soldier born in the Dominican Republic, was deeply disturbed by the "hideous provincialism of the *villareños.*"[47]

By this time the Spanish soldier-politician Arsenio Martínez Campos had arrived in Cuba at the head of 25,000 reinforcements. As the new field commander of the Spanish army, his fighting strength nearly reached 100,000 men in the first days of 1877.[48] Madrid had authorized him to implement a shrewd plan that coupled the pursuance of a vigorous offensive with peace overtures designed to cash in on the divisions and the declining morale of the rebels. The plan proved so successful that in only two months Martínez Campos pacified Las Villas and began to fall upon the Camagüeyans, whereupon he proclaimed an amnesty for all the insurgents (except the leaders) who presented themselves for pardon before the end of the conflict.[49]

Under the impact of these tactics the Cuban liberating army began to crumble, most especially because at this juncture (May 11, 1877) Vicente García chose to start another seditious movement against the insurgent government: he alleged that Estrada Palma wished to put him out of the way by sending him to replace Gómez in Las Villas. This time the consequences of García's action were massive desertions, widespread insubordination of officers and men, and generalized uncertainty and confusion. The situation was made even worse by the killing of two members of the House, the circumstance that Maceo (who was wounded) was nearly captured by the Spaniards, and the fact that Estrada Palma actually fell into their hands. Clearly the shadowy rebel republic was nearing its end. One of its officials attempted to save what was left of it by setting up a sovereign canton (in the Helvetian fashion) in Oriente.[50] The House, for its part, could think of nothing better than entrusting the presidency and the command of the army to García, the man who had done more than any other to destroy both institutions. By this time, of course, the only way that remained open to the rebels was to achieve some kind of negotiated peace. García and Martínez Campos met (February 5, 1878), and after exchanging proposals and counterproposals they ultimately reached an agreement whereby, among other things, Spain consented to "forget the past" and the rebels agreed to capitulate (February 11). Maceo denounced the Pact of Zanjón (as the settlement was called) because it contemplated neither the independence of Cuba nor the abolition of slavery. But he could go on fighting for only ten more weeks. By May 21 all had laid down their arms.[51]

The Ten Years' War was basically a regional conflict that never expanded beyond the eastern half of Cuba. Yet its ramifications reached every corner of the island and affected all sectors of society. It was a war in which the civilian population was often harshly treated by both sides, and in which most of the time little respect was shown for the lives and properties of the vanquished.[52] According to some reasonable estimates, the numerical strength of the Cuban liberating army never exceeded 15,000 men, not including the "irregular" units.[53] As a military force it was therefore relatively small, although it was apparently sufficiently aggressive despite its size to compel Spain to send to Cuba between mid-November 1868 and May 1878 a total of 186,849 troops.[54] Even so, it took these troops ten long years, the application of considerable material resources, and some say as many as 160,000 casualties (up to 60 percent of the Spanish soldiers were sick at times) to put down the insurrection.[55] Cuban deaths have been reckoned at 50,000,[56] a figure that seems somewhat exaggerated. What is certain, however, is that there was enough bloodshed and devastation, enough heroic sacrifices, and enough epic feats to provide the basic stuff of the martial tradition that thenceforward pervaded the Cuban national conscience.

Interlude between Wars

The Ten Years' War was ignited by members of the eastern creole elite—sugar planters and cattle barons like Céspedes, Agramonte, and Cisneros Betancourt. For all practical purposes, these men lost the leadership of the separatist movement after Céspedes was deposed at Bijagual, and this became evident as Cubans began to plot again to drive the Spaniards from the island shortly after Zanjón. The new leaders that emerged out of the violence of the war as a rule were men of modest social origins. A few, like Máximo Gómez and Manuel de Quesada, were professional soldiers. But most of them had been civilians, amateurs who had learned their military skills on the battlefield. By the end of the conflict they had definitely turned military. They had also smarted under what they had regarded as the nagging supervision of a provisional government that, in their view, had proved to be only a hindrance to military operations. Whenever necessary, they had ridden roughshod over that government. Cubans therefore no longer had to rest on the experience of other countries in order to rationalize their fear of unruly liberators. They had witnessed the dislocations caused by such liberators during the last phase of the war, and they labored under that unsavory memory throughout the post-Zanjón interlude.

What could be expected of the veterans of 1868 soon became clear to the Cuban émigrés in New York, which had become the new center of separatist agitation. From late 1878 there was widespread suspicion that the promises made by Spain in its agreement with the insurgents would not be kept. The old dictatorial colonial regime was dismantled, the insular army began to be reduced, and Cubans were allowed to elect deputies to the Spanish Cortes. But they were granted no other political rights. This type of regime, which condemned freedom of the press and assemblage, could perhaps be endured by the newly organized Liberal or Autonomist party, essentially made up of former reformists or supporters of annexation to the United States who contented themselves with political and economic reform within the Spanish empire. Basically, however, it was a political arrangement designed to guarantee that Cuba would be "always part of Spain" (as the reactionary elements of the Constitutional Union party insisted), and this could hardly satisfy the exiled former heroes of the war (who had been allowed to leave the island under the terms of Zanjón), some of whom were eager to resume the battle for independence.

This time it was Calixto García who began to plan for a new uprising, which he initiated when he arrived in New York after being released from prison by the Spaniards. In October 1878 he issued a manifesto inviting all Cubans to unite in the fight against Spanish tyranny, and from a people that was weary of a decade of killing and destruction he obtained a startling response. There were difficulties caused by betrayals, the recalcitrance of some conspirators, and the racism of others (who allegedly prevented García from entrusting the command of an expedition to Maceo). Notwithstanding these difficulties, on August 29, 1879, the "Guerra Chiquita" (Little War) erupted in Cuba, and for a few months especially Oriente and Las Villas bore a close resemblance to what they had been two years before. Nevertheless, owing to the decisiveness of the Spanish response, Maceo's absence, and the capture of García shortly after he landed in southern Oriente (eight months after the outbreak of the war), the fighting spirit of the rebels soon began to ebb and the revolt gradually lost momentum until it faded away. By September 1880, separatist Cubans were brooding over yet another failure.[57]

Indeed they had plenty to worry about. In some regions of Cuba the population had been hostile to the insurgents. Without their old leaders, insurgent officers had often appeared to be no more than bandits, and a few had occasionally behaved as such. Discipline had been practically nonexistent.[58] García and Maceo had been at odds over the issue of the expedition, Maceo claiming that García had yielded all too easily to the pressure of the white supremacists and that the true reason why he had been passed over was that García was jealous of his prestige and his ascendancy over the Oriente rebels.[59] There had been, furthermore, the matter of García's authoritarian political convictions. García believed that institutions such as those framed at Guáimaro ten years before could only subsist under "normal conditions,"[60] and therefore he did not even make a casual reference to such political constraints in the manifesto in which he called out separatist Cubans. Shortly after his landing in Cuba, the émigrés received a laconic cable whereby they were informed that a provisional government had been organized on the island and that the general was at its head, that is, that all civil and military powers were concentrated in his hands.[61] That meant that democracy was postponed until the end of the conflict. Meanwhile, free Cuba would be subjected to the preeminent authority of the general.

After the disasters of the Little War, Cubans abstained from active plotting for several years. By 1884, however, the economic and political situation on the island once again was propitious. More important, a rich Cuban merchant in New York promised $200,000 for a new revolution provided that Máximo Gómez would consent to put himself at its head. This was enough to encourage the general to submit to the "revolutionary centers" in the United States a plan to which he asked that they adhere beforehand as a "guarantee of success." The plan envisaged the creation of a "governing board" that might possibly form the basis of a future provisional government, but in reality its chief duty would be to raise and keep funds and to spend them as directed by the general. Actually Gómez demanded for himself "the most ample powers" and clearly specified their extent: "Unless it becomes absolutely necessary by force of circumstances, no civilian institutions of any kind [will] be created."[62] In short, he wanted the same dictatorial power that Calixto García had reserved for himself during the Little War and he got it, even from the crucial revolutionary club of New York. Thereupon he turned up in the Empire City accompanied by Maceo, who had immediately pledged his support to the new revolutionary venture and shared his political views.[63]

Upon their arrival the two generals learned to their chagrin that the $200,000 would not be forthcoming. The merchant had reneged on his promise. It was then that the émigrés understood what Maceo had meant when he used to say that Gómez regarded the Cuban war as his "exclusive property."[64] Pressed for financial support, Gómez never again mentioned the board that he himself had proposed. Instead, he began to issue orders in every direction and insist that they be obeyed without question. Some of the civilian coconspirators were inclined to overlook this turn in the general's conduct,[65] but not José Martí, a brilliant and free-spirited man of letters who had swiftly established himself as one of the leaders of the New York separatists.[66] Martí had agreed to go to Mexico with Maceo to procure funds, but when he tried to make some suggestions of his own Gómez told him to limit himself to his instructions or otherwise follow Maceo's directives. Two days later (October 20, 1884) Martí wrote the general announcing that he was withdrawing from the movement. In a carefully penned letter he severely reprehended him:

I have determined not to contribute one iota to establish on the island the despotic rule of only one person, which would be far more disreputable and doleful than the oppressive regime which it presently endures. . . . One does not found a nation, General, with commands as issued in a military camp. . . . What are we, General? Are we the heroic but humble servants of an idea . . . or the bold and fortunate caudillos who, whip in hand and spur on heel, are preparing themselves to bring war to a country with the view of subjugating it afterward? . . . [I will support] a war undertaken in obedience to the will of the country . . . but . . . to an adventure cunningly launched at the right moment to avail personal purposes that may be taken for the lofty ideals that actually will make it feasible; to a campaign conducted as the private enterprise of caudillos who merely pretend to pay homage to patriotism in order to attract the backing of elements or persons who might be useful to them in one way or another; to a purely military exertion, no matter how brilliant, magnificent, or successful it might turn out to be, or how great the honor it might bring to its leaders . . . to such an adventure, campaign, [or] exertion . . . I will never lend my support.[67]

This incident left a deep mark on Martí's feelings. Nearly a full year thereafter he was still insisting that Gómez and Maceo had not been "exclusively concerned with the good of the fatherland," and he was complaining about the "scornful insolence" of the two generals.[68] He was also writing words that would be repeatedly quoted by successive generations of Cuban revolutionaries: "The seeds that are planted at the time of war are the ones that fructify at the time of victory. Before answering the call to arms, a people has to know what it is pursuing, where it is going, and what is going to happen afterward."[69] This is precisely what Gómez had set out to do in the plan he submitted to the revolutionary centers, but then he was carried away by his dictatorial proclivities and failed to follow through. To him revolution and dictatorship were inextricably intertwined, and anyone who could not assimilate this truth and act accordingly was either an effeminate, a simple soul, or, worse yet, a meddler.[70] He thus devoted himself to caricaturing Martí's character in his correspondence with the émigrés,[71] a practice in which he was imitated by Maceo, who also has left quite a few unkind remarks about Martí's conduct. On June 14, 1885, for example, Maceo inveighed unreservedly against "Martí's retrograde tendencies," subtly implying that he was a vulgar intriguer and a slanderer. Venting his irritation over Martí's attitude, Maceo asked rhetorically: "Are these bad Cubans by any means worthy of being compared to the good ones just because they were born in the same land?"[72]

Subsequent to their disagreement with Martí, Gómez and Maceo succeeded in raising some money for their revolutionary initiative, but then they were overcome by a number of unforeseen difficulties. Discontent and dissension arose among the colonies of émigrés and the veterans involved in the project, and bitter disputes strained the relations between the two generals. On August 17, 1886, Gómez broke off his long friendship with Maceo. Things obviously had reached a point beyond which coordinated action was no longer possible. In December, convinced that "Cubans . . . do not want to hear a word about revolution," Gómez called off the movement.[73] Apparently, however, when Maceo was allowed to return to the island four years later, a large number of Cubans were willing to listen to him and indicated they were willing to participate in yet another uprising. But the general proved to be as inept as a conspirator as he was brave on the battlefield, and the agents of the Spanish police never had an easier time. Fully informed of every move made by the revolutionists, the Spanish authorities followed their activities for seven months and then, at the right moment, arrested and deported Maceo and other leading plotters (August–September 1890).[74] The new movement was thus nipped in the bud. It was a most astonishing demonstration of the fact that not even the craftiest and boldest of the Ten Years' War veterans were able to penetrate the oppressive armor with which Spain was defending the remains of its colonial empire. Within Cuba itself, many disappointed separatists began to lose hope. Outside Cuba, the movement deteriorated into an outpouring of passionate but helpless rhetoric.

At the beginning of 1891, therefore, the time was ripe for a new approach to the problem of Cuba's independence. José Martí seized upon this opportunity. He had begun his efforts to reorient the activities of the émigrés in the fall of 1887, constantly hammering on the need to check "the unlimited authority of a military or a civilian group, or of a particular region, or of one race over the other."[75] Then, in January 1890, he had busied himself with La Liga, a society for the instruction and advancement of poor black exiles, and this had allowed him to reach thousands through his weekly classes, frequent speeches, writings, and personal contacts. Thus, by the time that Maceo passed through New York after his deportation from Cuba, Martí's democratic and egalitarian message with its condemnation of militarists had gained many adherents. It was a period of intense proselytizing that culminated with the extension of his revolutionary preaching to the Cuban tobacco workers of southern Florida late in 1891. In Key West, on January 5 of the following year, the representatives of twenty-seven separatist clubs approved the Bases that Martí had drawn up. The Bases incorporated the reasons, justifications, and program of a new movement—the Cuban Revolutionary party (CRP). The program was ratified by a majority of the separatist clubs of the South, New York, and Philadelphia in late March, and in April Martí was elected to the position of Delegate, or head, of the party. That same month the organization was formally proclaimed in the various émigré centers, where its members could read the first issue of its unofficial organ, the newspaper *Patria*, which Martí had founded in New York the previous month. Alongside the full text of the Bases, *Patria* published an unsigned article (the author was easily identifiable) that summarized the Delegate's political creed. It proclaimed that the party would not lead Cubans to a triumph that would be subsequently tarnished by "the victor's exertions or factional ambitions."[76]

The CRP, insofar as such thing was possible for Cubans living in exile, was a mass organization. Its membership encompassed "as many elements of all kinds as could be recruited." It was also an organization that functioned democratically. Its most important characteristic perhaps was that its formation had resulted from the general agreement of the separatist clubs of the United States on the principles stated in the Bases. The goal of the party was to obtain "the absolute independence of Cuba, and to promote and aid that of Puerto Rico," but the Bases clearly specified that this goal would be attained through "a war of republican method and spirit." It was not the object of the party, the document went on to declare, "to perpetuate in Cuba, under a new form or through the implementation of changes more apparent than real, the authoritarian spirit and the bureaucratic structure of the colonial regime." Nor was its purpose to "unleash upon Cuba a victorious group prone to regard the island as its prey and domain." What the Bases foreshadowed was the establishment of "a new and honestly democratic nation."[77]

Party doctrine on civil-military relations therefore could not be more explicit, as befitted an organization exclusively directed by civilians. There were lesser veterans of 1868, men like Carlos Roloff and Serafín Sánchez, who had joined the party. But Martí, following a course that was contrary to all precedents in the Cuban revolutionary movement, had left the great military leaders (Máximo Gómez, Antonio Maceo, and the like) out of his plans. He knew well that he would have to secure the cooperation of these experienced and proven men before he could launch the military phase of the struggle. Yet he refused to turn to them until a strong revolutionary organization had been formed. It was only after the party had become the undisputed and supreme coordinating body of the new attempt (and after its tentacles had reached separatist groups inside

Cuba itself[78]) that he called in Gómez and Maceo. When he did so, he asked them to first recognize and accept the authority of the party.[79]

The Second War for Independence

Martí approached Gómez in August 1892, after the exile centers chose the general for the supreme direction of military affairs. Shortly afterward he set about enlisting the support of Maceo. Both generals ultimately agreed to serve, a fact that Martí subsequently reported in the most glowing terms.[80] There is no question that these three men were deeply committed to the cause of Cuba's freedom, but none of them—especially Gómez—had forgotten the incident of 1884,[81] and all of them still clung to their previous political beliefs.[82] What made the two generals bury their differences was their realization that independence had to result from a long and laborious process of preparation and organization and that both of them were incompetent to undertake such a task.[83] Martí, on the other hand, was already facing the skepticism of many Cuban veterans who could not understand how anyone could think of launching another war without counting on the services of the great chiefs. The rapprochement between Martí and the two generals, therefore, in many respects was nothing more than a mariage de convenance dictated by circumstance. Martí kept fearing and worrying;[84] and Gómez, who by this time had resumed his correspondence with Maceo, continued to think that "the old soldiers formed the principal part [of the party], the elements that will be responsible for the action."[85]

For the time being, however, neither Gómez nor Maceo interfered with the activities of Martí, who for all practical purposes functioned as the sole head of the revolutionary movement. He monitored the political situation, raised donations over and above regular party contributions, centralized the contacts with the separatists inside Cuba and elsewhere in the United States, controlled the war chest, organized expeditions, and little by little purchased armaments of all sorts. Only he knew where they were kept hidden. As the preparatory work picked up momentum, Gómez, Maceo, and the other military leaders learned what their individual responsibilities would be and where they would land with their men when the time came. But none of them was conversant with the overall plan: they were not familiar with the arrangements made to load the ships, nor did they know the port (Fernandina, near Jacksonville, Florida) from which they would sail.[86] The leaders on the island were no better informed. They had been told, of course, about the impending action and ordered to support and protect the landings. Nothing else was revealed to them.[87] Martí alone knew all the details of the plan and consequently the military chiefs had no alternative but to depend on him.[88]

Gómez had signed the order to begin the war and preparations for the embarkation of Martí's expeditions were nearly complete when U.S. authorities detained the ships and confiscated the war matériel (January 12, 1895).[89] This was a devastating blow. The movement itself kept going unchecked until it finally burst forth in an uprising on February 24. Yet Martí's position vis-à-vis the military leaders changed drastically, for it was he who now had to lean upon them and beg them to set off for Cuba in any way whatsoever. Martí's authority probably would have been whittled down anyhow at the onset of hostilities, but it is unquestionable that the Fernandina affair tipped the balance against him sooner than might be expected and worsened his predicament. Prior to the collapse of the plan, Gómez was going to land in Cuba thanks to Martí's efforts. As it happened, it was Gómez who condescended to include Martí in the small party that eventually accompanied him to the island (April 11). Martí never overlooked the significance of this fact. He knew that he was in free Cuba on sufferance of the military and that he had many enemies who were "already sharpening their teeth."[90] Therefore, he might be compelled to return to New York at any time[91] or even expelled from the movement. On the very day of his arrival in Cuba he instructed Gonzalo de Quesada, his close friend and disciple, to keep in a safe place his books on Latin American history, geography, and related matters. "If I emerge alive of this conflict, or if I am expelled," he explained, "I will need them to earn a living again."[92]

The difficult tasks that laid ahead of Martí must have had something to do with his assessment of the situation. At Montecristi, Dominican Republic, shortly before leaving for Cuba, he had issued a manifesto (cosigned by Gómez) setting forth the basic policies of the war that was already raging in the island. The document did not dwell at length on what was to become of Cuba in the event of a rebel victory, for it was essentially an attempt to broaden the appeal of the movement, but it did go beyond the usual assurances about independence. Martí stated that the "difficulties" caused by the wars of independence in Spanish America stemmed from the inability of the new republics to choose the right form of government. Such was, therefore, the pitfall that Cuba had to avoid. From the outset, it needed to find "a form of government equal to the task of satisfying, at the same time, the mature and sensitive intelligence of its civilized sons . . . the requirements that determine the assistance and respect of other nations [and the conditions] that permit rather than hinder the full development and rapid termination of the war."[93] Once, after he had already spent some time in Cuba, Martí hinted that it was possible to advance many suggestions as to what form of government would be the most appropriate.[94] Yet nowhere did he ever elaborate on these suggestions. What is certain is that the main reason he insisted on going to Cuba with Gómez is that he intended to organize a realistic provisional government.[95] When he attempted to do so, Maceo proved to be the most formidable obstacle.

Maceo had preceded Gómez and Martí to Cuba, and he was in a sullen mood because Martí had not given him as much financial assistance for his expedition as he had demanded.[96] He devoted his first few weeks in the island to assuming the supreme command of the Oriente insurgents, which he did at the expense of another general, Bartolomé Masó, who was far less competent than he was but had been one of the first to rise up in arms.[97] He actually eluded Gómez and Martí (who were looking for him) for nearly a month, and when the meeting finally took place it was almost by accident.[98] As the three men closeted themselves in the room of a house at the sugar mill La Mejorana, Maceo blurted out, addressing Martí: "I like you less now than I did before." Thereupon he proceeded to excoriate the rebel government during the Ten Years' War, adding that he would have none of that again. The new revolution, he stated, should be placed under the control of a military junta, a small group made up of the highest army leaders that would rule free Cuba with the assistance of a civilian secretariat. Such a plan, Martí thought, would transmute the government into an appendage of the army. He failed, however, to "ravel out any sense from Maceo's words," and when he insisted on the necessity of assembling the representatives of the insurgent forces, Maceo retorted that he would choose the four delegates from Oriente. "They will be people," he said, "who will not be easily entrammeled by Dr. Martí."[99]

The principle of civil supremacy suffered a severe blow at La Mejorana. Beyond keeping up with appearances, neither of the generals involved in the meeting later did anything substantive to attenuate this impression.[100] On the contrary, Gómez' attitude changed for the worse. Whether he sided with Martí or Maceo during their heated verbal exchange is a matter of speculation.[101] What is known is that before the meeting he treated Martí with deference, even going as far as to name him major general of the liberating army, indeed a bizarre gesture given Martí's unmartial background.[102] Gómez had also agreed to issue a call for an assembly of delegates in order to "unify the revolutionary leadership" and "structure the revolution along solemn, sober, and viable republican lines."[103] At La Mejorana, nevertheless, he supported Maceo when the latter insisted that Martí return immediately to the United States;[104] and subsequently, as they made their way up and down the Oriente hills looking for the forces of Masó, he made clear to Martí more than once that he did not relish the prospect of a rebel republic presided over by Martí. "Martí will not be president as long as I live," he declared with his usual brusqueness on one of these occasions.[105] This is no doubt the explanation for the pessimism and despair that permeated Martí's private thoughts at this time, feelings that ultimately persuaded him that he should "desist," that is, leave Cuba, in order to "have the moral strength that is required to cope with the danger [military authoritarianism] that I have been envisaging for so many years."[106] But he was unable to carry out his plans, whatever they were. On May 19, 1895, his party finally met with Masó (who also urged him to return to New York) and that same day he was killed in a skirmish of little consequence at Dos Ríos.[107]

The truth is, Gómez and Maceo were in complete agreement concerning Martí: neither of them thought very highly of him[108] and both opposed his doctrine of civilian control of the war. Less artful than Gómez, Maceo openly proclaimed that most of the power should be vested in the liberating army. Gómez shared this opinion, but he contented himself with operating within a system that afforded him freedom of action while maintaining the impression that supreme authority was in civilian hands. This way of thinking was the one that ultimately prevailed. At the time most advocates of independence in Cuba and abroad were confident that Cuban belligerency would be recognized by the United States and other nations upon the formalization of a rebel political organization.[109] On the other hand, the insurgents in Cuba had been informed by Tomás Estrada Palma—after his election to Martí's old party post in New York—that foreign powers would not accept an organization run by a general in chief alone.[110] If Cubans desired to receive outside help, as indeed they did, then they had no alternative but to institutionalize the insurrection and provide it with "a republican and democratic government." This is the reason the proposal to proceed along these lines came from Gómez himself, who thereby became the chief proponent of constitutionalism (as a wonder-struck Cisneros Betancourt, an old veteran of 1868, noted).[111] Even Maceo eventually came to partake of the sense of urgency about the importance of democratic government, as did practically everyone in free Cuba as a result of the constant urgings of its representatives abroad.[112]

Thus, only four months after Martí's death, what amounted to a makeshift constituent assembly set to work on September 14 in Jimaguayú, Camagüey, under the auspices and protection of Gómez. Neither Martí's name nor his political doctrine was even mentioned in the course of the deliberations.[113] A few delegates proposed the adoption of a modified version of the Guáimaro Constitution[114] but the proposal struck no responsive chord in the assembly,[115] which appeared to be more concerned with granting power to the men of arms than enhancing the role of the civilians. One of the young delegates in attendance even had the audacity to suggest that Gómez be proclaimed dictator,[116] a plan that for obvious reasons was killed by the general himself when he was consulted.[117] Regardless of legal definitions, Gómez believed, the key position was that of general in chief, and that was the position he wanted. Next to it in importance was the position that Maceo coveted, the rank of lieutenant general, or second in command.[118] The assembly applied itself to finding a political formula that would incorporate these ambitions, which it embodied in a new constitution two days later. The new goverment would be headed by the Government Council, a civil government body made up of a president, a vice-president, and four cabinet secretaries representing war, the interior, the treasury, and foreign relations. The Council would be endowed with supreme authority in the revolution; nominally, the army would be under its jurisdiction. But the constitution clearly specified that "all the armed forces of the republic and the direction of military operations" would be "under the control of the general in chief." In order to intervene in military matters the Council would have to do so, "without exception, through the nation's generals," and then only for the achievement of "high political ends."[119] Under the authority of these constitutional provisions, on September 18, Gómez was confirmed as general in chief and Maceo became the first lieutenant general of the liberating army.

The mere fact that the Jimaguayú assembly took place is perhaps the best indication that, after Martí's death, Gómez had become the de facto politico-military leader of the new insurrection. What the assembly did was simply sanction this fact, thus enabling the general to claim thenceforward that his post had been given to him "by the revolution itself."[120] The new Government Council took its responsibilities seriously, honestly thinking that "Caesarism" (to quote the secretary of the interior) had been interred at Jimaguayú.[121] But nearly everyone else in the rebel camp appeared to have understood what the assembly truly accomplished. Gómez, of course, kept proclaiming that military authority should be recognized as the "only and supreme authority while Cuba is not free."[122] Maceo, too, clung to his original view that "while the war lasts, there must be only soldiers and swords in Cuba."[123] The delegates themselves subsequently acknowledged that in drawing the constitution, they had tried to prevent civilians from intervening in military affairs rather than limiting the powers of the general in chief.[124] The constitution was, moreover, clearly made out and approved by newcomers and veterans alike;[125] and even Estrada Palma in remote New York sensed what had really happened at Jimaguayú, for he quickly acquired the habit of bypassing the Council and corresponding directly with Gómez.[126] So inconspicuous in fact was the role of Cisneros Betancourt (the new president) and his colleagues that rebel troop commanders generally refused to fill posts in the civil government. Not even the presidency itself with all its supposed prestige interested them.[127]

At this time Gómez dominated the Cuban insurgent movement as no one had dominated it before. His fundamental campaign plan had always been to march to the west in order to strike at the heart of Cuba's economy, the rich sugar plantation area of Matanzas and Havana. Central to this plan was a ruthless scorched-earth policy, for in his view this would transform the island into an economic liability that Spain would be forced to give up in order to stop the drain on its own resources.[128] From 1868 to 1878, during the Ten Years' War, he had to live through seven years of procrastination before he could attempt to carry out this project, and then he had to abandon it, owing to the insubordination of the *villareños*. In this second war for independence he succeeded in launching an invasion of western Cuba again after only six months of combat. It took him a while longer to impose his directive of total destruction, for there were other revolutionary military figures (Maceo among them) who at first balked at indiscriminately destroying Cuba's wealth.[129] Before the close of the first year of fighting, however, the rebels had marched from the eastern end of the island to the other end, reducing to ashes some of the most valuable property in the western provinces. This feat was achieved by a force that at no time numbered more than 4,500 men[130] and that fought against a vastly superior army. After the Little War,[131] the regular Spanish forces in Cuba had been gradually reduced for budgetary reasons to the point that by the outbreak of the new conflict there were only approximately 14,000 men.[132] However, large contingents of troops began to reach the island in the weeks and months that followed, and by mid-

January 1896 the reinforcements numbered 80,219.[133] General Martínez Campos, who had been sent again to Cuba in April 1895, could thus concentrate 25,000 troops in Las Villas alone for the purpose of stopping the western invasion. It was against these odds that Gómez' offensive prevailed.[134]

Upon the completion of the campaign the Cuban liberating army was reorganized and expanded to six corps and two special columns commanded directly by Gómez and Maceo. According to an estimate made by Martínez Campos on the basis of captured reports, the former then presided over a force that was 40,000 strong.[135] His ascendancy in the rebel movement consequently became greater than ever. Refusing to become a compliant instrument in his hands, nonetheless, the Government Council began to bid defiance to his orders. Taking advantage of his absence in the west (the Council had remained behind when the invasion began), it put into execution a few schemes of its own that clearly overlapped his sphere of activities. In addition, the Council demanded that "general campaign plans and their modifications" be submitted to it for approval before being carried out, and it imposed on the general the obligation of keeping it posted on all military activities. As a consequence, civil-military relations deteriorated to the point that for a number of critical months the specter of a coup d'etat hovered over the insurgent camp. It is very likely that the coup would have materialized—had conditions been the same as twenty years before.[136]

But the situation had changed considerably in 1896 and 1897, when the first two Pan American conferences were convened in Washington. At that time naked militarism of the type that had plagued Spanish America earlier in the century was repudiated nearly everywhere. Moreover, in the United States the Cleveland administration, which had been tenaciously opposed to the recognition of Cuban belligerence, was about to depart, and while William McKinley prepared to assume the presidency the friends of Cuba publicly recalled the Republican party's platform pledge to "give independence to the island."[137] Under the circumstances, the forcible overthrow of Cisneros Betancourt and his colleagues would have been most inopportune, particularly after Cleveland's last message to Congress in which he reported "on reliable authority that at the demand of the commander in chief of the insurgent army, the putative Cuban government [had] given up all attempt to exercise its functions, leaving that government confessedly . . . a government merely on paper."[138] This statement had been accompanied by a special written report from Secretary of State Richard B. Olney in which he emphasized the shadowy character of the insurgent gov-

ernment with some accuracy.[139] It would have been foolish, therefore, on the part of the "rascally Cubans" (as Cleveland disdainfully
referred to them in private[140]) to prove the U.S. president and his
secretary of state correct in their assessment of the situation in
free Cuba.

Gómez' position vis-à-vis the Government Council, on the other
hand, was supported by most high-ranking rebel officers (including
Calixto García, who had arrived in Cuba in March 1896 and been
appointed chief of the Oriente army corps the following month).[141]
Junior officers, for their part, were openly discussing among themselves different ways of putting Cisneros Betancourt and his cabinet
out of the way.[142] The Council was consequently under considerable
pressure, a situation that was made even more intolerable by the
fatalities that befell the insurgents in the second half of 1896. The
most painful loss by far was that of Antonio Maceo; but, in addition,
his brother José, General Serafín Sánchez, and Brigadier Juan Bruno
Zayas were all shot down by the Spaniards. Against the background
of these calamities, could the Council seriously consider doing
without the services of a commander of Gómez' stature? The only
one who could possibly take his place was Calixto García, and it
was well known that his attitude toward the Council was one of
utter contempt.[143] This was precisely the juncture chosen by Gómez
to put his putative superiors in the dilemma of either accepting
his resignation or submitting unconditionally to his authority. As
might be expected, the Council capitulated—as it solemnly declared, in order to avoid a clash that would "produce fatal consequences for the fatherland."[144] Shortly afterward Gómez took a step
that he had refused to take before. He issued a manifesto impugning
Cleveland's premature remarks about the subdual of the Council.
Without the slightest compunction, the general proclaimed that the
Council was "for all Cubans in arms the supreme authority that
they had constituted for the purposes that they themselves had defined and announced."[145]

Such was then the upshot of the civil-military crisis of 1896 and
1897—a reaffirmation of the political settlement worked out at Jimaguayú. The appearance of democracy was preseved and the military continued to pretend that it was the faithful servant of the rule
of law. But in reality it was in full control of the revolution. This
time the Council grasped the ultimate meaning of its acquiescence
to Gómez' wishes, and thenceforward there were no further disputes
of any consequence between the general and the civil government.
The Guáimaro Constitution was supposed to last no more than two
years, however, so by October 1897 it became necessary to gather a

new constituent assembly at La Yaya, Camagüey. The overwhelming majority of the delegates reflected Gómez' political views. Heeding the advice of the émigré centers, he favored the maintenance of the status quo. But there was a nearly complete change in personnel (Cisneros Betancourt was conveniently retired and Masó, upon Gómez' recommendation, was chosen to replace him), and a few modifications were made to strengthen the position and powers of the general in chief. The Council, for instance, was disenabled to designate the commander in chief. This meant that the person then occupying the position—Gómez—would continue to do so indefinitely.[146]

There is no doubt that the general's preeminence and prestige as a revolutionary leader peaked at La Yaya. By that time Martínez Campos had been relieved of his command, Captain General Valeriano Weyler had replaced him, and Spain had poured into Cuba a total of 200,000 officers and men.[147] More than that, Spain had been forced to turn to a brutal policy of total war that included the concentration of rural noncombatants in urban areas protected by Spanish troops. After the death of Maceo, Weyler had thought that the war in the west was over, and thus had moved 40,000 men into Las Villas to fall upon Gómez, who was in that province with fewer than 4,000 men under his direct command.[148] It was probably the hardest campaign that Gómez fought during the conflict. Yet somehow he managed to withstand the Spanish onslaught. His reputation as a warrior therefore had reached new heights when the La Yaya assembly met, an event that more or less coincided with the news that Weyler too would be recalled. Would the next captain general, Ramón Blanco, who was an appeaser, succeed where the "butcher" Weyler had failed? There was nothing in the offing at that time that seemed likely to endanger the general's leadership except the growing tensions between Spain and the United States. The irresponsible U.S. yellow journalists were already trumpeting war.

2. The Impact of U.S. Intervention

In transforming the Cuban struggle for independence into a Spanish-Cuban-U.S. war, Washington made a number of decisions, all of which tended either directly or indirectly to weaken or destroy the tenuous bonds that held together the insurgent polity. The most crucial of these decisions was, of course, President William McKinley's steadfast refusal to recognize the rebel government. The second was the War Department's determination to secure the cooperation of the Cuban liberating army in the approaching military operations. The third was dictated by Spanish naval strategy—or lack of it. It compelled the United States to concentrate its forces in the vicinity of Santiago de Cuba (the provincial capital of Oriente) instead of in the western portion of the island as originally planned. A Cuban historian has suggested that Washington policymakers deliberately intended to disrupt the rebel institutions.[1] This may or may not have been the case. If such was their purpose, however, their success surpassed their most sanguine expectations.

The Quandary of the Cuban Junta

The first piece of the rickety insurgent organization to be adversely affected by the United States' entry into the war was the so-called Cuban Junta, which had its headquarters in New York. The Junta was nothing but the delegation that had been officially appointed by the Jimaguayú assembly to represent the revolution abroad. Its chief spokesman was Tomás Estrada Palma, who was authorized to carry on diplomatic relations with other countries, especially, of course, with the United States. For this purpose, the Junta had set up a legation in Washington, with Gonzalo de Quesada as chargé d'affaires. The chief goal of the Junta had always been to obtain the recognition of Cuba's belligerency, and Estrada Palma had always believed that the attainment of that goal was within his reach.[2] The definitive rejection of such a possibility in McKinley's war message of April 11, 1898, was therefore a severe blow to the Junta's mission and prestige.

Still, because of the U.S. involvement in the conflict, the Junta's activities became more crucial than ever. Normally this should have resulted in a significant increase in the volume of correspondence between the Junta and the Government Council, but this is exactly the opposite of what happened. Either because Estrada Palma's reports failed to reach their destination or because he sent none at all,[3] President Masó and his cabinet did not hear from the Junta during the critical weeks that preceded the U.S. declaration of war. On January 12, 1898, riots erupted in Havana and a mob led by officers of the Volunteer Corps attacked the offices of three newspapers that advocated Cuba's autonomy from Spain.[4] Early in February the letter of Enrique Dupuy de Lome (Spanish minister to the United States) calling McKinley a "hack politician" was splattered over the front pages of the New York newspapers.[5] On the fifteenth of the same month, the U.S. battleship *Maine*, which had gone to Cuba with the mission of protecting U.S. lives and property, was blown up in the harbor of Havana.[6] Insurgent leaders inside Cuba began to sense what their representatives abroad had perceived some months before—that the United States was on the road to war.[7] Yet, aside from what they learned from newspapers and private letters, the members of the Council remained in the dark about Washington's moves and intentions.[8]

Increasingly concerned about the conduct of rebel foreign affairs, on April 4 they dispatched from their headquarters a letter to Estrada Palma demanding a thorough briefing on events in the United States.[9] But May came and nothing had been forthcoming from New York.[10] In the meantime, their anxiety had increased in view of some perplexing actions on the part of the Spanish authorities. On April 11, Captain General Blanco had unilaterally proclaimed a sudden truce in Cuba. Then, on the twenty-second (having already seen the U.S. fleet on the horizon outside Havana), he had written to Máximo Gómez proposing an alliance between Cubans and Spaniards. The erstwhile enemies were to join forces in order to repel the invaders from the north and thereby keep free "from a foreign yoke the descendants of a single race."[11]

Finally, on May 10, Estrada Palma's long-awaited report arrived in Cuba. It was a sketchy document (dated April 26) wherein the head of the Junta explained that the United States had acknowledged Cuba's right to govern itself and had determined to use its military and naval forces in order to obtain Spain's immediate relinquishment of authority on the island. Thus far the United States had taken no steps to recognize the legitimacy of the Cuban government. This fact notwithstanding, Estrada Palma went on, he had written to President McKinley assuring him of the full cooperation of the Cuban army and vouching for the Cuban republic's disposition to instruct its generals to obey the orders and put into execution the campaign plans of the U.S. commanders. In keeping with this pledge, he had held several meetings with General Nelson A. Miles, commander in chief of the U.S. Army, in the course of which he had given the general the best available information on the rebel troops, their strength in the various regions of Cuba, the equipment and horses at their disposal, and all the other particulars that had seemed relevant. At the same time, his military advisers, Brigadiers Emilio Núñez and Joaquín Castillo Duany, had discussed matters of strategy with Miles, apprising him of the arms and ammunition as well as food rations that would be required for the Cubans to take the offensive against the Spaniards.[12]

Indeed Estrada Palma had been exceedingly active in New York and Washington. The Junta could claim at least some of the responsibility for the passage of the Teller amendment, the congressional resolution whereby the United States had renounced any power over Cuba once the island was pacified.[13] Also, the Junta had concluded what appeared to be a working agreement with the U.S. military. Yet Masó and his colleagues on the Government Council were far from satisfied. They believed that the account of Estrada Palma's conversations with Miles had not been circumstantial enough, and they felt uneasy about the U.S. attitude vis-à-vis the revolution. Perhaps it was true, as Estrada Palma maintained, that the resolution passed by Congress "was tantamount to the recognition of the Cuban republic."[14] But all that most Cubans in a position of leadership had ever wanted from the United States was arms and supplies to drive the Spaniards out of their country. No one in the island had ever thought that U.S. armed intervention was a requisite for victory,[15] and therefore Washington's decision to step into the fray was an unexpected complication that had to be carefully considered. Would the intervention lead to the occupation of Cuban territory by the U.S. Army? If so, what parts of Cuba, for how long, and under what terms? Who would "keep order and tranquility" while the intervention lasted? Would the U.S. government respect "the order of things" established in the La Yaya constitution?

The first reaction of the Council was to demand from Estrada Palma a more comprehensive report.[16] But Masó and his cabinet must have grown increasingly concerned as the hours passed, for, upon meeting again on May 12, they resolved to send Vice-President Domingo Méndez Capote to the United States. Although on the surface Méndez Capote's was a fact-finding mission, such sweeping powers were vested in him that he seemed a modernized version of the *visitadores* (inspectors general) that the Spanish Crown used to send to the Indies in bygone eras. He was given full authority over Estrada Palma and his associates, and was instructed to undertake as many functions as he deemed necessary. His wide range of his prerogatives specifically included recommending the dismissal of the head of the Junta or any one of his aides.[17] Méndez Capote reached New York late in May, and it did not take him long to learn that the failure of the Junta to win the battle of Cuba's recognition was due to the refusal of the McKinley administration to tolerate any interference with its Cuban policy. Because of this and the fact that he was a prudent man, no ostensible changes resulted from his mission. Still, while he remained in the United States, he was the true representative abroad of the Cuban republic. The independence that Estrada Palma had shown in the handling of rebel foreign affairs and the formulation of the Junta's policies became a thing of the past.

The Isolation of the General in Chief

Like the Junta, Máximo Gómez was also relegated to a secondary role because of the chain of events triggered by the U.S. intervention. The general had never been as distrustful of U.S. aid as Maceo,[18] and when Captain General Blanco had invited him to make common cause with Spain against "the foreign invader" he had solemnly stated in his reply that

> up to the present I have had only feelings of admiration for the United States. I have written to President McKinley and General Miles thanking them for the American intervention in Cuba. I do not see the danger of our extermination by the United States to which you refer in your letter.[19]

Gómez had been extremely pleased, therefore, when at about the time that he wrote to Blanco he was somehow led to believe that he would soon receive the visit of an emissary from the U.S. War Department. Anticipating that the purpose of such a visit would be to arrange for military cooperation between the U.S. and Cuban armies, he proceeded—most uncharacteristically—to request the prior approval for such aid from the Government Council. This he did through a letter dated April 26, following which he dispatched another on May 2 in which he outlined in detail the plan of the campaign that would at last allow Cubans "to seize the beautiful laurel of conclusive victory."[20] These two letters reached the Council's headquarters before Estrada Palma's report on the situation in Washington, and thus added considerably to the uncertainty that then prevailed in the insurgent camp. But, after some reflection, the Council chose to bow to the inevitable. It not only endorsed the general's rejection of Blanco's offer (about which there had been no prior consultation) but it also authorized him to join forces with the United States and approved his military plans. At the same time, it issued the necessary orders so that the other rebel commanders, and most especially Calixto García, would lend him full support.[21]

The strategy of the general in chief included the landing of U.S. troops in Las Villas (his own theater of operations), wherefrom the island would be occupied from east to west until finally the city of Havana was captured. As this joint Cuban-U.S. maneuver progressed, it would be the duty of the insurgent regional commanders of Pinar del Río, Camagüey, and Oriente to pin the enemy forces to their positions so as to prevent them from rendering assistance to Spanish defenders elsewhere. Gómez counted, of course, on the support of the U. S. fleet, just as he counted on military supplies and food from the north. Moreover, he expected that U.S. contingents no less than 6,000 strong would help to tie down the Spaniards in the provinces unaffected by the invasion. One essential feature of the plan was the detachment of a sizable portion of the liberating army—between 1,500 and 2,000 men—from Oriente to reinforce Gómez's own troops in central Cuba. Back in March, the general had requested the transfer to the west of Brigadier General Mario García Menocal, one of Calixto García's most brilliant officers.[22] He now insisted that García Menocal should be at the head of the reinforcements on their long march westward.[23]

Initially the U.S. military had contemplated the landing of 70,000 troops in northern Cuba, at Mariel, the point from which they would move eastward to fight the decisive and final battle for the possession of Havana. Gómez's strategic ideas might have aroused General Miles' interest at this early stage of his planning. Gómez might even have been assigned the same supportive role that Calixto García was subsequently assigned in Oriente. At this critical juncture, however, communications between the two armies failed. The emissary that Gómez was expecting, a Lieutenant Whitney, did reach Key West, where the émigrés rendered him assistance; but he never showed up at the general's headquarters.[24] Eventually Gómez managed to have a talk with the U.S. consul at Sagua la Grande, Las

Villas,[25] although by this time events had made his cooperation superfluous. On May 19 the naval squadron that Spain had dispatched to the Antilles entered the Santiago de Cuba harbor almost unnoticed. This move drastically altered U.S. military thinking. What the United States needed to do now in order to achieve a quick victory was to blockade the Spanish flotilla where it was (instead of Havana, as McKinley had previously ordered) and to land the main bulk of the army in Oriente. The original western strategy was thus abandoned in favor of a concentration of force in the east.

Had Gómez been advised of this change perhaps he could have arranged to be present during the action in Oriente. Yet he was all but forgotten once the new campaign plan was adopted,[26] and thus he remained isolated in central Cuba playing the role of a mere spectator while other soldiers brought to a successful end the war he had begun. For a while he stuck to his guns, doggedly maintaining that regardless of U.S. strategy (of which he confessedly knew nothing), the war had to be won in western Cuba.[27] Events gradually forced him to recognize reality. Early in June, for example, he sent his chief of staff and another officer to Key West and Tampa carrying his military plan and memoranda to General Miles.[28] But this attempt yielded practically nothing, for all that the persistence of his subordinates got him was the last-minute addition of a detachment of some fifty black troops from the Tenth Cavalry for an expedition organized by the Junta. This expedition, moreover, was the last that he got during the war. The Junta had run out of funds to outfit additional volunteers and the War Department simply refused to underwrite new expeditions. The United States was no longer interested in Gómez's campaign.[29]

Not that the Cubans themselves had proved more cooperative. May, June, and the first part of July had gone by and the column of reinforcements that García Menocal was supposed to lead had never appeared on the horizon. This was partly due, of course, to the modification of military plans and Calixto García's new role in Oriente. But there were also the general's well-known recalcitrance and intense regionalism—two conspicuous personal tendencies that fed upon each other. At least since late August 1896 García had been saying that once he had liberated the interior of Oriente he would march westward at the head of 10,000 soldiers.[30] Yet he had never brought himself to put the project into execution. Once, in October 1896, compelled by Gómez's orders, he had laid siege and taken the eastern Camagüeyan town of Guáimaro, the historic place where the first Cuban constitution had been proclaimed. Never again, however, had he ventured beyond the borders of Oriente. In May

1897 he had boasted of the fact that he had 14,000 men under his command.[31] Nevertheless, just a few days earlier he had told his beleaguered chief (who was then under Weyler's attack) that he could not send him any reinforcements. His troops, he wrote, "were fading away"; and, besides, "the parochialism and love of home" so highly developed in Cuba made it impossible, in his judgment, "to take people from Oriente again to the west."[32] Gómez knew, of course, that these were also García's feelings. "When chiefs and officers so wish," he commented, "soldiers go everywhere."[33]

Despite his idiosyncrasies, however, García never relished the prospect of an open break with his commander in chief. Eventually, therefore, García Menocal joined Gómez's forces. But he only brought with him 150 men and he did not make his appearance until some time after July 9.[34] By this time the U.S. expeditionary force under General Rufus Shafter had set foot on Cuban soil, the only major engagement in which U.S. soldiers participated had occurred (San Juan Hill), and the Spanish battle fleet had been destroyed when it tried to break the U.S. naval blockade. A demoralized Spain was about to acknowledge its defeat and Gómez had played no part in this. Shortly before the surrender of Santiago de Cuba, the disillusioned general began to think about resigning his post,[35] and he finally did so precisely on the day in which the U.S. flag rose over the governor's palace in the city (July 17). In his letter of resignation he merely stated that he was giving up his post because it was "unnecessary."[36] Nevertheless, two days later he gave vent to his frustration in a more private missive:

> What [the Americans] need is to be helped; they are practical people and thus will care little about the way in which such help is rendered. Our own organization means nothing to them, as it also means nothing to us in view of the fact that in our camp discipline is a myth. The general in chief and the Council are but figureheads. I suffered a good deal, in fact too much, when I involved myself in the dispute with [Cisneros Betancourt]. Then I thought that Cuba's independence was in danger. But now I regard it as an accomplished fact and thus I believe that no one can demand from me unnecessary sacrifices.[37]

Curiously enough, there are hardly any traces of anti-U.S. feelings in this letter, or for that matter in any other of the known documents that Gómez wrote in this period. This is all the more surprising because he was aware at the time of the utter contempt the U.S. government had for the Cuban insurgents. Estrada Palma had minced no words in conveying this impression to him:

My pride has been so deeply hurt by the Cuban policy of this government that I cannot possibly conceal my wounded feelings. In formulating such a policy, the government has ignored the courage, abnegation, and bloody sacrifices of the extraordinary men who . . . for three years . . . have fought bravely, like true heroes, against the most formidable army that has ever crossed the sea. . . . In [the U.S. government's] opinion these men do not constitute an army, a people, or a government. They are looked upon as bands that have scattered throughout the island according to the exigencies of topography and the features of each region. Little is expected from these bands. [The Americans] hardly count on them for carrying out their campaign plan.[38]

The U.S. intervention had a divisive effect on the ranks of the insurgents, and in this context it was perhaps natural that for the time being Gómez should have blamed his subordinates rather than the United States for his inactivity and isolation during the last phase of the war. Thus, two weeks after his resignation (which the Masó government never accepted), he kept hammering on the fact that Calixto García had always refused to obey his orders.[39] He failed to realize that by then the politico-military scenario had again changed in Oriente and that García's was no longer the leading role.

The Eclipse of the Government Council

If the commander in chief and the Cuban Junta receded into the shade as a result of U.S. decisions, the Government Council all but passed into oblivion. Although it did not dissolve itself officially until a few months later, it lost even the nominal authority that it had exercised up to that moment. This was the upshot of the War Department's determination to bypass it and to establish relations directly with the rebel commanders. Once the commanders realized that they could receive U.S. aid without the agency of the unrecognized Council, they discarded all pretense and openly regarded it as a useless appendage to the corps of actual combatants. They readily agreed that the McKinley administration could not possibly consider the Masó government a legitimate political entity. Gómez himself frankly said so when he still entertained the hope of carrying out his military plan;[40] and García followed suit with similar statements. Of the two generals, because he was the leading insurgent commander in the area where the U.S. campaign was centered, it was García who was able to capitalize on the situation.

Throughout his career García had voiced his condemnation of militarism and despotism a number of times. As late as May 1898, he had emphatically told Méndez Capote: "In my opinion, the revolution and the government must not lean on the prestige and influence of two or more generals, but on good republican principles and solid instructions. What I ardently desire is that we Cubans quench once and for all the predominance of the saber over intelligence. I do not wish a Hereaux[41] to become the master of Cuba; I do not wish to see desperation and brute force prevailing over justice and reason."[42] Because of this and other statements,[43] and because he was careful not to involve himself in any serious dispute with the government before the intervention, García has often been portrayed as a thoroughly disciplined soldier.[44] But at bottom he felt little or no respect for the civilian heads of the revolution. He either scoffed at their lack of authority[45] or dragged them through the mud, dubbing them "a little government of jugglers and performers of dirty tricks."[46] Like Gómez, he never hesitated to order his subordinates to ignore the bidding of government officials.[47]

García especially disliked Cisneros Betancourt and Masó,[48] although it appears that his objections to the government went beyond personal animosities. His views were often contradictory. At times, for example, U.S. political sensitivities seem to have been uppermost in his mind,[49] while at other times he would simply laugh off U.S. hostility to militarism.[50] One month he would write to Estrada Palma stating categorically that he "would rather see the revolution lost than saved through the agency of a militaristic movement."[51] Then the following month he would voice the hope that the delegates to the forthcoming convention at La Yaya would set aside *civilismo*, that is, the preoccupation with civilian political preeminence.[52] It is not easy, therefore, to determine with certainty the basic tenets of the general's political thought. What is clear is that he condemned the existing form of the rebel government because it was oligarchic.[53] It is equally clear that what really concerned him was the civil-military crisis of 1896–1897, and that he sought to prevent the recurrence of such crises by reestablishing the constitutional mechanisms erected during the Ten Year's War.[54] In the days that immediately followed the U.S. declaration of war, García had also conceived a scenario of which, apparently, no other insurgent chieftain ever thought. In January 1898 an autonomist government had gone in effect in Cuba under the aegis of Spain. Equal rights between Cubans and Spaniards as well as universal suffrage had been proclaimed. Local government, with the right even to draw up its own budget, was now in the hands of a prime minister and a cabinet. There was also a local parliament divided into two chambers, the first freely elected and the second (a senate) partly nominated by the captain general, who continued to be responsible for internal order and foreign affairs. García reasoned that except for its illiberal senate and the fact that it stood with the metropolis this was not a bad government. What would happen if the officials of this government suddenly informed the United States that they were prepared to embrace independence and welcome the intervention? [55]

The prospect of being discarded after so many years of struggle obviously disturbed the general, who perhaps for this reason went on record about his intention to cooperate with the United States quite early. On April 18 he officially made this plain to the Government Council, adding that he aimed at rendering this help "unconditionally," that is, even without recognition of the Cuban republic by the United States. On this occasion he stipulated that he would refrain from cooperating with the United States if so ordered. [56] But subsequently he conveniently omitted any reference to the Council's attitude in commenting on his plans. To Estrada Palma he simply said that he proposed "to assist the Americans in any useful way." "It is true that they have failed to reach an understanding with our government," he added. "But they have recognized our right to be free, and for me that is enough." [57]

This explains García's reaction when Lieutenant Andrew S. Rowan unexpectedly appeared in his headquarters in Bayamo (which he had recently taken) for the purpose of requesting the cooperation of his forces in the forthcoming operations. Rowan also asked the general to make his requirements known to the War Department so that military supplies could be promptly dispatched. Up to this moment García had not yet received any instructions from his superiors concerning the delicate matter of the relations between the insurgents and the U.S. Army. Military discipline dictated that he should have referred Rowan to either Gómez or the Council. But evidently he thought otherwise. Carrying out his initial design, he committed himself to joining hands with the United States right then and there, without giving any sign of being "embarrassed" by the War Department's decision to ignore the rebel chain of command. [58] As a result, Rowan was already on his way home on the following day (May 2) accompanied by a military mission that carried information, maps, notes, and a message to be delivered to Secretary of War Russell Alger viva voce. In the note that he wrote introducing his officers to the U.S. official, García significantly hinted at "further intelligence" between the War Department and his forces. [59]

No one can reasonably assume that García would have been overruled had he consulted his superiors as duty directed. At the time neither the Government Council nor the general in chief was pre-

pared to reject the idea of the United States as an ally against Spain—
nor, for that matter, were any of the prominent insurgent leaders.
The Council, moreover, had gone on record on the matter when
Gómez had asked for instructions prior to Whitney's abortive mission, going even a step further and officially proclaiming the de facto
alliance of Cubans and the U.S. government (May 10). It may be argued, therefore, that García's decision was sanctioned retroactively.
Still, when the Council issued its proclamation it knew nothing
about Rowan's visit, and thus the fact remains that García acted on
his own initiative and snubbed both the government and the general
in chief.[60]

This was the pattern of the general's conduct from then on. Taking advantage of the comparative weakness shown by Spain in eastern Cuba, he had established his mastery over most of the interior
of the region, and this had enabled him to achieve a remarkable independence within the insurgent movement.[61] Now he asserted this
independence more and more with every passing day. No one could
accuse him of disobeying the directives of the Government Council,
for he was most anxious to cooperate with the United States. When
he finally learned, on June 6, that their plan was to disembark several thousand men in Oriente and then attack Santiago de Cuba by
land and sea, he reacted as the most alert and disciplined of soldiers.
"Since for me your wishes are a command that I obey with great
pleasure," he told General Miles, "I am taking the necessary measures to bring together an appreciable number of forces at the place
you indicate. . . . All my subordinates have orders not only to protect
the landing of the American forces and to render them whatever
services they need, but also to put themselves unconditionally under your orders."[62]

Meanwhile, he nearly forgot his immediate superior, Gómez, and
repudiated the authority of Masó and his subordinates. In a most
clever fashion he used the very orders that he had received from
the government for the purpose of justifying his disobedience of Gómez's. "Whom shall I obey," he asked the commander in chief when
pressed for the reinforcements that he was supposed to send west.
"Shall I obey you or the government? The latter has instructed me
to put myself at the disposal of General Miles and Miles has asked
me to commit all my forces to an operation in Oriente. Yet you are
demanding that I send two thousand men to the west."[63] On occasions such as this when he felt the need to justify himself García
would call upon the Government Council to clarify its directives.[64]
But it is obvious that these appeals were made only for the sake of

appearances. Had the Council backed Gómez it is likely that García would have stuck to his course anyhow. It is difficult to reach a different conclusion when one considers his reaction to what appeared to be a very sound piece of advice that he received from Estrada Palma shortly before the landing of Shafter's army in Oriente.

The head of the Junta had rightly concluded that it was not possible to persuade President McKinley to recognize, even informally, the rebel civil government. He had thought, however, that it might not be difficult to achieve in Cuba itself what could not be achieved in Washington. For this reason, he had encouraged the Government Council to join García's forces so that it would be close to the various towns, especially Santiago de Cuba, as they fell into the hands of the U.S. Army. In this way the Council might be able to capitalize on the situation and participate, directly or indirectly, in the organization of the local civil administrations that, of necessity, would take over the towns. This was an astute scheme designed to confront the United States with an accomplished fact, but its implementation required the cooperation of García. This is why Estrada Palma believed that it was necessary to appeal to his innermost feelings:

> You have been called, my dear Calixto, to play a very important patriotic role in the matter at hand. With the government at your side, you might be able to put to good use the prestige that you have attained as a victorious general, for you will be in a position to make possible— tactfully and without applying any pressure—a rational understanding between the general representing Washington and our government. That government, after all, is the true representative of the people of free and independent Cuba until such time as general elections are held.[65]

This letter was delivered to García by James Creelman, William Randolph Hearst's favorite reporter. It elicited a lengthy and disappointing response in which the general peremptorily ruled out the idea of bringing Masó and his cabinet to his side. Obsessed by the notion that the Council was inherently oligarchic, he made the mistake of attributing Washington's refusal to recognize it to a matter of principle (how could a "truly democratic government such as McKinley's recognize a body that was comparable to the Venetian Council of Ten or the Roman triumvirate"?). But he accurately predicted that Washington would not "retrace its steps." He also made abundantly clear that as far as he was concerned, the intervention had consummated the political liquidation of the Council. In this connection his logic was devastating:

Since we have agreed to the alliance with the Americans and are fighting together with them to expel the Spaniards from Cuba, have we not also accepted the intervention as a matter of fact? And if we have accepted it, then we have accepted too that in Cuba there does not exist a government such as the one that the Americans wish to establish. We cannot but acknowledge, in concurrence with them, that we have no government. The present Government Council is incapable of fulfilling the most elementary duties that institutions of its kind are normally supposed to fulfill. It is not merely that there is no longer any justification for its existence. It died at the hand of President McKinley the very moment in which he decided to intervene in Cuba. But there is more that can be said and this is quite odd. . . . the Government Council acquiesces to the intervention and directs the general in chief and the lieutenant general [García had been appointed to replace Maceo at La Yaya] to put themselves under the orders of the American commanders. Not only does it approve of the intervention, which amounts to a death sentence signed by McKinley, but it also relinquishes legally and in fact its authority over the heads of the liberating army. After all this, is there anything left for the Government Council to accomplish?

García obviously understood the anti-Council bent of the intervention better than most insurgents, and he did not hesitate to highlight this fact in order to trumpet his own independence. But probably owing to his early dealings with General Miles, he erroneously concluded that the United States really cared for the leaders of the liberating army, and this is what perhaps encouraged him to make his militaristic proclivities more explicit than ever:

The members of the Council could still play a decent role should they gladly lend themselves to face the risks and hardships of war together with the Americans. Unfortunately, they will not do that. You know that President Masó, despite the fact that he is the highest ranking officer of the army, makes no secret of his disinclination to occupy the position that he should be occupying at this moment. Sad truths these are indeed; they explain why I wish that the Council would remain in Los Chincheros, the place to which it withdrew when the rumor about the American landing began to circulate. It can run the course of its existence right there in complete tranquility and happiness without complicating any further the life of us who are fighting, that is to say, the life of the fatherland.[66]

At the time that García thus relegated Masó and his colleagues to the category of ciphers he was the only insurgent commander of note who was still operative. His attitude toward the government therefore was of the utmost importance, for if he refused to obey its orders, of what use was it to the insurgent movement? During the months that ensued, the Cuban civilian leaders consistently blamed the unruliness of the rebel army command for McKinley's nonrecognition policy. Such was the opinion of Masó;[67] and both Méndez Capote and Estrada Palma, despite their familiarity with Washington's politics, agreed with him.[68] But this view focused only on the Cuban side of the question. The other and perhaps more important side was the turn of mind of the United States, which in soliciting the cooperation of the military leaders on an individual basis and behind the back of the Masó government actually encouraged them to emancipate themselves and act as petty dictators in the areas of their commands. García's conduct during and after the Santiago campaign is the most conspicuous and illustrative example of this side effect of the intervention.

Calixto García's Chiefdom in Oriente

Eventually, of course, the general found out that the United States did not intend to recognize the Cuban army any more than it meant to formalize its relationship with the Council. In the beginning, during the first few weeks of operations, his dealings with the "allied army" proved to be satisfactory.[69] But friction between Cubans and U.S. representatives soon developed for a number of reasons. Some stemmed from the U.S. determination to assign the Cubans to a subordinate and ancillary role, a plan of action that immediately aroused García's indignation.[70] Others derived from cultural and racial differences, for which neither side had been prepared. Yet others resulted from the peculiarities of the Cuban organization, methods, and tactics, which for the most part were incomprehensible and unacceptable to the officers and men of a conventional army such as Shafter's. There were misunderstandings, accusations, and scorn for the Cubans on the part of the U.S. soldiers, and suspicion of the U.S. personnel on the part of the Cubans. The upshot was that García's troops were virtually ignored during the final stages of the siege of Santiago, and when the terms of surrender were agreed upon, no Cuban rebel representative was present. Cubans were likewise prohibited from entering the city and excluded from the local administration. For these reasons, García resigned his command and broke publicly with the United States, actions that should have determined the end of his prominence. Paradoxically enough, they only served to mark the attempt that he then made to establish his control over the rest of Oriente.

This attempt was related to the situation that had developed in

the region immediately after the U.S. declaration of war, when the
Spanish army had begun to evacuate the towns of the interior and
to fall back on the seaport cities.[71] This move posed a problem that
the insurgents had never had to face before. In the past, whenever
they had succeeded in taking a town of any consequence, they had
shortly abandoned it lest the enemy return in force. At present, however, it appeared that the garrisons were leaving for good. How
should the rebels proceed in order to fill the void left by the Spaniards? There were more than niceties of political theory involved
in this question, for cities and towns were the places where pro-
Spanish elements were more numerous, and there was always the
danger that through cashing in on the confusion that the Spanish
collapse would inevitably bring about, they would end up controlling government jobs and thus reaping the fruits of victory. "Our
dilemma is critical and difficult to resolve," pointed out General
Demetrio Castillo, one of García's closest collaborators. "If we move
away from the population centers our influence will diminish while
that of the Hispanophiles grows. If a government is formed one day,
it will be controlled by them without fail and we will be shut out
from all the offices."[72] That Castillo's was not idle apprehension
became evident later, after the U.S. occupation began and a new regime was created in Cuba. There was then a wholesale redistribu-
tion of offices at the higher levels, but on the lower levels many
former civil servants remained on their jobs.[73] This evoked complaints among the lesser former officers, who bitterly grumbled that
their worst fears had been realized.[74]

In order not to be passed over when the Spaniards began to withdraw, therefore, García had had to concern himself with the problems of local administration. Not that such problems had been entirely neglected by the insurgents until now. Since the adoption of
the Jimaguayú constitution there had been rebel local authorities—governors of provinces, lieutenant governors, and prefects, the
latter being in charge of small districts.[75] When apprised of the situation that had arisen in Oriente, the Government Council had expressed the view that this organization would be able to cope with
it. García, however, had thought otherwise, and shortly after occupying Bayamo (April 26), the first relatively important town that fell
into his hands, he had written to Secretary of the Interior Manuel
Silva representing his opinion:

> The present local authorities—governors, chiefs of districts, prefects,
> and assistant prefects—are not equal to the job of managing the towns
> that are falling into our hands. . . . Most of them are nearly illiterate,

and, without exception, they are countrymen. . . . We must proceed according to republican principles and imitate the United States. . . . Municipal councils must be organized and mayors must be designated. But all this must be accomplished through the free vote of the citizens. . . . It is your responsibility to build up the organization that we need. Meanwhile, I have appointed mayors to rule the most important towns and deputy mayors to take charge of the others. At the same time, steps have been taken to designate a rational number of councilmen in the former. . .[76]

Whatever its intrinsic merit, García's recommendation was at odds with the constitution, and thus the government could not possibly subscribe to it. But the general was in no mood for legalistic scruples. He had been threatening to resign his post and leave Cuba unless a new political apparatus to his liking was created,[77] and consequently he flew into a rage when he realized that Masó and his cabinet refused to go along with his proposal. Ascribing their negative attitude to slothfulness,[78] he proceeded to set up municipal governments as he saw fit.

This in itself was reprehensible, but no one could have ever accused García of being a militarist had he limited himself to placing the towns under freely elected mayors and municipal councils. The trouble is that in intertwining the various municipalities into a centralized provincial structure he forgot about the rights of the people and subjected mayors and councils to the authority of his senior troop commanders. This, by the opposite token, had all the earmarks of militarism. In the circular letter into which he incorporated his directives regarding the new local administration, the general made an effort to gloss over this fact. His officers, he promised, would always respect "the freedom of action of the principal governing entities." This was hardly compatible, however, with the powers that he vested in them, and hence in himself:

Given the necessity [the circular read] that a superior authority be charged with directing and making decisions in all matters, such a task is hereby assigned to division commanders and those placed above them. These officers will be the only ones entitled to issue orders to city government officials.[79]

Máximo Gómez (who was amazed by García's audacity and lack of political common sense) understood quite clearly the implications of his subordinate's move;[80] and, as events proved later, the Government Council fully grasped them too. By means of his circular, García had in effect proclaimed himself the sole ruler of the portion of Oriente that was occupied by his troops. In those chaotic days this portion included not only the interior of Oriente with most of its towns, but also the majority of the seaport cities. Banes, Puerto Padre, and Gibara had fallen to the insurgents, Manzanillo was about to surrender, and even the Spanish garrison of Puerto Príncipe, the provincial capital of Camagüey, had intimated its willingness to abandon the city. Indeed, the chiefdom that the general had carved out for himself was not inconsiderable.[81]

The most challenging aspect of García's circular, nonetheless, is that it was dispatched from his headquarters at Casa Azul, on the outskirts of Santiago de Cuba, on July 17, 1898. It was precisely on that day that Shafter took possession of the city and prevented the Cubans from participating in its occupation, and it was on that day too that García sent him the memorable letter in which he stated his refusal to keep serving under U.S. orders.[82] Moreover, it was also on July 17 that García sent Gómez his resignation as lieutenant general of the liberating army, a step that he took because, as he put it, he was "no longer disposed to keep on obeying the orders and cooperating with the plans of the American army." "I do not want it said," he added, "that I am disobeying the orders of my government. I have no other way of protesting against the attitude of the American government than to submit my resignation."[83] Can political ambitions be fairly imputed to a general who through his actions had just given up the second highest position in the rebel army? Given the U.S. attitude in the case of Santiago, could García reasonably assume that he would be allowed to remain in control of the rest of Oriente?

These are indeed puzzling questions, albeit only superficially so. In the first place, Cubans were remarkably slow in penetrating the intentions of the United States toward the island. They knew that McKinley had refused to recognize the insurgent polity, but they had no clear and precise information about which parts of the country were to be occupied by the U.S. Army, for how long, and under what conditions. García knew that as far as his troops were concerned Santiago was out of bounds, yet he did not know then that the permanent occupation of the other towns and cities by the liberating army was also out of the question.[84] Second, it is obvious that the general never really intended to step down nor to desist from prosecuting the war. In fact, as the reference to his government's orders suggests, his letter of resignation was more than a bit pharisaical, and, as far as he was concerned, amounted to nothing more than a bureaucratic transaction.[85] Barely a month later he was boasting that, on August 16, he had led his men in the last engagement of the war.[86] To all appearances, he resigned simply because he did not wish to remain in the vicinity of Santiago after Shafter's disposition of the city and because he balked at impressing on the United States that he was acting on his own. Thus the only course open to him was to officially relinquish his post. He probably calculated that by resigning he would be free to expand the area of Oriente under his authority, which is what he set about to do immediately after he went his way.[87]

Everything seems to indicate, therefore, that García indeed undertook to preside over an autonomous chiefdom during the final phase of the war. What he hoped to accomplish with it, however, is far less clear. Even in the days in which he had trusted U.S. motives, he had insisted that Cubans should fight side by side with their allies on the front lines and should never "permit the American flag to fly without having at its side a Cuban flag."[88] Now that his early high hopes had faded and he no longer took U.S. good will for granted, he was even more emphatic about warning his forces not to give any ground to the "army of the intervention." He included a special admonition on this point in his Casa Azul circular letter, and thus perhaps it was his intention in drawing that document to create for himself a position of strength from which he could negotiate with the invaders—as McKinley considered the expeditionary forces in Cuba.[89] If so, his purpose was truly commendable. But he had acted in violation of the insurgent law, and this the moribund Government Council was not ready to condone. On August 13—the very day in which the Council received a cable from Estrada Palma announcing that he had accepted the armistice proclaimed by McKinley the day before—Masó and his colleagues passed a resolution cashiering the general because "he no longer deserved the confidence that the Council had put in him."[90] Here is what Secretary Silva had to say upon recommending such a drastic step:

The existence of a civil government in Oriente has been a myth. The chief of this military department has mischievously destroyed the organization that I vainly attempted to create. . . . Abusing the military authority, coercing in an untold manner civil officials, and publicly disowning the law passed by the Government Council, he has persecuted with rancorous ferocity the government employees who, in discharging their duties, have attempted to uphold the interests of the administration. . . . General García has designated special delegates, with powers that really pertain to civil authorities, and has placed them under the direct and immediate supervision of his officers. Thus he has . . . openly infringed . . . the constitution. . . . Ignoring the resolution that the Council passed at my request on May 10, he has absolutely nullified its terms by decreeing that local officials in the towns evacuated by the enemy be appointed by military authorities, and by subjecting these officials to no orders or laws other than those emanating from himself. In this fashion he has created a political dualism in our territory as a result of which there are presently two centers of power: the one that was legally established by the constituent assembly of 1897 and the one that General García has illegally created. . . . The existence of the latter . . . reflects a dictatorial tendency that ought to be completely eradicated. General García is the incarnation of such a tendency today.[91]

It was on this note that Cubans ended their second major effort to attain independence from Spain. The officers who served under García later gave currency to the idea that the general was dismissed by the Council because it sought to disassociate itself from his differences with Shafter.[92] Estrada Palma and Méndez Capote, who was still in New York, made some public statements in this direction. But the Council kept silent.[93] The sad truth is that, from the standpoint of civil-military relations, Cubans were in 1898 in exactly the same situation that they had been at the end of the Ten Years' War. As the struggle had dragged on, the civilian leadership had waned and the military chieftains had gained the upper hand. The only difference was that in 1898 there was an extraneous factor that also contributed to bringing about this result, and that factor was the armed intervention as carried out by the McKinley administration.

3. The Liberators As a Political Force

In the fall of 1898 the liberating army was the only organized political force that was still operative on the Cuban scene. Annexationism was no longer viable, and both the pro-Spanish and the autonomist parties had lost their raison d'être. Cuba lay in ruins. The population had been decimated; the economy was in a shambles; the backbone of the class structure had been shattered. There was not a single force on the island, either political or social, that could dispute the supremacy of the liberators, unless it was, of course, the power of the nation that was about to assume control of its government.

The Liberating Army at the End of the War

The liberating army was the most compact and substantial component of the independence movement. It had been born during the protracted struggle against Spain under the shadow of the excesses perpetrated more than half a century before by its Spanish American counterparts. For this reason, considerable efforts had been made to provide it with a legal framework and a consensual basis. The constitutions of Guáimaro, Jimaguayú, and La Yaya, and, above all, the organization of the Cuban Revolutionary Party by José Martí, testify to such efforts. Yet none of them had proved effective enough to curb the aggrandizement of the military leaders who had immediately begun to appear in free Cuba. Not the quixotic legislature created at Guáimaro but first Carlos Manuel de Céspedes and then Ignacio Agramonte and the two Garcías (Vicente and Calixto) had dominated the liberated portions of the island over the course of the Ten Years' War; and not Salvador Cisneros Betancourt or Bartolomé Masó but Máximo Gómez, Antonio Maceo, and again Calixto García had been in control in 1895–1898. If on the eve of the U.S. invasion of Cuba Calixto García could veraciously claim that his powers were "nearly absolute,"[1] can we take seriously the laws, rules, and regulations drawn up by Masó and his cabinet or, for that matter, the last-minute resolution dismissing the general from his post? García was of course right when he responded publicly to his dismissal shortly after the war ended. Upon being questioned by a U.S. correspondent about the rebel political organization he sharply replied:

> Provisional government? What are you talking about? There is no such government. . . . [What you refer to] is merely a clique of civilians that the army has invariably ignored. We allowed them to draw up laws in Camagüey provided that they remained quiet and abstained from interfering in our affairs. But we never cared about them. They are not fighting men, and the true revolutionary party in Cuba is made up exclusively of fighters. Have you ever heard of Bartolomé Masó as a fighter, or Mr. Capote in a battle? . . . These men are not the leaders in Cuba. . . . We deny that the provisional government has the authority to interfere in any way with the actions of the general in chief. The provisional government has been and is nothing more than a figurehead.[2]

But even if the army had accepted the civilian claims of authority, this would have meant little. The insurgents had consistently pretended that they constituted a republic, and at least until the United States entered the war they invariably adhered to this piece of make-believe. Ultimately, they would have surely objectified their triumph as the triumph of their republic. Yet even assuming that their assemblies were freely elected and functioned without extraneous interferences—hypotheses that are somewhat controversial[3]—it is apparent that the authority of the political institutions which these bodies created issued solely from themselves. Thus, what passed as constituent assemblies at Guáimaro, Jimaguayú, and La Yaya were nothing more than army assemblies. Publicly, as in Gómez's impugnment of President Cleveland's message to Congress, the insurgents stressed the broad popular base of their government. But they never deceived themselves about this. Gómez himself was acutely aware of the fact that Masó and his associates were not "the product of an assembly of the people but of the army,"[4] and that consequently they made up a revolutionary government rather than the government of the republic. "It has always seemed foolish to me," he said, "when I read 'Republic of Cuba' in our official correspondence."[5] This was also García's private belief. "We are an armed people fighting for independence and liberty. As such we should be looked upon as a people of soldiers."[6]

This "people of soldiers," moreover, merely formed a minority within the Cuban people as a whole. This was true from the point of view of sheer numerical strength. In 1899 the population of Cuba was 1,572,797 inhabitants,[7] of which 418,000 were males of voting age, as defined by the 1899–1900 electoral system.[8] The insurgents, on the other hand, as disclosed in a report prepared at approximately the same time, totaled only 69,800, a number that perhaps should be reduced by the 9,000 who joined the ranks after the U.S. intervention took place. Another illustrative piece of information is that the number of casualties, although admittedly incomplete, did not exceed 5,000.[9] The number of the insurgents therefore was never very large. Gómez once calculated that those who served at one time or another during the entire war came to 53,774,[10] but even the most fervent defenders of the insurgents view their effective combatant force as never more than 30,000 strong,[11] and, in any case, when the liberating army was disbanded, fewer than 40,000 men received payments. The figure agreed upon at the time was 33,390.[12]

It is true that there were perhaps an equal number of unarmed men in the insurgent ranks[13] and that their cause was supported in the cities by an indeterminate number of civilians.[14] But it is also true—although Cuban historians rarely dwell on the fact—that there were many Cubans fighting on the Spanish side, a circumstance that proves conclusively that the desire for independence was not as widespread as it is often said. There were Cuban-born officers in the Spanish regular army just as there were Spaniards occupying prominent positions in the liberating army.[15] Yet where the native contribution was more noticeable was in the markedly Cuban guerrillas, the body of irregular forces that was first organized by Spain in 1869 and subsequently revitalized by Weyler when he took command of the captaincy general early in 1896. The guerrillas represented no more than 6 percent of the total Spanish strength, but they made up approximately 51.5 percent of the mobilized forces and constituted the core of most of the Spanish columns that crisscrossed the Cuban countryside. The units that operated in isolation from the regular troops were responsible for many abuses and cruelties, but other units rendered important military services to Spain up to the siege of Santiago de Cuba. According to some estimates, their numerical strength at the time was close to 16,000;[16] according to others it nearly reached 25,000.[17] One of its most distinguished units was the so-called Santa Catalina del Guaso squad, which operated in the Guantanamo region. This squad was composed primarily of native blacks.[18]

To a large extent this was also the racial composition of the liberating army. Edwin F. Atkins (1850–1926), a sugar baron from Boston who owned the Soledad mill in Las Villas, reckoned the liberators as 80 percent black.[19] Blacks themselves subsequently claimed that this proportion had been as high as 85 percent,[20] although other estimates would reduce it to only 70 percent.[21] Whichever estimate we choose, the truth is that blacks were the backbone of the insurgent columns, which were completely integrated units where men of all colors fought side by side. Blacks were also well represented in the senior commissioned ranks of the army: they accounted for approximately 40 percent of the total,[22] while 22 of the 140 rebel generals were black.[23] This is after all what might be expected in a movement led by army veterans of humble social origins and—under them—by professional men and middle-class intellectuals. Despite the fact that some leading members of the old Cuban landed oligarchy (particularly those ruined as a result of the crisis of the 1880s) joined the insurrection, the liberating army consisted chiefly of peasants and other rural elements.[24] Among them the blacks were overrepresented. Since they made up only about 32 percent of the entire population,[25] it is obvious that the army also constituted a minority from a racial standpoint.

The type of war waged by such an army had to be, almost of necessity, a revolutionary war. What else could be expected when in a certain area the rebel commander was the former slave of the local plantation?[26] In order to understand this dimension of the conflict, there is no need to consider Martí's ill-defined social concerns, which were all but forgotten after his death, or Gómez's scorched-earth policy, which was basically a military strategy. It is likewise unnecessary to mention the general's decree of July 4, 1896, ordering the division of confiscated enemy property among "the defenders of the Cuban Republic against Spain,"[27] for such a decree was nothing more than a measure devised to compensate and reward his soldiers, probably inspired by the example of Bolívar.[28] Instead it is critical to recognize that the popular extraction of the rebels determined the character of the 1895–1898 Cuban war of independence, although we will never be able to gauge with any degree of accuracy the extent to which this factor would have transformed society had the war been able to run its course. The U.S. intervention made this impossible. Contemporaries, however, were fully aware that it was rather more than a mere attempt to cast off Spanish domination. At the very least the Spaniards living in Cuba would have been right in fearing that their property would be expropriated and that they would be expelled from the island. Such had been the fate of the

Spanish-born population elsewhere in Spanish America earlier in the century.[29]

Postwar Economy and Society

Aside from the U.S. military, there was not a single group, institution, social class, or political organization strong enough to prevent an insurgent takeover or to keep the authority of the liberators within bounds. After three and a half years of ruthless devastation by both sides, the once prosperous island had been turned into a wasteland. "There is nothing left in Cuba," Gómez informed Estrada Palma, ". . . its land is barren, deserted, and the nearby brush has crept up over the plain."[30] Largely owing to Weyler's policy of concentrating the peasants in urban areas, roughly 300,000 people— or close to 20 percent of the prewar estimated population of about 1,800,000—had been wiped out.[31] In the larger cities and towns the situation was somewhat better, but partly as a result of the blockade of the Cuban ports by the U.S. fleet, starvation and disease were rampant everywhere. Local government had virtually ceased to function; mail service was paralyzed and nearly half of the public primary schools had closed.[32] In the interior, many small towns had been reduced to ashes; others had been sacked and simply were uninhabitable. The country roads had been transformed into ditches and the few railroads were in complete disrepair. Bridges and telegraph lines were down or totally inoperable. A substantial portion of the rural and village population was sick from malaria. Previously flourishing regions were now depopulated, for they had become a haven for brigands and people were afraid to return to their farms for fear of the Spanish guerrillas who were still in the hills.[33]

For the weakened and anemic Cubans who survived the war the future was bleak. The war, combined with the Spanish American tariff conflict of the 1890s, had destroyed two-thirds of Cuba's productive capacity.[34] The activities that made up the economic base of Cuban life were either at a standstill or appeared at an end. Commerce and manufacturing had been interrupted. Mining had come to a halt. Agriculture, above all, seemed to have suffered most. Before the war there had been 90,000 farms and plantations on the island; in 1899 the number had dropped to only 60,000. In 1895 there had been well over 1,300,000 acres under cultivation; only 900,000 of these were returned to production with the advent of peace.[35] Cuba had been self-sustaining in livestock at the beginning of the conflict. But after more than three years of uncontrolled consumption and pillaging, only an eighth of the cattle remained and under a sixth of the horses.[36] The production of tobacco also had declined considerably. The 1894–1895 crop reached 62 million pounds; the 1897–1898 crop plummeted to less than 10 million.[37] Meanwhile, the production of coffee, which for various reasons had been steadily decreasing since the middle of the century, received a finishing blow. After the war, coffee accounted for less than 2 percent of the cultivated area on the island.[38]

The speedy reconstruction of war-torn Cuba therefore necessitated vast amounts of capital. Yet Cubans had none, nor access to sources of credit. Rather they were heavily in debt. Ever since the sugar crisis of 1884 the value of real estate had declined on the island, and consequently in many areas the amounts of cash advanced on mortgages had come to exceed the declared value of the encumbered properties. Such had been the situation especially in the cities. As the economy further deteriorated under the impact of the war, an increasing number of property owners found it difficult to meet their obligations—interest rates of 20 to 40 percent were not unusual at the time.[39] This forced the colonial government into action, and on May 15, 1896, a loan payment moratorium was decreed. This was followed by another one, which went into effect two years later.[40] But the relief thereby accorded to debtors proved insufficient, and between 1898 and 1900 many of them had to sell their properties in order to escape foreclosure.[41] The number of farms that were sold in this way averaged 3,700 a year during this period.[42]

This picture of ruin and desolation was nowhere more apparent than in the sugar industry, the fulcrum of Cuba's wealth and therefore the chief target of the scorched-earth tactics of Cubans and Spaniards alike. An indeterminate number of sugar mills had been destroyed,[43] thousands of hectares of cane fields had been repeatedly burned, and crop cultivation had been neglected. Many of the mills that survived were unable to operate for want of cane. There was no fuel, equipment, or capital to resume operations. In the cities, factories connected with the sugar industry were idled. As a result, sugar production fell from a little over 1,000,000 tons in 1894 to 335,668 tons in 1899.[44]

The disturbance was so severe that it delivered the coup de grace to what was left of the Cuban sugar aristocracy, the master class that had traditionally dominated the island's economy and society. The plantation system upon which this class had based its preeminence had begun to disintegrate years ago, at the time of the Ten Years' War. The conflict had destroyed over a hundred backward, slave-operated sugar mills in eastern Cuba,[45] and Spain's confiscatory measures had deprived a number of insurgent or proinsurgent mill-owners of their property.[46] But what had really driven the industry into a structural crisis and decimated the ranks of the planters had been the pressure for modernization and consolidation generated by the competition from European beet sugar, which had steadily increased during the war. This process (which clearly exceeds in importance the end of slavery in 1888[47]) had culminated early in 1884, when prices dropped badly, so much in fact that it became impossible for small, inefficient mills to operate at a profit. Mortgaged to the hilt and unable to mechanize and expand as the times required, they were forced to halt grinding.[48] The belle époque of the Cuban "sugar nobility" therefore came to an end during the postwar years, and although prosperity returned in the 1890s, by then only the owners of the larger mills had been able to survive. They now had to share social hegemony with a different type of magnate—the group of parvenus, largely war profiteers, who had acquired estates in Cuba.[49] On the eve of the 1895–1898 war they had to face yet another crisis, this time resulting from a drop in world prices that coincided with the resumption of a 40 percent duty on all sugar entering the United States, on whose market Cuba had come to depend. Their situation became extremely precarious, for they had overextended in response to the bonanza that had antedated the crisis. It was precisely at this juncture that they were overtaken by the ravages of the war.[50]

With the decline of their mills, the sugar barons lost their leadership role in society. Unlike most Spanish American nations, therefore, Cuba set about severing its ties with Spain without the stabilizing influence of a strong civilian elite.[51] Nor could it rely during this critical period upon the Catholic church, an institution endowed with prestige and authority in the other republics.[52] Weakened by the wave of anticlerical excesses that swept Spain in the first half of the nineteenth century[53] and thoroughly Hispanicized by the Concordat of 1851,[54] the Cuban church had nevertheless been able to prevent the total identification of its bishops with the Spanish side when the Ten Years' War broke out. Yet, upon the restoration of Alfonso XII (1874), it had cast its lot with the dynasty, and Cubans had resented the consequent attitude of the hierarchy and the clergy—all of whom were overwhelmingly Spanish and thus tended to view Hispanicism and Catholicism as one and the same.[55] As a result, the church had lost ground to libertarian deists, free-thinkers, and masons. On August 4, 1880, Raymundo Fernández Piérola, bishop of Havana, had officially reported that fewer than

3,000 out of a total of 200,000 people attended mass in the city, whereas the same population managed to support more than fifty masonic lodges.[56] When the struggle for independence resumed in 1895, Cuba's prelates had followed the lead of the Holy See and the peninsular bishops and looked upon the insurrection as an anti-Catholic masonic conspiracy. Havana's bishop, Manuel Santander, had publicly and repeatedly characterized the insurgents as violent men moved by a satanic hatred against humanity and religion.[57] This unreservedly pro-Spanish posture proved to be fateful. For, despite the fact that a number of native priests supported the insurgent cause,[58] when Spain was humbled in 1898 its defeat was also the defeat of the church. Forced to beat a retreat and politically discredited as an institution, it reached the nadir of its prestige on the island.[59]

In 1898, then, Cuba's social structure was in a state of flux. In addition to the depressed oligarchs and the uncared-for clergy, there existed on the island, to be sure, other more or less clearly defined social groups.[60] One of them was formed by loyalist merchants, speculators, army suppliers, and corrupt government officials. Another, which passed as a colonial middle class,[61] consisted of largely Spanish bureaucrats, armed forces personnel, and retail merchants. For obvious reasons, neither of these two groups could hope to play a significant role in independent Cuba. Nor could any such role be played by people of lesser social standing—for example, the small group of tobacco workers or the impoverished, half-famished, and geographically dispersed peasants. Cuban society had been built upon subjugation and servitude, and only recently had been subjected to the harshness of Weyler's counterinsurgency methods. The mass of the population was inarticulate, illiterate (about 60 percent of the total[62]), poverty-stricken, and—insofar as it had not been involved in the war—politically apathetic. It was consequently extremely vulnerable to the ambitions and lack of scruples of would-be "saviours of the fatherland," a weakness made all the more evident by the existence of a sizable black or mulatto minority (then estimated at roughly 500,000[63]) that included perhaps 70,000 former slaves and many more first-generation freemen.[64] This minority was the largest illiterate segment of the population (72 percent could neither read nor write[65]), the poorest,[66] the most susceptible to the social ills of the time,[67] and the least apt to break through the existing social barriers.[68] Noncombatant blacks and mulattoes did not benefit from the racial fraternity that was observable in the liberating army.[69] For the most part they could only aspire to occupy a passive and secondary position for the foreseeable future.

Alone among noncombatant Cubans, the ones who might have proven capable of exercising some sort of leadership at the time, were those who had been active in autonomist politics throughout the postwar interlude and even while the war raged. These elements were the more affluent and best educated, and they comprised planters, property owners, merchants, members of the professions, law professors, and magistrates. Among them there were men of recognized ability: astute politicians, high-caliber intellectuals, and dedicated public servants who, under different circumstances, would have doubtless counted themselves among those presiding over the period of transition. But after the recrudescence of Spanish intransigence under Weyler, many deserted the ranks of the party and sided openly with the insurrection, in Cuba and abroad; a minority embraced the lost cause of annexation, or that of the U.S. protectorate, which seemed the only feasible one at the time; still others were persistent, stouthearted, or shortsighted enough to return from exile to assume positions in the home rule government inaugurated by Spain on January 1, 1898. Among these were many ranking members of the old party leadership, men who thereby disqualified themselves for a role of any consequence in an independent Cuba. They and their colleagues had insisted for too long (in the case of the prime minister of the new government, José María Gálvez, for nearly twenty years) on reform within the Spanish system; their identification with the policies emanating from Madrid had been too close. As in the case of the church, Spain's defeat was also their defeat. They too had to look forward to brighter and more auspicious times.[70]

This left the separatists as the only viable political movement in Cuba. Colonialism and autonomism were things of the past, spent forces that had already gone down in history; separatism was oriented toward the future. At the fringes of the separatist spectrum, especially among the expatriates who served the cause abroad, there were many who were advocates of annexation or the protectorate.[71] But in the areas of Cuba controlled by the insurgents, separatism was synonymous with self-determination,[72] and there was no nationalist party (or parties) on the island at the time that possessed any degree of independence from the liberating army. Even the Cuban Revolutionary party, the political organization that had initiated the armed struggle, had turned into an appendage to the army.[73] The soldiers made up the chief separatist politico-military agency, and their leaders were the most forceful exponents of the cause. Separatist government therefore meant government by the liberating army. Upper class and educated Cubans, whose views passed as public opinion at the time, seem to have understood well this reality. Aware of the weakness of their position, they were ready to give in to the liberators. Contemporaries tell us that before they learned of Washington's plans for Cuba, many of them contemplated a dictatorship by General Máximo Gómez as a distinct possibility.[74]

4. The Disbandment of the Liberating Army

The likelihood, then, is that not consent but military power would have been the foundation of the Cuban republic—had it been allowed to go its own way.[1] As things happened, however, the Cuban liberators, because in 1898 the United States set itself in opposition to them (nearly as much as to Spain), suffered the consequences of defeat largely as though they had actually been overcome on the field. They ceased to exist as an armed body, and their leaders had no alternative but to yield to the new master of the situation.

The removal of Spanish authority, moreover, did not leave a political vacuum on the island, as had occurred elsewhere in Spanish America earlier in the century. Unlike their mainland confreres, therefore, Cuba's liberators lost rather than gained control of the country that they had fought to liberate. They had to show conformity to the foreign presence, cooperate with the new authorities, and share the fruits of victory with their former adversaries. Thenceforward, acquiescence rather than rebellion marked out the road to independence. Any other course would have been unrealistic and perhaps suicidal.

The Postwar Strategy of the Liberators

There is no need for speculation in order to ascertain what would have happened in Cuba in the case of an unqualified insurgent victory. Even after the U.S. Army began to occupy the island, Calixto García's practice of moving into the towns and villages evacuated by the Spaniards was widely followed by other insurgents. Consequently parts of Cuba fell under the sway of the liberating army. At first this was possible because the U.S. Army was chiefly interested in acquiring control of the island's customhouses and thus tended to neglect the population centers located in the interior.[2] The liberators had their biggest opportunity when, as a result of the peace negotiations between Spain and the United States, Cuba was in effect temporarily partitioned. In the province of Oriente, which remained under U.S. sovereignty by right of conquest, there was little that the liberators could do. Here García's plan immediately clashed with the U.S. decision to be the sole holder of authority over Cuba. A week had not elapsed after the end of hostilities when General H. W. Lawton, newly appointed military commander of the province, wired the War Department: "These people [the liberators] still maintain their organizations, are scattered through the country in vicinity of city, are threatening in their attitude, and keep the inhabitants stirred up and panicky by threats and acts of violence."[3] In a dispatch to Washington sent on the same day (August 16), General Shafter put it far more clearly: "A dual government can't exist here; we have got to have full sway of the Cubans."[4] These messages elicited a quick response from Washington, making it clear that interference would not be permitted and that Cubans had no choice but to recognize the absolute dominance of the region by the United States.[5] As might be expected, the implementation of García's plan came to an abrupt halt.

But the other Cuban provinces to a large extent were up for grabs in the period between the signing of the peace protocol on August 12, 1898, and the establishment of U.S. control of the island on January 1, 1899. Although still included in the orbit of Spanish rule, according to the protocol Spain had already committed itself to relinquish all claims of sovereignty and title to them. Furthermore, the Spanish army was under the obligation of withdrawing from them by the time of the transfer of power to the United States. This was carried out during the closing months of 1898, and because U.S. troops did not move immediately to occupy the abandoned territory, Cuban army units were able to break through the dikes. As the Spaniards gradually marched away from the interior they quickly replaced them, taking charge of the evacuated regions and functioning there as an interim government. It is difficult to estimate the magnitude of the area over which the insurgents gained local mastery in this way. Yet there is little doubt that it amounted to a substantial portion of the island. A U.S. observer said that "in every small town and in every village, the Cuban soldiers were in charge";[6] and General James H. Wilson, who became the military commander of Matanzas after the United States assumed full responsibility for the government of Cuba, was able to list some 350 towns in this province alone occupied by Cuban troops.[7]

This systematic occupation of the island probably would have been the upshot of the collapse of Spanish authority in any event, but as it happened the liberators were merely following the example and advice of García, who urged them to prove to the world that Cubans were as orderly a people as any, and that therefore they should be permitted to proceed freely to create a republic.[8] Their performance, it must be noted, was not always irreproachable, for it appears that some of them behaved "immorally" in the towns evacuated by the enemy. This led Máximo Gómez to dispatch a circular from his headquarters setting penalties for such offenses.[9] As a rule, however, the liberators did some valuable work in the urban areas that they transiently controlled. Generally speaking they took upon themselves the task of preserving peace and bringing about a condition of order; and as General John R. Brooke, Cuba's first military governor, subsequently testified, they performed their police duties well. Amid the considerable confusion incidental to the withdrawal of the Spanish troops and their replacement with U.S. forces, the liberators managed to maintain order.[10] Likewise, they worked in harmony with U.S. officers and men during the several weeks that it took the Brooke administration to extend its authority to all parts of the island.[11]

The liberators' initial reaction to the occupation, therefore, was to demonstrate how they would have behaved had they been the masters of the situation. According to their leaders, their conduct would have been nothing short of exemplary. The generals would have retired to their homes, either to rest on their laurels, as Gómez professed,[12] or to work and be a model for their subordinates as García said he would do,[13] and the mission of governing the country would have been entrusted to intellectuals, men who no doubt were better qualified to run public affairs than the uncouth and untutored warriors.[14] Having succeeded, after a fashion, in expelling the Spaniards from Cuba after thirty years of struggle, the insurgent chieftains seemed to be satisfied. García explicitly said so, adding emphatically: "Neither today nor ever will I be capable of troubling our fatherland."[15] Gómez, for his part, philosophically concluded that he had done "all that [he] could humanly do to help Cubans" and that his mission, as he saw it, was "nearly fulfilled."[16] In a proclamation that he issued from Yaguajay, Las Villas, upon the termination of the war, he gave Cubans this solemn piece of advice: "We must never forget that although the sword is a most useful instrument for directing and governing affairs while at war, it is not very good for performing such tasks while at peace. What people must be told in peacetime is what is written in the law, and the military mind is too tough to interpret the spirit of the law with the necessary compassion."[17] Indeed, it appeared that both generals, authoritarian and ill-disposed to tolerate criticism and dissent as they were, stood ready to make themselves as unobtrusive as possible. "It is not inconceivable," Gómez wrote to Estrada Palma, "that one of these days I will suddenly throw myself into your arms and bid you farewell."[18]

It seems, then, that in the contingency of a rebel takeover, non-combatant Cubans, either neutral or pro-Spanish, as well as the Spaniards who lived in Cuba would have had nothing to fear. The reassuring statements that the insurgent leaders made in this connection seem to leave no room for doubt. García, for example, once told Estrada Palma that the "armed people that is fighting in Cuba wishes to create a free and honest fatherland for all Cubans . . . for those who are here [in Cuba], for those who are there [abroad], for those who have sided with the *godos* [the Spaniards] and repent, and even for the *godos* themselves if they choose to remain or come here."[19] However, it was Gómez who, as Spain began to wind up its affairs in the island, most decisively adhered to a policy of concord and unity among all its inhabitants. Calling to mind all of a sudden the solemn pledges that he and Martí had made in the long forgotten Manifesto of Montecristi,[20] he embarked on a campaign that few would have expected from the ruthless soldier who, barely a few months earlier, had ordered that sugar mill owners identified as milling in violation of his war decrees be hung immediately without a trial.[21] Shortly after the peace protocol was signed, for example, he stated in a public letter to Estrada Palma that he "would prefer that no one ever again speak of vanquishers and vanquished";[22] and even more startling pronouncements may be found in his proclamation of Yaguajay, where he had this to say about the future rulers of Cuba:

In order to move faster along the road of national organization, select as masters of your destiny proven men of outstanding virtues, without asking them first where they were and what they were doing while Cuba was shedding blood fighting for its independence. . . . We must stop relating our past exploits. That task must be left to the majestic discipline of history. Otherwise, we would be annoying those who should have performed similar deeds and did not. The talk about our own exploits involves an implicit accusation that is irritating and predisposes people to disunion and discord.[23]

A few months later the general returned to the same subject in a series of manifestos and other public declarations addressed to the liberating army and the Cuban people in general. "The revolution . . . ," he said in one of them, "solely looks for honest men regardless of their political extraction or what their birth certificate states."[24] In another he clearly extended the olive branch to the Spaniards: "I did not wage war against the Spaniards," he protested. "Those who have said that I did so have slandered me. I fought against Spain, against the Spanish administration. . . . [Now] concord between Spaniards and Cubans must prevail."[25] Further on he expressed his joy that this was already happening: "We are getting closer to each other, we know each other, we love each other. Long live the Spaniards! Long live the republic!"[26]

Indeed, Martí himself could not have sounded more open-minded or more conciliatory. Still, baffling as Gómez's repeated statements were, his words could not but make an impact on the insurgent camp, and soon some of his most distinguished lieutenants publicly endorsed his preaching.[27] The Government Council, although tottering on the brink of its political grave, also followed the general's lead and went on record as an advocate of harmony and brotherhood. This it did, by the way, in a most interesting fashion, for Masó and his associates found no better way of allaying the fears of their fellow citizens than to quote from the Bases of the Cuban Revolutionary party in which Martí had assured Cubans that they would not be victimized by a "victorious group susceptible to regarding the island as its prey and domain."[28] It seemed as though the frail little man of genius who had launched the war could not be left out of the new scenario that the insurgents were now envisaging. The republic "with all and for the good of all" of which he had dreamed appeared to have finally captured the imagination of even the most battle-hardened veterans.[29]

According to García, this republic would have to be the work of "a great assembly, a great convention composed of representatives of all Cubans, regardless of their political tendencies or convictions."[30] Gómez held similar views. The war had not yet ended when he began to recommend to the Government Council the convocation of such an assembly,[31] and he continued to insist during the months that followed that the definitive structure of the republic should be the handiwork of this body.[32] Thus there can be no question that the two generals committed themselves to the observance of republican and democratic modes of procedure. True, neither of them, their statements to the contrary notwithstanding, ever showed the slightest inclination to withdraw from the Cuban political scene.[33] But both went on record about their willingness to accept without reservation any political arrangement that was sanctioned by a majority vote. "I will accept anything," García said, "except comic opera dictators shored up by puppet governments."[34] Gómez put it in stronger terms: "If the people want another Weyler for president of the republic," he told a close friend, "I will regret it in silence, but nothing else."[35]

Yet the more the matter of this "great assembly" is examined the more it seems that Martí's grand design would not have been viable—at least not in 1898. Gómez's diary and correspondence clearly evidence that for all his professed belief in unity and concord as the cement of the Cuban nationality, the thought of delivering the nascent republic to his "erstwhile enemies" never crossed his mind. The general thought that the task of "consolidating peace," as he liked to refer to the transitional period ahead, could not be trusted to these elements,[36] and therefore it is apparent that he viewed the upcoming period as one in which the insurgents would play the role of a "preponderant political force."[37] The preoccupation of other insurgent leaders with the control of government offices was by no means foreign to him.[38] Like his comrades in arms, he dreaded the ambitions of the "bad Cubans, *guerrilleros* [pro-Spanish Cuban irregulars], and autonomists." People like them, he noted, had succeeded in monopolizing governmental posts in Central America after independence, and he was not in the least disposed to allow them—disloyal, avaricious, and conniving as they were—to achieve a similar success in Cuba and to push those who had been "good patriots" into a corner. To be sure, rancorous feelings and vindictive thoughts had to be set aside, for the Manifesto of Montecristi had said that the hatchet would be buried and that promise had to be kept. Still, it would be a mistake to grant a bill of indemnity too soon to guerrilleros and autonomists.[39] Before the liberating army slackened its grip on them, it was necessary to establish a center of insurgent power in the country capable of keeping them at bay and preventing them from tipping the scale in their favor. It was to bring this center of power into being that Gómez urged the Government Council to convoke the assembly, and such being the case it is obvious that problems of representation did not worry him excessively. As far as he was concerned, a "more or less representative" body was right to meet the needs of the moment.[40]

Evidently most of the insurgents shared the views of their commander in chief, for when the Council finally acted upon his recommendation on August 14, 1898, no one was troubled by the fact that only members of the thirty-one corps of the liberating army were asked to send delegates to Santa Cruz del Sur, the small Camagüeyan town where the assembly met on October 24. At the time, delegate Manuel Sanguily remarked that the liberators amounted to nothing more than a "handful of patriots" who had risen up against Spain and who should dissolve the meeting and return home as soon as possible.[41] But apparently the rest of the forty-four general officers and colonels in attendance[42] went about their business without paying too much attention to Sanguily's words or to the fact that their meeting was merely a replica of those previously held at Jimaguayú and La Yaya, that is, it was strictly an army assembly. Sure enough, it styled itself a preliminary proceeding destined to pave the way for a future constituent assembly representing all Cubans; and, in convoking it, the Council had once again insisted on the absolute necessity of forgetting past differences. "Genuine peace makes it indispensable," Masó and his colleagues declared. "Our people need a total and complete peace, a condition that would not obtain if a triumphant party instituted a regime of exclusion and vengeance. Such behavior would imply committing the crime of giving new forms to an old struggle."[43]

Nevertheless, in justifying their summons to the delegates, the Cuban civilian leaders disclosed further political motives. The Council, they stated, had been constituted to preside over the war. Hence its authority had terminated upon the arrival of peace, and this made it imperative to decide about the "governmental entity that [should] aspire to direct public affairs pending the convocation and gathering of the general constituent assembly."[44] This "entity" was foremost in Masó's mind, to the extent that he found it necessary to go back to the subject in his message greeting the delegates. The Council had endeavored, he explained, to elicit as much public support as possible for the assembly, with the goal of emphasizing the importance of its mandate. The delegates would of course have to define the posture of the liberating movement vis-à-vis the ambiguous attitude of the United States and to make an attempt to clarify Washington's intentions. But it would also be their duty "to provide on an interim basis the governance and structure of the republic until the definitive constituent assembly convenes." This, Masó added, was tantamount to saying that thenceforward the delegates would have "the power to decide all matters related to the revolution or pertaining to the island of Cuba."[45]

In order to confirm this power, the Council dissolved itself then and there. But the provisional government that was supposed to succeed it (and which must not be confused with the Executive Committee that the assembly did appoint) was never created. This was due, of course, to the fact of the U.S. presence, which was formalized only two months later. The consensus within the ranks of the liberators was clearly to assert their political supremacy with the exclusion of "bad Cubans, guerrilleros, and autonomists"; and everything they did after the cease-fire—and before they realized that their claims were useless—was part of a political strategy devised to achieve that end. Although a good deal of their rhetoric at the time was obviously inspired by the peculiarities of the situation in which they saw themselves, it is impossible to determine with any degree of accuracy if every pronouncement of the military leaders (who contradicted themselves often enough[46]) or every statement of the Council (including the abrupt unearthing of Martí's preaching) would have been made in the absence of the U.S. intervention. By the same token, however, it is unimaginable that such a consequential event had no influence whatsoever on what was said and done at the time. Ever since the first American soldier set foot on Cuban soil, or better yet, ever since the McKinley administration resolved to appropriate the Cuban struggle for independence, the frame of reference of political activity had changed drastically on the island. Everything that occurred from then on was affected by this change.

The Road to Disarmament and Disbandment

This new correlation of forces became manifest initially in Oriente, where peace between vanquishers and vanquished was immediately superseded by a potential conflict between the two victorious armies, both of which laid claim to sovereignty over the divided province. After the fall of Santiago de Cuba, the original cooperation between García's and Shafter's troops had given way to an adversarial relationship which, if anything, had grown worse following the armistice. Shafter's explanation of his cavalier treatment of the Cubans upon the occupation of the city (fear of reprisals against the Spanish population[47]) had merely added fuel to the fire, and tensions had reached the breaking point after General Demetrio Castillo was appointed as mayor only to be dismissed shortly afterward because of the "hungry, vengeful horde" that followed him.[48] The final insult had been the designation of a former Spanish officeholder to replace Castillo, a step that exacerbated the resentment of the Cubans and made an unpleasant incident appear inevitable. Doubt, suspicion, and apprehensiveness had spread widely among the insurgents, and some of the officers had begun to talk gloomily about the necessity of having to resume the struggle, this time against the United States. General Pedro Pérez, the commander in the Guantánamo area, went on record about his willingness to fight another thirty years if necessary; and General Juan E. Ducasse also acknowledged publicly that he had already started to stockpile arms and supplies for the approaching conflict.[49] These officers, of course, were merely echoing the attitude of their chief, Calixto García, who saw "only darkness on the horizon." "No one can be held responsible for what may happen in the future," he somberly told Estrada Palma.[50] "I think that the United States will keep its word," he wrote on another occasion. "Otherwise there will always be time to die, if not to win."[51]

As a result, rumors about an anti-U.S. uprising began to circulate and to add their weight to the worries, misinformation, petty rivalries, and recriminations that clouded the end of the "splendid little war." Washington, aware through Shafter that the Oriente insurgents might "lead to complications of grave character,"[52] was subsequently informed that "Cubans had no love for Americans" and that they looked forward to "a conflict between themselves and the U.S.," having "expressed a readiness to participate in such conflict when it did come."[53] On the strength of these reports, late in August 1898 the United States took steps to reinforce its military forces in Cuba and to prevent the liberating army from receiving any outside help. A blockade of the island was proclaimed, and Cubans were alerted to the fact that they would not get any food supplies nor be appointed to any jobs as long as they remained under arms.[54] It seemed as though Cuba and the United States were about to come to blows.

But the situation in Cuba was quite different from that in the Philippines, where another disillusioned group of patriots also helped by the United States was preparing to challenge the imperial designs of the U.S. expansionists. Calixto García, who was then fifty-nine years old, had devoted nearly half of his life to fighting for Cuba's independence, and he was not physically capable of imitating General Emilio Aguinaldo, the Filipino leader, and renewing the struggle against the United States. Consequently, along with his fears and misgivings, he had also conveyed to Estrada Palma his desire for assistance in reaching some sort of understanding with the U.S. authorities in Santiago. Clinging to his long-held opinion that Masó and his cabinet did not constitute a true government, he had basically agreed with the U.S. plan to organize a stable government in Cuba; and most important, he had concurred with the need to disband his men. It had always seemed ridiculous to him that a general should be left without any troops to command at the very moment of victory;[55] but as one of his most distinguished officers, General Enrique Collazo, subsequently put it, his "glorious soldiers," deprived of the source of supplies and provisions on which they had depended during the war, had gradually been transformed into "an army of beggars living on public charity and relying on the generosity of friends in order to shed the rags of war."[56] Under the combined pressure of starvation, illness, and unemployment, García's army had begun to disintegrate.

But the dissolution of the liberators was happening too slowly for the McKinley administration, which did not relish either the prospect of yet another armed clash in Cuba and was anxious to expedite the process. How could this end be achieved, given the deep-seated animosity between García and Shafter? The opportunity presented itself when General Lawton assumed the military governorship of Oriente, at which time he was instructed to take the necessary steps to improve relations with the rebel chieftain. This directive resulted in a number of conferences between the two generals, during which Lawton apparently succeeded in persuading García that the United States would honor the congressional pledge to respect Cuba's independence. So it was that, on September 23, the general finally entered Santiago with his troops as a guest of the Americans, who met him outside the city and then escorted him as he marched through the streets along which thousands had gathered to celebrate the event. Lawton had told him that Cuban cooperation was essential to speed up the transition to self-government, and he rose to the occasion with an emotional speech in which he expressed his gratitude to the United States, which he called "a grand nation." "A grand nation it must be," he added, "when sons of millionaires, who have nothing to gain in Cuba save the glory of the soldier, have nonetheless come here to die side by side with the Cubans." For this reason nothing could ever diminish Cuba's gratitude toward the United States.[57]

It appears that a few days later García (who was as destitute as his soldiers) was offered and accepted a municipal job at a modest salary;[58] and it was at this time too that he made public his view that no government should be recognized in Cuba but that of the United States,[59] a statement that led some to report that he advocated annexation.[60] Nothing, of course, could be farther from the truth, as he subsequently made clear, and by the beginning of October he was threatening war if General Leonard Wood (the former governor of Santiago who had succeeded Lawton as governor of Oriente) did not provide work and rations for his men. This Wood flatly refused to do as long as the soldiers remained under arms,[61] thus demonstrating that Cuban resistance to U.S. authority could not go beyond rhetorical outbursts. García's army (about 14,000 strong[62]) then proceeded to disintegrate rapidly, perhaps encouraged by a liberal furlough policy instituted by the Government Council.[63] Some of the men became brigands. The majority, however, slowly gave up their arms, seeking to take advantage of the food-and-jobs-for-guns policy established by U.S. officials at the outset and now actively promoted by Wood with a public works program.[64] As a result, by the end of October it appeared that the eastern corps of the liberating army had ceased to exist, and so Wood reported to General Brooke when the latter inquired about the situation some months later. He must have been thunderstruck when a subsequent investigation uncovered the fact that several thousand armed men had been meeting in Oriente every fortnight for drill and review, and then dispersed until the next muster![65]

While the eastern liberators were resorting to these expedients in order to preserve a semblance of unity, liberators in the central and western parts of the island were busy raising Cuba's single-starred flag over the areas evacuated by the Spaniards. They had even less incentive than their confreres in the east to dissolve their military organization, for the United States had not yet even attempted to move into the territory under their control and, after all, despite the fact that the withdrawal was proceeding apace, there were still many thousands of Spanish soldiers left on the island. Then there was the question of the lack of candor of their putative ally. Contrasted with the impervious posture assumed by U.S. agents and military personnel in Oriente, the resounding phrases of the congressional resolution authorizing McKinley to terminate the war in Cuba did not seem reassuring enough. Moreover, upon returning from his sojourn in the north, Vice-President Méndez Capote had reported to his colleagues on the Government Council that there existed in Washington "great fears and marked prejudices" concerning the real intentions of the Cuban insurgents and of their actions.[66] Upon first learning the news of the U.S. intervention, officers and men had cheered in the rebel camps,[67] but they were now in a sullen mood, full of resentment and bitterness toward the United States. Would their humanitarian and liberty-loving friends from Washington be duplicitous enough to disavow their previous commitment to the independence of Cuba? As in the east, the ominous thought of a new war against the United States crossed the mind of the leadership.[68] For the time being, however, the decision in which everyone concurred, field commanders and Council alike, was to resist the pressure to disband and to keep the men organized under arms.[69] All the remaining agencies of war—the Cuban Junta, the Cuban Revolutionary party, and the local patriotic juntas—were equally kept alive insofar as it was possible.

To maintain the insurgent forces banded together was truly a Sisyphean task, for conditions were at least as bad in central and western

Cuba as in the east. Even before the end of hostilities, because of the U.S. blockade,[70] the suffering of the men had become tenfold as great. While fighting the Spaniards, they had exposed themselves to danger; they had endured exposure, hardship, and sickness; and they had gone without medicine, shoes, adequate food and clothing, and, above all, pay.[71] Like veteran troops everywhere, they had taken food and whatever supplies they needed wherever they had been able to find them. With the end of the war all these extralegal activities had necessarily come to an end. "While at war," an officer of Las Villas recalled later, "we exchanged blood for food, but afterward we had to observe very rigid disciplinary measures designed to show that we respected and guaranteed the life and property of those who previously had been neutral or even those who had been our enemies."[72] As a result, the half-famished liberators found themselves "in the saddest situation that men had ever experienced in the world."[73] First they began to eat horses and mules, *jutías* (Cuban rodents), and *majases* (Cuban snakes), then they had to experiment with all the plants that they assumed could provide some nourishment,[74] and when even these meager and often repugnant sources of food were depleted they began to go without their daily sustenance.[75] In certain places they actually began to die of starvation.[76] "Hunger causes in our ranks more casualties than enemy bullets caused!" cried an officer in desperation;[77] and watching how his destitute men "could find no way of satisfying that great need of life—to eat," another gave way to his anguish asking himself: "What to do, great God?"[78]

As in the east, some of the men sought relief from their sorry plight by selling their horses and equipment, others simply deserted and resumed foraging, and yet others turned into highwaymen. Unlike in the east, however, there were no U.S. officials on the scene ready to create jobs and positions for needy veterans. The Government Council and the troop commanders therefore found themselves in the situation of being solely responsible for the fate of the soldiers, which is no doubt the reason why the issue of the payment to the army assumed such a paramount importance at the time. The men had to return home with at least some resources to facilitate their transition to civilian life, and after three and a half years of fighting the only source to which they could appeal was the military to compensate them for their service.[79] In theory, all of them had been earning a monthly wage according to a resolution that the Council had passed on December 4, 1895;[80] and since at that time it had been specified that payment was to be made after victory was achieved, the consensus was that the obligation had already matured.[81] Had the insurgent government been able to collect the revenues of the island it would have been able to pay off the troops itself. But as the United States had taken over the customhouses and consequently appropriated the chief source of these revenues, it was clear that the necessary funds could only be secured through the agency of the U.S. government.[82]

To request a "reasonable" amount for this purpose was precisely one of the main objects of the Cuban commission that went to Washington in November 1898. The group was headed by Calixto García, who was now on excellent terms with the McKinley administration, and it included, in addition to other prominent officers and civilians, Gonzalo de Quesada, the chargé d'affaires in Washington,[83] and the Cuban Junta's lawyer, Horatio Rubens. It had been appointed by the Santa Cruz del Sur assembly after the assembly had gone through the formality of accepting the resignation of Masó's government and constituted itself as the ultimate source of political legitimization in Cuba. Among the instructions to the commission was, of course, that it continue the inquiries about the intentions of the United States toward Cuba that the insurgents had been making since first learning about the intervention. But the commission also had the duty of informing Washington that the assembly (whose authority in this connection had been recognized by General Máximo Gómez[84]) was ready to demobilize the liberating army, unless the United States was counting on its assistance to maintain order. The commission was to point out, nevertheless, that under no circumstances would the men be discharged without first being paid for their services as they had been promised. Washington therefore was to advance enough money to satisfy at least a substantial part of this obligation and to cover other accumulated debts, a loan that would be guaranteed by the future revenues of the Cuban republic.[85]

Since McKinley knew that a major goal of the commission was to discuss the disbanding and paying of the army, García and his colleagues were expeditiously invited to the White House, where the thorny issue immediately became the chief topic. The group proved irrevocably divided over the policy to be pursued in paying the soldiers. The majority favored the idea of the loan and wished it to be large enough to meet as much of the army debt as possible—the larger the better. But García feared that such a loan would cripple the republic at its very inception—perhaps even delaying its day of independence—and consequently he stood for the payment of just sufficient money to enable the men to return home and engage in useful pursuits.[86] Realizing that in granting the loan he would be tacitly recognizing the liberators' assembly as the legitimate representative for the future republic (which was one of the purposes underlying the proposal, after all[87]), McKinley immediately ruled out such a possibility. Yet, anxious as he was to get rid as soon as possible of the only tangible threat to U.S. government on the island, he stated that he was prepared to offer an outright gift in order to facilitate the demobilization of the insurgents. Thereupon he asked the Cubans how much money would be required for this purpose, and García quickly replied: "Three million dollars." Just as quickly, the other Cubans protested, stressing that what was really needed was more than twice that amount, but as far as McKinley was concerned the general's words were final. Although he was favorably disposed to assist the veterans in other ways,[88] from that moment on he clung to the figure mentioned by García, as did his representative, Robert P. Porter, to whom he turned over the negotiations after the first interview. The $3 million was the remnant of the appropriation from Congress for the war against Spain and could be spent at the president's discretion. To request a special congressional appropriation in order to settle the Cuban army issue was out of the question. Thus, no matter how hard the Cuban representatives argued in favor of a larger sum, Porter always gave them the same answer: "All there is is three million dollars; you can take it or leave it."[89]

García therefore had his own way in the matter of the army debt, but ended up by sharing the bitter disappointment of his associates in the face of the reaction of one of the first legislators whom they approached as they negotiated with Porter. Alabama Senator John T. Morgan, Democratic member of the Senate Foreign Relations Committee, in the past had been an advocate of the extension of belligerent rights to Cuba and was generally regarded as a friend of Cuban independence. He consequently shocked the commission when, showing his true expansionist colors, he declared himself a supporter of the indefinite military occupation of the island and of the exclusive sovereignty of the United States over its territory during that period. He also told the dismayed Cubans that in his opinion the Teller amendment was not legally binding on the United States. Throughout the meeting, Morgan was blunt to the point of unkindness, and thus his statement elicited from the Cubans a vehement rebuttal signed by García, dismissing Morgan's analysis of the amendment and vigorously rejecting the thesis that the future of Cuba was "at the discretionary power of the American government." The Cuban response ended in a veiled threat. Cubans would not oppose violently the ambitions of the U.S. imperialists, but they had other ways of showing their disapproval of the U.S. government that violated their ideals and aspirations. In such an eventuality, the commission warned, "we will see the necessity of standing to one side, of not cooperating in the government and policy of the American military authority, leaving to it the most absolute responsibility for the results . . ."[90]

This act of defiance cum frustration was the last of García's career, for he died after a brief siege of pneumonia a few days later (December 11, 1898). His untimely death brought to an abrupt halt the work of the commission, which after the funeral returned to Cuba to report the results of its activities to the assembly and to put in its hands McKinley's rather small bonus. The commission recommended that the bonus be accepted in principle, emphasizing at the same time that work to increase the amount should be continued. Obviously dissatisfied, the assembly limited itself to tabling the recommendation[91] while its disconsolate members brooded over the rest of the report:

> It was absolutely impossible for the commissioners, despite their determination and insistence, to obtain any explanation but only vague manifestations, and even phrases more or less evasive, either from the President, or the Secretaries, or from other persons whom they consulted . . . ; although everyone stated that they were resolved to comply faithfully with the resolutions of Congress of April 19, 1898, they never let a word escape regarding the means they would adopt to obtain this result, nor the duration of the occupation of the island, as though they really had no definite political program.[92]

The commissioners had received only noncommittal answers to their questions, of course, because ambiguity was intrinsic to U.S. policy at the time, as it became evident that same month when McKinley sent his annual message to Congress. In the section devoted to Cuba he promised that once the island had been "pacified," at the earliest moment, Cubans would be assisted in forming "a government which shall be free and independent," "just," "benevolent," and capable of performing all its international obligations. It would seem, therefore, that those who feared for Cuban independence could rest assured that their dream would come true—if only they had faith in the good intentions of the United States. For thereupon McKinley had attached the following caveat to his pledges: "Until there is complete tranquility in the island and a stable government inaugurated, military government will continue."[93] Since it was up to the United States to judge whether Cuba was fit to be independent according to these standards, as some U.S. newspapers were quick to point out, it was entirely possible that the day of Cuba's emancipation from military tutelage would be indefinitely postponed.[94]

The Gómez-Porter Deal

Either because of the failure of the Cuban commission to Washington or because Cuban expatriates had returned to the island by the thousands,[95] by December 1898 the insurgent polity had begun to fray at the edges. Deprived of the contributions of their members, most of whom were back in Cuba, many of the local patriotic clubs that had played such an important role in supporting and advancing the war effort had ceased to exist. In October, General Emilio Núñez had discontinued the department of the Junta charged with supplying the armies on the field (the Department of Expeditions);[96] and in December, at the initiative of Estrada Palma, the New York delegation announced the dissolution of the Cuban Revolutionary party—on the grounds that its work had been accomplished—and with it the remaining local organizations.[97] A few isolated voices were raised in protest here and there, but the leadership stood firm and Martí's political organization went down in history.[98]

But the core of the rebel movement kept its unity and the concomitant system of allegiance, and when the transfer of government from Spain to the United States took place in Havana on January 1, 1899, a good many units of the liberating army—40,000 men?[99]—remained in their camps where, as General Máximo Gómez remarked, the last shot had been fired and the sword had been returned to the scabbard.[100] If anything, the situation in Cuba had changed for the worse since the return of the commission, for General Brooke, fearing that fighting might break out between the Cubans and the Spanish forces that were still boarding their transports on the Havana waterfront, placed a ban on the parade of insurgent troops through the city that the insurgent patriotic committees had planned for the day of the transfer as the most important part of a five-day celebration. The upshot was that the celebration was never held, serious ill will marred Cuban-American relations, and tensions heightened considerably. At Brooke's invitation eight Cuban generals were present when, in the so-called throne room of the old palace of the Spanish captains general, the last of them turned over the island of Cuba to the government of the United States. But Gómez, the legendary Old Man, the seventy-three-year-old warrior who had led the Cubans throughout the bitter fight against Spain, was conspicuously absent. From his headquarters at Narcisa, Las Villas, he had announced that he would not come to Havana unless he could be received there by his army.[101]

Gómez's arrogant words could not but have an unsettling effect on U.S. officers appointed to run the military government of the island, much more so since it was known that the general had instead visited the city of Cienfuegos, Las Villas, where "nothing was said about the Americans" in the celebratory speeches, "only that the Cubans could have conquered Spain without [their] assistance."[102] In addition, there had been intermittent friction between Cubans and U.S. citizens—susceptible of degenerating into a larger conflict at any time—and Cubans had developed practices that, to say the least, were embarrassing to those who were supposed to be exercising their "belligerent right over conquered territory," as McKinley had succinctly put it.[103] The Cubans in effect "were massing around the cities and towns, producing more or less unrest in the public mind,"[104] and considered "themselves exclusively under the control of [their] military chiefs," exempt, as it were, from the obligation to obey mayors and other civil authorities.[105] As Leonard Wood later remarked, this made it indispensable "to teach them that in a really stable government the civil power must be absolute and supreme."[106] For the time being, however, it was a matter of taking the necessary military precautions. The United States thus sent to Cuba between December 13, 1898, and February 17, 1899, a force larger than the entire body of men who had fought against Spain—fifteen regiments of infantry volunteers, one of volunteer engineers, and four battalions of artillery. From 24,000 officers and men at the outset, the occupation army grew to 45,000 by March 1899.[107]

It has been suggested that Gómez really intended to remain under arms until the United States transferred the sovereignty of the island to the Cubans themselves.[108] But the truth is that there was never a chance that he would have behaved like Aguinaldo and openly challenged U.S. power. He was too old and, like Calixto García, he had fought too many battles to become involved in yet another desperate struggle against an even mightier enemy. Moreover, deep down he was convinced that Cuba's powerful neighbor would be true to its promises.[109] He had seen nothing that would "belie its solemn pledge" to free the island, and he therefore felt "that after so many struggles and privations [it was possible] to wait a little longer."[110] What actually troubled him was that throughout the Santiago campaign and its aftermath he had been totally ignored and discarded, a fact that he resented bitterly. "The war was declared and the peace signed," he complained to Estrada Palma, "and I have not received even the slightest official attention from the Americans. They have been very rude to me."[111] His indignation about the treatment that he had received was so deep that it permeated most of his writings of this period. To his wife he said plainly that he had been "abandoned by the Cubans and the Americans."[112] Comparing himself to Prometheus, he wrote to an old Dominican friend that forces beyond his control had prevented him from completing his work in Cuba.[113] Shortly before the transfer of government, he did not hesitate to ascribe the plight of the liberators to the "niggardliness" of the United States.[114] They, he wrote in his diary in commenting on the ceremony that took place in Havana, had "embittered, with their tutelage imposed by force, the joy of the victorious Cubans."[115] Consequently no one could expect that he would enter Cuba's capital to witness the formal lowering of the Spanish flag and the raising of the U.S. flag. "Ours," he said, "is the Cuban flag, the one for which so many tears and so much blood have been shed, and the one that will be run up if, setting aside spurious and selfish passions and guided only by the good of the country . . . we unite in order to bring to an end this unjustified military occupation."[116]

Indeed, the alarm and worries of Washington and the occupation authorities would have increased had they learned of statements such as this, or like the one that the offended general made to one of his aides:

> I am worried and offended. I can set aside my being offended, but not my preoccupation with the plight of the army and independence. What is going to be done about independence? The Americans are not thinking about independence. Even if they finally give it to us, it will be as a gift, while we have earned it with continuous efforts during more than half a century. I am obliged to be grateful to the Americans, but only when they fulfill their promises and provided that they do so with decency and without aggravation to the Cubans. The Cuban army cannot dissolve itself unless I receive the assurance, honorably promised, that independence will be given to Cuba and that it will be given as the just reward of Cuba's efforts, suffering, constancy, and spilled blood.[117]

On another occasion Gómez asked his officers: "Where is independence? I do not see it. . . . A declaration of the American Congress is not enough; it is indispensable that the organized Cuban people, that is to say, the liberating army, remain prepared to reclaim the promise. While we are not assured of independence, our work is not complete."[118] The general's attitude, however, seemed most menacing when he announced that those leaving the ranks of the army without authorization would be tried as traitors,[119] and when he urged the Executive Committee of the Santa Cruz army assembly to convoke a constitutional convention as soon as possible for the purpose of establishing a government to which the United States could relinquish its authority. The U.S. occupation, Gómez said in justifying his adjuration, "constitutes a danger to the absolute independence of Cuba."[120] If Gómez ever gave the impression of being ready to take action, it was at this time.

The Executive Committee must have known better, however, for in its curt reply to the general it told him to hold his tongue and mind his own business. There was little to worry about, the committee informed Gómez, not knowing yet the contents of the report of the commission to Washington. Relations with the United States were good and growing better. The committee, furthermore, knew what it was doing. The best way to cut short the intervention, Gómez was reminded, "is in avoiding words or acts that give our enemies the opportunity to accuse us of impatience or evil feelings and our allies of jealousy or perfidy."[121] In other words, the general should keep quiet and leave the matter in the hands of the committee, an injunction that he accepted with uncharacteristic equanimity. This attitude was far more in keeping with the tone of his public pronouncements, which although cast in firm terms had always been partly conciliatory. In the most important of them, the so-called Narcisa proclamation to the people and the army signed at his headquarters two days before the transfer of government, he explained why he had chosen not to move from the place where he had engaged the enemy for the last time. The Spanish soldiers had not departed yet from the island, and perhaps his absence would help to smooth the transfer at Havana. He then added that the period of transition was about to end, and that although Cuba was "neither free nor independent yet" because of the forthcoming establishment of U.S. sovereignty on its soil, it was necessary to dedicate themselves "to bringing about the disappearance of the causes for the intervention." This he stated, should be achieved by means of peaceful cooperation, and no one should doubt that the liberators would figure among the first to work for the restoration of order and prosperity to the country. But the demobilization of the army was contingent upon the success of the negotiations to procure funds to pay the soldiers for their services. "Until this is settled," the commander in chief declared in closing, "I shall remain in a suitable place, always ready to help Cubans to conclude the work to which I have dedicated my life."[122]

His decision to hold the army together placed a heavy burden on Gómez's conscience, for he knew better than anyone else that it would only worsen the precarious condition of his poverty-stricken men and their families.[123] In the case of heads of household, he had no choice but to issue them furloughs so that they could return to their homes.[124] But, generally speaking, he tried to provide his veterans with some means of support by appealing for relief to whomever he thought could afford it. First he submitted a request for food and supplies to the American Evacuation Commission;[125] then he dispatched Enrique Conill to deliver a personal plea to McKinley, explaining the suffering in the Cuban countryside;[126] finally, he sought the assistance of the army assembly—assistance that the helpless body was hardly in a position to give.[127] At the same time he kept hammering on the subject of the soldiers' pay in his correspondence, public statements, and appeals to the Cuban émigrés. His approach to the problem was based on his personal responsibility. Most of the officers and men had gone to the field in obedience to his orders, and in doing so they had lost everything they had. He therefore could not desert them at this critical juncture. If he could not obtain for them at least part of the arrears of pay from custom receipts or other sources, he had to do his best to find some other way of restoring them to their prewar condition, to the positions they had abandoned to take up arms for independence.[128] If a loan was required for this purpose, then it was necessary to negotiate a loan. "Cuba is wealthy," he told Estrada Palma. "It can consequently easily pay for the bread that the Americans may give us on credit."[129]

Regardless of Gómez's opposition to demobilization, by the time that the failure of the Cuban commission to Washington became known on the island, it was obvious that the disappearance of the liberating army was only a matter of time. On the one hand, there was the appointments policy of Brooke, who used patronage to lure officers and men away from the ranks of the army.[130] On the other, there was the hopelessness and disappointment generated by the certainty that no relief would be forthcoming soon from any quarter. Many hungry veterans forsook their units and returned to their old ways. Others simply could not stand still while civilian offices or administrative positions were distributed to those who had supported Spain or stood neutral during the conflict. Not all the liberators, furthermore, conformed to the heroic image subsequently forged by Cubans. Among them there were an indeterminate but sizable number of self-serving opportunists who had joined the army at the last minute in order to share the spoils of victory,[131] and there were also individuals of this type among the more seasoned insurgents. These were the officers who, according to Calixto García, took leave to visit Estrada Palma in New York "just to run away"

from the enemy or "happily lingered away the war awaiting the arrival of independence achieved through the efforts of others, or better yet, handed over by the American intervention, from which they
expect everything."[132] The general must have had these elements in
mind when, on the eve of the U.S. landing in Oriente, he told his
troops that "it would be shameful if the Cubans who are loitering
about did not cooperate with [the American] efforts to defend their
fatherland on the battlefield."[133] It was clear that none of these fa-
bled revolutionaries would have adhered for long to an inflexible
policy such as Gómez's, which called for even more hardship and
self-immolation.

Meanwhile, however, a substantial part of the liberators held
together in response to their commander in chief's directive, a situation that was aggravated by the inaction of the new military governor, who made no attempt to communicate with Gómez. Apparently Brooke considered it beneath his personal dignity to take the
initiative in establishing a rapport with the insurgent leader.[134] Thus
the month of January wore on and the question of disbanding the
army remained unresolved. Evidently the body would eventually
dissolve itself, but this would be a gradual process and Washington
was beginning to grow impatient. It was then that McKinley, acting
it seems upon the recommendation of Estrada Palma, decided to
send Robert P. Porter to Cuba to confer with Gómez and break
the impasse.[135] This decision, which implied bypassing the army
assembly—the only body with legal authority to approve the discharge of the soldiers—was in line with the U.S. policy of ignoring the insurgent political organization.[136] Still it is erroneous to
accuse the U.S. president of having deliberately attempted to capitalize on the general's proclivity to ignore the established insurgent
institutions.[137] The opportunity was clearly there, for the assembly,
which Gómez had not attended, tended to ignore and rebuff him,
and he for his part had replied with his usual acrimony.[138] Yet shortly
after Porter departed for Havana, McKinley was persuaded that it
would be useful to permit the representatives of the assembly to
participate in the disarmament of the rebels; and even though subsequently Porter limited himself to dealing with the general, it was
solely because the new instructions arrived in Cuba too late.[139]

McKinley's special representative met with Gómez on February 1
at Remedios, Las Villas, where the general had moved his headquarters. Porter carried with him a letter from Brooke inviting the insurgent leader to Havana to discuss the payment to the army.[140] He was
accompanied by the Cuban chargé d'affaires in Washington, Gonzalo de Quesada, who was armed with another letter in which Es-

trada Palma reiterated his faith in American promises and urged his old friend to cooperate and accept the offer of assistance that would be extended to him.[141] Had the general been less aware of the insurmountable difficulties attending Cuban resistance to the U.S. occupation, or had his former attitude been unrelated to his amourpropre, Porter and Quesada would have faced an impossible task. As it happened, however, they encountered a man who was not only profoundly realistic, but who was also anxious to be recognized and to retrieve his undisputed leadership of the Cuban independence movement. True, Washington had ignored him up to this moment; now, however, Washington showed itself disposed to make amends and to deal with him with the respect and deference that was due to his revolutionary rank and his generalissimo status. Such an opportunity he simply would not let go by.[142]

Thus Gómez was the most receptive of men when he received Porter after a preliminary conversation with Quesada, in the course of which the latter persuaded him that Cubans should "look upon the Americans as [their] real friends and trust them."[143] On the strength of what he had just been told, the general said in his opening statement, he was prepared to cooperate with the U.S. government. Porter then presented to him the same $3 million bonus that he had previously offered to the Cuban commission in Washington. This amount, Porter went on, was not to be regarded as a partial payment of the soldiers' overdue wages. The United States, he made it clear, was not accepting responsibility for any Cuban revolutionary obligations. But the president strongly desired to have disbanding the liberators completed, and hence his wish to facilitate it by offering this relief fund. Porter added that the return of the soldiers to useful occupations would in any event be beneficial to Cuba, and he closed by indicating that perhaps later on some of them could be used for a national police force similar to the Rural Guard that General Wood had organized for the purpose of suppressing banditry in Oriente.[144]

Gómez graciously agreed with most of what Porter said. But even to him, whose ideas on the subject were moderate compared to those of the assembly, the $3 million seemed a bagatelle. Quesada nevertheless urged him to accept Porter's offer and not to delay demobilization any longer, whereupon the general, reasoning that after all the exiguity of the bonus was not his fault, determined that he would do the best he could with it. He therefore accepted Porter's offer, adding only two conditions: the first was that Brooke rather than himself would be in charge of the money; the second was that Cuban officers must have a part in its distribution to the men.[145]

That same day, at Porter's request, Gómez cabled McKinley that he had been informed of and satisfied with his wishes,[146] and, in another cable to Brooke, he assured the military governor that he soon would be coming to Havana.[147] Then, in the evening, the three men attended a reception and ball in the local theater, where after speeches by Porter and Quesada[148] the general personally led the dancing, which lasted until early morning. Indeed, things seemed to be going so well that Porter returned immediately to the United States, leaving Brooke to handle the actual negotiations about when demobilization should begin. Gómez, for his part, left for Havana shortly thereafter, although instead of going directly to confer with Brooke he first made a triumphal tour of Las Villas and Matanzas, reviewing parades, presiding over ceremonial functions and rallies, and arousing outbursts of patriotic emotion wherever he went. He felt "like the happiest man in the world,"[149] and it was at this time that he most insistently urged Cubans to be forbearing and forgiving and to bury the past, a message that instantly struck a responsive chord in the population. Thus, by the time he finally entered Havana on February 24, 1899, the fourth anniversary of the 1895 uprising, he had clearly become the idol of the Cuban masses. There were an estimated 150,000 people in the streets waiting to greet him, and pandemonium broke loose when they saw him riding at the head of an insurgent cavalry and later reviewing his soldiers (about 2,500 of them) from the balcony of the governor's palace. On that day, the municipality officially thanked him for all he had done to promote the cause of Cuban freedom.[150]

Gómez versus the Army Assembly

While Gómez had been sweeping across Las Villas and Matanzas, however, things had been going less than well in Havana. Shortly after Porter's departure, on February 5, hostilities had broken out in the Philippines and, haunted by the specter of a similar uprising in Cuba, U.S. officials had begun to worry about the leisurely pace of the general's trip to Havana and his delay in getting down to business with Brooke. Then a misunderstanding over the position of the insurgent representatives at the final burial of Calixto García (which took place on the eleventh) had aroused ill will among Cubans in general and especially among the liberators who were supposed to escort the corpse to its resting place—and did not, as a result of the incident.[151] Finally, the army assembly, now in session again at El Cerro, a suburb of Havana, had already learned through press releases of the Gómez-Porter deal. Despite the fact that he had been repeatedly asked to confer with the delegates and even warned not to act on his own, the general had done precisely that in negotiating with McKinley's representative. Moreover, he appears to have misled members of the assembly into thinking that he would cooperate with them.[152] This had understandably infuriated them, not only because they had been ignored and to an extent befooled, all of which was aggravating enough, but chiefly because they had not given up their hopes for getting a large sum through a loan from private U.S. bankers. Gómez's unilateral acceptance of McKinley's bonus obviously threatened to ruin the negotiations that were already under way.[153]

Thus the stage was set for what turned out to be a bitter confrontation between the general and the occupation authorities on the one hand and the assembly and a number of lesser insurgent officers on the other. Hardly had Gómez worked out with Brooke the details of the plan to distribute the $3 million to the soldiers ($100 to each man whose name appeared on the official rolls of the liberating army)[154] when, on March 9, he was visited by an assembly committee which advised him that on that very day the delegates had voted to approve a transaction with a group of U.S. bankers represented in Havana by a certain C. M. Coen. The Cubans would be receiving $12,400,000 in return for Cuban bonds in the amount of $20,000,000, which were to pay 5 percent interest and to be redeemed at face value within thirty years.[155] The assembly, the general was told, expected him to adhere to its decision to hold out for more money and lend his approval to the transaction. This Gómez flatly refused to do. In the course of a violent argument during which both sides exchanged harsh phrases and epithets, he made clear to the committee that rather than go back on the word that he had given to the United States, he would pay off the army himself. He also stated that he was strongly opposed to the loan, pointing out that its terms were too unfavorable, that the sum involved was too large, and that the burden that it would impose on the Cuban people was too heavy. More than that, he asserted, the loan scheme would open the door to a vast amount of graft and corruption.[156]

In the face of this challenge the army delegates could have chosen to recognize reality and accommodate themselves to circumstances, as a few of them suggested at the time.[157] But the majority of them foolishly opted for measuring swords with the man who was at once the most popular public figure of his day and persona grata to the true masters of the situation. This they did, furthermore, in a graceless, most unseemly way. For nearly two days, as they worked themselves up to a frenzy of anti-Gómez sentiment, they heaped uncomplimentary remarks and even outright insults upon the general. Many intimated that he had been bribed into accepting McKinley's gift; Martí's old friend and fellow conspirator, Juan Gualberto Gómez, overlooking that the Dominican had dedicated most of his adult life to the cause of Cuban independence, shamefully brought up the question of Gómez's citizenship; and General José Lacret Morlot went so far as to volunteer his services as head of a firing squad that would execute the commander in chief, for which several members of the assembly had called. "If someone is needed to shoot General Gómez," cried out Lacret Morlot, "here is a general."[158] Out of the uproar and confusion caused by violent declarations such as this, there eventually emerged a resolution, based for the most part on arguments supplied by Manuel Sanguily,[159] dismissing the Old Man from the post he had held since the beginning of the war. The army grade that he occupied, the resolution stated, had become "unnecessary and prejudicial" and therefore the assembly had determined to abolish it. At the same time, Gonzalo de Quesada was removed from his position in Washington because of his role in the Porter mission.[160]

The reaction to Gómez's dismissal took diverse forms. That of the people was swift and angry. In Havana, stunned by the news of the assembly's action, crowds burned or hanged in effigy several of the most prominent delegates. Many gathered outside of the general's residence to cheer him and thunder against the villainous assembly members. Meantime, a wave of protest swept the rest of the island and, as telegrams of support poured in to Gómez, an avalanche of letters was sent to the press denouncing the ungrateful men who had had the temerity to affront the hero who had sacrificed so much for the fatherland. Indeed, had Gómez encouraged the mobs that rallied in front of his home, the Havana police would have been hard pressed to prevent the lynching of some of his erstwhile comrades in arms.[161]

But the general sought to placate the irate *habaneros*. His reply to the assembly, published on March 12, was a paragon of moderation and restraint which began by conceding that by virtue of their supreme authority the army delegates certainly had the right to remove him. He then informed the people that his dismissal was due to his opposition to the loan approved by the assembly, and that he had taken this stand because he was convinced that such a transaction would later jeopardize the financial and political interests of the new nation. Thanking the delegates for making it possible for him to return to his home in the Dominican Republic, he noted that although he was a foreigner, he had not come to Cuba as a mercenary but rather as a defender of the cause of justice. "Nothing is owed me," he added in closing, "and I retire happy and satisfied for having done everything that I could for the benefit of my brothers. Wherever fate forces me to set my tent, Cubans will always be able to count on a friend."[162]

Privately, nevertheless, Gómez believed that the assembly should be dissolved.[163] This was also the opinion of General Brooke, who not only announced at once that he would continue to recognize the old soldier as the only representative authorized to speak for the liberating army but wired Washington requesting permission to abolish the troublesome body by decree.[164] Had this permission been granted, it is likely that the delegates would have resigned themselves to their fate, as they did a month later. But in those days Washington was in no mood for drastic solutions, and thus it advised the military governor against taking such action. As time passed, however, it became evident that the assembly's was a lost cause, and that not even U.S. overcautiousness could endow it with new life. Realizing that the assembly had lost all popular support and that its authority had all but disappeared, on March 14 Brooke wired the Secretary of War that action of the nature he had previously suggested would probably not be necessary.[165] Whether or not this cable emboldened the McKinley administration, which until then had limited itself to reappointing Quesada the Cuban representative in Washington, the fact is that it began to act more decisively. Reacting swiftly to the news that Coen had promised to get the president's approval for the loan that he had offered the assembly, for example, it flatly denied on the following day that anyone was authorized to communicate with the army delegates on behalf of the chief executive, and confirmed once and for all that he did not recognize the assembly. Such was also the substance of the War Department's reply to Brooke on March 17, when the latter reported that a new assembly commission to Washington was in the making. The department said that the "so-called assembly or any part of it [would] not receive recognition by this government under any conditions whatsoever."[166] It could have been neither more clear nor more emphatic.

But the assembly did not immediately signal its readiness to buckle under adversity. Although the language it used was conciliatory,[167] its determination was unyielding, and furthermore, it had possession of the rolls of the liberating army, without which no payment could be made to the soldiers. By refusing to relinquish them either to the occupation authorities or to Gómez, it managed to hold fast throughout the month of March. Meanwhile it made a futile attempt to assuage the furor of Cuban public opinion by issuing a "document of justification" for the removal of the commander in chief. It was a noteworthy statement in the sense that for the first time it officially brought to light and analyzed the differences that had marred the relations between the general and the Government Council during the war. Such differences, it maintained, had been primarily caused by Gómez's proclivity toward insubordination, his scorn for legality, and his dictatorial tendencies. Although the insurgents had passed over them, it had only been because to depose their leader halfway through the conflict—"justified, useful, and even necessary" as it might have been—would have given encouragement to the enemy. Serious as these accusations were, they did not make much of an impact, for they referred to events that now belonged to the past, and Cubans—including those who had a penchant for history[168]—demurred at musing over them. As to the general's more recent transgressions—beginning with the agreement with Porter—which were naturally reviewed at great length in the document, they remained similarly unmoved. Few actually read the delegates' self-justification in its entirety,[169] and except for one or two troop commanders, no one stepped forward to support them.[170]

It was clear that the assembly was completely isolated, a predicament that led some of the delegates to waver in their determination and propose that the body be dissolved and the army disbanded without pay. But the majority resolved to make a last-ditch effort.[171] This was made through a second commission to Washington (this time a two-man commission) that was appointed and sent to the U.S. capital for the purpose of working on behalf of the Coen loan. The transaction required McKinley's approval, and thus the commissioners were instructed to request it in order "to raise the funds which are indispensable . . . so that [the Cuban troops] may be disbanded without difficulties or apprehension."[172] Having managed to get an interview with Secretary of State John Hay, they heard what turned out to be the final words on the matter. Speaking for McKinley, Hay told them that it was out of the question either to authorize any loan or to increase the $3-million-dollar bonus. Evidently "the assembly could hope for nothing from the American government," and the delegates finally so understood it when their emissaries wired the news to Cuba.[173] It was only then that they decided to give up the fight. During the heated debate that culminated in this decision, some of them insisted that the soldiers retain their arms, while others recommended that the arms be turned over to the municipal councils. In the end, however, they came to realize that such gestures of defiance were not suitable to the realities of the occupation and, on the evening of April 4, voted to disband the army, dissolve themselves, and deliver the army rolls to Brooke so that he and Gómez could implement their plans. As Sanguily put it, they had been "finally vanquished by uncontrollable conditions." It was only natural therefore that their mood should be somber and pessimistic. In their view, the future of Cuba was "clouded and dark." That the island would some day be free and independent was no longer sure by any means.[174]

Against this background, it was to be expected that Brooke and Gómez would face problems in trying to proceed with their arrangements. One of them was to determine the number of soldiers to be paid. Back on March 18, Brooke's headquarters had ordered all U.S. departmental commanders to report the number of Cuban troops in each department that were still organized, and, according to the reports that were then received, they numbered only a few thousand. At the time this total had seemed too low, although no one was prepared for the 48,000 veterans who now appeared on the rolls. Since the sum of money available was fixed and there was no way of verifying the accuracy of the rolls, Brooke and Gómez decided not to pay anything to the officers and men who already held jobs in the military government. This reduced the number of troops to fewer than 40,000, which would make it possible for each man to receive $75. Upon being paid, they would have to surrender their arms to a mixed Cuban-U.S. commission.[175]

But many Cuban officers objected to the idea of the soldiers turning over their arms to a commission partially made up of U.S. citizens and in fact none of those chosen by Gómez to aid in the job agreed to serve. Pressured by Washington to get through with the vexatious business, Brooke then borrowed one of the recommendations made by the delegates at the final session of the assembly and suggested that the arms be deposited with the mayors of the municipalities where the payment was made rather than surrendered directly to the mixed commission.[176] After some hesitation Washington approved this plan, and on that basis payment finally began on May 27, a task that even after so much haggling proved strenuous. For one thing, owing to a boycott organized by a group of Cuban diehard officers, the soldiers were slow in coming to be paid. Some refused to accept the money and went home with their arms. Conversely, some troop commanders demanded that all of their men be paid regardless of whether they were listed on the rolls. For the most part, however, the veterans collected their money without giving any trouble and things ran smoothly.[177] Even so, it took all summer to distribute McKinley's bonus. Ironically, when the project was completed there was an unexpended balance of $445,250. Brooke and Gómez had agreed that in such an event the surplus would go to disabled officers according to a list to be made up by the latter. But the list was never prepared and the funds were ultimately returned to the U.S. Treasury. When Gómez subsequently tried to retrieve them, his request was denied on the grounds that the money had been transferred to the Treasury and was consequently beyond the control of the War Department.[178]

Such was the way in which the Cuban liberating army passed out of existence. As Gómez wrote in his farewell manifesto to his men (which he issued on June 5, after the plan for the payment of the soldiers had been completed), the time had come for them to put the war behind them. "We no longer need soldiers to wage war," said the General. "What we need at this time is peace-loving men for the maintenance of public order and for the rebuilding of public wealth." He used some infelicitous language in referring to the United States, calling its people "those rich northerners, owners of a continent." But although grateful to the U.S. government for the role it had played in terminating the war, he expressed no satisfaction with its rule. Mincing no words, he proclaimed, "None of us thought that [peace] would be followed by a military occupation of the country by our allies, who treat us as a people incapable of acting for ourselves, and who have reduced us to obedience, to submission, and to a tutelage imposed by force of circumstances." Resistance, nevertheless, was not the answer to the problem. What Cubans ought to do was to cooperate peacefully with the occupation authorities so as to "make useless the presence of a strange power on the island." For this purpose they should unite, organize politically, and "form a central board, a committee, a government—the name is not important—in order to direct public opinion and, at the same time, be its legitimate representative." After noting that there were no longer autonomists and conservatives in Cuba but "only Cubans," Gómez added emphatically: "Today there can be but one party in Cuba with only one goal in mind: to put our blood-stained flag where it belongs and where at present it is not."[179]

Unfortunately, the general was calling for something that could not possibly come to pass. For, given the circumstances attending the dissolution of the army, there were many former insurgent leaders who were not prepared to join the all-inclusive party that he envisioned. His own actions and U.S. policy had irrevocably split the revolutionary forces, and there was no way of healing the breach, which continued to divide the liberators until the end of the occupation. It would be unfair, however, to go a step further and blame

Gómez for having enabled the United States to tighten its hold over Cuba. Doubtlessly carried away by the passions of the moment, Manuel Sanguily once remarked that after Gómez accepted Porter's proposal, the general "went over to the side of the United States, neglecting Cuba."[180] But even as clear-witted an observer as Sanguily was susceptible to attaching too much importance to McKinley's gift and its effect on the subsequent course of Cuban-U.S. relations. The crucial issue for the liberators at the time was not to choose between the gift and Coen's loan, but whether to disband and cooperate with the United States or to remain under arms and resist, and on this matter Gómez and the assembly were of one and the same opinion. Both agreed that the needy condition of the men required a quick demobilization, and neither of them was prepared to stay in the woods and resume fighting. The factor that really forced the liberators to reach this conclusion was the reality of the U.S. intervention carried out by the McKinley administration. With or without the general's collaboration, the outcome would have probably been the same, or worse, which is what happened in the Philippines—and this is what perhaps Gómez perceived more acutely than any of his colleagues. It is indeed difficult to add even one iota to the summary of the situation that he presented to a group of friendly Cuban generals. "We must recognize," he said, "that the only power today in Cuba is the power of those who have intervened, and therefore, for the present, thoughts of a Cuban independent government can be no more than a dream."[181]

The Search for Victory in Defeat

Contemporary nationalists were able to pick Gómez as their scapegoat because to all appearances he was the one who made possible the liquidation of the army and thus removed once and for all the possibility of a Filipinolike insurrection in Cuba—if such a possibility ever existed beyond the imagination of the Washington politicians. Yet the record shows that as soon as the Brooke administration was inaugurated the liberators began to leave the "wilds," as the general used to say, first to attend the lavish receptions that were held in Havana during the early days of the U.S. takeover for veterans of the war,[182] and then to grasp at the opportunity which presented itself when the occupation authorities showed their disposition to staff with insurgent officers the positions of the new civil government. General Wilson, the military governor of Matanzas, had advised Brooke that "the officers of the successful revolution should have preference for civil employment over those who supported the Spanish regime or stood neutral between it and those who were contending for independence,"[183] and up to a point Brooke had followed Wilson's recommendation. Hence from the very beginning there had been army veterans filling offices in his administration. Among them were the heads of two of the departments that he organized, Domingo Méndez Capote and José Antonio González Lanuza; five of the six civil provincial governors; more than a dozen mayors of important cities and towns; and many more.[184] It is true that there was a large contingent of former expatriates who made their way into positions under the occupation government.[185] Still, the veterans who held jobs prior to the official dissolution of the army had to be counted by the thousands. When Gómez and Brooke decided to remove them from the list of those eligible to be paid out of McKinley's bonus, the total of potential payees dropped by more than 10,000.[186]

The number of office seekers increased dramatically, of course, as a result of the formal order of disbandment. At the time some remarked that the liberators simply craved the spoils of political office and the comforts associated with them.[187] But the fact is that their eagerness to take advantage of U.S. patronage was basically due to their inability to find any other way of earning a living on their desolate island. Most were jobless and penniless. All that Brigadier Rogelio Castillo, for example, had with him upon returning home were his machete and his revolver.[188] Colonel Orestes Ferrara arrived in Havana to procure supplies for the starving men of his brigade with no money whatsoever in his pockets.[189] General Lacret Morlot let it be known that he was a "pauper" and that he needed to work "soon and hard."[190] Another general, Alejandro Rodríguez, complained that he could not start any business nor restore his farm for lack of funds. "I cannot have my family at my side," he wrote, "for want of means to support it."[191] Even those who were able to secure jobs, like General Carlos Roloff, or who were property owners, like Masó, could not dispel their uneasiness about financial matters. "What do you want me to do here if I lose my job?" Roloff asked Gonzalo de Quesada. "Without question I will have to look for another job, since my family is in need and I do not have clothes to wear, nor the means to betake myself from one place to another."[192] Masó was not as despairing, although he too could not avoid musing over his straitened circumstances. "I plan to go to Manzanillo," he confided to a friend, "and the first thing I intend to do is to build a *bohío* [the typical Cuban peasant hut] on my old farm; then I will quietly work content with my penury."[193] Again, however, it was Gómez who provided the most eloquent and pungent testimony of the destitution of the liberators. A few days after having been publicly and solemnly thanked for his efforts on behalf of Cuba's independence, on March 8, 1899, he was forced to beg for assistance. "I am shamefully living on public charity here," he wrote to Quesada, "and thus I am unable to give aid and comfort to those who turn to me believing that I can help them. Talk to Tomasito [Estrada Palma] and see whether there is a way to procure a loan of $5,000 pesos, which I think I will be able to repay within the next four months at the very latest."[194] At the time the general was living at a residence that had been given him by Brooke, [195] and, according to U.S. sources even he had ended up accepting a "gratuity," which was only a little less than the pay and revenue of the military governor himself.[196]

But escaping from poverty and despondency was not the only reason why the liberators sought out government jobs under the occupation. Ever since Calixto García had launched his ill-fated attempt to control the Oriente municipalities, Cuban leaders—including Gómez—had been convinced that in order to abbreviate the rule of the U.S. proconsuls, Cubans had to prove that they possessed the aptitudes necessary for self-government. Under the circumstances, perhaps the best way to achieve this end was to help the military authorities put the country on a solid and stable foundation, and therefore the veterans were exhorted to act in conformity with the U.S. presence, to cooperate with the foreign administration, and to seek positions that could be used to demonstrate that Cubans really had the ability to govern themselves.[197] It is hard to ascertain whether it was this sort of patriotic virtue that led them, for example, to assail Colonel Tasker H. Bliss, chief of customs in Havana, to the extent of making him complain that had he yielded to their demands, he "could . . . have discharged and appointed the personnel of the Havana customhouses ten times over" in a period of just three months.[198] But there is no doubt that they indeed collaborated with the military government, even going as far as to allow themselves to be used to do the "dirty work" of the intervention, as a contemporary wit duly recorded.[199] This, nevertheless, was only incidental to their fate. It was far from the bitterest pill they had to swallow.

Next to defeat at the hands of Spain, perhaps the worst that the liberators could have possibly envisaged was a scenario that entailed sharing the fruits of victory with "bad Cubans, guerrilleros, and autonomists." Yet this is precisely what happened under the occupation and, even worse, they were asked to respect the personal security and well-being of the Spanish residents of the island and to guarantee them a place in Cuban society. These concessions, which were utterly implausible after the war of extermination that Cuba had just lived through, were imposed upon them for two related reasons. One was Washington's decision at the onset of its occupation to win as many supporters for its policies as possible among the local population.[200] The other was the inclination shown by Spanish and pro-Spanish elements—businessmen, property owners, professionals, officials, and the like—to flock around the U.S. authorities in search of protection against insurgent reprisals.[201] The result was that no preference was initially given to the members of the liberating army in the distribution of jobs. In Oriente Wood filled most offices with Spaniards and conservative Cubans, and the same happened later in the rest of the island, where a large number of provincial and municipal positions remained in the hands of the Spanish or pro-Spanish officeholders and some Spaniards—including some notorious guerrilleros—received early appointments.[202]

It was against this background that Gómez proclaimed the need "to forget past antipathies and disagreements" and to develop a new rapprochement between insurgents and loyalists.[203] His purpose was again to remove obstacles from the way to independence, and there were many veterans who understood it very clearly. One of them was Colonel Ferrara, who devoted almost the entire newspaper *La Nación*, which he published in Tunas de Zaza, Las Villas, to defending the general's policy of national reconciliation.[204] But there were other veterans who were embittered by their failure to secure jobs and who assumed a threatening attitude to the extent of becoming a "truly grave danger for everyone in Cuba."[205] They vented their frustration in a number of ways. Some accused the Cuban members of Brooke's cabinet of preferring men without revolutionary record in their appointments.[206] Others talked about emigrating because Hispanophiles and annexationists had obtained the most lucrative posts in the occupation.[207] Still others simply thought that the victory of the revolution had been incomplete.[208]

Yet the sad truth is not that victory had been incomplete, but rather that there had been no victory at all. For, regardless of their martial accomplishments and their success in defying Spain's power, the liberators had failed to assert their political supremacy. Instead they had lost control of the state apparatus to a putative ally, and as a result had been denied access to the most important source of resources that was left in their ruined island. Thus, after nearly thirty years of exhaustive struggle, they saw themselves reduced to the condition of men who were not even masters of their own personal destinies. Unquestionably, they benefited from the lack of perspicacity of the Washington politicians, who lost sight of the differences between the situation in Cuba and that in the Philippines. But even so they were forced to yield to the crushing power of the foreign occupiers on a number of vital questions. They were driven to disband their army, thereby giving up their only means of extracting concessions from the Americans, and they were compelled to reassure their former adversaries and to share with them the scant employment opportunities that were available. These were indeed painful adjustments, bitter renunciations apt to create rupture and division and which in fact did so, shattering once and for all the semblance of unity that held together the insurgent polity. Transformed into an amorphous multitude of would-be public officials, the once proud veterans began to vie with each other to become the objects of U.S. largess, not hesitating to challenge the patriotic credentials of their former comrades in arms whenever it seemed expedient. The most frequent frictions were between former soldiers and those who had served abroad,[209] but generally speaking the situation was one in which ideals tended to pale and survival took precedence over patriotism. This time it was General Enrique Collazo who summed up the seediness of the Cuban political milieu in a few poignant words. "We are becoming a nation of petty office seekers," he complained in February 1899. "We no longer have a political personality."[210]

There is little doubt, therefore, that the U.S. occupation drove the liberators into a nether world, a limbo that was somewhere between defeat and victory but probably closer to defeat than victory. As a result, Cuba's situation for the time being was similar to that of annexed Puerto Rico or the wartorn Philippines. In the case of Cuba, however, there was a solemn congressional pledge that interposed itself between the wealth and beauty of the island and the ambition and cupidity of U.S. expansionists, and so Cubans were entitled to some hope. It was an intangible expectation that was contingent upon a maddening paradox. In the past Cubans had sought to become independent through violence, bloodshed, and rebellion, whereas their hopes for freedom now rested on orderliness, cooperation, and submission. That was precisely the crux of Gómez's—and most other insurgent leaders'—formula for attaining victory in defeat, namely, to avoid giving the expansionists any excuses for prolonging the occupation indefinitely or for preventing in any other way the establishment of a Cuban republic. The general has been occasionally accused of being politically naive in his often publicized view that the occupation was an "honorable mission [that the United States had] assumed by force of circumstances,"[211] and in proclaiming his conviction that Washington would shortly fulfill its promises and leave Cuba to govern itself.[212] It is true that he lacked the political acumen of José Martí and that he obviously failed to understand the broader and darker aspects of U.S. imperialism. Still, he was a crafty old man who was thoroughly familiar with the realities of power. What else could he have preached to his huge constituency in Cuba if in fact there was no alternative to acquiescence to U.S. authority? In time events would prove him right, although he could not possibly have had any inkling of the new twists that they would take.

5. The Estrada Palma Interlude

Because of their generally cooperative attitude, the liberators were not completely eliminated from the Cuban political scene. They were prevented from monopolizing political life, as their Spanish American counterparts did on the mainland after independence, but they played a larger and more visible role in Cuban politics than any other group, organization, or party. Whatever the significance of their activities, however, they saw themselves compelled to function within the lines of demarcation drawn by Washington and by the often arbitrary dictates of an autocratic military governor (Leonard Wood) bent on "Americanizing" the island as a preliminary step to annexation. Their contribution to the configuration of the new republic was consequently somewhat limited. They had undertaken to attain nationhood and had to settle instead for a protectorate that tended to preserve colonial structures that otherwise might have been swept away.

Transformed into veterans, they could have expected to advance their cause and strengthen their political position once the foreign occupation ended. Indeed they took an important step in this direction when they succeeded in electing one of their own as the first president of Cuba. But, in furthering at the same time their policy of acquiescence to U.S. predilections, they chose a conservative with strong pro-U.S. sympathies who was no sooner elected than forgot his political debt to them. Claiming to be president of all Cubans and oblivious to previous political loyalties, he sometimes ruled as though his authority stemmed from U.S. approbation rather than the support of his people. For this reason, his administration appeared to be an outgrowth of the U.S. occupation, a fact that was nowhere more evident than in the institution to which he entrusted the task of maintaining order. There was no resemblance whatsoever between Cuba's Rural Guard and the armies that took upon themselves the mission of defending the new Spanish American nations against reconquest by Europe earlier in the nineteeth century. Basically the Guard was a police force, and although largely officered by former liberators, one of its salient characteristics was its obedience and faithfulness to U.S. authorities.[1] To all appearances, Cuba was destined to be an exception in the postindependence history of the region.

The First Cuban Government

The first name that came to the minds of the liberators when they began to think about the first president of Cuba was that of Calixto García.[2] Then, when he died and it became evident that Máximo Gómez was the most popular man in Cuba, their eyes turned in the direction of the Dominican.[3] But Gómez, who was acutely aware of his dual condition of foreigner and unlettered man,[4] declined the honor, suggesting instead the name of Tomás Estrada Palma, Martí's successor as head of the Cuban Revolutionary party and chief of the Cuban Junta throughout the war. Estrada Palma's patriotic credentials were indeed impeccable, although he was far from the ideal man to run for public office.

Captured by the Spaniards in 1877 when he headed the insurgent government, he had spent the rest of the Ten Years' War in a prison in Barcelona. Upon his release after Zanjón, instead of returning to Cuba he had gone to live in Honduras, where he married the daughter of President José Santos Guardiola. A few years later he moved to the United States, making his home in Central Valley, New York, where he founded a school for Cuban children. By the time the war ended, he was in his late sixties and had been away from his native land for over twenty years, most of which he had spent in the United States. He had become a naturalized U.S. citizen. He played an important role in the movement for independence by raising funds (some from the mortgage of his own home), arms, and munitions and occasionally by recruiting men for the liberating army. Nevertheless, outside of the insurgent leadership he was little known to Cubans. A converted Protestant who had spent a long time with a Quaker family while teaching at Central Valley, he had come to identify closely with his adoptive country. He had little faith in the ability of his fellow Cubans to govern themselves, and perhaps for this reason he decided upon the advent of peace that his commitment to Cuba had ended and that he would never live on its soil again.[5]

At heart, moreover, he probably was still an annexationist. He had definitely been an advocate of annexation at the time of the Ten

Years' War, when he had been deeply disturbed by the convulsions and anarchy that had victimized the other Spanish American republics.[6] Back then he had been firmly convinced that union with the United States was the only way out of Cuba's misfortunes, and although he had subsequently toned down his views it was only because of the growth and solidification of Cuban nationalism after Zanjón. But he had never really ceased to look upon the U.S. government as the guarantor of internal peace on the island, nor had he ever been remiss in postulating the advisability of Cuba's dependency on the United States. Barely two months before his nomination for the presidency, for example, he did not hesitate to proclaim that in his opinion "the natural destiny" of the island was to become "part of the United States."[7] Such was Cuba's only alternative, as he explained in detail to a friend toward the end of his life:

> It has always been my view, since I actively participated in the Ten Years' War, that independence was not the ultimate goal of our noble and patriotic efforts. What we were determined to accomplish was rather to establish a stable government strong enough to protect life and property and to guarantee the natural and civil rights of whoever resided on the island, whether native or foreigner. In this way, we could be certain that the enjoyment of freedom would never turn into agitation, lawlessness, or, worse yet, violent disruptions of the public order. I have never found it embarrassing to state nor feared to raise my voice to proclaim that it is a hundred times better for our beloved Cuba to be a political dependency where the gift of liberty may be enjoyed peacefully than to be an independent and sovereign republic, though ruined and disgraced by the baneful legacy of periodic civil wars.[8]

That the man who wrote these words should have become the first president of Cuba can only be attributed to the U.S. occupation and the policy of collaboration instituted by Gómez and his followers. It is not that the liberators had become too submissive or come to accept blindly the injunctions of the U.S. proconsuls. From time to time they gave evidence of their old combative spirit, organizing rallies and mailing campaigns, publicly criticizing Wood and his methods,[9] spearheading protest demonstrations, and showing their ability to stir up trouble in various other ways. When annexationism became active in the United States late in 1899, for example, they revived their old threat of resorting to armed resistance should any steps be taken in this direction;[10] and they reacted with similar vigor and intensity when Wood attempted to placate them shortly after he took over as military governor (December 20, 1899). At the time, General José Miró Argenter, Antonio Maceo's former chief of staff, openly accused Wood of working for annexation rather than Cuban independence.[11] During no other period, however, did the liberators show greater commitment to self-determination than throughout the long months during which the Cuban constitutional convention that assembled on November 5, 1900, agonized over the acceptance or rejection of the Platt amendment.[12] Many of the veterans (who made up the vast majority of the delegates) objected to the constitutional appendix whereby the United States planned to curtail Cuban sovereignty, but none achieved the dignified tone and sheer brilliance of the *Report to the Convention* written by Juan Gualberto Gómez,[13] the mulatto who had been Martí's chief aide during the conspiratorial phase of the war. Gómez's *Report* was adopted by his colleagues in March 1901, an action that marked the peak of nationalism in the assembly.[14]

But the very fact that only two months later the body bowed to U.S. pressure and accepted the amendment is the best indication that the basic principle of cooperation with the U.S. authorities was never truly abandoned. As none other than Manuel Sanguily put it, independence with restrictions was better than continued occupation, and so most of the delegates voted accordingly.[15] Máximo Gómez, who had refused to be a delegate to the convention, was saddened by this outcome. "The republic will certainly come," he complained, "although not with the absolute independence that we had envisioned."[16] The general, however, had been sufficiently concerned about the prolongation of the occupation to abstain from playing any role in the fight against the amendment, and even— according to Wood's dispatches[17]—supported the U.S. position and used his influence to obtain acceptance of the appendix among the delegates. Since he later indignantly denied the press reports about his backstage maneuvering, perhaps the best that can be said about his posture in the amendment debate is that it was equivocal.[18]

This certainly was not the case regarding Estrada Palma's attitude. The former head of the Cuban Junta also refused to seek a seat on the convention, but unlike General Gómez he put his views in writing for the avowed purpose that they be shown to all the delegates. In a letter from the United States to Gonzalo de Quesada, who had been elected to the convention, he began by deploring the "brusque, dictatorial manner" with which the controversial appendix was being forced upon the Cubans. To reject it, he hastened to add, would nonetheless be an ill-advised move. In his opinion, it embodied a fair compromise of U.S. and Cuban interests. The United States, after all, had acquired the right to some guarantee of order in Cuba, and he himself had told the U.S. political leaders before the passage of the congressional war resolutions in 1898 that the intervention in the Cuban war would provide them with a base from which to ensure internal peace on the island.[19] Once again, therefore, Estrada Palma had spoken the kind of language that U.S. expansionists liked to hear. At a time in which Máximo Gómez believed that Cuba was undergoing a greater danger than when the insurgents had faced Weyler and his 250,000 soldiers,[20] could anyone be surprised that he should have thought of his old friend and companion when the question of the presidency arose during the meetings of the constitutional convention? Eventually the amendment would have to be incorporated into a permanent treaty between the United States and Cuba. It was obvious that no radical nationalist could be the first president of the new republic.

Estrada Palma may have been Washington's first choice for the position,[21] and Gómez may have discussed his candidacy with Wood before making public his view on the matter,[22] but it was the general who was the architect of his electoral victory. In late June 1901, some time after the final vote on the amendment by the convention, Gómez announced that he would not run for the presidency himself but that he would support the election of Estrada Palma, whom he hoped to persuade to accept the nomination in a forthcoming trip to the United States. Upon his arrival in New York, Gómez must have succeeded in his mission relatively quickly, for he was able to refer to Estrada Palma at a dinner as the "holdover president of Cuba," an allusion to the fact that he had been elected to that office during the Ten Years' War. Gómez also voiced the hope that the old Junta chief would be the one to occupy the position of president when it was set up upon the withdrawal of the U.S. troops.[23] It was thus that Estrada Palma's presidential campaign was launched, in Manhattan rather than in Havana, as was perhaps to be expected given the grip that the United States had on Cuba.

Despite the untoward circumstances, by this time what passed for political parties had already sprung up on the Cuban scene. At first the liberators had talked about uniting under a single banner, but this had proved infeasible not only because of the controversy over the disbandment of the army but also because of certain ideological differences.[24] As a result, they had grouped into a number of political organizations, the most important of which were the Cuban Nationals, formed on March 11, 1899; the Federal Republicans, a regional party centered in Las Villas and also established in 1899; the Republicans of Havana, organized in April 1900; and the Union Democrats, also organized in Havana in 1900.[25] With the exception of the latter, all these parties had endorsed the Platt amendment with varying degrees of resignation, and it was perhaps for this reason that in a published letter issued upon his return from the United States, Gómez stated that the acceptance of the amendment by the convention had dispelled the doubts about Cuba's political situation, and that it was time for the Cubans to put that issue behind them and busy themselves with the task of establishing their own government.[26] It was his belief that for this government to be reasonably strong it had to stem from a united political front, and he came back determined to do his utmost to work out a national ticket apt to be supported by most factions.

But the broad political coalition that Gómez envisioned was not to be. Even before his trip to the United States, General Bartolomé Masó, former president of the insurgent government, had repudiated the Platt amendment in a letter to his colleague General José Lacret Morlot, which had been amply publicized and commented on in the Cuban press.[27] The letter had evoked enthusiasm from a heterogeneous group of politically unaffiliated "independents" that included a number of ranking liberators, and this group had published a manifesto on June 2, 1901, nominating Masó for the presidency of the republic. The members of the group had very little in common except their personal allegiance to Masó and their opposition to the amendment. But Masó apparently believed that repeal of the odious appendix was an important and popular issue, so when he was offered the vice-presidential nomination by Gómez's associates, he declined. The battle lines were thus drawn in the Cuban political arena.[28]

On August 18, a number of prominent Republicans (from both Havana and Las Villas) and Nationals met with General Gómez at the home of General Emilio Núñez, governor of the province of Havana, in order to deliberate about the forthcoming election. They agreed to write to Estrada Palma asking for his political views and the way in which he proposed to deal with the many issues confronting Cuba. The reply came in a lengthy letter dated September 7 that was read on the twenty-seventh to the same distinguished gathering, also at General Núñez's residence. The letter was not very enlightening in the sense that it largely reflected the positions of its addressees on the Platt amendment and Cuban-U.S. relations, their conciliatory attitude toward former colonialists, and their interest in commercial reciprocity with the United States. But it did reveal some thought-provoking aspects of its author's convictions, such as his passion for fiscal austerity, his cautious approach to the matter of the veterans' back pay, and his curious hope that "the orderly practice of democratic institutions" by the Cubans would one day allow him to abolish the armed forces on the island.[29] These were sensitive issues, especially the one concerning the amount to be paid to the liberators—on which Masó's view was diametrically opposed to Estrada Palma's—and perhaps Gómez and his colleagues would have done well to request some sort of clarification from the candidate. Apparently, however, the die had already been cast, for on the following day, September 28, a manifesto to the people of Cuba was issued in which Estrada Palma was presented as the epitome of civic virtue and the most appropriate man to rule Cuba in the critical period ahead.[30] So that everyone could verify that such was the case, his letter was appended to the manifesto, which was signed by more than ten generals of the liberating army. Heading the list there appeared the signature of Gómez, who was obviously the driving force behind the nomination and the National Republican alliance that was formed to support it.

Opposing the alliance was the so-called Masoísta coalition, made up of Union Democrats, whose strength lay in Havana, and a conglomerate of splinter groups, regional organizations, and local factions. There were former autonomists as well as pro- and anti-Platt amendment elements on both sides, although, curiously enough, the most conspicuous cases of ideological transpositions were found among the Masoístas. One of Masó's chief campaigners, for example, was the autonomist Rafael Fernández de Castro; and his coalition's nominee for governor of the province of Pinar del Río was Joaquín Quílez, a political figure of the day who was characterized by some observers as "an instrument" of General Wood.[31] This is an indication that the alignment of forces at this critical juncture of Cuba's political history was dictated as much by personal preferences and animosities (such as the old Gómez–Cisneros Betancourt feud) as by other considerations, a fact that no doubt was a contributing factor to the insults, personal attacks, and violent clashes that marred the election campaign from the beginning. Not even Gómez himself was spared by the rabble rousers. On two occasions (in Camagüey, home of Cisneros Betancourt, and Manzanillo, home of Masó), he was greeted at political rallies with shouts of "death to the traitor," and on both occasions he was stoned by angry Masoístas, who thereby deeply wounded the feelings of the old general.[32]

This was indeed a bad start for postindependence Cuban politics, especially considering the anticlimactic way in which the heated campaign ended. For, as the day of the election (December 31, 1901) drew nearer, the Masoístas began to realize that the followers of Estrada Palma had the capability of padding their own vote while lowering that of their opponents. The possibility was real because the Masoísta alliance had not coalesced until relatively late in the electoral process, and for that reason its members were not represented in the Junta Central de Escrutinios or any of the other electoral institutions charged with preparing the voter lists, watching the polling places, counting the ballots, and generally monitoring election procedures. That the Masoístas had reason to worry was warranted by the known fact that the results of voter registration had been illegally altered in Las Villas. They therefore decided to appeal to Wood, requesting among other things that the Junta Central be reorganized so as to include at least one supporter of Masó. They got nowhere. Wood naturally disliked Masó, and in his effort to prevent his election had even gone so far as to dismiss, early in the campaign, a number of mayors who backed his candidacy.[33] Consequently, as might be expected, he rejected the request of the Masoístas, who then turned to Washington for justice. But Washington did not look with favor upon Masó's cause either, and this second appeal, which included a petition for a one-month postponement of the election, was also rejected. Charging that the United States intended to rig the vote, Masó refused to participate further in the campaign and formally withdrew his candidacy. He made the announcement on December 21, a week before the scheduled election.[34]

As a result, Estrada Palma won an uncontested victory on a quiet day during which not a single incident hampered the electorate. Some U.S. newspapers reported that the vote had been "the lightest of the light,"[35] but the truth is that out of 335,699 registered voters 213,116 cast their ballots, a significantly larger number than voted in the constitutional convention election.[36] Regardless of the lack of opposition, therefore, Cubans were not totally indifferent to the outcome of the election. No one has ever ventured the opinion that Masó would have been the winner had there been no irregularities and had the U.S. authorities been truly impartial. By this time Masó had lost some of his intellectual vigor and thus became prone to error, as was amply demonstrated during the campaign.[37] There were, furthermore, many Cubans who feared that his success would have postponed the evacuation of the island by the U.S. personnel and doomed the prospects of a reciprocity agreement with the United States. Finally, it is necessary to consider the ascendancy and popularity of Gómez, which was probably the decisive factor. With the Gómez backing, Estrada Palma's candidacy did not need any additional buttressing; he would have emerged triumphant in any event. Yet the fact remains that his was a rather unusual election. Not only was there only one candidate but the victor did not make a single appearance throughout the campaign; moreover he waited until barely a month before the vote to renounce his U.S. citizenship.[38] For a nation that had been looking forward to self-government for so long, it was indeed an inauspicious beginning.

Estrada Palma and the Veterans

Initially the new president gave no inkling of what his rule would be like, for rather than returning to Cuba immediately after his election became official in order to learn for himself about the changes that twenty years had wrought in the country, Estrada Palma chose to remain in the United States and to have two friends (Domingo Méndez Capote and Diego Tamayo) come up from Cuba to brief him on the situation there. Toward the end of March 1902, he traveled to Washington to make the final arrangements for the transfer of power to the Cubans. It was only after they were satisfactorily concluded and it was decided that the long-awaited event would take place on May 20 that he readied himself to leave his Central Valley home. He arrived in Cuba on April 20, landing in Oriente, where he made stops at Bayamo, his birthplace; Manzanillo, where he had a pleasant meeting with Masó; and Santiago de Cuba. Then he began to move slowly toward Havana, riding a wave of popular enthusiasm that crested upon his arrival in the city, on May 11. On the morning of that day, he was solemnly greeted by Wood, Gómez, and the municipal council, and in the afternoon he met with the Las Villas Republicans, who began to press him to include some of them in his cabinet. The meeting did not go well, for Estrada Palma ended up by proclaiming angrily that the appointment of the secretaries was his prerogative and that he would not be coerced in his decisions by anyone. As he was leaving the meeting, General José Miguel Gómez,[39] the Republican leader, was overheard as he grumbled, "This old man is going to be very troublesome indeed!"[40]

This became more and more evident as quick-witted Cubans began to sneer at Estrada Palma's almost daily meetings with Wood and Máximo Gómez, and to insinuate that they were tutoring rather than briefing sessions. In addition, these were days in which, as might be expected, celebrations, patriotic ceremonies, and rallies were quite frequent; joint appearances of Gómez and the new president were mandatory on such occasions; and almost inevitably the loudest cheers were always for the old warrior, who as a rule was also asked to deliver the most important speech. For him, this was a pleasurable state of affairs that he certainly seemed to enjoy. But Estrada Palma felt deeply offended. He regarded the preference shown by Cubans to Gómez as detrimental to his dignity as chief executive, and he interpreted it as a resurgence of the caudillo tendencies that he had to cope with during the Ten Years' War. One day, trying to erase the impression that he owed his election to his old friend, he tersely informed the press: "No one will dominate me. I am free to act as it pleases me. I did not have to make any promises in order to obtain my position."[41]

Because of this conviction, from the day of his inauguration Estrada Palma ruled Cuba as though he had his own political base. He was upright—he once observed that he was the only honest man in the country—but he was also irritable, obstinate, and as dogmatic as he was upright. Once he made up his mind about the source of his power, he clung to his belief with the fiercest of determinations. In order to advance the cause of his supporters even to a moderate extent, he would have had to implement a liberal fiscal program and take a flexible and, at times, even ingratiating attitude. He would have had to acknowledge that the army veterans and their problems (back pay, employment opportunities, and the like) were one of the major issues of Cuban politics. Nevertheless, nothing could be in more direct opposition to his political self-image and his rigid and deep-rooted conservatism. On the one hand, he was an advocate of thrift, tight money, and balanced budgets; on the other—aware of the revolt-ridden trajectory of Cuba's sister republics—he valued to a high degree obedience to authority. Not that he believed in the virtues of autocratic rule—far from it! Indeed he was convinced that Cuba's future was democratic, yet he was likewise convinced that such a state of affairs would have to evolve from education and training. In his view, the island's chief problem lay in the insufficient preparation of its people for self-government. Democracy, he maintained, was sane and disciplined; and since Cubans had an overpowering inclination to confuse liberty with license, they would have to learn orderliness and restraint in public affairs before the system could operate effectively in their land. It followed then that Cuba ought to have "more teachers than soldiers" (the maxim that he adopted as the motto of his administration), for it was in the schools that a new generation of citizens imbued with the true values of democracy would eventually be shaped. Meanwhile, the government of the island ought to be in the hands of a responsible and enlightened elite capable of serving as a deus ex machina that would bring about public tranquility and prosperity.[42]

Obviously, there was little room for the liberators—most of whom were uncultured and poorly educated men—in the soldierless and elitist republic that Estrada Palma envisaged. This became apparent as soon as he made his first moves as president. Owing to his long exile, he had never been involved too deeply in the factionalism within the insurgent movement. Nor had it been necessary for him, because of the approach taken by Máximo Gómez in the matter of his nomination, to affiliate himself with any of the political parties that had backed him in the election. Moreover, his opponent, the genial Masó, had welcomed him with open arms upon his return to Cuba. He was thus able to shun party labels and to act the part of the nonpartisan and neutral president, the president of all Cubans without distinction of previous political loyalties. From this comfortable position, he proceeded to choose the members of his cabinet, all of them men of considerable administrative ability but also known for their conservatism. One of them, Carlos de Zaldo Beurman, belonged to a family of bankers; another, Emilio Terry Dorticós, was one of the wealthiest planters on the island.[43] Half of the secretaries were erstwhile autonomists—Zaldo, Terry, and José María García Montes. Two were Cuban Nationals—Diego Tamayo and Manuel Luciano Díaz; two were Republicans—Zaldo and García Montes; and two were the president's personal friends—Terry and Eduardo Yero. None of them was a high-ranking liberator.[44] Not even the highest-ranking among the liberators, the commander in chief himself, had a role in the new administration. As the mastermind of Estrada Palma's victory, the old general expected to be the éminence grise of the regime, a role that suited his lack of intellectual background and the fact of his Dominican birth. But the president soon showed no disposition to seek Gómez' advice on the problems of the country and the relations between the former friends turned cool.[45] At least on one occasion Gómez was publicly slighted by Estrada Palma in a way that those present could hardly fail to notice.[46]

Of course, there was nothing that Estrada Palma or any other politician could do to prevent Gómez and his colleagues from bringing into view their political muscle whenever the opportunity presented itself. This became evident very early in the life of the young republic (November 1902), when a period of considerable labor unrest marked by violent clashes between law enforcement agents and the striking workers made some fear that the U.S. Army might return to restore order and possibly terminate the Cuban experiment. In the face of such danger (which seemed real given the activities of some provocateurs[47]), Máximo Gómez, Juan Gualberto Gómez, Manuel Sanguily, and other leading veterans formed a commission for the purpose of settling the dispute and removing what they felt was a threat to Cuban independence. They asked the workers to return

to work and to choose a delegate in each factory to act on their behalf in a negotiated agreement with the employers. They also asked
that all factories be compelled to hire native workers, regardless of
race, and not to give preference to Spanish immigrants, as had been
happening up to that moment, especially in the tobacco industry.[48]
But the center of veteran influence under Estrada Palma was Congress. Approximately one-third of the senators and congressmen
were former officers of the liberating army or men that, in one capacity or another, had been associated with the insurgent movement.[49] Eventually these men and their colleagues proved to be the
stumbling block of the administration. After a time they evinced
scant inclination to pass any laws except those granting themselves
immunity or pecuniary or political advantages, yet they became the
most bitter critics of the government. With a vengeance, they
blamed it for the state of the economy (which was not so bad, after
all), for spending too much money on public works in Havana, for
being excessively friendly to U.S. citizens, for striving too hard to
accumulate millions in the treasury, and, last but not least, for being
insensitive to the demands of the patriots in Congress. Clashes between the president and the legislators were frequent, and sometimes the latter lost, as when they attempted to reestablish the lot-
tery that had operated under Spanish rule. But it was Estrada Palma
who, more often than not, had to bow to their wishes. Such was the
case when a congressional immunity act was passed to protect Mariano Carona, a congressman from Oriente who had murdered a
newspaperman;[50] and such was the case when the question of payment to veterans for their military service was revived on the day
that the House of Representatives met for the first time.

The battle over the veterans' payment illustrates the basic political contradiction that handicapped the Estrada Palma administration—whatever opinion we may have of the intrinsic merit of
its policies. The president's position on the matter had been clear
since the inception of his candidacy. He believed that the monthly
wage that the insurgent Government Council had offered to pay
the officers and men was too high and ought to be reduced; and he
further believed that the resulting amount ought to be paid out of
savings from surplus revenues.[51] Yet, in taking this position, the
Cuban head of state showed his lack of foresight, for he should have
anticipated that no Cuban government could realistically expect to
inch along in meeting the republic's obligations and responsibilities
to the liberators. It did not take long for them to show him their
unquestionable strength as a political force. A few of the more
impatient among them expressed their dissatisfaction by resorting

to open revolt, but for the most part the pressure sprang from Congress, which gave the matter the highest priority. If there was anyone in Cuba who stood a slim chance of heading off the veterans' drive, it was Máximo Gómez. On this occasion, however, the general sided with his comrades in arms; and although he strove to assuage their impatience and anger and even opposed certain high-flown money-raising schemes suggested by the politicians, he let it be known that he was in favor of floating a loan to pay off the army provided its terms were reasonable and would not place Cuba too deeply in debt.[52] One wonders if at this point anyone dared to point out to Gómez that his position was now closer to that of Masó than to Estrada Palma's.

Eventually the pressure mounted to the point that the administration could not bear it (Colonel Ferrara was nearly lynched at a theater in Havana for speaking against the loan[53]), and Estrada Palma had no alternative but to consent to expedite the payment as demanded by the veterans. The law providing the necessary authorization to the chief executive was passed on February 13, 1903, and negotiations for the procurement of the funds began shortly after the law was modified by another of January 25, 1904. Since by this time the credit of the country was already well established, and, furthermore, Washington appeared to look with favor upon the transaction,[54] it did not take long for a contract to be signed with Speyer and Company, a New York banking house, for a loan of $35,000,000 payable in forty years and bearing 5 percent interest annually. The sum that the Cuban government actually received amounted only to $31,675,000. This money, as it turned out, proved sufficient to pay only half of the army debt. For although the bond bill went through on the basis of a dollar for each day of service for the privates, which was in fact a pittance, extravagant sums—running well into the thousands for those of higher rank—were approved for officers. In addition, many who had never served in the field were entered as veterans on the rolls; the length of service of others was made to appear greater than it actually was in order to inflate the bonus checks; not a few were listed with a superior rank to that which they had attained for the same iniquitous purpose; and then numerous names on the records were purely imaginary. Still, all this was condoned by Estrada Palma, who, in the interest of appeasing the clamorous veterans, went along with the additional steps that were taken to redeem the remaining 50 percent of the debt without uttering the faintest protest. This was partially accomplished through yet another bill, enacted on August 29, 1905. No foreign loan had to be obtained this time, however, because an increase in customs duties (authorized by a law of January 1904) had permitted the austere president to build up a surplus in the treasury; but even so a domestic bond issue of $11,250,000 was necessary to supplement the Speyer loan so that a further partial payment could be provided to the army.[55]

Such was the way in which the liberators began to wrest from the administration the reward for their sacrifices. But the men in the ranks received only a small share of the bounty available to them. The ones who really profited from the distribution of the money were a number of officials high up in the government and a coterie of legislators who were veterans who contrived to delay the payments so as to make the more humble veterans, the majority of whom were illiterate, believe that they were never going to be paid. As a result, approximately half of them sold the certificates of service with which they had been provided before payments were made at only 40 or 50 percent of their true value.[56] Among the speculators were José Miguel Tarafa, who had been a colonel in the insurgent army, and Alfredo Zayas, leader of the Cuban National Party and the man who solemnly greeted Estrada Palma on behalf of the municipality of Havana upon his arrival in the city after his election. It also appears that about $16 million worth of certificates somehow found its way into the portfolio of U.S. investors.[57] Both Tarafa and Zayas were arrested for their improprieties, of which Estrada Palma was well aware. Although innocent of any wrongdoing himself, he nevertheless found it necessary to put his stamp of approval on the activities of the scalpers (and of those who, like Zayas, had added fictitious names to the lists of veterans in order to claim the money for themselves), which he did through an executive order whereby the purchasers of the certificates were allowed to collect the money in lieu of the original holders. Another executive order authorized lenders to attach up to 50 percent of the amount owed to the men.[58]

The Rural Guard

Of all his traits, perhaps Estrada Palma's most salient was his obstinacy, the dogged determination with which he stuck to his course in the face of contradiction and adversity. Thus, true to form, despite the setbacks inflicted upon him by the unruly Congress, he remained adamant in pursuing his economic policy, the cornerstone of which was cutting back on unnecessary government expenses and keeping the government payroll at a minimum. His passion for frugality reached new heights after the $35 million loan became a fact, when he redoubled his efforts to build up enough reserves to pay it off as soon as possible. These were years in which his administration enjoyed a growing income as the economy recovered from the wartime and millions began to accumulate in the treasury, which soared from less than $1 million when he took over from Wood to close to $25 million at the end of his term in office.[59] Once the loan was repaid, his plan was to keep the bonds in the treasury while continuing to collect the same amount of revenues, which he intended to spend on education and public works. He had already managed to spend 25 percent of the national budget on education, and he had thus been able to increase the number of schools and teachers to the extent that there were over 500 more teachers than soldiers in the country. But he obviously wished to do more in this area.[60]

Owing to Estrada Palma's economic policy and to his antimilitaristic prejudices, Cuba remained a country without a standing army. "Public tranquility and security rest on the discipline of the country itself," he had declared when he delivered his first message to Congress on May 26, 1902.[61] Thus the only measure that he took concerning military matters was that of strengthening the Rural Guard, a body that he had inherited from the U.S. occupation, whose budget he increased to approximately $1.5 million a year.[62] As a result, the force nearly doubled in size; by 1905, its officers and men numbered 3,020, while the Artillery Corps, a largely ceremonial unit that had been incorporated into the Guard in 1901, reached 700. There were plans, moreover, to recruit an additional 1,000 men, an increase that would have brought the Cuban armed forces to a total of almost 5,000.[63]

Of these changes, the most significant was the expansion of the Artillery Corps, which had been organized in 1901 to assume command of coastal fortifications. At the time, as planned by U.S. officials, it had "consisted of 150 white Cubans recruited under the same conditions as to qualifications that [obtained] in the United States."[64] But in 1904 Estrada Palma had added new men, organized them into six companies, and placed the unit under his personal command. When he set out to restructure the Artillery Corps, one of his purposes seems to have been to rid himself of the eight batteries of U.S. artillery that remained in Cuba after the occupation ended.[65] It is clear, nonetheless, that he wanted the force to serve also as a sort of palace guard that he could trust, and this appears to have hurt the feelings of General Alejandro Rodríguez, head of the Guard. The general, who was an annexationist and had promised Wood that the body "would always be loyal to the government that had done so much for Cuba,"[66] called on U.S. minister Herbert G. Squiers to complain about Estrada Palma's action, to which Squiers reacted by immediately demanding the dissolution of the corps. This was one occasion on which Estrada Palma refused to give in to the minister's importunities. "I want a body of men near me," he explained patiently, "on whom I can rely absolutely in time of danger."[67]

Yet apart from this modest effort the Cuban president did little to provide himself with a military fulcrum of power. To create a truly strong army simply did not fit into his plans for the country, and thus he decided to depend on the Rural Guard, which had only been and still was essentially a colonial constabulary. It was established at the time the United States assumed responsibility for maintaining order in a country in which, Máximo Gómez's denial notwithstanding,[68] banditry became widespread upon the arrival of peace.[69] At this time, as Wood later reported, "many restless and disorderly spirits . . . resumed their irregular and lawless lives, and to such an extent did they carry their depredations that they became a serious menace to public order, life, and property."[70] As a result, "people were afraid to go into the country and make any start with cattle or in other directions," as another U.S. military commander also reported.[71] Therefore something had to be done to restore law and order, especially in the eastern part of the island where the problem seems to have been particularly acute. But law enforcement misunderstandings attributable to language and cultural differences would have arisen if the U.S. troops themselves had undertaken to pursue and arrest the brigands, and the occupation authorities were only too aware of this.[72] Sensitive as they were to developments in the Philippines, they were anxious to avoid any situation potentially capable of precipitating hostilities in Cuba.[73] Consequently they assigned the U.S. Army a behind-the-scenes role, that of providing the sinews of the intervention, turning to the Cuban veterans for the job of directly enforcing the authority of the military government, particularly in districts remote from the locus of its power.

This proved to be a sensible policy decision for a number of reasons. In the first place, it helped to clear the way for the demobilization of the liberating army, providing the soldiers with employment and allowing them to continue to bear arms in the service of their country. Second, it softened the impact of the sudden release of thousands of men, many of whom might have taken to brigandage themselves had they not been gainfully employed in some manner. Finally, it allowed the U.S. rulers to count on men who were acclimated, largely immune to the diseases of the country, and thoroughly familiar with the areas that they policed. As a peace-keeping force and an instrument to control the rural population (and unruly

U.S. troops as well), the liberators-turned-Guards rendered inestimable services to the occupation authorities. At first they served as part of informal auxiliary units under U.S. officers, but very soon they began to be organized as adjunct forces to assist departmental commands at the local level.[74]

The first of such forces, made up of 20 men, was formed by Wood when he became head of the military district of Santiago de Cuba late in July 1898, a few days before the signing of the peace protocol with Spain. The following month another small unit was created to police the region around Guantánamo, and it did not take long before this unit reached 40 men. At about the same time there emerged yet another detachment based at Baracoa, and shortly afterward, in Manzanillo, Colonel Whiteside followed Wood's example and organized his own force. By December 1898, this force had grown to approximately 50 men. That same month a local constabulary was likewise formed in Holguín, following the same pattern. Before long all the U.S. officers who had been named provincial and municipal chiefs had organized similar makeshift forces with Cuban veterans, upon whom devolved the responsibility of patrolling the countryside in all of the island's six provinces. But as late as the fall of 1899 less than a third of Cuba's 3,500 constables were in Rural Guard units. Conspicuous among them was the force organized by Wood in Oriente after he became governor of the entire region. This force, which was shaped up with the advice of the veteran Colonel Francisco Valiente, was purposely modeled on the Spanish Guardia Civil and Mexican President Porfirio Díaz's Guardia Rural.[75]

Since the function of all these local constabularies (all of which were tacitly approved by the War Department) was the same and their jurisdictions were tangled, it would have seemed logical to merge them into a single national body. In fact, the organization of such a body—a "colonial army" composed of 10,000 veterans—had indeed occurred to President McKinley, who had proposed it while discussing the fate of the liberating army with the Cuban commission that had come to Washington in December 1898.[76] Upon his visit to Máximo Gómez the following February, Robert P. Porter had reiterated the same idea, holding out the possibility of converting a large cadre of the Cuban army into a sort of national police force of the type created by Wood in Oriente.[77] These proposals had stricken a responsive note in the Cubans, who had also been thinking along the same lines. Months before the Gómez-Porter meeting, both the general and the army assembly had suggested the organization of a native militia to facilitate the disbandment of the liberators. Not unnaturally, the scheme had resurfaced when such an event appeared imminent. At that time Gómez's idea was to add several regiments made up of his own soldiers to the U.S. occupation forces, and as he later explained in a manifesto to the people and the army, the fact that it had not been implemented was not for lack of interest on the part of the U.S. president. What had paralyzed the project were the quirks of insurgent politics, the political storm caused by his acceptance of McKinley's bonus, and his removal from the command of the army.[78]

On the U.S. side, as might be expected, Wood himself had been the main advocate of enlarging and extending his Guard since the beginning, and during the early months of the occupation he had advanced this plan periodically. But despite McKinley's inclination to try it, and the fact that Elihu Root supported it when he came to the War Department, nothing was ever done to bring it into being. On the one hand, the project, in many ways, had been predicated upon and responsive to difficulties anticipated in the dissolution of the liberating army, and no such difficulties had arisen when the liberators were disarmed and sent home. On the other, Brooke had always opposed the creation of a native military institution. He made this clear on the two occasions on which McKinley took up the matter with him. On the second, he wired Washington that he had polled his departmental commanders and found only Wood in favor of the project. Fitzhugh Lee, William Ludlow, and James Wilson thought that all police forces should be controlled by civil authorities, preferably at the municipal level, and Wilson went so far as to assert that a disciplined armed force in a new nation could very well be the point of origin of future military dictatorships.[79] The maintenance of internal order, the general reasoned, could be achieved merely by increasing and strengthening the already existing constabularies, and the funds that would be spent in organizing and supporting a national force could be put to better use in acquiring oxen, farm implements, and other paraphernalia for the reconstruction of the war-torn peasant dwellings.[80] The opposition of Brooke was based on the assumption that the implementation of Wood's plan would make a bad impression on the Cubans. It would lead them to think, in the first place, that the United States could not cope with the Philippine insurrection without turning to native support elsewhere. Second, it would generate distrust about U.S. intentions. This last point, the military governor declared, had suggested itself to some of his subordinates as well as himself.[81]

Wood, however, had the opportunity to have his own way when, culminating a series of maneuvers that he designed to displace and replace Brooke, he finally succeeded in becoming the proconsul of

Cuba late in December 1899. Thereupon he embarked on a general program of reforms with the hope of "Americanizing" the island in the shortest possible time, and, as part of this program, he set out to create a national rural guard. He viewed such a force as an agency for spreading U.S. influence and for establishing a friendly bond between Cubans and U.S. citizens, and it was in this light that he once again insisted on the need to unify the various local units into an islandwide military organization. Since by this time Root had become enthusiastic about the type of colonial forces that the British had developed in Egypt, he experienced no difficulty in carrying out his project.[82]

Shortly after he replaced Brooke he decreed that the existing Guard members would be the principal executors of the law in all his military departments. He also made certain that they would be adequately trained, equipped, and generally developed into a high state of efficiency, spirit, and discipline, for which purpose he detached a member of his staff, Cavalry Captain Herbert J. Slocum. Under Slocum's supervision, the constabularies were gradually shaped in the image of the U.S. cavalry, and within a year of Wood's appointment they had been transformed into a 1,200-man force in which the provincial units had yielded to national companies, the first step toward unification under a central command. Then, in January 1901, Wood summoned the provincial Guard chiefs to Havana for the purpose of developing a new and sweeping reorganization proposal, and this resulted, after several months of deliberations, in the issuance of Military Order 114 of April 5, 1901, the Organic Law of the Rural Guard. The jurisdiction of the body, according to this ordinance, extended to all areas where there was no urban or municipal police. Its mission was to enforce the decrees of the central government and the decisions of the courts. Unlike the local constabularies, it was under the direct control of the military governor, whose prerogative it was to select officers and men. Composed of four regiments and headed by a lieutenant colonel, its men were distributed into small detachments through the six provinces of the island in accordance with crime rates, the relative proportion of rural and urban population, the efficiency of communications, and the concentration of private property. Major General Alejandro Rodríguez, who had commanded the Fifth Corps of the liberating army, was appointed chief of the united force with the rank of colonel.[83]

The nationalization envisaged by Wood was completed in April 1902, when the Artillery Corps and the Guard were consolidated under one command, with General Rodríguez as the head of both organizations. By then, barely a month before national sovereignty was transferred to Cubans, the body had expanded to 1,604 officers and men, stationed at 247 posts, with a monthly budget of $75,000.[84] At best it was a force of a paramilitary nature; it did not constitute by any means a regular military organization. Its mission was neither to defend Cuba's international integrity nor to underwrite the viability of the legally constituted Cuban authorities. Through the Platt amendment the United States had appropriated such responsibilities. The efforts of the Guard were to be devoted to police work—to protect property in rural districts, to keep the peace in these areas, and to make itself available to judges and civil governors for apprehending suspects, transporting convicts, and other law enforcement duties. The training of the Cuban Guard members was centered on the successful performance of this type of work. Militarily, they were incapable of carrying out even company-size operations.[85]

Such was the armed support with which the occupation endowed Estrada Palma's republic. To a large extent, the members of the force were former insurgents, and the veterans held virtually every high position in the body. Yet the Guard was not by any means a byproduct of the liberating army. Not only were the majority of the veteran Guard members white,[86] but because they primarily rendered assistance and protection to agriculture, cattle-raising, and other branches of wealth, they were also men who had strong links with the rural economic sector. For the most part Guard outposts were on privately owned lands, and frequently post chiefs owed their appointment or reappointment to the intercession of grateful planters.[87] Then there was the matter of the force's recruitment system, which tended to strengthen the ties of its members with propertied interests. Members of the Guard had to be men of good character, literate, physically fit, and recommended by "at least two well-known citizens of good repute, preferably property owners." In addition, upon enlistment they had to pay for uniforms and mounts.[88] This made it extraordinarily difficult for the most turbulent and rambunctious individuals—and indeed for most blacks—to be included in the ranks. Certainly commissioned ranks were out of reach as far as they were concerned. It is no wonder that at the time mounted guards seemed to be "members of the best Cuban families." According to a U.S. observer, "some of them had been wealthy, some looked like former prosperous businessmen."[89] Evidently these men were no longer made of revolutionary stuff. Whatever they had been while fighting against Spain in the woods, they were no more.

Nor was the institution to which they belonged more than superficially and indirectly related to the advancement of Cuban nationalism. The system of allegiance upon which the Guard was built was vastly different from that which underlay the formation of the liberating army. Carefully chosen from among an abundance of recruits as the "best material" in the insurgent contingents,[90] the majority of the Guard members looked with favor upon the work of the occupation, and consequently had no qualms about taking the required oath of allegiance to the United States. The officers were selected by and were responsible to U.S. commanders, and all of them, whatever their rank, knew that their authority was determined by and derived from the military government. If they had power, it was because, as Slocum put it, "the strong arm of the government of the intervention was supporting them";[91] and if they were members of an elite force and had smart uniforms, good pay, respectable status, and prestige, it was because in many ways they were part and parcel of the government. As though to emphasize this point, Guard members frequently accompanied U.S. troops on maneuvers, so as to "let the people see that if necessary, they would work together in harmony to preserve peace."[92] The Cuban armed force was therefore closer to the foreign occupation than to its nation-building fellow Cubans, and its set of loyalties was arranged accordingly. Anyone who overheard General Rodríguez bidding farewell to Leonard Wood on the day of his final departure from Havana could have confirmed this fact.[93]

What Estrada Palma inherited as the underpinning of his regime consequently was a force that was militarily weak and of dubious fidelity. It remained to be seen whether it would be capable of keeping tight control over unruly elements, the very kind of people who had been prevented from joining its ranks. Quite perceptively, Secretary Root remarked in 1899 that the maintenance of law and order in Cuba under the occupation had been basically the result of the U.S. military presence.[94] Without the backing of "a strong government," as Slocum wrote,[95] the Rural Guard would be powerless, a fact that Wood himself was forced to recognize. True, the record shows that in his view the Guard was "ample to maintain public order in the rural districts of Cuba even after the withdrawal of the army of occupation."[96] But he must not have been absolutely sure of the efficiency of the force that he had brought into being, for otherwise he would not have suggested to Root in 1901 that a small U.S. contingent should remain on the island after the transfer of power to the Cubans for the purpose of underwriting stability and order. Such a contingent would be "a moral force to hold these people to their work until the decent element assumes its normal position in the government of the island."[97] As it happened, nevertheless, when at the urging of Estrada Palma the last U.S. artilleryman returned to the United States, the responsibility of holding in check potentially disruptive forces devolved on the Guard alone. The body appears to have been utterly unprepared for that task. With the departure of its U.S. patron, its effectiveness and morale began to deteriorate rapidly. Its head, furthermore, distrusted the new administration. He feared that under its rule the Guard would be unable to remain above politics.[98]

6. The Beginnings of Factionalism: The 1906 Uprising

Neither the disbandment of the liberating army nor the antimilitaristic bent of the Estrada Palma administration could keep Cuba from the turmoil that afflicted its sister republics in the nineteenth century. Like a stream, the tendencies historically associated with such ills merely went underground for a brief period, only to resurface later, full force. Owing to the demobilization imposed on them by the United States, the liberators metamorphosed into veterans. Technically therefore they came to be civilians, just like the Cubans who remained passive while the wars were fought. But they still represented the same forces that took over government elsewhere in Latin America and, insofar as it was possible within the limits of the Plattist protectorate, they conducted themselves in a similar fashion. They concentrated their efforts on achieving control of patronage and public revenues, and, if dissatisfied with the functioning of the established mechanism for the transfer of power, they did not hesitate to resort to violence. They rose.

The Issue of Reelection in 1905

Ultimately it was the millions that Estrada Palma began to accumulate in the treasury that determined the fate of his administration. On the one hand, the tight money policies from which they resulted antagonized the host of politicians who were constantly pressing the government for political jobs and other favors. On the other, they whetted the appetite of the former generals and other higher-ups who, as the president's term drew to a close, made no secret of their desire to get their hands on them. In a way, this was to be expected. Since the revolution had not been allowed to run its course, public office was about the only recompense to which the impecunious liberators could aspire for their services.[1]

For his part, persuaded that his programs could not be bettered and fearing—with reason, as events subsequently proved—that his precious millions would be squandered or misappropriated by his eventual successor, Estrada Palma resolved that none of the would-be presidents on the scene would have such an opportunity.[2] It also appears that he was further encouraged in this determination by the belief, not entirely without foundation, that his policies had met with Washington's approval and that he was the object of U.S. preference. In his message to Congress of December 6, 1904, President Theodore Roosevelt had in effect singled out Cuba among the Caribbean nations as a paragon of progressive and stable government,[3] a feeling that he had reiterated to the Cuban president in a personal letter late in January of the following year. After stating that he was proud of his role in the struggle for Cuban independence, Roosevelt congratulated Estrada Palma for the wisdom and courage that he had evidenced in guiding Cuba during its critical initiation into nationhood.[4] The extent to which this letter influenced the course of events in Havana is a matter of conjecture, but it was approximately at this time that the possibility of a second term began to be seriously discussed at the presidential palace.

Once the basic decision was made, Estrada Palma took a number of steps, all of them noteworthy and consequential. To begin with, he abandoned his previous neutrality and affiliated himself (February 1905) with the Moderate party, one of the political alliances that had emerged when the existing factions had begun to realign themselves over the issue of the presidential nomination the previous summer and the one that seemed most sympathetic to his legislative goals and economic conservatism. Second, he expressed his willingness to become the head of the Moderate ticket, a perfectly legal decision under the constitution. Third, he showed himself well disposed to countenance most, if not all, the measures, legal or otherwise, necessary to ensure his electoral victory and solid support for him in both houses of Congress. These measures—which were deliberately leaked to the opposition for intimidation purposes[5]— were to be taken by a new cabinet appointed by the president in March that, appropriately enough, was soon dubbed the "Fighting Cabinet." Some said that the reason for this sobriquet was that the majority of its secretaries were veterans of the war.[6] General Fernando Freyre de Andrade, the former president of the army assembly, was by far the strongest character among them. He was secretary of the interior, and as such he had under his control the police, the Rural Guard, the stewardship of provincial and municipal governments, and the supervision of the electoral process. Next after him in prominence was the new secretary of public works,

General Rafael Montalvo, a violent and still young former liberator, "brave in war and aggressive in peace."[7] The Department of the Treasury was entrusted to General Juan Rius Rivera, who had been a member of Wood's cabinet and had commanded the Western Corps of the liberating army after Antonio Maceo's death.

Cuban politics entered a new phase as a result of the involvement of the head of state in partisan politics. Owing to the rigidity of his judgment, his sensitivity to personal criticism, and his mania for economizing, he had lost not a few of his backers (among them Máximo Gómez, the prime mover of his election) and made many enemies. He had also clashed with the veterans as a political class and other ambitious elements. Yet in large measure his antagonists had remained unorganized and acephalous. Presently, upon becoming the visible head of a political faction, he had turned that faction ipso facto into the party in power. This, as might be expected, gave rise to the first opposition party in the history of Cuba, a political coalition that incorporated the remaining factions, the most important of which were the Republican wing formed by the followers of General José Miguel Gómez and the National Liberals led by Alfredo Zayas, who was not a veteran but had represented the insurgents in Havana during the war. Miguelistas and Zayistas formerly had been hostile to each other. Under the circumstances, however, they saw fit to merge into what was called the Liberal party, an amorphous organization that was soon joined by a number of lesser groups, among them what was left of the once vociferous Masoístas. The new party almost immediately received the blessing of Máximo Gómez and Bartolomé Masó, who thereby transformed it into a nearly invicible electoral machine—or so it seemed at the time.[8]

Of course, the emergence of this alliance had very little to do with principle or any issue worthy of that name. Nor was it brought into being by incompatibilities caused by social or economic cleavages. At the time most Cuban property owners had no connection with politics, and the politicians in general were a group apart.[9] Parties were scarcely more than groups of friends, fellow provincials, or pursuers of spoils, and their leadership uniformly included rapacious former generals and former colonels from whom the adrenaline of independence had already drained away, leaving them with the engrossing, overriding preoccupation of sharing in the plenty of peace. This was what truly separated the Liberals from the Moderates— personal and regional loyalties, party interest, ambition for jobs, and of course the eagerness to "administer" the surplus amassed by Estrada Palma. Which of the two factions would eventually capture the prize could almost be predicted from the congressional elections of February 1904, the first that were held by the republic. Violence had been used only sporadically and the day of the elections had passed with reasonably good order. But campaign issues had been reduced to differences of leadership; vote-rigging had been common; and returns had been generally favorable to whichever group held local power. Consequently, the prospects that the presidential elections scheduled for December 1, 1905, would be fair were dim indeed; and considering the Moderates' resolution to take no chance of failing, they seemed even dimmer.

When Cubans had begun to talk about a possible successor of Estrada Palma during the preceding months, they again had first thought of Máximo Gómez, whose popularity never appeared to subside. But the old general, while vigorously rejecting the reelection of government officials (because in his opinion it smacked of monarchism, regardless of what the constitution said), once again declined the nomination.[10] This cleared the way for various aspirants: General José Miguel Gómez, governor of Las Villas; General Emilio Núñez, governor of the province of Havana; and Alfredo Zayas, who had a following despite the aura of corruption that enveloped his name. For a few months the two governors, who appeared to be the chief contenders, bided their time. Núñez trusted that in the end his former commander in chief (who disliked José Miguel) would tip the scale in his favor, while the governor of Las Villas, who figured among the most faithful supporters of the administration, hoped that he would become the candidate of the government's coalition. Eventually, however, the president's determination to run again forced José Miguel Gómez and his Republicans into the opposition, and it was then (March 1905) that a round of conversations began that ultimately culminated in the creation of the Liberal party. Publicly censured at the time by another old friend of the Ten Years' War, Salvador Cisneros Betancourt, Estrada Palma hesitated for a moment. Yet he recovered quickly, making the fateful decision to match the resources at his disposal against the hold that Máximo Gómez and his other opponents appeared to have over Cuban public opinion.[11]

The resources available to the government were not inconsiderable, for the constitutional provisions for bipartisan election boards had not been implemented, and therefore the one who controlled local governments also controlled the elections. On the other hand, Congress had not passed a law covering the election of provincial and municipal officials either, which meant that the administration still retained the power to remove them under the old Spanish codes. This became the tactic of the Fighting Cabinet, which henceforward not only embarked on a wholesale purge of public functionaries in appointed positions at all levels but also dedicated itself to the systematic dismissal of all the Liberals who had been elected to provincial and municipal office. As a result, thousands of veterans who had been holding jobs since the days of the U.S. occupation again found themselves struggling for survival. Thirty-two mayoralties (including that of Havana) changed hands, and one Liberal governor was displaced in order to make room for a government supporter. The purge was most thorough in the Liberal strongholds of Pinar del Río and Las Villas, where it penetrated down to the lowest levels of the local administration. In these provinces teachers, public clerks, and even street cleaners were fired and replaced by Moderates.[12]

Máximo Gómez attempted to stop the government in its tracks with a public document in which he condemned its "immoral and unjustified" policies and candidly stated that he feared for the future of the republic, which was becoming "victimized by the mistakes of her sons."[13] His remarks, however, went unheeded, as Freyre de Andrade (who was the spearhead of the aggressive Moderate campaign) and his colleagues apparently became more convinced than ever that they could count on the backing of the United States. As a result, the opposition soon began to respond with street demonstrations, riots, and counter-intimidation and, as the political atmosphere heated up and the conflict grew more intense, talk of revolution began to be heard in antigovernment circles. The first to mention openly the dreadful possibility were the National Liberals, who announced in a manifesto published in April 1905 that they "would use all the means within their reach to resist as tenaciously as possible the behavior and designs of the government."[14] But no one made much of the threat until Máximo Gómez himself, at a political rally on the seventeenth of the same month, electrified the audience by loudly proclaiming: "The situation is extremely serious. I can already feel the beat of revolution in the air!"[15] In fact, he went much farther than that, for right then and there he served notice that he intended to concentrate 30,000 veterans in Havana and to lead them in a march on the presidential palace for the purpose of demanding from the government the immediate cessation of its illegal campaign tactics.[16]

Would U.S. gunboats have shown up in the harbor of Havana, as Estrada Palma forewarned, had the old warrior carried out his threat? He did not do so because the government solemnly promised to mend matters, indicating once again that he was the one man who could head off the self-destructive tendencies that were running amok in the country. Unfortunately, Cubans could not count on his services much longer. While he was stumping at Santiago de Cuba he fell mortally ill, and by the time he was transported back to Havana on June 8 he was already moribund. He died on June 17.[17] The repercussions of his illness and death became immediately apparent, for while he agonized on his deathbed, the negotiations between Gómez's Republicans and the National Liberals reached a successful conclusion, and shortly thereafter the new party named José Miguel and Zayas as its slate (May 23). Deprived of Máximo Gómez's support, Emilio Núñez (who was no friend of José Miguel[18]) was left entirely out of the picture, whereupon he determined to cast his lot with the Moderates in exchange for positions for himself and his friends. His sudden switch of allegiance highlights the true nature of the ongoing struggle between the Moderates and the Liberals.[19]

From then on both sides lost whatever sense of restraint was left in them. The Liberal-dominated Congress refused to approve the 1905–1906 budget, thereby provoking a fiscal crisis. A clumsy attempt was made on Estrada Palma's life as he traveled toward Santiago de Cuba. Gómez's followers reduced to ashes the city hall of Vueltas, a small town in Las Villas, rather than allow the government to conduct an investigation of municipal financial affairs.[20] Meanwhile, as the preliminary elections to choose the members of local electoral boards approached (they were scheduled for September 23), the Fighting Cabinet began to show more and more that it was ready to use force if that was necessary to ensure its victory. Freyre de Andrade prepared well for this eventuality. In Las Villas, for example, where José Miguel Gómez had dominated the Rural Guard detachments scattered throughout the region, his adherents had been able to secure open Guard backing in their bid for office during congressional contests. Freyre de Andrade made sure that this would not occur again. Detachments suspected of Miguelista sympathies were transferred; officers loyal to the Moderates were selected to serve in the most crucial districts; and those who were not trusted for any other reasons were either compelled to retire or denied promotion. The secretary, in sum, built a new set of loyalties into the Guard's structure. Earlier, local interests, either political or economic, had controlled the Guard posts. Now the 250 or so that existed on the island were converted into strongholds that permitted the weight of the government to be felt in even the most remote municipalities.[21] This is what was uppermost in José Miguel Gómez's mind when, early in June, he strongly protested the mistreatment of the Liberals in Las Villas. What he could not accept, he wrote, was that the administration had reassigned to the municipality of Cruces a certain Lieutenant Iglesias, who was guilty of the murder of two unfortunate local workers, "a crime for which he had never been brought to justice."[22] Gómez knew, of course, that if the lieutenant in question remained in Cruces he could not possibly hope to carry that district.

Yet it was not in puny Cruces but in the thriving city of Cienfuegos where the drama of the 1905 presidential campaign reached its climax in the days that preceded the preliminary elections. On September 17 the Liberals had made a show of force by staging a massive rally in Havana, a move that the government countered with a drive designed to jail the more militant Liberals and wipe out the few who might still be left on the payroll of the executive departments. On the nineteenth, the Cienfuegos Moderates assaulted the local Liberal club and shortly afterward attacked the U.S. consulate, hoping no doubt that their opponents would subsequently be blamed for the outrage. Daily life began to turn somewhat dangerous in the city, and as local families began to leave seeking safety elsewhere, the ranking Liberal on the scene, Congressman Enrique Villuendas (who had been a colonel in the liberating army), let it be known publicly that he had received death threats.[23] He was not stretching the truth, for on September 22, as he was discussing the untoward circumstances with his associates, he was brutally assassinated as a result of an incident that also caused the violent death of the Moderate chief of police.[24] During the hours that ensued Cienfuegos lived in the grip of terror. Not surprisingly, therefore, at noon on the following day, while Villuendas was being hurriedly buried and the Moderates were casting their ballots, the local Liberals decided to withdraw from the election. Two days later José Miguel Gómez resigned as governor of Las Villas and presidential nominee of the party in a letter which the daily *La Lucha* published on the twenty-seventh. It was a document filled with foreboding but at the same time ambiguous. In it, after lamenting the demise of Villuendas and advising the party to give up a struggle that it could not possibly win, he stated:

We have yet another choice, which is the same one that all peoples of the world going through analogous circumstances have—to exercise the right to rebel. But Cuba is a very special case, and an armed struggle would bring about, inevitably, foreign intervention. Before it could take place, however, the material prosperity of the country would be seriously endangered. The properties that in such great numbers are in the hands of foreigners would be destroyed. . . . I once had the courage to rebel against the Spanish government, a hundred times stronger than Mr. Estrada Palma's. Yet I do not wish to assume moral responsibility for plunging my country into a war . . . [25]

Despite the fact that soon afterward the candidate left for the United States, the Liberal national assembly refused to accept his resignation, apparently wishing to fight to the bitter end. But its attitude underwent an abrupt change as soon as it learned the disastrous outcome of the preliminary elections, which predictably resulted in a total Moderate sweep. In full control now of the enrollment mechanism, the winners were able to pad the voters' lists as they pleased. In Las Villas alone, which was widely recognized as Liberal territory, the electoral registry showed that 99,662 citizens were affiliated with the Moderate party, that is, a few hundred more than the total number of persons of voting age in the whole province (99,313). Many of the names entered in the registry were those of newly born babies, deceased citizens, and nonexistent persons. This last practice—that of adding imaginary names to the lists—was apparently commonly used throughout the island, for out of a total of 429,730 names in the registry no less than 150,000 were fictitious.[26] Under such circumstances, not even the most optimistic among the Liberals could realistically hope that the party would have a fair chance of winning the forthcoming contest. Bowing to the facts, therefore, on October 15 the Liberal leadership formally announced that the party would abstain from going to the polls on December 1.

The government, of course, had no choice but to go through the motions of the election. As might be expected, it attained a crushing victory. Estrada Palma received an overwhelming 306,874 ballots, and all the other Moderate candidates were equally successful. Not a single Liberal candidate—national, provincial, or municipal—was elected.[27] So lopsided was the result that the balance of political interests in the country was completely disrupted, and as a consequence the pattern that had prevailed until then for the allocation of public resources was drastically altered. The veterans, the architects of the new nation, were especially affected, for although some of them, including a few of the old leaders, figured in the Moderate camp, "the flower of the liberating army, the most widely known warriors,"[28] were on the Liberal side. The Moderate veterans, in any case, espoused Estrada Palma's philosophy and were not true representatives of the concerns and aspirations of veterans as a class. The severity of the setback for the liberators became immediately clear when Estrada Palma, upon being officially informed of his reelection, emphatically declared that he would continue his policies "even in a country without citizens, like Cuba."[29] In other words, his second term in office would be a replica of the first, which meant that the veterans would continue to be shut out of the power structure as well as denied the perquisites of political eminence. Instead of making progress toward the attainment of these goals, they seemed to be retrogressing.

The Liberal Revolt

Estrada Palma inaugurated his second administration on May 20, 1906, and it was at approximately this same time that the Liberals set up a Central Revolutionary Committee. Four generals were on the committee: José Miguel Gómez (who had returned to Cuba early in January), José de Jesús Monteagudo, Demetrio Castillo Duany, and Calixto García's son, Carlos García Vélez. Juan Gualberto Gómez, Alfredo Zayas, Pelayo García, and Manuel Lazo were also members of the committee. Months before, Liberal plots had been formed, and there had been several minor outbreaks as well, among them an attack on the Rural Guard post in Guanabacoa, only a few kilometers from Havana. Since at the time the Liberals were waiting for the new Congress to ratify the elections, however, it had taken only a slight show of force to restore order, although there had been casualties.[30] But, by May, the Liberal leaders became convinced that they could not hope for a peaceful settlement, and so they went ahead with their plans. What they had in mind was a swift coup d'etat that included the seizure of police stations and government buildings; an attack on the presidential palace; the abduction of the president and the vice-president; and the staging of a number of supportive provincial insurrections. At the same time, personalities and institutions devoted to the Liberal cause were to make public statements in order to create a favorable political climate. It was a well-planned move which the Revolutionary Committee hoped to execute quickly enough to prevent a U.S. intervention. The organizational work was conducted in a rather careless fashion, however, and as a consequence the government was able to arrest the chief plotters on August 17, two days before the date set for the coup. Among those who managed to escape was a former colonel of the liberating army, Faustino "Pino" Guerra, who had served under Maceo. Perhaps because he disobeyed his orders, Guerra succeeded in slipping into the Pinar del Río countryside, where he exchanged a few shots with the Rural Guard the very day that the arrests took place. It was thus that the so-called guerrita de Agosto (August's Little War) broke out.[31]

Despite its inauspicious beginnings, the war soon gathered an alarming momentum. In Pinar del Río, several hundred men quickly enlisted under the banner of Guerra; General Enrique Loynaz del Castillo and Colonel Ernesto Ashert were similarly successful in the province of Havana; Colonel Orestes Ferrara and General Eduardo Guzmán[32] likewise managed to organize powerful rebel columns in Las Villas; and, in Camagüey, General Tello Sánchez was also able to raise some men. There were flare-ups of revolutionary activity in Oriente too, Matanzas being the only province to remain calm and loyal to the government.[33] Within days, the Liberals had 2,000 men on the loose, and by the end of the month there were between 14,000 and 16,000 of them in the field. As a rule, they were ill-equipped and lacking in resources; few had rifles and ammunition, and fewer still had really serviceable weapons. The majority were armed simply with machetes and revolvers, but all of them were mounted either with horses of their own or with animals that they had expediently appropriated.[34] Most, of course, had taken to the woods in the second war of independence and some had been in the first: this was true, at any event, of the former generals, colonels, majors, and captains who joined their officer-heavy army (where self-promotions were frequent), but it was also largely true of the privates, whose arms were usually those they had retained when the liberating army was disbanded.[35]

Given their background, therefore, it is not surprising that in waging war the rebels followed the traditions of Cuban warfare of the past forty years. Thus, generally avoiding pitched battles, they dedicated themselves to carrying out property raids, skirmishing, and disrupting communications, threatening at the same time to burn out landholders for the purpose of creating an atmosphere of impending violence in the country.[36] Yet, as in the days of the earlier wars, combat was not entirely evaded. Occasionally, the self-styled Constitutional Army (as Liberal chieftains called their forces) clashed with the Rural Guard, and whenever this occurred the government was defeated more often than not. The Guard had proved extremely useful as an instrument of political partisanship. It had effectively hindered the Liberals, arresting and detaining scores of them and preventing others from voting whenever it had been ordered to do so. Still it was one thing to carry out political chores efficiently and another to put down a full-fledged revolt. Despite the increase in its size, the body had continued to be an army only in the sense that its members wore uniforms and were armed. With the exception of the Artillery Corps, which had been armed and trained as infantry, it was not in a position to take action immediately against an enemy force. The way in which it was deployed throughout the national territory prevented it from doing so.[37] Moreover, General Rodríguez, who had remained as chief throughout Estrada Palma's term in office, was an ineffectual commander. He was a brave man and, as his U.S. advisers had taught him when the Guard was first organized, he was always ready to uphold the authority of the incumbent government. But he lacked organizational skills; under him discipline had been lax.[38]

By September it became clear that the rebellious Liberals could very well succeed in toppling Estrada Palma. They did suffer a few reverses. In Havana a Guard patrol surprised the largely black force headed by the seventy-three-year-old veteran General Quintín Banderas, and finished him off with machete blows while he was asleep in his hammock.[39] In Las Villas Guzmán and his cohorts were put to flight a couple of times. But aside from the cities and Matanzas province the government had scant support;[40] the rebels rode about with impunity in the greater part of the island, most especially in the areas where they had operated while fighting against Spain.[41] In Pinar del Río, Pino Guerra, who by now was a self-proclaimed general, was even able to take the towns of San Luis and San Juan y Martínez. He took advantage of the opportunity to telegraph a pair of challenging messages to the president and to give a press conference in order to publicize the goals of the rebels. What they wanted, he affirmed, was to reestablish the rule of law, to render void the elections, and to install the legislators chosen by the popular will.[42]

Estrada Palma and the Moderates were taken aback by the rapidity with which the insurrection grew, a clear sign that the overwhelming sentiment of the popular masses in the country favored the Liberal cause. With greater insight, they would have recognized that the successful use of coercion in the Porfirio Díaz style inevitably requires, first, the ability to count on someone like Díaz, and, second, force necessary to quell the rebellion that inexorably breaks out. This was what should have been expected given Cuba's "long history of insurrection," and the "natural tendency" of its people to have recourse to arms.[43] But, convinced that the Platt amendment stood as a guarantee that peace would be kept at all costs, they had injudiciously thought that they could operate with impunity and thwart the choice of the people without the support of a strong standing army.

At least, once reality exposed the naiveté of their views, they should have made immediate adjustments. The situation called for the rapid mobilization of a powerful military force—something like the 20,000 men that the Cuban secretary of state, Juan O'Farrill, assured the U.S. chargé d'affaires, Jacob Sleeper, would be raised so that the revolt could be crushed in two months' time.[44] But this entailed making use of a good many of the millions piled up in the treasury, and the president would have none of that. It also appears that he blindly clung to the belief that the United States would do whatever was necessary to pacify the country and keep him in power.[45] He thus limited himself to raising appropriations for military expenditures to $2,984,100, about 13.4 percent of the national budget.[46] With these funds, he then undertook to increase the Guard by 2,000 men, to organize a national militia, and to establish the so-called *cuerpos francos*, groups of veterans devoted to the Moderates or friendly to his cause.[47] In addition, steps were taken to create a bizarre Foreign Legion of Artillery, commanded by U.S., English, and German personnel, for the purpose of handling the government's Colt machine guns.[48] Most of these efforts were dismally unsuccessful. The ill-disciplined Guard (troops in Havana had recently mutinied because of allegedly bad food) found no recruits or only undesirable ones. With the exception of the corps organized by veteran General Jesús Rabí,[49] the liberators proved utterly unenthusiastic about joining the *cuerpos francos*; and, despite the low standards for recruitment, the widespread unemployment prevailing at the time, and the great incentives offered to volunteers, enlistees in the militia were few and far between. Worse yet, many militiamen began going over to the side of the insurrectionists with arms and ammunition—something that policemen, for their part, had begun to do earlier.[50]

By this time the government had unified the command of its various forces and put it in the hands of General Montalvo. But not even a man of his credentials could do anything to stem the tide of the revolt. While economic conditions deteriorated rapidly—commerce came to a standstill and merchants ceased to restock their shops—the hordes of rebels kept growing, to the point that they began to encroach upon the urban areas. In Havana it was not necessary to travel far beyond the city limits in order to see their camps; and the same was the case in Las Villas, where the residents of Santa Clara, the provincial capital, or Cienfuegos, at times could easily catch a glimpse of the rebel columns roving in the adjacent countryside. At first all the Liberal commanders had actually been quite diligent in keeping their men away from foreign properties—often easily identifiable by the flags that flew over them—and the damage caused, if any, was no more than the loss of horses and supplies.[51] Yet, as the conflict assumed more menacing proportions and lawlessness and disorder spread, planters began to despair of protection and claims for indemnity started to pile up on the president's desk. However, the situation was never as bad as it was described in the rumors that circulated around Havana, often disseminated by Estrada Palma's own friends. One day it was rumored that the central railroad had been destroyed; the next insiders swore that a particular foreign-owned plantation had gone up in flames; forty-eight hours later the bad news was that the rebels had paralyzed navigation around the island by turning off the lighthouses. In the midst of all the uncertainty and confusion attending this newsmongering, perhaps the only report that had some factual foundation was that the Liberals were prepared to reach an accommodation with the government provided the December elections were nullified. This prompted into action the elements that thus far had remained neutral. Sensing that perhaps there was a peaceful way out of the civil war, they began to press the administration to meet its opponents halfway. Among those who moved in this direction was an important group of veterans who, answering a summons from Bartolomé Masó, met at Manzanillo in order to formulate a peace plan. The spokesmen of the group were Generals Agustín Cebreco and Mario García Menocal, upon whom eventually devolved the responsibility of implementing the plan. Of the two, Cebreco was the first to call on Estrada Palma, on September 1.[52]

The president, who thought it beneath his dignity to make concessions to the insurrectionists or even to negotiate with them, never expected the veteran's mediation to lead anywhere.[53] Nevertheless, for the sake of appearances he talked to Cebreco and a few days later held a long meeting with Menocal, who had quickly availed himself of the support of other ranking liberators who were also in Havana. Initially Estrada Palma was merely willing to permit the rebels to return home unmolested if they laid down their arms before they returned. But subsequently he was persuaded to agree to a truce and to allow Menocal and other mediators to confer with the leaders of the uprising. When on September 8 he was informed of their peace terms (essentially the holding of new elections for all elective offices except that of the president), Estrada Palma even appeared to be amenable to persuasion. Yet later on he abruptly returned to his original position, seemingly concerned with nothing but the sanctity of his own authority and the humiliation that was implicit in accepting all or part of the Liberal proposal. From then on he showed no further inclination to budge. As if to discourage Menocal and his colleagues from making any further attempts, the president gave a statement to the press reaffirming that the only basis for peace was the unconditional surrender of the rebels. And he called off the truce. Menocal then was compelled to admit publicly that the veterans' mediation had failed.[54]

Oddly enough, this seems to have whipped the skeptical president into a frenzy of activity. On the same day that he held his last meeting with the mediators (September 10), he placed the provinces of Las Villas, Havana, and Pinar del Río under martial law. He ordered the arrest of all the Liberal senators and congressmen who were still at large, and he called an extraordinary session of Congress to be held on the fourteenth. At this time a law was passed appropriating additional funds for the war and increasing the Rural Guard to 10,000 men and the Artillery Corps to 2,000.[55] To all appearances the government had finally decided to suppress the revolt by force of arms. What remained to be seen was if there was still time for doing so. In Las Villas, Guzmán had put his threats into effect and had begun to wreck locomotives, burn railroad stations, and blow up other facilities. How long would it take before he put a big plantation to the torch? In Pinar del Río, Pino Guerra seemed unstoppable in his relentless march toward the capital. In the province of Havana, coinciding with the congressional meeting, what turned out to be the most important engagement of the conflict had just taken place. At El Wajay, not far from the city, four hundred Guards under the personal command of General Alejandro Rodríguez had been routed by the combined forces of Loynaz del Castillo and other rebel chieftains. Not without some justification, the more timid spirits began to think that soon these forces would be able to carry their destructive action into the urban area itself and launch a direct attack on the government's seat of power. By then, however, the beleaguered Estrada Palma had already called upon the United States to forcibly intervene in Cuba.

The Taft-Bacon Pacification Mission

It is evident from Estrada Palma's correspondence that in begging the United States to throw its support to his side, he was prompted by a number of facts and considerations. In the first place, he knew that a week after the outbreak of the insurrection the U.S. military began to prepare for the eventuality of an intervention in Cuba. Second, he believed that the destruction of the sugar mills in Las Villas could begin at any moment. Finally, he was convinced that as the legally constituted authority in the country and as the representative of a government officially recognized by the United States, he could rely on full U.S. support. He was apparently unaware of the fact that President Roosevelt was interested in quieting the anti-U.S. sentiment that his imperialist policies had aroused in the hemisphere, and that therefore he was ill-disposed to become involved in the Cuban imbroglio.[56]

His actions were not entirely devoid of duplicity, for he approached the U.S. consul general, Frank Steinhart, for the first time when he was still involved in the negotiations with Menocal and the other veterans.[57] In fact it was on September 8, precisely the day on which he became acquainted with the Liberal peace proposal, that Steinhart cabled Washington, at the request of the Cuban secretary of state, urging Roosevelt to send immediately two vessels: one to Havana and the other to Cienfuegos. "Government forces," the cable explained, "are unable to protect life and property. . . . Congress will ask for our further intervention."[58]

Estrada Palma must have been appalled when he learned, through the subsequent exchange of messages between Assistant Secretary of State Robert Bacon and Steinhart, that there was "reluctance" on the part of the United States to intervene in Cuba, and that Roosevelt had even ruled out "actual immediate intervention."[59] It was no doubt for this reason that four days later, coinciding with the arrival of the requested warships (the U.S.S. *Denver* to Havana and the U.S.S. *Marietta* to Cienfuegos), he renewed his request, this time with an added sense of urgency. Claiming that his government could no longer prevent the rebels from entering cities and burning property (with or without the remittance of the five million cartridges that the United States had promised), he asked Roosevelt to "send to Havana with the greatest secrecy and rapidity two or three thousand men to avoid [a] catastrophe in the capital."[60] Meanwhile, by describing the situation in dark colors, he managed to persuade Chargé Sleeper to arrange on his own for the landing of a party from the *Denver*. This maneuver was executed on the following day, when 125 sailors with three artillery pieces disembarked and stationed themselves on the square in front of the presidential palace.

But the Cuban president was not the only one to capitalize on the presence of the *Denver* in the harbor of Havana. On the very night of its arrival, the commander of the ship received the visit of a Liberal delegation, which stated that the rebels would surrender if the United States guaranteed that serious negotiations with the government would ensue. This proposal was consonant with the Liberal view that it was the responsibility of the U.S. government to put an end to the Cuban situation, a view that Liberals had held ever since José Miguel Gómez and Alfredo Zayas had called on Minister Squiers on September 28, 1905, following the murder of Enrique Villuendos.[61] At the time, the two leaders had left the U.S. legation empty-handed, but Gómez had continued to harp on the subject while touring U.S. cities during the next several months and, although he had invariably protested that he abhorred intervention, he had never failed to add that if conditions did not change in Cuba he would not hesitate to appeal directly to Roosevelt.[62] After Gómez was jailed at the outset of the revolt, various Liberal field commanders trumpeted the party's message, a duty that they fulfilled with great force and clarity, never forgetting to mention the property they held hostage. Pino Guerra went so far as to send emissaries to the United States for the purpose of "inviting" it to intervene. Most leaders, however, confined themselves to their Cuban audience. Of them, Colonel Ernesto Ashbert used the bluntest language. "My orders are," he said to the veteran-mediators who contacted him early in September 1906 "to launch an extremely active revolutionary campaign on the fifteenth, destroying trains and burning property, including that of foreigners, if the government does not accept our demands. . . . We would prefer a new American intervention that would guarantee the holding of new elections."[63]

Although they were doing so for different reasons, the two sides of the Cuban conflict clearly were pursuing the same objective in their relations with the United States. The rationale of the Liberal strategy, nevertheless, was subtler and far more astute than that of Estrada Palma and his Moderate advisors. The Liberals calculated that Roosevelt would not fight to keep in power a weak and unpopular regime established by rigged elections. They anticipated that the U.S. president eventually would be forced to intervene, for he could not allow the risk of general disorder and destruction to grow in Cuba. But intervention was bound to work in the Liberal interest, because it would not be violent nor lead to the permanent occupation of the island. In time, free elections would inevitably be held under U.S. supervision and then, as surely as the sun rises every morning on the horizon, the party would earn its victory. As José Miguel Gómez had confidently predicted, it would be amply demonstrated that at least 80 percent of the Cuban people were Liberal.[64]

Ironically, it was Estrada Palma's rigidity and exaggerated sense of his own dignity that paved the way for the ultimate success of the Liberal scheme. He was displeased, of course, when Roosevelt countermanded Sleeper's orders and, as a result, the sailors of the *Denver* had to clear their position in front of the palace.[65] But his annoyance turned into deeply felt mortification and bitter resentment when he learned that the commander of the ship had consented to talk to the representatives of the rebels. From then on his attitude hardened considerably. On September 13, he sent Washington via Steinhart yet another appeal for intervention, this time announcing that he would resign irrevocably in favor of whomever Roosevelt designated as soon as the U.S. troops landed in Cuba.[66] This message was followed by a fourth request a day later (coinciding with the defeat of

El Wajay), in which Steinhart elaborated on the Cuban president's plan. Estrada Palma and his vice-president would resign and the cabinet ministers would do likewise. In such a situation the Cuban Congress could provide a constitutional presidential successor, but since there would be no one legally empowered to convoke it, it would be impossible for the body to take any action. The republic would be acephalous. "The consequence," Steinhart commented, "will be the absence of legitimate power and the continuation of the current state of anarchy unless the government of the United States decides to adopt the measures required to prevent this danger."[67]

But Roosevelt was not yet ready to send in the troops. Instead, after a lengthy meeting with a group of advisors, he resolved to send to Havana Secretary of War William H. Taft and Robert Bacon with the assignment of assisting the warring Cubans to patch up their differences and secure peace. At the same time, aware as he was of the true goals of both Liberals and Moderates, he decided to divulge his misgivings and reservations about the whole affair, which he did on September 14 by means of a public letter to Gonzalo de Quesada, who was still Cuba's diplomatic representative in Washington. The missive included a paragraph that could be interpreted as a more or less veiled threat, for Roosevelt wrote that the only way in which Cuba could preserve its independence was by showing that its people could tread peacefully along the path of progress. For the most part, however, the letter was a disclaimer, an explanation of why the responsibility for intervention, should it become necessary, would not be Roosevelt's but should be ascribed to the "enemies of Cuba," that is, to those who were disturbing the public order and creating a situation of impending chaos on the island. The president further said that, according to reliable information he had received, U.S. properties had been damaged and even destroyed. The civil war therefore had to stop and the country had to be pacified. It was precisely for that purpose that he was sending Taft and Bacon to Havana, to try to attain that end through mediation. Full-scale intervention as contemplated in the Platt amendment was to be undertaken only as a last resort. It would happen only "if Cuba herself shows that she had fallen into the revolutionary habit, that she lacks the self-restraint necessary to ensure peaceful self-government, and that her contending factions have plunged the country into anarchy."[68]

The impact of Roosevelt's letter in Havana (where it was also published) was nothing short of miraculous—or so it seemed for a fleeting moment. The government immediately suspended hostilities; the rebels made a show of doing so shortly afterward; and Menocal and the other veterans renewed their attempts at reconciliation, as a result of which a number of political prisoners were released. On the surface, therefore, the political climate could not have been more propitious when Taft and Bacon arrived on September 19 and began their quest for peace. Nevertheless, whether they knew it or not at the time, their mission was doomed to failure, and Roosevelt himself was partly responsible for that.[69] By then, following the arrival of the first warships and two landing parties (the *Marietta* had also put a party ashore), the Liberals were as intransigent as the Moderates, both parties being solely interested in what they could gain from further U.S. involvement. More than that, both began to exert as much pressure as possible in order to force the hand of the U.S. president. Estrada Palma, more adamant than ever in his rejection of a compromise with the rebels, kept threatening to resign and take the whole government down with him unless the U.S. Army campaigned for him and broke the revolt. The Liberals, for their part, also intensified the war of nerves by brandishing the torch, their most fearful weapon. As yet, despite the rumors of chaos and destruction that they themselves had cunningly encouraged, they had actually destroyed little property.[70] They had likewise shown the U.S. landing parties how cooperative they could be whenever the opportunity presented itself. After they saw what they construed as the prelude to intervention, however, they let it be known that they would soon begin burning the highly flammable sugar estates in earnest.

It is a matter of record that Taft, who was generally recognized as the virtual head of the peace mission, was of the opinion that the Liberals were "only an undisciplined horde of men under partisan leaders"[71] and that there was not a single one of them who was "fit to be president."[72] Even the remote possibility that they could become a de facto government made him shiver.[73] Both he and Roosevelt had a fellow feeling for the conservative, elitist control of Cuban affairs that Estrada Palma advocated, and they were fully aware of the "bad precedent" that sanctioning rebellion—that is, making concessions to the rebels—would set in Cuba.[74] Yet they could not bring themselves to support the tottering Moderate regime once they conducted an inquiry in Havana. During this investigation, which took the best part of two days, Taft and Bacon talked to dozens of persons, among them, of course, Estrada Palma as well as Zayas, the Liberal representative, and very soon reached a few inescapable conclusions. There was no doubt that the Cuban government had "flagrantly and openly used and abused its power to carry on elections and in so doing removed many municipal officers in many parts of the island."[75] This had "made a deep impression on the minds of the people," and it was for this reason that the Liberal movement was so "large and formidable and command[ed] the sympathy of the majority of the [Cubans]."[76] The Moderates had neither the military strength nor the moral support or following required to cope with this challenge. Their government was "nothing but a house of cards,"[77] weak both politically and militarily, and it was obvious that armed force alone could keep it in power. Should the United States decide to provide such a force, however, it needed to be understood that it "would be fighting the whole Cuban people."[78]

Taft could have condoned the fraud and coercion employed by the Moderates in 1905, for after all, as he himself wrote, the elections had been "held under the forms of the law and [had] been acted upon and recognized as valid."[79] But he concluded very quickly that neither his mere mandate nor one charge of U.S. cavalry would be sufficient to disband the rebels then assembled at the gates of Havana.[80] To lend armed support to Estrada Palma would entail involving the United States in a protracted and costly counterguerrilla campaign similar to the one in the Philippines, and such a campaign would indeed be immeasurably unpopular with U.S. voters. For Taft, who was close to becoming a candidate in the forthcoming presidential elections, this was a matter of considerable importance, as was the question of the eventual fate of U.S. interests in Cuba. Taft knew that if force were used these interests would be "the first to suffer" and, as he wrote to his wife soon after his arrival on the island, that meant that "some $200,000,000 of American property [would] go up in smoke in less than ten days."[81] A story about the burning of three large sugar plantations in the neighborhood of Cienfuegos—the rebels had threatened to torch them if their demands were not accepted—would indeed make unpleasant reading in the U.S. press![82]

Considering the pressure he was under, Taft's decision to "temporize"—as some outspoken contemporaries have charged[83]—and his inclination from the beginning to favor the Liberal position are quite understandable. On the very day of his arrival, he learned from Generals Menocal and Eugenio Sánchez Agramonte the details of the veterans' mediation plan (which the Liberals had accepted and Estrada Palma had rejected, as will be recalled), and he made it the basis of his own compromise proposal. This proposal included, in addition to the annulment of the 1905 elections and the scheduling of new elections, the resignation of Moderate officials with the exception of the president and vice-president, and a review of the laws relating to the judiciary, municipal government, and elections. Upon its acceptance, the rebels would lay down their arms. As might be expected, Estrada Palma felt the concessions to the rebels were too great (he had already told Roosevelt's emissaries that he distrusted the veterans' efforts). At another meeting held at the presidential palace on the evening of the same day, Estrada Palma rejected the U.S. proposal in its entirety because it did not include the prior disarming of the insurrectionists. By then, Taft had characterized Estrada Palma as "a good deal of an old ass"[84] and Estrada Palma in turn had formed the opinion that the two commissioners were nothing but recent rebel recruits.[85] Instead of leading to a solution, therefore, the meeting grew more tense with each passing minute until it ended on a sour note, with the Cuban secretary of state, Juan O'Farrill, angrily wanting to know: "Is it for this that you Americans have come here? We could have settled this matter ourselves, put down the revolution unaided. Yet you come here and deal with men in arms against the government."[86]

The matter did not end there, however, because the United States persisted for a while in its attempt to shake Estrada Palma's obstinacy. But all efforts proved fruitless. On September 25, the Cuban president spurned one last appeal from Taft and Bacon (an exertion to have peace "at any cost," as he sarcastically called it[87]), and soon afterward he also rejected somewhat more politely another one from Roosevelt himself.[88] At the same time he summoned the Congress to meet in an extraordinary session on the twenty-eighth. It was obvious that he was going to put into effect his long-announced decision to scuttle the government and to leave the republic without legitimate authority. This triggered a series of frantic negotiations between Liberals and Moderates, with the participation of the peace commissioners and the veterans, for the ostensible purpose of finding a suitable replacement for the chief executive. But these negotiations came to nothing essentially because no one really wanted them to succeed. On the surface, neither side favored the intervention; at bottom, both wanted it. On the twenty-seventh, resigned to the inevitable, Taft gave a statement to the press acknowledging that the peace mission had failed and declaring that preparations had been made by the United States to intervene and establish a provisional regime.[89] On the following day, Estrada Palma submitted to the Cuban Congress the resignation of his secretaries and then his own, together with that of his vice-president. That afternoon there was a last-minute attempt on the part of a few congressmen to persuade the president to change his mind; and while Congress recessed to allow for this final—and, as it turned out, futile—effort, Havana lived through hours of confusion and anxiety owing to rumors of impending rebel marches and attacks, Moderate plots and counterplots, and conspiracies to assassinate certain congressmen. Finally, as darkness set upon the city, the Congress was unable to reconvene at the appointed time for want of a quorum and thus failed to act upon Estrada Palma's resignation or to elect a successor. Consequently, the political drama played itself out exactly as the stubborn old man had planned: the country was left without a government.

On the following morning Taft issued a proclamation (the wording of which he had previously cleared with Roosevelt[90]) taking over control on behalf of the United States and naming himself provisional governor of Cuba. But even before this happened he had begun to act as such, for during the evening he had received a letter from Estrada Palma placing in his hands custody of the national treasury, and he had ordered the landing of a squad of marines in order to discharge this responsibility. By this time the treasury had been considerably depleted and amounted to only $13,500,000 (over a million of which was in Cuban bonds). It had been reduced by half from the $26,000,000 that had been accumulated prior to the Liberal insurrection.[91] The affair, therefore, had been a costly one, but even though the republic had been lost, the closefisted president had at least managed to save some of his millions. Such, for the time being, appeared to be the situation.

7. "Keeping Cuba Quiet": The Second Intervention

The second U.S. occupation of Cuba ended with the electoral victory of the Liberals in the fall of 1908 and their subsequent ascension to power early in the following year. So it was that the "flower of the liberating army," the former warriors who made up the core of the party, finally succeeded in gaining control of Cuban politics. At the conclusion of the war of independence, they were stymied by the imperial designs of the United States. Before a decade had passed, nonetheless, a U.S. administration unwilling to risk criticism at home changed course and actually helped them to attain their goals. It may be argued that this probably would have happened anyhow. But, as events actually unfolded, it is impossible not to discern a direct relationship between the second occupation and the rise to power of the Liberal faction of the Cuban veterans.

The Rise of the Liberals

Soon after the intervention was formally proclaimed, the Liberals approached Taft about the offices that the Moderates held in the government. Pointing out that there were many "undesirables" in the various executive departments, the Liberals suggested that such persons be replaced with Liberals. Taft replied "that it was not the intention of the provisional government to oust faithful servants to make places for Liberals, however deserving." He added, however, that he was aware of the disproportionate number of Moderates on the public payroll, and he promised that whenever vacancies occurred Liberals would be shown preferment until some sort of balance was restored.[1] This was tantamount to saying that the party would not be allowed to monopolize patronage nor permitted to dominate the elections that would eventually be held.

This apparent setback did not chill the ebullient mood of the Liberals nor hinder the round of celebratory activities that they began at the end of the revolt. These included collecting contributions in order to erect a statue to Roosevelt; presenting a gold watch to Commander J. C. Colwell, captain of the *Denver;* and attending a banquet in his honor organized by the appreciative members of the Revolutionary Committee. The apex of the festivities was a victory rally that took place at the Payret Theater in Havana on October 15, two days after Taft returned to the United States. Evidently the jubilant Liberals believed that the insurrection had been successful, that Washington had intervened in Cuba on their terms, and that their ability to bring pressure to bear upon the provisional government was considerable.[2] Hours before the issuance of Taft's proclamation taking over the government of Cuba, Roosevelt had told his emissary that the rebels should disarm because they would have "practically all the advantages they would have had if [Estrada] Palma had gone into the original agreement to which they [had] assented."[3] Actually it seemed as though the Liberals had been able to read this cable.

But this was not really necessary for them to have a reasonably clear picture of the situation. All they had to do was to reflect on their own experience and read the Havana press, most especially Enrique José Varona's dispassionate analysis of the rebellion and its denouement. What had occurred in Cuba, the noted Cuban philosopher wrote,

> was precisely the contrary of what it was reasonable to expect . . . The government of the United States, acting through the illustrious delegates of its distinguished president, after a very quick investigation, has sanctioned the complaints of the Cuban insurrectionists and has proposed them as a basis for an agreement to the government de jure of this republic. In short, the government of the United States has exacted of the government of Cuba . . . that it abdicate before an armed insurrection.[4]

Why had this happened? The more sagacious and best informed among the Liberals must have known or at least sensed that the intervention had been precipitated by a number of factors. They must have heard of Roosevelt's concern for Cuba's stability and progress, his constitutional and legal responsibilities, and his wish to keep the European powers out of the Caribbean. Perhaps they were also aware of the U.S. Army's experience in the Philippines and how distasteful it was for U.S. authorities to resort to Weyler's methods to put down a rebellion in Cuba. Nevertheless, as Cubans they were more acutely conscious of what they themselves had done, and they knew that there was a great deal of truth in what Varona wrote in attempting to further explain the paradox of U.S. policy:

> The cause lies in Cuba's economic situation. Cuba . . . is no longer a colony, but it continues to be exploited. Until very recently it was a factory ruled and exploited by Spain; today it is a factory governed by Cubans and exploited by foreign capital. This capital—the four hundred million that Americans, British, Spaniards, and Germans have invested in sugar mills, tobacco farms, tobacco factories, railroads, and mining enterprises—is the formidable force that has been acting at the bottom of this chaos, the one that brought the naval squadron presently anchored in our harbor, and the one that led the mediators until they sat as arbiters between the factions blinded by rage.
>
> The arbiters did not come, therefore, to decide which of the two sides was right . . . they came to save the properties threatened with destruction, to save them as quickly as possible, and with a minimum of forcible intervention. The rebels, whether they knew it or not, had discovered the Achilles' heel of our situation, and concentrated their efforts on that vital point. For President Roosevelt's emissaries, their only important duty is to stop the hand that may deliver the finishing blow. This is, in my view, the key to solving the enigma . . . [5]

Of course, the Liberals did know that they had discovered the Cuban "Achilles' heel," but any doubts they entertained in this connection began to be dispelled when Taft published his initial proclamation. He made it clear that the occupation was only an alternative to anarchy, and that it would last only until order could be restored and elections be held. Meanwhile, the provisional government should be considered a Cuban government. The Cuban flag would continue to fly, the public administration and the courts would function as they had under the republic, and all laws would remain in effect.[6] Two days later, speaking at the opening exercises of the University of Havana, Taft sounded even more reassuring, telling his audience that Cuba had simply stumbled "in the progress toward self-government" and that therefore it had become necessary for the United States to assist it once again to move forward. But no one should misunderstand U.S. intentions. The United States was in Cuba to lend a helping hand, not to take advantage of the Cubans. When he concluded his address hailing "la República de Cuba,"[7] it was difficult not to see that the United States intended to pacify the island by means other than the force of arms.

This intention was confirmed when the provisional government undertook to disarm and disband the insurgent forces. On the same date that Taft assumed his new duties, the Revolutionary Committee formally agreed that the Constitutional Army would disband, surrender its arms, restore the property that had been taken for military purposes (mostly horses), and return to lawful pursuits.[8] The governor then appointed a Disarmament Commission made up of neutral Cuban veterans and U.S. officers to make the necessary arrangements for the execution of the agreement with the Liberal generals.[9] The sugar harvest was drawing near, and the pull of work in the cane fields was supposed to facilitate the work of the commissioners. But not even under such favorable circumstances could they claim to have been completely successful. The Liberals retained the horses, kept the serviceable weapons, and in the following spring were again roaming the countryside in two provinces.

The matter of the horses was by far the most deplorable, and not only because of the scandalous behavior of the Liberals. Since it was almost impossible to prove ownership of the animals (frequently on account of the various ways in which their possessors had managed to disguise them), it was decided to allow each rebel to take the one in his possession back home, with a certificate describing the horse and showing his right to keep it until its owner claimed it.[10] The certificates were supposed to specify that "ownership [would] be determined later." But owing to a mysterious typographical error, the phrase was omitted when the certificates were printed and they appeared to vest title in the temporary holder. Before the error could be corrected, the rebel officers distributed the certificates to the men, who thereby understood that their illegal appropriation of the horses had been sanctioned.[11] Because they believed that the rebel possession of the animals would encourage them to surrender their arms and go home, the U.S. commissioners, General Frederick Funston and Major E. F. Ladd, agreed to this irregularity,[12] as did Taft also, albeit reluctantly.[13] Taft overcame his unease about the lack of respect shown for private property by persuading Roosevelt to indemnify the owners.[14] To Cubans, nevertheless, it appeared that the United States had put its official stamp of approval on horse stealing.[15]

Aside from the fact that certain municipal funds also misappropriated in the course of the insurrection were not returned either,[16] the process of disarmament was not marred by any further improprieties. But this does not mean that things went smoothly. The commissioners were so interested in the rapid dispersal of the rebel bands that they did not bicker over the number or the serviceability of the arms the insurgents turned in as long as the men were returning to civilian pursuits. Loynaz del Castillo's troops, for example, surrendered only about 12 percent of their weapons. No ammunition, no pistols, and no machetes were found in Asbert's camp, where 693 rusty rifles were all that could be secured from 7,000 men. As Asbert himself later acknowledged, the good arms, especially those in the possession of their lawful owners, were usually kept,[17] and that must be what also happened in Las Villas. In this province the insurgents, still afraid of possible ill-treatment on the part of Moderate officials, refused to go home without their weapons. They therefore had to be permitted to proceed fully armed to the vicinity of their dwelling places under the supervision of their brigade commanders, who then were supposed to confiscate the arms and deliver them to the provisional government.[18] How many insurgents managed to circumvent these arrangements and remain in a state of readiness for the next rebellion? On October 24 the authorities attempted to dramatize the successful completion of the surrender by towing the weapons that had been turned in out of the Havana harbor and dumping them in the Gulf of Mexico off Morro Castle.[19] The truth is, however, that only 3,153 weapons had been collected from a total of 24,479 insurrectionists and that for the most part they were practically worthless. Obviously, most of the arms had remained in the hands of the people, and the government knew it.[20]

At the time this appeared to be a small price to pay for the quick disbandment of the rebels (carried out in less than two weeks), which was the primary goal of the government. But even this goal was imperfectly attained, as Taft's successor had the opportunity to verify during the *tiempo muerto* of 1907, a period of unemployment, strikes, political tension, rumors of revolt, and even one attempt at such. When the Disarmament Commission members set to work to disperse the various insurrectionist columns, Loynaz del Castillo, for example, told his men that the Constitutional Army would not be dissolved but would only appear to be and that they would be able to keep their arms, for the insurgents knew "that the American government is willing to grant almost anything before having to fire a gun in Cuba."[21] It was hardly surprising, therefore, that this rebel chieftain should have been the one to organize the "Constitutional Militia," a shadowy army that began to roam the countryside in the provinces of Havana and Matanzas at the end of the sugar harvest for the ostensible purpose of intimidating conservative elements and deterring them from resorting to violence.[22] Other chieftains did not go that far, although they too showed their intention to imitate Loynaz del Castillo at the slightest provocation. Among them figured General José Luis Robau, who had, according to U.S. intelligence officers, eight hundred thousand cartridges and a large number of rifles stored in Las Villas. It is difficult to find anything more indicative of the predisposition of the provisional government than what Robau was told when his little arsenal was discovered. Lieutenant Colonel Robert L. Bullard warned him, of course, that any uprising would be crushed without hesitation. But he was also promised more public works for his province.[23]

Evidently the Liberals were correct in assessing the temporizing and compromising position taken by the United States. The Roosevelt administration had no intention of arousing a storm of criticism in the United States by undertaking to pacify Cuba militarily. Therefore, in order to achieve its avowed goal of restoring representative government on the island, it had no choice but to keep Cubans quiet by speaking softly rather than brandishing a big stick. This applied primarily to the Liberals, who had the greatest potential for seriously disturbing the peace, and it implied a willingness to grant them "almost everything," to virtually let them have their way. Once this all-important premise is understood, considerable light is shed on the course of the occupation that followed when Taft and his coarbiter were left with a full-scale intervention on their hands. If there is any one person who can be blamed for the permissive treatment of the Liberals, Roosevelt is certainly that person. But it was presidential hopeful Taft who set the tone of the provisional government.[24]

The Army of Cuban Pacification

When it became apparent that the United States would have to assume the responsibility of governing Cuba, a hastily organized marine brigade was landed from the fleet that by then had assembled in Havana harbor and sent to various parts of the island to protect plantations and railway facilities and to guard trouble spots. This brigade was subsequently joined by an expeditionary army, the two forces thus combining to make up what Taft called the Army of Cuban Pacification because he thought it was impolitic to use the word *intervention* in its title.[25] By October 25, this body, already 6,000 men strong, was garrisoning the country, with its members stationed at some twenty-seven posts throughout the national territory.[26]

Given the administration's policy, the role of this army was even more inconspicuous and passive than that of the forces which occupied Cuba under the first intervention. Especially in the days of Wood's governorship, the U.S. military had enjoyed an authority and status they now lacked, for this time the troops were not permitted to march along the streets of the capital even once and they never performed any military operations.[27] As Roosevelt made clear at the outset, their mission was to provide the "moral force" behind the provisional government,[28] and they strictly conformed to the norm during the two and a half years that the occupation lasted. They occupied key locations, engaged in practice marches in rural areas, established an intelligence network, mapped the island, and became involved in building roads.[29] If they contributed to the task of suppressing disorder, they did it merely by intimidating the population with their presence and the knowledge of their availability. Roosevelt had specifically dictated that "no blood [should be] shed between Americans and Cubans,"[30] and he was fully obeyed.

Because the pacification army was to remain in the background, law enforcement had to be assigned to another force and the only other force that existed in the country was the Rural Guard. The Guard, however, owing to its political role in the 1905 elections and its military defeats in 1906, was completely discredited and demoralized. As Taft's successor reported, it was viewed with disfavor by most Cubans.[31] Consequently, if it was to retain its constabulary functions of keeping order, arresting law offenders, and in general maintaining peace on the island as Roosevelt and Taft wanted, it was imperative to breathe new life into the institution—to return it to its proper duties, to inculcate professionalism in its members and regulations, and to restore public confidence in it. Taft himself took the first steps. Soon after the intervention became official he publicly announced that the Guard repudiated its past activities on behalf of the Moderates, and then proceeded to transfer certain detachments in order to lessen local tensions.[32] He also made the more questionable decision of retaining Alejandro Rodríguez in the same position to which he had been appointed by the Estrada Palma government on September 14—commander of the Rural Guard and Artillery Corps with the rank of major general.[33] It also appears that he gave the general a salary increase.[34]

The justification for this apparent mistake appears to have been Taft's conviction that although the Guard no doubt was guilty of political activities, "this service was contrary to the desire of a large majority of the officers and enlisted men."[35] Consequently, overhauling the Guard would not require a large purge. What had to be done was to put it again through the teachings and training that it had received under Wood, so as to cure its ills, revive its old ideals, and increase its level of military proficiency. To this end, the provisional government detailed an able and experienced group of U.S. Army officers. Most of them had served either in Cuba or the Philippines. The chief advisor was Herbert J. Slocum, who had helped to organize the Guard under Wood and was now a major. He was detailed to assist General Rodríguez at Guard headquarters.[36]

There is no question that the Guard made some progress under the supervision of the U.S. officers. Active patrolling was reinstituted and carried out as much as the Guard's police duties permitted. Measures were taken to correct the worst features of the outpost system, which was nonetheless retained. Weapons were standardized; army schools were established in Havana, Matanzas, Camagüey, and Santiago de Cuba; and specially designed programs for officers were developed. Efforts were made to improve the troops' welfare and, at the same time, standards for recruitment and commissioning were made more selective. A promotion system exclusively based on merit was set up, and more rigorous training under the prodding of the U.S. advisors resulted in discharge of the unfit.[37] No attempt was made, however, to change the basic structure of the body, which continued to be formed of three regiments each with a two-province area of responsibility. A year after the end of the revolt, the regiments had been able to increase the number of their posts to the extent that there were more than three hundred of them scattered throughout the national territory.[38] Most were located in the sugar-growing areas.[39]

The Artillery Corps, which was also subjected to the program of reconstruction, primarily received artillery instruction. One company was equipped with pack howitzers, and a new machine gun company armed with ten Colts was created. The Artillery Corps showed its readiness when the provisional government called upon it at the time of the 1906 railway strike.[40]

Because of these reforms, the morale and efficiency of the Guard began to rise perceptibly. Yet the chief goal of the U.S. advisors was to transform it into an apolitical force, immune to personal influence and social rank in enforcing the law, respectful of the inviolability of person and property, and, most especially, averse to carry out political chores of any kind. The Guards were assumed to be "soldiers of the state"; consequently, as the provisional government decreed in March 1907, partisanship within the ranks was not acceptable and political activity would be thenceforward a court-martial offense.[41] In keeping with this principle, the men who had most notoriously involved themselves in politics previously were eliminated. Also, the Guard was denied police authority in municipalities unless it obtained proper local authorization.[42]

It was the consensus of the U.S. advisors that the depoliticization of the Guard was never as thorough as it should have been.[43] Still, after only six months of tutelage, the advisors rendered a favorable report underlining the improvements that had taken place, and the provisional government expressed its satisfaction with the body as a peace-keeping force.[44] Whether it had regained its old prestige and the confidence and goodwill of the public was an entirely different matter. Because it did not undergo a drastic purge, the Guard still contained many of the political appointees that it had accumulated during the Estrada Palma years. The reforms, furthermore, although well-advised and unassailable in themselves, had been carried out in the spirit of the Wood regime, to which some of the U.S. officers (Slocum being the best example) were still committed. What they had striven to do was to "Americanize" the Guard—to instill U.S. values in its members and to place it under the control of the occupation authorities. From an institution cast in this mold, those whom Wood used to call the "better elements"—the conservative and frequently foreign elite that dominated economy and society—could expect everything. But not the Liberals, the rebel chieftains who had been responsible for the demise of Estrada Palma's demilitarized republic. At the first opportunity they turned against it.[45]

Character and Policies of the Provisional Government

One of the most important consequences of the appeasement policies of the Roosevelt administration became apparent when Taft returned to Washington to resume his post as secretary of war. Among the possible successors for his position as provisional governor was Leonard Wood, who had a following in the Cuban conservative sector.[46] But Roosevelt did not want to send to the island a military man who might antagonize the Cubans with his autocratic methods and provoke another rebellion. With the concurrence of Taft and Secretary of State Elihu Root, he decided that the type of official that was presently needed to take over in Cuba was a civilian governor, an experienced administrator with expertise in Hispanic law, a gift for compromise and personal diplomacy, and sensitivity to policy and politics. He would also need to be a malleable man who would be responsive to the orientations emanating from Washington. Taft suggested the name of Beekman Winthrop, his former private secretary who was then governor of Puerto Rico. At Root's recommendation, however, Roosevelt chose Charles E. Magoon, a Nebraska lawyer who had been governor of the Canal Zone and had just completed a tour of duty as a minister to Panama.

Magoon appeared to be well qualified to become Taft's successor in Cuba. He was good-humored, courteous, and inclined to trust people. Owing perhaps to his agreeable disposition and his ever-present desire to offend no one, he had been highly successful in Panama, where he had shown great skill in the art of placating ungovernable people and winning goodwill. But he was essentially a paper-shuffling bureaucrat, a man quite unlike Wood. Instead, Magoon apparently resembled Wood's predecessor, General Brooke, who, as rumor had it, allowed his Cuban secretaries to dominate him. Magoon nevertheless had one outstanding qualification for the Cuban position, and that was his more than ordinary knowledge of the Hispanic codes. Therefore, despite the fact that he did not speak Spanish and lacked brilliance, he was ideally suited for the day-to-day administration of Cuban affairs in the manner that would best serve the political interests of Roosevelt, and, most especially, Taft—from whom he took general orders through the Bureau of Insular Affairs[47] and with whom he was in constant communication, not only by correspondence but also through four personal conferences. On October 6, 1906, Magoon arrived in Havana, where he spent the next few days familiarizing himself with the Cuban situation. He was inducted into office on the thirteenth, whereupon he issued a proclamation advising the people of Cuba that he would exercise the powers and perform the duties contemplated and provided for by the third article of the appendix to the constitution of Cuba.[48] He ruled by decree and his authority had no other limits than his own discretion and that of his superiors in Washington. It included the Army of Cuban Pacification, which, as Taft made clear at the beginning, was under his orders and through him those of the administration.[49]

It was the consensus of U.S. officials in Cuba at the time that the money hoarded in the treasury by the thrifty Estrada Palma had been too strong a temptation for the power-hungry Liberals, and had been the ultimate cause of the uprising. It would have been much better, they reasoned, to have expended the money along lines that would have advanced the republic, and so they decided that the provisional government should expend money rather than permit it to accumulate.[50] Such was the rationale behind Magoon's spending policy during the twenty-seven months of his rule, which made him appear as an example of unrestrained profligacy when compared with his predecessor and even with Wood. It is true that he had to meet a number of extraordinary obligations, such as claims for damages incidental to the civil war or accrued in earlier years.[51] He also was forced to spend large sums on an emergency basis to extirpate yellow fever (which had reappeared in Cuba in October 1905) and to cope with other unforeseen difficulties, such as droughts and hurricanes. But he definitely favored a high level of public expenditure, which became evident when his administration embarked on a public works program—greater than any that had been planned in Cuba before—that included the improvement of harbor facilities; the construction and repair of state buildings, sanitation works, and water supply and drainage systems; and, above all, the building of highways, waterways, and other means of transportation and communication. There is no doubt that the republic received benefits essential to its welfare and development as a result of these improvements.[52] Nevertheless, it is obvious that, at the same time, the program helped to provide employment and hence prevent potential trouble during the economic standstill of the *tiempo muerto.* That Magoon's public works were undertaken in response to legislation passed by the Cuban Congress in the time of Estrada Palma is therefore irrelevant. What matters is that he believed (rightly or wrongly) that were it not for his road building, the United States would have had to expect another Philippines in terms of time, lives, and cost,[53] a conviction that clearly brings forth the direct relationship that existed between his public spending policy and the paramount objective of "keeping Cuba quiet." In other words, since it had been governmental parsimony that had impelled Pino Guerra and his colleagues to take to the woods, the wise thing to do now in order to maintain tranquility in the country was to loosen the purse strings.[54]

Inevitably, such a policy had to redound to the benefit of the Liberals and the interests they represented. From the day he assumed office, Magoon (like Roosevelt and Taft) viewed the problem of administering Cuba as a problem of patronage, bringing into office the faction hitherto excluded from it as rapidly as vacancies occurred or could plausibly be made.[55] One of the problems to which he first directed his attention was thus that of the municipalities the Liberals claimed had been arbitrarily taken over by the Moderates in 1905 and 1906. He carefully reviewed each case on its merits, and quickly reestablished Liberal administrations in twenty-two of the thirty-two that had been illegally interfered with by the Fighting Cabinet. As might be expected, his action met with the approval of the most vocal Cubans.[56]

But then things turned topsy-turvy, for the "great Cuban politicians"—as the governor ironically referred to the "heroes" of the August revolt[57]—descended upon him, as they had previously descended upon Taft, like a plague of locusts. Magoon saw himself deluged with petitions for jobs, and since he knew little of the entanglements of Cuban politics and had no cabinet to advise him (he had made the chief clerks of the various departments acting secretaries), he had no choice but to set up a committee to assist him in the selection of Liberal officeholders. The committee was composed of the leading members of the Liberal Revolutionary Committee and the most important rebel chieftains: Pino Guerra, president, Eduardo Guzmán, vice-president, Ernesto Asbert, secretary, Alfredo Zayas, José Miguel Gómez, Juan Gualberto Gómez, Tomás Recio, Demetrio Castillo Duany, José de Jesús Monteagudo, and Carlos García Vélez.[58] In theory, these men were supposed to nominate qualified candidates for jobs whenever vacancies occurred. In practice, however, they wanted every vacancy filled with a Liberal, and it took only a few months before they split into Miguelistas and Zayistas, among other things, over the issue of patronage control. Each faction recognized the rights of the other, yet each accused Magoon of favoritism whenever he gave an appointment to a member of the other faction.[59]

The governor listened patiently to the complaints and demands of the two groups, and since he was a "yes-man extraordinary"[60] who "did not know to say 'no,' always said 'Amen' and signed the papers,"[61] soon there were not sufficient vacancies in the provisional administration to satisfy the importunities of all job seekers. The vacancies were limited to those created when the Moderates had arbitrarily removed the Liberals in 1905 and 1906, and consequently new positions had to be created. After a while Magoon began to dish out *botellas* (sinecures) with amazing rapidity. The charge that he was responsible for the introduction of *botellas* in Cuban politics is, of course, senseless.[62] Still, although there is no way of verifying the number of such offices that the governor granted or of identifying the persons holding them, the fact is that *botellas*—few or many—were certainly given out. The post of secretary of the Advisory Law Commission (which he appointed to make studies on legislative matters), given to Juan Gualberto Gómez, was probably a *botella*;[63] and, since the provisional administration formally took over responsibility for legislation upon itself, it is obvious that the Cuban congressmen who were retained on the government payroll (about one-third of them) held *botellas* too.

The truth is that in Cuba, as one U.S. officer dryly remarked, pacification meant "dealing out the pie,"[64] a practice that became widespread in the field of public instruction, where *botellas*, officials carrying their mistresses on the payrolls, falsified reports, kickbacks on supply contracts, and promotion for sexual and political favors were common happenings.[65] When Lieutenant Colonel Robert L. Bullard became acting secretary of public instruction in 1908, he thought that his task was to cover up the corruption in the department until the occupation ended.[66] The chief sanitary officer, Major Jefferson R. Kean, on the other hand, made strenuous efforts to depoliticize public health and to appoint men as sanitary officers exclusively on the basis of their professional qualifications, yet he failed most lamentably. As Magoon bluntly informed him, "Everything on this island is political, and the political chiefs must be consulted."[67] Thus through the governor the "chiefs" controlled patronage, a power that they never hesitated to use to their own advantage whenever the positions concerned were consequential enough, as occurred when the provisional administration determined to "strengthen" the executive branch in 1907. At this time, the Liberal Justo García Vélez was entrusted with the Department of State, his brother Carlos became inspector of prisons, and Demetrio Castillo Duany was named chief of the national penitentiary. No one could have said that these men were incompetent. Yet both Carlos García Vélez and Castillo Duany sat on the Committee for Appointments, as the Liberals shamelessly called the advisory board on patronage. Both, as members of the top leadership of the party, had also been among the signatories of the revolutionary pact that formalized the conspiracy against Estrada Palma.[68]

But granting soft jobs was not the only way in which the provisional administration sought to further the policy of pacification despite the hazards involved. Whenever turbulent spirits threatened to stir up trouble, for example, the governor provided reasons and funds to send the individuals concerned off on extended excursions abroad.[69] He also accommodated José Miguel Gómez, Zayas, Asbert, and other prominent Liberals by signing an unusual number of pardons, unmindful of the fact that Taft had released all political prisoners upon assuming the governorship and had decreed an amnesty on October 10, 1906, covering the crimes related to the revolt.[70] Most of the convicts pardoned by Magoon were common criminals. The number of those who benefited from his generosity was so great that according to some estimates he lavished more pardons than any other Cuban chief executive between 1902 and 1924.[71] Apparently Magoon was aware of his vulnerability in this respect, for he tried to defend his record by pointing out that up to September 30, 1908, he had granted 1,110 pardons, commutations, and remissions, an average of 555 a year, which was below the 648 instances of executive clemency per year during the first two years of Estrada Palma's rule.[72] Still, as even his staunchest defenders conceded, Magoon granted too many pardons,[73] although the accusations that he participated in the handsome profits of the pardon "rackets" of some Cuban attorneys and political chiefs were unjustified. He neither sold pardons nor accepted bribes. He simply set another bad precedent.

These and other aspects of Magoon's efforts in "keeping Cuba quiet" were severely criticized by the Cuban press (a fact that Taft, his immediate superior, could not possibly ignore), but when he retired from the island after a new Cuban president was inaugurated the reaction was at first favorable, although a diversity of opinion was already noticeable. The city of Havana made him an "adopted son," and the day in which he departed a huge crowd headed by the chief executive and other dignitaries went to bid him farewell. A U.S. journalist who witnessed the event in a paroxysm of enthusiasm called him "Magoon the Magician,"[74] and for a moment it seemed as though his Panamanian experience was going to be repeated. But later plaudits were forgotten and denunciations of his administration turned more caustic. Barely six months after his departure, the Cuban cabinet reviewed a number of his public works contracts and secured their rescission because, as the cabinet minutes set forth, they were based on "profound immoralities." Soon the condemnation of his administration became a firmly established tradition in Cuban historiography,[75] to the extent that even his personal integrity was questioned.[76] After some investigation and debate, posterity has finally vindicated his name, for it has been shown that he was painstakingly honest in the handling of his personal finances, and that he was worth less when he died in 1920 than when he went to Cuba.[77] Yet, for Cubans he has retained his bête noire reputation,[78] a circumstance that can only be explained by the fact that he symbolizes the ills and shortcomings of the policies he had to implement in order to suit Roosevelt's political preoccupations and Taft's presidential ambitions. It is impossible to verify whether Taft's sole instruction to Magoon was to keep things quiet so that no "Cuban question" would disturb his race for the presidency in 1908.[79] Nevertheless, Magoon acted as though such were the case, as if his task were "to do not so much what was right as what was expedient."[80] And that is precisely what he did. Magoon granted *botellas*, granted pardons, launched an unprecedented public works program, and crowned his work by leaving Cuba the legacy of a thoroughly politicized army.

Inception of the Cuban Army

One of the first conclusions that Taft drew upon his arrival in Havana as a peace commissioner was that Estrada Palma's near overthrow by the Liberals was attributable to the president's lack of a large enough military force. If political stability and national order were to be preserved in Cuba, therefore, the republic would need a military force sufficiently strong to make it a difficult task to bring about a revolution. Otherwise, he feared, the United States would be unable to pull out even after the restoration of government by the Cubans, indeed a most unpleasant prospect in view of Roosevelt's avowed intention of administering the island for a few months only.[81] Thus as early as October 31, 1906, he instructed Magoon to make plans to strengthen the Rural Guard, which seemed to him the natural and most expedient way to solve the problem.[82] Magoon then asked for recommendations, which ranged from a modest proposal for a 1,000-man increase submitted by Major Slocum and General Rodríguez to the creation of an armed force of 9,439 men suggested by a board of U.S Army general staff officers then serving in Cuba.[83] The governor's own idea was to recruit up to 10,000 additional Guards (that was the limit the Cuban Congress had approved back in September), which would make it possible to protect the cities and defend the interior at the same time.[84] "Of course, this . . . will cost more," he wrote and, showing that the intricacies of Cuban politics were still beyond his grasp, he added not without a touch of naiveté: "The Liberals should not object, because the Rural Guard will keep them in power after the election."[85]

Yet, as it turned out, the Liberals did object. Basically unconvinced that the Guard, still commanded by Rodríguez and other politically tainted officers, had been divested of its previous partisan attachments, they flatly opposed any increase in its size. To their good fortune, they did not stand alone in their position. When Magoon, after conferring with a group of Liberal leaders—Guerra, Monteagudo, and Carlos García Vélez—publicized the U.S. plan, public reaction was decidedly contrary to the creation of a too powerful armed institution. Many people, the governor learned to his discomfort, doubted that a standing army would assume in Cuba a U.S.-like, nonpolitical attitude. Should such a military force be created, they feared, the country would be inexorably exposed to the "dangers of militarism" and eventually suffer under its excesses as the other Caribbean islands and the Central and South American republics had suffered.[86] This negative reaction became a political uproar when it was learned a few days later that Roosevelt, unmoved

by the adverse public opinion, had directed Magoon to implement
the plan anyhow. Surprisingly enough, on this occasion the protests
of the Moderates nearly drowned out those of the Liberals. Even the
Spanish newspaper *La Lucha*, whose owner and editor, Antonio San
Miguel, customarily sided with the provisional government, joined
the chorus denouncing the proposed enlargement of the Guard.[87]

Taking advantage of this favorable turn of events, the Liberals
then submitted to the governor a counterproposal whereby they recommended the organization of an entirely new military force, a permanent Cuban army. This alternative plan was presented to Magoon
on February 7, 1907, by a majority of the Liberal leadership: Zayas,
Juan Gualberto Gómez, Monteagudo, García Vélez, Recio, and Asbert. There is no way of ascertaining, of course, whether these men
were sincere when they invoked public economizing to support
their initiative (which called for an army of foot soldiers, less expen-
sive to maintain than mounted Guard members) or when they
claimed that a constabulary such as the Rural Guard could not be
relied upon to become the military underpinning of the Cuban government. One might also find it mildly amusing that in the course
of the discussion, Recio should have chosen to bring up the perils of
militarism. But one thing was certain: the Liberal party, despite the
reforms introduced by the provisional government, remained im-
placably hostile to the Guard. After all, as Juan Gualberto Gómez
pointed out, the officer corps as it was still constituted was guilty of
all the irregularities of the regime that had been overthrown. For this
reason, and because of the wickedness and abuses that had been
committed, the force had lost forever the confidence of the majority
of the people. How, then, could Cubans enjoy tranquility if public
power was delivered into hands that were suspect if not positively
criminal?[88]

At this juncture, Magoon sought the advice of the U.S. officers
attached to the Guard, who, as might be expected, doggedly de-
fended the institution that they were reshaping in their own image.
Unmindful of the most telling aspects of the Liberal criticism of
their wards, they launched a sharp attack on the army project in the
course of which they proved to have a clearer vision of Cuba's future
than the Cubans themselves. Slocum, for example, openly stated
that the proposed military force had no other purpose than to reward
the Liberals and strengthen the party's leadership. If Zayas and his
colleagues wanted to bring it into being, he went on, it was only
because they had realized the futility of their efforts to fill the Guard
with their cronies. In all likelihood, therefore, the new army would
be composed from those who had recently taken part in the insur-

rection; it would be "a machine of [the Liberal's] makings and work-ings."[89] Captain James A. Ryan expressed himself along similar lines. Given the existence of the Platt amendment, Cuba only needed an army to keep internal order, and a loyal, professional constabulary answered this need fully and completely. Such a constabulary, fur-thermore, was more apt to protect the sugar estates than a Havana-based, barracks-bound army. If the Liberal proposal was accepted, the country would be instead endowed with a political army, and "an army dominated by politics," Ryan gravely remarked, "is ru-ined. In proportion to its freedom from interference by politicians is proficiency proclaimed. History repeats itself from Rome to South America, and the use of politics has ruined every army, every mili-tary force, with which it has been connected."[90]

There were other U.S. citizens on the scene, like the planter H. E. Havens, who had seen his estate threatened by the torch during the revolt and feared that the proposed army would be used by the Lib-erals "to protect against their rascalities, and also to control elec-tions and maintain themselves in power." Havens went so far as to maintain that upon withdrawing from Cuba the United States should "leave the people the remedy of revolution against the inevi-table abuses of the factions in the ascendancy."[91] The Cubans them-selves, however, did not appear to share these pessimistic feelings. Almost overnight, spokesmen of nearly all political persuasions muted the fear of militarism that had possessed them only a few days before and began to hail the new regular army as the guarantor of peace and stability. This abrupt change in the public mood (which no doubt had to do with the fact that the Rural Guard plan appeared to be "American" while the regular army plan looked "Cuban") could not but play into the hands of the Liberals. Acting now with their usual dexterity, the Liberal leaders approached Magoon with a new proposal, suggesting what in effect was a compromise solution: the Guard would be preserved but provision would also be made for a permanent army as a separate body, the latter to be a mixed brigade (infantry, cavalry, and artillery) of 4,000 men. In defending this new reorganization plan, the Liberals put forward an argument they had not used before. Cuba, they said, need not fear military oppression, for the August uprising had succeeded not because of the weakness of the Estrada Palma regime but because of its unpopularity. "When the government has the country against it," they declared, "the number of bayonets of which it may dispose matters little; the result is always the same, since no people worthy of unity fails to throw off the yoke that it deems insupportable."[92]

While listening to his visitors Magoon must have remembered

what Pino Guerra had told him barely a month earlier. According to the flamboyant general, had a sufficient force been available to the Moderates in 1906, the revolution would not have lasted forty-eight hours. Nevertheless, when the issue of the country's future military establishment was under discussion, coherence, steadfastness, and adherence to convictions and principles meant practically nothing. The essential fact was that the Liberals regarded the Guard as a menace to them, as Guerra had also hinted to the governor.[93] If the provisional government insisted on transforming the force into the chief agency for political stability, then it could no longer count on their full cooperation. This they informed Taft himself without equivocation when he visited Havana in April 1907.[94]

By this time it appears that the Roosevelt administration, following the path of least resistance, had brought itself to consider the feasibility of a Cuban army. In Washington, the War Department had even already worked out a reorganization scheme of its own incorporating the separation of the Guard and the army, as the Liberals had proposed. But Taft did not receive the staff papers in time to discuss the compromise plan with Magoon, and thus he made no public decision while in Havana. Having apparently been unable to find any other alternative, six months later, in October, he directed the governor (upon his request) to act on the matter. At Magoon's request, the plan was included in the agenda of the Advisory Law Commission, the body that the provisional administration had appointed to revise and codify Cuban law. The commission took it under consideration in January 1908 and, as might be expected, approved it after only an hour-and-a-half session.[95] Few of the laws thus passed actually went into force before the end of the occupation.[96] Yet on the matter of the War Department's plan there was no thought of allowing the incoming Cuban Congress to complicate the underlying issues any further. Consequently, on April 4, Magoon promulgated the law approved by the Commission. It was, in fact, the first law approved by the Advisory Law Commission that went into effect before the restoration of self-government on the island.

The law organized the Cuban military into three separate branches. The least important of them was the militia, an innovation that merely meant that all male citizens between the ages of twenty-one and forty-five would have thenceforward some sort of military obligation. The other two were the Rural Guard and the Permanent Army. The Guard, consisting of about 5,180 officers and men distributed in 380 detachments,[97] was preserved without modification; even General Rodríguez remained at its head. The Permanent Army was composed of an infantry brigade that would subsequently be strengthened by the transfer of other troops. Pino Guerra was selected as its commander in chief. The law did not assign any specific missions to the different forces, although it was not difficult to ascertain what their missions were to be. As Magoon later reported, the commission had visualized the Guard as a "body of surveillance and safety [rather] than a military force."[98] The Guard, therefore, was to be strictly a police organization; the army, on the other hand, was intended to be a "real military force."

Were it not for the fact that the army was provided with a separate command, this would have been a perfectly acceptable division of responsibilities. But given this fact and others that were in everyone's mind—the Guard's past activities, the expected electoral victory of the Liberals, and the consequent probability that the officers and men of the army would be mostly Liberal—it was clear that the latter institution was to have an additional, extramilitary (that is, political) and quite unprofessional function to perform. On April 17, Magoon wrote to President Roosevelt that the separate command of the army had been designed to reduce the danger of militarism and to discourage any combined use of the two principal branches of the armed forces against the chief executive.[99] This meant, in plain language, that it would be the task of the army to protect the next Cuban government from any future interference on the part of the Guard. The creation of a large force for just that purpose had been precisely what Juan Gualberto Gómez had called for when the Liberal leadership had discussed the military question with Taft.[100] Indeed, it is difficult to conceive of a more senseless military system than that which the provisional administration established to please the Liberals. Not only did it politicize the Army ab initio but it also brought into being side by side two armed institutions which, as Captain Edmund Wittenmeyer (another Rural Guard advisor) had warned his superiors, were likely to succumb to jealousy and discord if politics crept up on them, as was bound to occur after the U.S. withdrawal.[101]

Unmindful of these major flaws, Magoon conveyed to Taft a Panglossian assessment of the impact of his military reform. He felt that it "had given general—I might say, universal—satisfaction." Public opinion was pleased; General Rodríguez, his officers, and the more conservative elements were in good spirits because the Rural Guard had been upheld; and the Liberals of course were also delighted because the Permanent Army that they had advocated had been created.[102] Actually, the only ones that had reasons for being gratified were the Liberals. On the central issue—the formation of a separate regular military force—they stood as the outright victors.

Moreover, inasmuch as the provisional government left the task of organizing the new force and working out the details to them [103]— the overwhelming favorites to win the coming electoral contest— they could rest assured that they would dominate it and be able to transform it into their party's army. Finally, they had received an ironclad guarantee that such would be the case when Pino Guerra was chosen for the post of commander in chief. Guerra had been politically inactive for a whole year, and this is perhaps the reason why Magoon was optimistic about his appointment and Taft praised it.[104] Cubans, according to the rosy reports dispatched to Washington, had widely acclaimed it too. "This puts an end to insurrections; nobody will want Pino to go after them; he would not bring in prisoners—he served too long with [Antonio] Maceo for that"—such was the tenor of the comments generally made by Cubans, the governor buoyantly noted.[105] Magoon overlooked the fact that Guerra, for all his supposed military prowess (he had been a congressman between the war of independence and the August revolt), had only joined the army just at the time of becoming its head. He also chose to ignore that the Liberals were already irreconcilably divided and that Guerra was a Zayista. It was obvious that the Miguelista faction would see a political threat in a force led by him.

The Conquest of Power by the Liberals

At the outset it was expected that the second U.S. occupation of Cuba would be so brief that elections would be held in January 1907. Soon, however, it was thought advisable to put them off until May, so that the political campaign would not coincide with the sugar harvest, and further delays were dictated by the need to take a census and draft additional laws. Finally, during Taft's stay in Havana in April, it was decided that municipal and provincial elections would be held after a voter registration based on the census. If these elections took place in an orderly and peaceful manner, then presidential and congressional elections would follow in six months. Following this timetable, on May 25, 1908, Magoon issued a proclamation announcing that municipal and provincial elections would be held on the first day of August.

By this time a Liberal triumph could no longer be equated with the natural order of the universe. At first the general impression was that the Liberals would be easy winners because of their undisputed popularity, the fact that theirs was the faction upheld in the civil war, and Washington's tendency to show them preference and look upon them as though they were the sole spokesmen for the entire

Cuban people. But Liberal prospects changed considerably after the party split over the issue of patronage and the schism deepened more and more as the elections drew near. The governor could not but frown upon this development, for the division threw into doubt who would win the election, and it is only reasonable to assume that the U.S. authorities wanted to see a Liberal victory. After all, such a victory afforded the prospect of self-congratulation. It would justify the stand taken by the Roosevelt administration when the Taft-Bacon peace commission was dispatched to Havana; it would vindicate the policies of the provisional administration; and it would amply demonstrate that the Colossus of the North had acted in good faith and had not attempted to ride roughshod over the hot-blooded and high-strung natives of tiny Cuba.[106]

Inasmuch as opinion has invariably been unanimous that the Liberals ultimately rose to power as a result of orderly and fair elections, it is apparent that the provisional administration cannot be accused of having undertaken any unconscionable manipulations in order to secure the political success of the party. Still, throughout his life General Mario G. Menocal—the man who eventually ran against the Liberal candidate and subsequently served Cuba as president from 1913 to 1921 with the blessing of the United States—clung to the belief that he lost in 1908 because the occupation authorities had been biased in favor of his antagonists.[107] If what Menocal (who died in 1941) had in mind was the fact that the Liberals had the advantage because Washington had supported their party and placed a good many of them in office, he was probably right. Moreover, the Liberals were also indirectly aided by two decisions made by the provisional administration when it set out to reshape the Cuban electoral process. The first, for which Magoon was responsible, had to do with the official dissolution of the old Moderate party (November 1906) and the failure of the efforts that conservative elements made shortly thereafter to organize themselves against the ascendant Liberals. The governor wished these elements to regroup, and thus in the spring of 1907 he called them in, encouraged them to do so, and even promised to give them a voice in the patronage.[108] As a result, a Conservative party was formally launched in the summer. This meant, of course, that Cuban voters would have some choice other than the candidates of Miguelistas and Zayistas. But it also meant that there had emerged a political opposition in the country that in time might force the two Liberal factions to unite.[109]

The other decision was made by Taft, and was incorporated into his plan to hold two elections. When he drew it up, the fortunes of the Liberal cause may have been far removed from his mind. Yet, as it turned out, the plan made the Miguelistas and Zayistas realize that within the framework of the U.S.-style party system that Magoon had somewhat artificially created in Cuba, neither could expect to win if they persisted in their differences. This became evident when Cubans went to the polls to elect provincial governors, councilmen, mayors and municipal councilors on August 1, 1908. The result was a stunning victory for the Conservatives, who were able to elect three governors and twenty-eight mayors. Having finally seen defeat in continued division, the Liberals determined to reunite and nominated Gómez and Zayas, a repeat of the slate of 1905. This time, given the potential strength that they had already evinced, it was clear that they could not possibly lose. When, after a clamorous campaign, national elections were held on November 14, their ticket secured a solid majority in all provinces of the island. In addition, fifty-one of the eighty-three representatives elected were Liberals, as were all the newly elected senators. One of the reasons why their victory was so overwhelming was obviously that in the mind of the people, theirs was the party favored and sustained by the United States. Cubans, of course, wanted to be on the winning side.[110]

Had the Conservatives won, the finale of the tragicomedy that was the second intervention would not have been consonant with the introductory scene. But the vagaries of Cuban politics combined with the kinks and twists of U.S. policy to bring about an acceptable denouement, and thus it was the effusive and smiling José Miguel Gómez and not the elegant and reserved Menocal to whom power was transferred on January 28, 1909. After all, Gómez had been the sacrificial lamb in 1905. In recording the events of the twenty-eighth, contemporary chroniclers tell us that the new president, after taking the oath of office, opened the palace doors and shook hands with the crowd until his fingers became swollen—so joyful was he at having finally achieved his ambition![111] Then he went out and saw Magoon off to the United States on the new battleship *Maine*. Indeed he had reasons for being grateful to the provisional governor as well as his superiors in Washington. For, throughout the twenty-odd months that the occupation lasted, most of the major political decisions made by the American authorities had been, or turned out to be, favorable to his party; and this had been so down to the last days. On January 20, General Rodríguez had been removed from the command of the Rural Guard and General José de Jesús Monteagudo, who was perhaps closer to the president-elect than any other man, had been named to replace him.[112] So, as the

Maine and its escorts left the Havana harbor amid the firing of salutes, Gómez could rest satisfied that after the departure of the U.S. troops that had been left behind to ensure a peaceful transition, nobody would do to him what had been done to Estrada Palma and what he himself attempted to do to Menocal some years later. True, Pino Guerra was a Zayista, and, despite their transient electoral alliance, there had never been real cordiality or teamwork between the two Liberal factions. Consequently, the chief executive could not feel at ease with such a man as commander in chief of the new army. But this force had yet to be organized, and the controls available to the presidency could always be manipulated to strip Guerra of effective power and reduce him to a mere figurehead. Somehow too—violently or otherwise—it might be possible to put him out of the way. Meanwhile, thanks to Magoon, Monteagudo would see to it that for the next four years Gómez and his followers would go about reaping their reward for all the sacrifices they had made for Cuba.

8. The Republic under Its Liberators

The rise of the Liberals to power in the wake of the second U.S. intervention ushered in the era of the veteran-presidents (1909–1933). Throughout this period, not all the politicians were veterans of the wars of independence, but every dominant leader with a substantial following either had been a prominent warrior or had the backing of such an individual. Thus the Cuban liberators, despite the setback of the first intervention and its offshoot, the Estrada Palma administration, ultimately attained a measure of control in political affairs that was comparable to that achieved by their Spanish American counterparts in the nineteenth century.

Because of U.S. tutelage, the island did not go through the vicious cycle of dictatorship and revolt, tyranny and chaos that afflicted so many of the other republics. But this only means that the level of political violence was not as high in Cuba as elsewhere. Compelled to keep an eye on Washington's actions and reactions, the Cuban veteran-politicians had to refrain from certain excesses and strive to give a democratic tone to the government. Yet, since they were men who had been schooled in violence during the struggle for independence, violence continued to play a role in the methods they used for the transfer of power, and it was this circumstance that brought the Cuban armed forces into politics. It was thus that the militaristic tradition, one of the key developments in Cuba in the twentieth century, came into being.

The Internal Mechanisms of Cuban Democracy

During this period national elections were held regularly every four years, as prescribed by law, and, of the six that took place between 1908 and 1928, each of the two major political parties—Liberals and Conservatives—won three. But the regularity of this electoral sequence and the political balance that it appears to suggest is entirely misleading, because none of these elections was ever won by an opposition candidate. José Miguel Gómez, the winner in 1908, had the tacit approval of the provisional administration. He, in turn, because of his aversion to Zayas—the vice-president under him—gave his support in 1912 to the Conservative Menocal, who served for two consecutive terms after he chose to reelect himself in 1916. Four years later, in 1920, wishing at all costs to humble Gómez, who had taken up arms against him, Menocal threw the weight of the government behind the candidacy of Zayas, who thereby finally succeeded in occupying the presidential chair. Lacking a political base of his own, Zayas was the weakest of this series of presidents. He wished to retain the presidency, but he found out that Menocal again coveted it for himself. Thus, unable to secure the Conservative nomination and prevented from using coercion indiscriminately because of Menocal's influence with army officers and his tendency to shun physical danger,[1] he resolved to back General Gerardo Machado, the Liberal candidate (Gómez had died in 1921). Had Zayas not been in the palace to safeguard the interests of the Liberals, Machado might have been "robbed" of his victory. Yet even Zayas was able to neutralize the Conservatives and secure the presidency for him in 1924. Having thus become the custodian of the fulcrum of power, Machado faced no serious difficulty in engineering his own reelection at the end of his first term in office.

The methods that incumbent governments usually employed to control the vote and assure victory were electoral fraud and coercion, in that order. No objection can be found, of course, to the elections of 1908, and perhaps the same may be said of those of 1912, although it appears that military intimidation was then used in one crucial province for the purpose of tipping the balance in favor of Menocal.[2] But in 1916, when the Conservative leader ran for a second term, fraud made its appearance on a large scale, and it became worse in the ensuing years. True, in 1924 Menocal, after having been overwhelmingly defeated by Machado in yet another bid for power, took the unheard-of step of writing a letter of felicitation—not too cordial, it must be noted—to his victorious opponent. Even in that election, however, the same unlawful methods as before were put in practice. These methods included strong-arming voters whenever necessary. Yet as a rule Cuban politicians preferred such tactics as buying votes and placing fictitious names in the registration books (as the Moderates did in 1905). At times they closed the polls early or delayed the voting to keep opposition voters from getting to vote. Another tactic was burning a polling place or destroying its records if the vote of a particular precinct was adverse. The election of Zayas in 1920 was largely due to the utilization of these simpler and less coercive devices. Coercion played a far greater role when, after an expedient constitutional reform, Machado was reelected in 1928 to a six-year term. In order to silence the opposition he had to deport or have liquidated a number of labor leaders, political opponents, and students critical of his regime.[3]

It is clear, then, that the government and not the people controlled the transfer of power in post-Magoon Cuba. This state of affairs was compounded by the fact that Cuban administrations, largely because of external constraints, had little to do with the trajectory of the island's economy and society. Politics as such was divorced from the latent and manifest issues of the day, and consequently it was not necessary for political parties to concern themselves with such issues. Unmindful as the parties were of electoral platforms, matters of principle, or questions of a validly doctrinal sort,[4] it was only by an arbitrary extension of the term *party* as it was more meaningfully used in other countries that it could be assumed that such organizations existed at all. Properly speaking, there were no political parties in Cuba. The Liberals tended to attract the urban vote, generally appealed to blacks and mulattoes, and stressed their revolutionary heritage and their credentials as freedom fighters and founders of the republic. The Conservatives, for their part, were usually supported by business interests, had a considerable following in rural areas, and admitted into their ranks former autonomists. But there was no ideological differentiation between the two organizations beyond these largely rhetorical dissimilarities. As a contemporary Cuban wit put it, "There is nothing more like a Conservative than a Liberal and vice versa."[5]

This is what explains why top party leaders shifted their allegiance from one party to the other at their convenience, keeping in mind only the relative advantages of alignment with the ins or the outs. Such was the case, for example, of Governor Asbert of Havana, a longtime Zayas supporter who chose to deliver the vote of his province to Menocal in 1912 rather than to his erstwhile crony. Another example is Zayas himself, who, raising political opportunism to unprecedented heights, had no qualms about joining forces with the Conservatives in 1920 provided Menocal would back him for the presidency. The truth is, Cuban parties in the decades that followed the second U.S. occupation were nothing more than factions organized around a particular political leader. Therefore, quite fittingly, they took their popular designation from the leader's name, family or Christian. Thus the Conservatives were truly Menocalistas, while the Liberals and members of the Popular party (the splinter

organization that Zayas formed when he went over to Menocal)
were in point of fact either Miguelistas or Zayistas. Subsequently,
after Gómez died and Zayas also disappeared from the scene, the
leading wings of the Liberal party dubbed themselves Machadistas
and Mendietistas, the latter being the followers of Colonel Carlos
Mendieta, a veteran of the 1895–1898 war who had been the Liberal
vice-presidential candidate in 1916. Organizations such as these
were of course purely personalist, and their chief goal was to foster
the political ambitions of their leader or to support him once he was
in power. Inasmuch as their membership was largely composed of
those dependent on him for patronage or expecting to get it should
he be successful, the organizations or factions could otherwise be
described, in the caustic words of the same writer, as "cooperatives
organized for bureaucratic consumption."[6]

Why, then, should stump orators have bothered to argue about
programs and ideas while campaigning for office? There being no
authentic issues to discuss, they confined themselves to exalting
the party candidates, denigrating those of the opposition, rousing
their audiences with slogans and appeals to patriotism, and invoking
the names of the heroes of the wars of independence, whose spiritual
successors they invariably claimed to be. The sole object of the political scramble was to gain power, and that contest was fought—
and decided, exceptionally, by the voters—on the basis of personalities. Of course, power was enticing because it was the source of
concrete personal gain. Most of the best-known Cuban politicians
of this period retired from political life in considerable comfort.[7]

Because all important decisions were made at the top by the man
around whom the party was organized and his cronies, the electorate
usually had few candidates to consider. Election after election the
same names kept appearing on the official ballots. This pattern, indicative of the emergence and development of a political class, was
even more marked insofar as the presidency was concerned, for, as
though from force of habit, only the names of former generals of the
liberating army were customarily listed as choices for this exalted
position. Power during this remarkable phase of Cuba's historical
existence was apparently beyond the reach of those who had not
achieved prominence in the struggle against Spain. It is true that
Zayas, who never wore a uniform in his life, figures among the ten-
ants of the presidential palace in this period. But he could certainly
claim that because of his activities in Havana on behalf of the insurgents, he had been deported from Cuba at the time of the war and
spent some unpleasant days in Ceuta, the Spanish enclave in northern Morocco. His election, moreover, was the handiwork of Meno-

cal. Had it not been for this contingency, he might have never been able to interrupt the succession of veteran-presidents that took political charge of the island after the second U.S. withdrawal.

What was the mental attitude of these men, who had ostensibly returned to civilian pursuits and at least pretended to be duly elected? Is it really permissible to equate conditions in Cuba with those that prevailed in the other republics after they shook off Spain's domination? Actually, none of the Cuban veteran-politicians ever stopped being soldiers. This they amply demonstrated with the Liberal revolt of 1906 and continued to do so in the Gómez period. In 1910 and 1911 there were two attempts to begin revolutions, one in Havana headed by former liberator General Guillermo Acevedo and another in Oriente led by his colleague Vicente Miniet.[8] Also in 1911, in August, a far more serious movement was launched. Prone to use violent tactics, this group demanded the ouster of pro-Spanish elements from political positions. Since it was supported by the National Council of Veterans and its leader was the influential General Emilio Núñez,[9] the movement has gone down in the annals of Cuba as the Veteranist Movement (its most important public pronouncement was signed by twenty-seven former officers of the liberating army, among them fourteen generals[10]). Prominent veterans proved far less willing to cooperate, however, when the independent black political party called the Colored Independents, claiming that not enough political favors had been accorded the blacks who had participated in the Liberal insurrection and the struggle for independence, took the road of armed protest in 1912.[11] Still, the leaders of the rebellion were Evaristo Estenoz and Pedro Ivonet, two men who had been active in the trade union movement among construction workers but had also been noncommissioned officers in the liberating army and fought against the Rural Guard in 1906. As it was, they were able to draw a good many rank-and-file black veterans to their side.[12]

This tendency of the liberators to take to the woods and lead insurrections against the constituted authorities remained unaltered over the years during which Menocal, Zayas, and Machado governed Cuba. It was Gómez himself—along with Pino Guerra, Asbert, Machado, Guzmán, Mendieta, and several other distinguished veterans—who led the Liberals when they again revolted, in February 1917 after Menocal rigged the 1916 election.[13] It was the veteran Colonel Federico Laredo Brú who rose near Cienfuegos, Las Villas, after the so-called Association of Veterans and Patriots issued a call for veterans all over Cuba to protest the corruption of the Zayas administration.[14] And it was Menocal and Mendieta who, early in

August 1931, headed the first serious attempt that was made to unseat Machado after his regime degenerated into an outright dictatorship.[15] By the time the Veterans and Patriots and Menocal-Mendieta movements were formed, new and aggressive urban-based forces in Cuba had begun to play a role in the country's political life.[16] Still, not even the most radical of these forces were yet ready to eschew the leadership of the men of 1895. Indeed, between the end of the second U.S. occupation and 1931, these men not only controlled the government but also monopolized the challenges to constituted authority and even the methods of mobilizing political violence. All the political disturbances that took place during this period followed the familiar pattern of the insurrectional efforts against Spain. The leaders would slip into the *manigua* (Cuban colloquialism for the open country) and, once there, put themselves at the head of a band of more or less well-armed men with the ultimate aim of stirring a general rebellion that would compel the incumbent regime to abdicate. The anti-Machado revolt of 1931 was the last such attempt headed by survivors of the wars of independence.[17]

The Role of the Armed Forces

Since throughout the era of the veteran-presidents a respectable military machine existed in Cuba, it remains to be explained why the leaders of this machine accepted a secondary role during the period. Nothing would have been easier for an ambitious army officer than to seize power by taking advantage of the turmoil and confusion that the liberators sometimes caused in trying to relive their martial accomplishments. Yet in these years the Cuban military only rarely failed to carry out its function of sustaining the incumbent government, and whenever this happened the military was under the banner of a veteran caudillo. This relatively restrained behavior cannot be attributed to the development of professionalism.[18] A truly professional force would never have intruded into the realm of political affairs even at the instigation of a more or less charismatic hero. What happened in Cuba at the time was plainly that the armed forces were nothing more than a political instrument of the veteran-presidents, an extension of the personalist parties organized to elevate the candidates to the presidency and to keep them there as long as circumstances permitted.

Several factors conspired to bring about this situation. One of the most important was the fact that the majority of senior army officers were veterans themselves, men who in many cases had fought under the political leaders and therefore tended to accept their authority.[19] Another was the bureaucratic character of the Cuban armed forces, which very soon became just another agency of the government under the patronage of whichever faction was in power. Not only did their size expand at a more rapid pace than the growth of the population as a whole,[20] but they also ate up approximately one-fifth of the national budget, at least until the Zayas period when the deterioration of the economy forced the government to cut back on military expenses.[21] Even then these expenses never dropped below $9 million per annum, and they were always so sizable that by the end of the period (1933–1934) their total surpassed the amount spent on education.[22] Three significant trends underscored the role of the armed forces as a mechanism for the distribution of public office and the disbursement of public funds: (1) more than 45 percent of the military budget was earmarked for salaries, while less than 3 percent was provided for the purchase of materials, equipment, and supplies; (2) in proportion to the size of the economies of the two countries, officers and men were paid higher salaries in Cuba than in the United States; and (3) despite the relative reduction of military expenses carried out by Zayas and Machado, the officers' share of the military budget increased appreciably after 1923–1924, due not only to salary increases and the payment of special bonuses but also to an increase in the number of officers.[23]

Although attempts were made at professionalizing the Cuban armed forces (begun under Gómez but most significant under Menocal), it is undeniable that such attempts were conditioned and sometimes rendered ineffectual by their obviously political character and purpose. Few facts are more revealing in this connection than the frequency with which the head of the army was changed, eight times during the period;[24] and, although complete data are not available concerning the officer corps, it is clear that it also suffered from the same lack of stability. There was an average of 342 officers in the army between 1903 and 1918; nevertheless, it is known that, from 1900 to 1917, at least 207 officers were discharged for various reasons, whereas no less than 560 were promoted during the shorter period from 1910 to 1917. This means that there were at least 767 personnel status changes in the body during the Estrada Palma–Gómez–Menocal period. During those fifteen years, the officer corps increased by 218 percent, from 164 in 1903 to 521 in 1918.[25]

The main reason for these and other changes is to be found, of course, in the successive reorganizations that the armed forces underwent as a consequence of alterations in the political picture. It all began with the law that Magoon presented to the Liberals, which left to the incoming Gómez administration the task of putting together the new Permanent Army. Things occurred exactly as the U.S. advisors of the Rural Guard had predicted. No sooner was the smiling José Miguel Gómez sworn in as president than he asked for an appropriation of more than $6 million—19.56 percent of the national budget, as it turned out—for the organization of the new military institution.[26] Not that he had any intention, of course, of allowing Pino Guerra to use this money as he saw fit. On the contrary, he surrounded the new army chief with officers hostile to him—including some civilians whose sole professional qualification was party loyalty—and further undermined his authority over posts and subposts by appointing Miguelista officers to assume charge of these detachments. Thus Guerra's power was effectively neutralized. Meanwhile, Rural Guard officers who had sympathized with the Miguelista cause in 1905–1906 were promoted to senior grades, while those who had remained loyal to Estrada Palma were summarily dismissed. In some cases, moreover, such as that of one Captain Manuel Lavastida, dismissal was followed by the actual shooting of the officer concerned.[27] Despite these measures, however, Gómez did not rest until he got rid of Guerra, whom he finally was able to dislodge from his post with the help of a would-be assassin, who wounded Guerra in December 1910. Thereupon, as might be expected, the president made General Monteagudo chief of the army, and shortly afterward, early in 1911, he united the two most important branches of the armed forces—the Guard and the Permanent Army—under his friend's command. Thus was accomplished what Cuban military historians have identified as the first reorganization of the armed forces.[28]

It made sense to put the Guard and the army under a unified command, for that was certainly the best way to prevent friction between the two forces and to eliminate the possibility of one of them eventually being persuaded to confront the other.[29] But the unification facilitated the transformation of the Guard into an elite cavalry force, which after a time became so thoroughly politicized that it was even suited to play the role of Gómez's palace guard.[30] At this time, the purge of anti-Gómez elements reached its completion and hundreds of army positions were distributed to Gómez's adherents. Consequently, by 1912 the Cuban military was made up almost exclusively of Gómez's Liberals. Also, because of the chief executive's largess, its total strength approached 12,500 officers and men.[31] Even so, Gómez's army was not a formidable force. The officer corps was already far too large and military discipline was subject to political caprice. Court martial decisions were often reversed by the president, and this naturally tended to blunt the edge of the senior commander's authority. Still, this was a Cuban army that was intended for use only against other Cubans. Militarily it performed well when the Colored Independents launched their insurrection,[32] and politically it performed even better. When Gómez determined to support Menocal's presidential candidacy, it proved extremely good at blocking the opposition from voting.

The Liberal character of the armed forces posed no problem for Menocal when he first succeeded Gómez. After all, General Monteagudo, the chief of the army and the Rural Guard, was one of the most enthusiastic backers of his bid for the presidency among the Liberal leaders.[33] Yet the situation changed drastically after Monteagudo died (1914) and the Conservative caudillo began to think about reelection. In 1915—the year in which it began to be rumored that he would run again—he once again reorganized the military services, consummating the incorporation of the Guard into the regular forces and placing loyal Menocalistas in key positions. There still remained, however, a powerful Miguelista faction within the armed forces, and members of this faction first campaigned actively against the government ticket in 1916, and then supported Gómez and the other Liberal leaders when the 1917 revolt broke out. Betrayals, miscalculations, and poor leadership aborted the action of the Miguelista officers in Havana.[34] But defections were virtually unanimous in eastern Cuba, where the rebels gained control of Oriente province and almost all of Camagüey province. According to rather low official estimates, approximately 1,000 officers and men enlisted under the Liberal banner on this occasion.[35]

These defections gave Menocal the opportunity to redirect the political loyalty of the armed forces once the insurrection was crushed. Using indiscriminately all the instrumentalities at his disposal—dismissals, transfers, leaves of absence, missions abroad, promotions, new commissions, retirements, and the ratification of emergency commissions—he managed to reshape the military institution into a largely Menocalista organization. He has been accused of having been apathetic concerning political and administrative matters, but his dedication to the military has been widely recognized,[36] and he worked diligently to create a Conservative consensus among the men in uniform. As a result, once he was done with his second reorganization what had hitherto been a basically Miguelista institution had vanished. There were still some Liberal partisans in the army, yet as a whole it had been drawn into Menocal's orbit. It was by far the strongest military force that had ever been put together in Cuba. By 1919 there were about 18,000 officers and men in the ranks,[37] an unprecedented number of whom—on the basis of the lessons learned from the recent uprising—were assigned to garrison and reinforce key locations in the interior provinces.[38] According to some estimates, a little less than one-fourth of the national budget was allocated to support this machine.[39]

Fearing that a Miguelista victory would be inimical to its best interests, and obediently following the directions of the government that had brought it into being, the Menocalista armed institution intervened decisively in the election of 1920 so as to hand over the presidency to Zayas.[40] This, by the way, placed the new incumbent in the same uncomfortable position the Conservative leader had been in eight years before. For, once again the constituted order was threatened by the antithetical loyalties inherent in the politics of the new administration and the partisan leanings of the military. Actually Zayas' predicament was worse—in fact, far worse—than Menocal's. Not only was he a sinewless civilian in a land dominated by war heroes and strongmen, but his term, because of the sugar crisis of 1920, coincided with a period of depression during which government receipts fell off significantly. As the price of sugar plummeted and bankruptcy overwhelmed speculators, Zayas had to resort to cuts in the budget, and these unavoidable economies ultimately affected military appropriations. From 17.4 percent of the total in 1920–1921, they dropped successively to 16 percent and 15 percent.[41] As a result, the armed forces were reduced by at least 2,000 men, a new military district that Menocal had created in Holguín (Oriente) was eliminated, and salaries were generally slashed. A good many officers became supernumeraries, and company strength was reduced from 140 to 60 men.[42]

Despite these drastic measures, two years later Zayas had to face yet another crisis, although this time trouble originated in the Congress. For the purpose of earning the goodwill of the sergeants of the old Rural Guard (the only ones who had served for more than twenty years in the Cuban armed forces and the ones whose allegiance was still crucial for winning elections), a group of legislators introduced a bill promoting sergeants to officer rank provided they had served at least twenty years. The bill also proposed the creation of a special school for sergeants with less seniority, which would make them eligible for promotion after they had taken a number of superficial six-month courses.[43] Beyond a doubt, it was a politically inspired and fiscally irresponsible piece of legislation that was submitted without any prior consultation with the General Staff or the Department of War, one that Zayas rightly refused to sign upon the recommendation of General Armando Montes, the Secretary of War. Congress nevertheless overruled the president's veto, but even so the ill-advised measure was never fully implemented chiefly because of lack of funds. As it turned out, only a little over 100 sergeants were eventually promoted in obedience to its provisions.[44]

All these difficulties notwithstanding, the men in uniform stood solidly behind the government when the more bellicose spirits among the Veterans and Patriots could contain themselves no longer and arose in arms. Indeed, throughout the 1924 political campaign the army remained remarkably quiescent. On the one hand, it appears that prior to the election Machado managed to convince the army chief of his sympathy and support for the military, and promised certain privileges for the officers if he were elected.[45] On the other, as the campaign ran its course, it became evident to everyone not blinded by partisanship that the Liberal candidate was sure to win in an honest election. Thus, shrewdly enough, Zayas refrained from even attempting to use strong-arm tactics to produce a Machado victory. To be sure, arms were very probably distributed at different strategic locations to be used in case of emergency, pro-Machado military supervisors were appointed to various electoral districts, and many government employees known to be sympathizers of Menocal were removed from their positions.[46] But these were merely precautionary steps that were taken against possible aggressions by the other side. Except perhaps for assisting Machado in vote buying (a practice in which both sides indulged unashamedly), the government did not interfere with the free expression of the popular will. Nor did Menocal's army, which insouciantly beheld the spectacle of its former leader's defeat at the hands of the Liberals. Inasmuch as military officers were for the most part supporters of the Conservative party or at any rate hostile to Zayas, it is unlikely that they would have used the forces under their command to follow the line of the incumbent regime. Yet, to all appearances, either because of Machado's preelection maneuvering or for some other reason, they were quite willing to allow the rise to power of a candidate who, after all, seemed inclined to cater to them as Menocal had done in the past.

Despite his smashing electoral victory (he lost only one province and then by only two hundred votes[47]), the new president did not feel at ease with an army controlled by Menocalistas. For some time he even feared that a military coup might prevent him from being inducted into office.[48] He had been inspector general of the Rural Guard under Monteagudo and commander in chief of the Permanent Army briefly following the attempt on Pino Guerra's life, and he knew well that in order to be truly functional his power would have to be based primarily on the military. He therefore resolved to follow in the footsteps of Gómez and Menocal and fashion a politically loyal armed institution. At the time of his inauguration the economic situation of the country was not conducive to fiscal extravagance—in 1925 Cuba produced over five million tons of sugar, but prices had fallen severely and consequently financial resources were tight. However, he somehow managed to build up military appropriations steadily. From 1925 to 1929, his first term in office, they fell to an average of 13.13 percent of the annual budget, but they increased considerably after 1928, soaring to nearly a quarter of the total national income in 1932 and 1933. From 1929 to 1933, they climbed to an average of 14.53 percent of the budget.[49]

With these funds, Machado was able to angle for military support with a silver hook. New housing units were built for garrisons throughout the island, training facilities were markedly improved, and even an Aviation Corps was created, thus adding air power to the armed forces.[50] Officers were regally treated. Not only did they receive generous bonuses—a minimum of thirty-eight cents a day plus food—but also their pay was regarded as immutable. If a company was supposed to be 150 men strong, for example, the commander received pay for that many soldiers, even if the actual number was smaller. This enabled the commander to pocket the difference, whatever it was. In September 1926, moreover, a government decree expanded army jurisdiction to secondary schools, and as a consequence military supervisors were installed in these centers for the purpose of superintending gymnastic drills and marching exercises and teaching elementary military science. Later on, as the new role of the armed forces was further enlarged—which, in effect, transformed the armed forces into an extra civil service—officers became overseers in all government departments, national and local. In time, as Machado's stranglehold on the presidency tightened, they displaced provincial governors and mayors all over the country, tried civilians for certain offenses, and even ran the meat and milk monopolies. As might be expected, graft permeated the institution.[51]

Machado, of course, mixed subornation with other expedient methods to achieve his goal. As in the days of Gómez and Menocal, officers of questionable partisan sentiments, especially Menocalistas, were forced out of the army or given unimportant posts. Senior grades were filled with trusted Machadistas, and, whenever necessary, old Miguelistas were asked to return to active duty. By this time the Cuban army was already twenty years old. The president, however, was able to make all these moves because Congress had enacted a law on March 2, 1926, that allowed him great latitude in carrying out the last reorganization of this period. Not that he was excessively concerned with legal niceties, for he never hesitated to contravene the law whenever he saw fit. Promotion to lieutentant colonel, for example, was regulated by a ratio of three executive appointments to one advance through seniority. Nevertheless, of the six officers promoted to lieutenant colonel between 1926 and 1932, Machado named five. By the same token, promotion to major was governed by a one-to-one ratio. Again, of the eleven majors who were commissioned during the same period, ten were presidential designations.[52]

On July 20, 1926, an executive order authorized a new peacetime strength for the army of 11,772 officers and men.[53] Not all of them, to be sure, were ardent Machadistas. In fact, there was a group of about 150 young men—career officers, trained in U.S. military schools—that was apparently immune to bribery and that the president consequently found intractable. These men, after the electoral farce of 1928, began to plot against him.[54] The plotters, however, were few in number and invariably failed to garner much support. Furthermore, Machado managed to undermine their authority by appealing to the interests of the noncommissioned and enlisted ranks above them.[55] Thus they were effectively neutralized, and for that reason it is no exaggeration to assert that by 1928 the Cuban armed institution as a whole was as solidly Machadista as it had been Miguelista and Menocalista before. It is no wonder then that the 1931 attempt at insurrection failed as ignominiously as it did. Menocal and Mendieta started it counting on the backing of certain sectors of the army; naively, as it turned out, they also took for granted that the small navy that President Gómez had created[56] would side with them. Yet when they took to the woods in the usual Cuban fashion, none of the expected defections materialized. Firmly united behind Machado, the armed forces easily crushed the outbreak. The two old caudillos were captured without a shot being fired.[57]

The Policy of Preventive Intervention

Although the failure of the Menocal-Mendieta conspiracy in 1931 was to be expected, the same cannot be said of the 1917 Liberal revolt. In 1917 rebellion spread like fire throughout the island, and for a moment it appeared as though the Menocal administration would be unable to quell it. How is it that such a powerful movement disintegrated into glorified vagrancy in three short months? This is perplexing indeed, as it is also perplexing that the threatening attempt at rebellion made by the veterans in 1911 aborted as abruptly as it did. Why did General Núñez and his followers, who had been saying openly that they would hang pro-Spanish officeholders unless they retired from their positions, suddenly decide to drop their violent campaign against these elements? Why, to mention still another example, did Menocal remain quiescent when he was defeated by Machado in 1924 and refrain from starting the armed protest that the Conservatives had vowed would erupt if their candidate was "deprived of the election"? Since in republican Cuba the armed forces were usually committed to a political leader other than the one occupying the presidential chair at a given moment, it might be assumed that violence often played a role in the transfer of power. Also, given the fact that these leaders as a rule succeeded in pulling the military institution into the orbit of their parties at some point during their incumbencies, it likewise might be assumed that they frequently attempted to perpetuate their power. Periods of dictatorship should not have been uncommon. Yet no successful revolution took place in post-Magoon Cuba before 1933, and all the presidents in this period served their full terms in office. Moreover, except for Menocal's second term, during which he ruled as a virtual dictator, Cubans did not really suffer from government repression until the illegal extension of Machado's governance in 1928. Why?

The answer to this question is provided by the immediacy of U.S. influence, which during this period conditioned nearly every facet of Cuba's life as a nation. Gone were the days in which a U.S. president, in the face of a serious disturbance on the island, would procrastinate until full-scale intervention was practically thrust upon him. Owing no doubt in part to the lesson learned in Cuba in 1906, the United States took the position that it should intervene to protect its interests rather than wait until the incumbent government disintegrated. Such was the substance of the notorious "preventive policy" developed by the Taft administration as the political component of "dollar diplomacy," a policy that was also central to the Wilsonian determination to refuse recognition to regimes established by other than constitutional means. Since its object was to deter the use of violence as an instrument for settling political disputes, the policy clearly tended to work to the advantage of the government in power.[58]

Insofar as Cuba was concerned, this meant that the case of Estrada Palma was not to be repeated. This goal was to be attained through a "constant and critical watchfulness" over Cuban affairs and the exercise of a variety of direct or indirect controls. At times, if the matter at hand was simply to protect a U.S. investor or prevent the ruling administration from enacting undesirable legislation, a piece of "friendly advice" from the U.S. minister sufficed to set things straight.[59] But in other cases more severe diplomatic pressure was exerted. It was a stern note from Secretary of State Philander Chase Knox expressing the "grave concern" of the United States, for example, that lessened the aggressiveness of General Núñez and the veteranists and ultimately led them to come to terms with the Gómez administration. And it was the so-called González's notes—indeed a salient point in Cuban republican history—that allowed Menocal to clip the wings of the Liberals in 1917 with such relative ease. In this series of notes, which U.S. Minister William Elliot González handed out to the press while ignoring the Cuban secretary of state, Washington announced that it supported the government, that in its considered opinion the insurrection was "lawless and unconstitutional," and that its excesses would "not be countenanced." More than that, Washington made clear that it would hold the leaders of the movement responsible for any damage to the person or property of foreigners, and menacingly stated that it would study what attitude should be adopted toward those participating in the disturbances. As might be expected, the strong tone of these representations could not but dampen the spirits of the Liberals, whose "powerful" revolution came to naught in short order.[60]

When several years later, after the fraudulent election of Zayas, the leaders of the party again seemed to be toying with the idea of civil war, all it took to make calmer views prevail was for Washington to formally recognize Zayas' victory (April 17, 1921), and to intimate that there might indeed be an intervention if a legal government was not in office by May 20. At that time, furthermore, Cuba was under the proconsulate of General Enoch H. Crowder, who, without formal prior notice to the Cuban authorities, had turned up in the Havana harbor in January on the USS *Minnesota* as the special representative of President Wilson. Circumstances, therefore, were not particularly propitious for the launching of another revolt. Crowder's influence (he went so far as to force upon Zayas a so-called honest cabinet[61]) was paramount in Cuba until 1923, when he gave up his post as special presidential agent to become the first U.S. ambassador to Cuba. As such he could only speak when Secretary of State Charles Evans Hughes permitted him to do so, and Hughes was a man who worried about the international image of his country. Even so, it is said that in 1924 it was Crowder who, after a long conference, persuaded Menocal to acknowledge defeat. The gesture, of course, thoroughly muzzled the Conservative diehards who were then prating about revolution.[62]

In some instances Washington's meddling in Cuban affairs took more concrete forms. When the Colored Independents rose up, U.S. Marines landed in Cuba, against the express wishes of President Gómez, to protect foreign-owned mines and sugar estates.[63] In 1917, to add strength to Minister González's peremptory notes, ten thousand rifles and five million rounds of ammunition were sold to Menocal; and, as though this were not enough, the marines landed again. At first they occupied only Santiago de Cuba (where the U.S. Navy engaged in some indiscreet negotiations with the local rebels[64]), but subsequently they also stationed themselves at Guantánamo, Manzanillo, and Nuevitas, a town located in Camagüey near the Oriente borderline. In addition, a detachment was sent inland to keep watch over the mines of El Cobre. As it turned out, these troops remained on the island for a long time, for the United States wished to protect sugar mills, mines, and railroad facilities while World War I raged in Europe, and Menocal had no choice but to grant Minister González's request to this effect. Thus 1,600 marines were established in Oriente and 1,000 in Camagüey in what amounted to a partial military occupation beyond the scope of the Platt amendment. This occupation lasted until 1922.

Consequently, the marines were gone by the time the Veterans and Patriots challenged Zayas' authority. Washington, however, did not send them back. Instead, before the new movement could gather headway, an embargo was placed on the sale of arms and ammunition to the rebels, whose representatives had traveled to the United States for the purpose of purchasing an airplane, among other things. Although these men were arrested and the material they had purchased intercepted, Zayas was allowed to buy military supplies from the U.S. government itself. Such was Washington's way of vetoing the incipient revolt, which, as might be expected, quickly lost its impetus. Indeed, during this era of unrestrained interference, the Colossus of the North cast a long shadow over tiny Cuba! So commanding was U.S. influence that Machado, before embarking on the adventure of constitutional reform and reelection, thought it proper to pay a visit to the United States (1927) in order to sound out President Coolidge about his plans. He resolved to carry them out only after the taciturn occupant of the White House told him that such matters were "a question for the Cuban people and their government to decide."[65]

Besides U.S. policy, other factors also contributed to the preservation of the rhythm of presidential succession in the young Cuban republic. On some occasions, as in 1931, it was essentially the effectiveness of the Cuban army that upheld the integrity of Cuba's shaky institutions. At other times, as in 1917, it was the resolute attitude and courage displayed by a president who persuaded Washington of his ability to defend his government.[66] On the whole, however, Cuba did not plunge into the anarchy and chaos that characterized the "apprenticeship to freedom" elsewhere in Spanish America primarily because of the U.S. protectorship. It was under its aegis that the appearances of constitutionalism developed on the island.

But this only meant that Cubans were unable to bypass the "useless forms" as cavalierly as other Spanish American nations did in the nineteenth century. Politically, the most important consequence of the second U.S. occupation of Cuba was the legitimization of the claims of the veteran-politicians to the spoils of independence, and the U.S. protectorship did practically nothing to check the forces that were thereby released on the Cuban scene. On the contrary, if anything, some of those forces, especially when not in power, were encouraged to keep gambling on intervention (as the Liberals had done in 1906) as the best way to political success.[67] Cubans therefore were not completely deterred from resorting to violence, but only from carrying it to the point of endangering foreign lives and property. Thus they could rig elections in order to seize power; they could make a show of reelection for the purpose of perpetuating themselves in office; they could use coercion to silence the opposition or put the government on the defensive; and they could rule for their own personal benefit. In short, they could play the game of politics much as it was played in the other republics during the post-independence period. Outwardly, Cuba between 1909 and 1933 was a republic in which the popular masses presumably had something to say about the government's policies, programs, and activities. In reality, the men who had the last word in Cuban affairs were those who could claim the credit for having created the new nation. Such was the fate of the other Spanish American countries upon the attainment of political emancipation and, to a large extent, such was the fate of Cuba.

Concluding Remarks

This was clearly understood by a conservative Cuban who, in November 1906—barely two months after the second U.S. occupation began—conveyed to his friend General Leonard Wood the following thoughts: "When the last soldier of the wars of independence is dead . . . when there is no longer left any soldier or general of the rebellion of 1906 . . . then and not until then will it be wise for the United States to trust us with a second experiment in self-government."[68] Regardless of what we may think of the unabashed pro-Yankeeism of this Cuban, he proved quite perceptive in pinpointing the origin of one of his country's most serious problems. Yet, despite his acuity, he failed to realize that Cuba's path had already been laid out. Cuba, like its sister republics, had inherited a tradition of military involvement in politics, and this tradition survived long after the effects of the wars of independence subsided. Its chief component, the regular use of violence as a means to attain political ends, has been a constant in the country's history.

This became evident once again at the end of the veteran-presidents' era, when the anti-Machado army officers finally prevailed and, with Washington's approval, ousted the dictator (August 1933). At this juncture, new civilian groups had already displaced the liberators as the leading force in Cuban politics and a genuine revolutionary situation had developed on the island. Acute social and economic conflicts that had been festering for decades came to a head, and nationalistic feelings reached an unprecedented intensity. Since the authors of the coup, the first in Cuban annals, did not seize power, a political vacuum developed that was filled by a stopgap government that resulted from hastily conducted negotiations between Sumner Welles, the U.S. ambassador, and the rebel officers. But the new government commanded so little authority that it was incapable of arresting the revolutionary fervor aroused by the excesses of the deposed dictatorship and the widespread unemployment caused by the sugar crisis of 1930. Then a group of noncommissioned officers mutinied at Camp Columbia, on the outskirts of Havana. This in itself was not surprising, given the prevalent economic difficulties and the conditions of uncertainty and near-chaos afflicting the republic. Yet the August coup had shattered the command structure of the armed forces (already weakened and demoralized by their previous association with Machado) and, because of the dictatorship's military policies, discipline had almost completely broken down. The mutiny consequently spread rapidly to the remaining military installations in the capital and the interior. Originally the goal of the mutineers was simply to obtain compliance—by force if necessary—on a number of demands related to the status and welfare of the troops. Upon learning what was happening, however, a group of civilian revolutionaries rushed to Camp Columbia and talked the sergeants into widening the scope of the movement. Thus, what had begun as a mere act of insubordination was transformed into a triumphant revolutionary takeover. The officers were removed, the provisional government was overthrown (despite its connections with Welles), and a revolutionary junta assumed the responsibility of introducing radical reforms in Cuba.

The sergeants' revolt, which took place on September 4, 1933, marked a turning point in the evolution of twentieth-century Cuba, for the two major groups that competed for political supremacy in the Cuban political arena until 1958 emerged from this episode. One of them consisted of the reform-minded and intensely nationalistic elements that became prominent during the period of revolutionary struggle that preceded Machado's downfall. Eventually the bulk of this group coalesced into what came to be known as the Auténtico party, whose leader was Ramón Grau San Martín, a physician and professor at the University of Havana. The other group, the new sergeant-dominated army, was by far the more powerful. Its recognized head was the leader of the Camp Columbia mutineers, Fulgencio Batista y Zaldívar, a desk sergeant who had never had any troops under his command and who went about his new duties as a political boss rather than a military chief. Thenceforward, the Cuban military institution distinguished itself by its lax discipline and, especially above certain levels, a peculiar chain of command based on an exchange of graft for loyalty rather than on respect for rank and authority. For all practical purposes, the revolt converted the army into a political party, subject to the same patronage pressures and built around the same personalist system of allegiance that typified the other political organizations. Despite some halfhearted attempts at professionalization, it essentially preserved this character until it was destroyed by Castro in 1959.

Before this happened, however, as is well known, Batista and the army ran Cuba during most of the quarter-century that followed the sergeants' revolt. They took over after Grau San Martín and his associates held power for four short months in the fall of 1933, and they pushed Cuba back into a military dictatorship on March 10, 1952, when they cut short the disappointing interlude of Auténtico rule that had begun in 1944. It is indeed debatable whether these instances of military interference in the political sphere, which began after the veteran-politicians had begun to decline, may be laid at the doorstep of the United States and its second occupation of Cuba many years before. But it is obvious that after that time, even though the Platt amendment remained in effect for nearly three more decades, the United States no longer concerned itself with the need to curb militarism on the island or to build up responsible armed forces capable of guaranteeing orderly constitutional processes. Subsequently, especially after the 1930s, the United States became interested in stability rather than legality, in securing reliable governments "well disposed toward the United States" (as Welles put it[69]) and faithful to their client status.[70] This is why Batista, a symbol of order and stability to many people in the United States, became one of the key elements of the relations between Cuba and the United States from 1934 to 1959.

During this period Washington took a number of steps that added to Batista's prestige as a political figure. In January 1934, for example, it extended recognition rather quickly to the puppet government with which he replaced the revolutionary regime of Grau San Martín. Shortly afterward, it secured a stable market for Cuban sugar and tobacco through a new reciprocity treaty, and it also finally agreed to abrogate the hated Platt amendment. It promptly declared that it "could not intervene" when Batista had a president "impeached" for refusing to follow his policies; and when Batista paid a visit to the United States soon thereafter, in the fall of 1938, he was received as though he were the head of state. President Franklin D. Roosevelt and Secretary of State Cordell Hull talked to him, and he was taken to review the cadets at West Point. World War II allowed him to enjoy a very close relationship with the United States after he became president in 1940, and this relationship remained intact even after he staged a coup in 1952 three months before a national election on a flimsy pretext. Barely two weeks later (March 27), Willard Beaulac, the U.S. ambassador in Havana, visited the new Cuban foreign minister to put the U.S. stamp of approval on Batista's regime. It took six years and a full-fledged revolution for Washington to publicize its lack of faith in Batista by finally announcing on March 14, 1958, that it was suspending arms shipments to Havana because the Cuban government was not using the weapons for external defense.

The historical significance of all these events is quite apparent. Whatever the factors that determined the transformation of the Castro revolution into a socialist upheaval, it was Batista's 1952 coup that set it in motion.

Notes

1. The Struggle for Independence

1. García to Tomás Estrada Palma, March 22, 1898. Cuba, Archivo Nacional, *Boletín del Archivo Nacional* (hereinafter referred to as *BAN*) 35 (1936): 102–103. All issues of *BAN* are from January to December unless otherwise specified. All translations in this work are by the author unless otherwise noted.

2. For a short biography of General García see Jaime Suchliki, *Historical Dictionary of Cuba*, pp. 114–115.

3. Francisco Figueras, *Cuba y su evolución colonial*, pp. 116–119; Duvon C. Corbitt, *The Colonial Government of Cuba*; José Luciano Franco, *Apuntes para una historia de la legislación y administración colonial en Cuba, 1511–1800*.

4. Ramiro Guerra, *Manual de historia de Cuba*, p. 303; Allan J. Kuethe, *Cuba, 1753–1815: Crown, Military, and Society*, p. xiv.

5. Eric Christiansen, *The Origins of Military Power in Spain, 1808–1854*; Stanley G. Payne, *Politics and the Military in Modern Spain*, pp. 5–101.

6. Vidal Morales y Morales, *Iniciadores y primeros mártires de la revolución cubana*.

7. José Luciano Franco, *La reacción española contra la libertad*, pp. 31–39.

8. So long as they served the king, there was never a disciplinary breakdown in the ranks of the Spanish American troops; see John J. Johnson, *The Military and Society in Latin America*, pp. 18–20.

9. Guerra, *Manual*.

10. Roque E. Garrigó, *Historia documentada de los Soles y Rayos de Bolívar*.

11. Guerra, *Manual*, p. 305. On the Permanent Executive Military Commission see Joaquín Llaverías, *La Comisión Militar Ejecutiva y Permanente*.

12. Richard Henry Dana, Jr., *To Cuba and Back*, p. 240; Louis A. Pérez, Jr., *Cuba: Between Reform and Revolution*, p. 103.

13. For press censorship under Vives see Larry R. Jensen, *Children of Colonial Despotism*, pp. 97–106.

14. See Martí's eulogy for the poet José María Heredia in *Páginas escogidas*, pp. 96–106.

15. For Vives' views on the reliability of native Cubans see his report of June 23, 1825, in Hortensia Pichardo, *Documentos para la historia de Cuba*, 1:291.

16. For a study of the Spanish insular army during this period see Octavio A. Delgado, "The Spanish Army in Cuba, 1868–1898," 1:65–82.

17. The Spanish constitution of 1812 had been restored as the result of a revolt of the sergeants of the royal guard.

18. Tacón's most prominent victim was the distinguished political writer José A. Saco (1797–1879).

19. For some of the remarks made by some deputies about Tacón's methods see Morales y Morales, *Iniciadores y primeros mártires*, 1:218.

20. Ramiro Guerra et al., *Historia de la nación cubana*, 4:4.

21. One of the most poignant descriptions of Tacón's despotism was made by Lorenzo in the manifesto that he subsequently published. See his *Manifiesto del general Manuel Lorenzo a la nación española sobre los acontecimientos de Santiago de Cuba*.

22. Delgado, "The Spanish Army in Cuba," 1:83, 235–236.

23. See, for example, Cirilo Villaverde, *Cecilia Valdés o La loma del ángel*, pp. 146, 152–153.

24. Full text in Pichardo, *Documentos*, 1:358–362.

25. Havana had the aspect of a "military city" according to Samuel Hazard, *Cuba with Pen and Pencil*, p. 235.

26. Payne, *Politics and the Military in Modern Spain*, p. 67.

27. Antonio Pirala, *Anales de la guerra de Cuba*, 1:385.

28. Luis Otero Pimentel, *Memoria sobre los Voluntarios de la Isla de Cuba*, p. 177.

29. Delgado, "The Spanish Army in Cuba," 1:250.

30. The most infamous excess of the Volunteers was the execution of eight medical students on November 27, 1871.

31. Besides Otero Pimentel, *Memoria*, see, on the Volunteers, José Joaquín Ribó, *Historia de los voluntarios cubanos*, and Eugenio Vandama Calderón, *Colección de artículos sobre el Instituto de los Voluntarios de la Isla de Cuba*; for a severe criticism of the Volunteers by a Cuban historian, see Emilio Roig de Leuchsenring, *1895 y 1898, dos guerras cubanas, ensayo de revaloración*, pp. 42–58. The best available modern account is that of Delgado, "The Spanish Army in Cuba," 1:235–260.

32. Delgado, "The Spanish Army in Cuba," 1:236–260.

33. Vidal Morales y Morales, *Hombres del 68: Rafael Morales y González*, pp. 172–76.

34. Francisco Ponte Domínguez, *Historia de la Guerra de los Diez Años*, pp. 83–87.

35. Quoted by Carlos Márquez Sterling, *Ignacio Agramonte, el bayardo de la revolución cubana*, pp. 110–111.

36. Quoted by Ponte Domínguez, *Historia de la Guerra de los Diez Años,* p. 107.

37. Antonio Zambrana, *La república de Cuba,* p. 37. The text of the constitution is included in Andres María Lazcano, *Las constituciones de Cuba.* A basic work for the study of the assembly and the origins of the first Cuban republican government is Cuba, Secretaría de Instrucción Pública y Bellas Artes, *Comunicaciones de la Cámara de Representantes desde el día 10 de abril de 1869 hasta el día 10 de junio del mismo año.*

38. Herminio Portell Vilá, *Céspedes, el padre de la patria cubana,* p. 163; Zambrana, *La república de Cuba,* p. 91.

39. Ramiro Guerra, *Guerra de los Diez Años, 1868–1878,* 1:396.

40. This description is based on the testimony of Manuel Sanguily y Garrite, *Obras de Manuel Sanguily,* 6:90, 206–207.

41. On Agramonte's "dictatorship" see Ramón Roa, *Con la pluma y el machete,* 1:172–73. On Calixto García's regionalism see Gerardo Castellanos, *Tierras y glorias de Oriente, Calixto García,* pp. 71–75. Regionalism and its leading exponents have also been studied by Elías Entrialgo, *La insurrección de los diez años, una interpretación social de este fenómeno histórico,* pp. 31–37.

42. Céspedes to his wife, Ana Quesada, October 18, 1871, Carlos Manuel de Céspedes y Quesada, *Carlos Manuel de Céspedes,* pp. 123–129.

43. See, for instance, Sanguily, *Obras,* 6:90, 206–207.

44. Céspedes y Quesada, *Céspedes,* p. 181. Other firsthand accounts may be found in Enrique Collazo, *Desde Yara hasta el Zanjón,* pp. 46–57, and Gonzalo de Quesada, *Ignacio Mora,* pp. 134–139. Céspedes' deposition had nothing to do with the problem of slavery. See letter, Céspedes to Ana Quesada, February 10, 1874, Carlos Manuel de Céspedes, *Cartas a su esposa Ana de Quesada,* p. 213.

45. On Lagunas de Varona see Collazo, *Desde Yara hasta el Zanjón,* pp. 67–72, and Guerra, *Guerra de los Diez Años,* 2:233–41. On the Las Villas invasion see Máximo Gómez, *Convenio del Zanjón,* pp. 6–12; also Ignacio Mora's diary as quoted by Quesada, *Ignacio Mora,* pp. 155–56. For an attempt to defend the behavior of Vicente García see Florencio García Cisneros, *El león de Santa Rita, el general Vicente García y la Guerra de los Diez Años,* pp. 57–82.

46. See the letter that Maceo wrote to the rebel government in May 1876 apropos this campaign. Quoted in full and translated by Foner, *A History of Cuba,* 2:259–60.

47. Máximo Gómez made this comment in his *Diario de campaña,* p. 103.

48. Delgado, "The Spanish Army in Cuba," 1:89.

49. Text in T. Ochando, *El general Martínez Campos en Cuba,* pp. 37–52.

50. Gómez, *Convenio,* pp. 29, 30; Collazo, *Desde Yara hasta el Zanjón,* p. 107.

51. See Fernando Figueredo, *La revolución de Yara, 1868–1878,*

pp. 227–308; also, Francisco Ibarra Martínez, *Cronología de la Guerra de los Diez Años*, pp. 169–236.

52. See Rafael Fermoselle, *The Evolution of the Cuban Military*, pp. 64–65.

53. Ibid.

54. Delgado, "The Spanish Army in Cuba," p. 93.

55. Fermoselle, *The Evolution of the Cuban Military*, p. 70

56. Hugh Thomas, *Cuba: The Pursuit of Freedom*, p. 269.

57. A basic work for the study of the Little War is Camilo García de Polavieja, *Relación documentada de mi política en Cuba*. At the time Polavieja was the Spanish commander in Oriente.

58. In this connection the correspondence of the *villareño* General Serafín Sánchez is revealing. See Cuba, Archivo Nacional, *Documentos para servir a la historia de la Guerra Chiquita*, 1:203–204; 2:58–60. See also Rebeca Rosell Planas, *Factores económicos, políticos y sociales de la Guerra Chiquita*, p. 56.

59. Leonardo Griñán Peralta, *Maceo, análisis caracteriológico*, pp. 132–133; Gonzalo Cabrales, *Epistolario de héroes*, p. 184; Maceo's letter to Gómez of August 31, 1886, in *Epistolario*, pp. 100–105; José Duarte Oropesa, *Historiología cubana*, 2:18.

60. Octavio R. Costa, *Perfil político de Calixto García*, pp. 18–19.

61. Francisco Pérez Guzmán and Rodolfo Sarracino, *La Guerra Chiquita: una experiencia necesaria*, p. 271.

62. Text in Máximo Gómez, *Revoluciones . . . Cuba y Hogar*, pp. 223–226.

63. Maceo to José A. Rodríguez, November 1, 1886, Cabrales, *Epistolario*, p. 197.

64. Jorge Mañach, *Martí, el apóstol*, p. 183; José Luciano Franco, *Antonio Maceo, apuntes para una historia de su vida*, 1:271.

65. As, for example, the physician Eusebio Hernández, who helped to write the manifesto that Gómez would issue upon his landing in Cuba and that confirms the dictatorial character of the enterprise. Text in Eusebio Hernández, *Maceo: dos conferencias históricas*, pp. 150–152.

66. Martí's definitive biography remains to be written. Mañach's *Martí* is probably the best of the existing lives in Spanish. The most recent is Alberto Baeza Flores, *Vida de José Martí*. There are a good number of studies available in English, the most recent of which are Peter Turton's *José Martí, Architect of Cuba's Freedom*, and Christopher Abel and Nissa Torrents, eds., *José Martí, Revolutionary Democrat*. The best study thus far of Martí's thought is Paul Estrade's *José Martí, 1853–1895: des fondements de la democratie en Amérique latine*.

67. José Martí to Máximo Gómez, October 20, 1884, José Martí, *Obras completas*, vol. 1, pt. 1, pp. 78–81.

68. Martí to Manuel Mercado, September 13, 1885, Martí, *Obras*, 3:857–861.

69. Martí to J.A. Lucena, October 9, 1885, ibid., vol. 1, pt. 2, pp. 353–356.

70. See, for instance, the note that Gómez wrote on the back of Martí's letter of resignation. The full text may be found in Duarte, *Historiología*, 2:33. See also Gómez, *Diario*, pp. 180, 192–193.

71. See, for example, Gómez to Juan Arnao, January 20, 1885; full text in Carlos Ripoll, *José Martí: letras y huellas desconocidas*, pp. 89–90.

72. Martí refused to help Maceo in the task of raising funds for an expedition, and the general reacted accordingly. See letter, Maceo to Juan Arnao, June 14, 1885. Full text in ibid., pp. 92–94. Further details about Martí's differences with Gómez and Maceo may be found in Eusebio Hernández, *El período revolucionario de 1879 a 1895*, p. 31, and Enrique Trujillo, *Apuntes históricos, propaganda y movimientos revolucionarios cubanos en los Estados Unidos desde enero de 1880 hasta febrero de 1895*, p. 16.

73. Gómez, *Diario*, p. 223.

74. Manuel J. Granda, *La paz del manganeso*, pp. 53–60; Polavieja, *Relación*, p. 109.

75. Martí, *Obras*, vol. 1, pt. 1, pp. 90–95.

76. Ibid., vol. 1, part 2, pp. 418–424. On *Patria* see, among other works, Joaquin Llaverías, *Los periódicos de Martí*. For a recent biography of Sotero Figueroa, the editor of *Patria*, see Josefina Toledo, *Sotero Figueroa, editor de "Patria."*

77. Martí, *Obras*, vol. 1, pt. 2, pp. 299–300.

78. For Martí's instructions to his secret agent in Cuba see letter, Martí to Gerardo Castellanos, August 4, 1892, ibid., vol. 1, pt. 2, pp. 574–577.

79. There is no dearth of materials on Martí's party. Among the most recent is Eduardo Torres-Cuevas, Mario Mencía, and Augusto E. Benítez, *El alma visible de Cuba: José Martí y el Partido Revolucionario Cubano*.

80. These reports appeared in *Patria*. See, for example, Martí, *Obras*, vol. 1, pt. 2, pp. 539–44. Martí's formal invitation to Gómez may be found in ibid., vol. 1, pt. 1, pp. 99–102. Gómez's reply was published in Cuba, Archivo Nacional, *El Archivo Nacional en la conmemoración del centenario de José Martí y Pérez*, p. 315. Martí described his visit to Maceo in a letter to Gómez of August 29, 1893, Martí, *Obras*, vol. 1, pt. 1, pp. 113–118. There is an extensive literature on the Martí-Gómez conference of September 1892, which is largely hagiographic in tone.

81. Gómez, *Diario*, p. 282; see also the letter that he wrote to Serafín Sánchez barely a month before his meeting with Martí. Quoted by Duarte, *Historiología*, 2:72.

82. As for Martí, see what he wrote in *Patria* on September 3, 1892, quoted in Duarte, *Historiología*, 2:72–73. Gómez simply believed that he, Maceo, Flor Crombet, and "the remaining generals" were "the revolution." See Ramón Infiesta, *Máximo Gómez*, p. 135.

83. Maceo to Angel Guerra, February 9, 1893, quoted by Mañach, *Martí*, p. 240; Gómez to Serafín Sánchez, n.d., in Emilio Roig de Leuchsenring, ed., *Ideario cubano*, vol. 2, *Máximo Gómez*, p. 121. Also, Gómez, *Diario*, p. 268.

84. See the letter that he wrote to his childhood friend Fermín Valdés Domínguez on April 18, 1894, Martí, *Obras*, vol. 1, pt. 1, pp. 151–152.

85. Gómez to Maceo, November 12, 1893, and February 12, 1894, Cabrales, *Epistolario*, pp. 125–127.

86. See, for example, Martí's instructions to Maceo about his expedition, Martí, *Obras*, vol. 1, pt. 1, p. 226.

87. Rebeca Rosell Planas, *Las claves de Martí y el plan de alzamiento para Cuba*, p. 6.

88. Ibid. See also Emilio Roig de Leuchsenring, "La guerra de independencia de 1895: el plan de alzamiento de Fernandina," Cuba, *BAN* (1948):16–25.

89. The best account of this episode is, of course, Martí's own; see Martí, *Obras*, vol. 1, pt. 2, pp. 227–232.

90. Martí to Gonzalo de Quesada, February 15, 1895, ibid., vol. 1, pt. 2, pp. 232–235.

91. Martí to Quesada and Benjamín Guerra, April 15, 1895; Martí to Federico Henríquez y Carvajal, March 25, 1895, ibid., vol. 1, pt. 2, pp. 247–249, 251–255.

92. Martí to Quesada, April 1, 1895, ibid., vol. 1, pt. 2, pp. 3–6.

93. Ibid., vol. 1, pt. 2, pp. 240–247.

94. Martí to Manuel Mercado, May 18, 1895, ibid., vol. 1, pt. 2, pp. 271–273.

95. Martí to Henríquez y Carvajal, ibid., vol. 1, pt. 2, pp. 251–255.

96. Martí left an account of Maceo's demands in his letter to him of February 26, 1895, ibid., vol. 1, pt. 2, pp. 235–236.

97. See the general order to the forces in Oriente issued by Maceo upon his arrival. Text in Roig de Leuchsenring, ed., *Ideario cubano*, vol. 3, *Antonio Maceo*, p. 29; also Rufino Pérez Landa, *Bartolomé Masó y Márquez*, p. 94. See letter, Cisneros Betancourt to Estrada Palma, December 6, 1895, Cuba, *BAN* 22 (1923): 184–197.

98. Benigno Souza, *Máximo Gómez*, p. 163.

99. Neither Gómez nor Maceo ever made more than oblique references to this meeting. Martí is the only one of the participants who left an account of what happened in his diary. Martí, *Obras*, vol. 1, pt. 2, pp.285–286.

100. This is what romanticized versions of the event would like us to believe, as does Manuel Isidro Méndez's *Acerca de La Mejorana y Dos Ríos*, p. 13. One of the few dispassionate studies published thus far on this matter is Carlos Ripoll's "Grandezas y miserias de La Mejorana."

101. For a sample of this sort of speculation see, for instance, Gerardo Castellanos, *Los últimos días de Martí*, pp. 255, 258, or Francisco Ponte Domínguez, *La idea invasora y su desarrollo histórico*, p. 18.

102. See letter, Martí to Quesada and Guerra, April 30, 1895, Martí, *Obras*, vol. 1, pt. 2, pp. 259–263.

103. Ibid.

104. Castellanos, *Los últimos días de Martí*, pp. 258–259.

105. Martí, *Obras*, vol. 1, pt. 2, p. 294.

106. Ibid., p. 296.

107. Martí's death has been exhaustively studied, as for example, in Rafael Lubián y Arias, *Martí en los campos de Cuba libre*.

108. For Maceo's opinion see Ripoll, "Grandezas y miserias." Gómez stated his own in a letter to Estrada Palma of August 22, 1895, Cuba, *BAN* 22 (1923): 209–211.

109. See, for instance, Cisneros Betancourt's letter to Masó of August 20, 1895, Cuba, *BAN* 21 (1922): 130–132.

110. Estrada Palma to Masó, July 17, 1895, quoted by Pérez Landa, *Masó,* pp. 113–114.

111. Cisneros Betancourt to Estrada Palma, August 22, 1895, Partido Revolucionario Cubano, *La revolución del 95 según la correspondencia de la delegación cubana en New York,* 1:60.

112. Maceo to Masó, July 14, 1895, Roig de Leuchsenring, *Ideario Cubano,* vol. 3, *Maceo,* pp. 42–44; Landa, *Masó,* pp. 111–112.

113. See Joaquín Llaverías and Emeterio Santovenia, eds., *Actas de las Asambleas de Representantes y del Consejo de Gobierno durante la guerra de independencia,* 1:1–32. For some pertinent comments see Ramón de Armas, "La revolución pospuesta: destino de la revolución martiana de 1895," pp. 56–57.

114. Cisneros Betancourt to Masó, July 16, 1895, Pérez Landa, *Masó,* pp. 112–113.

115. On the social composition of the assembly see Miguel Varona Guerrero, *La guerra de independencia de Cuba,* 1:630; also Enrique Collazo, *Cuba independiente,* p. 195.

116. The delegate in question was Enrique Loynaz del Castillo, *La constituyente de Jimaguayú,* p. 19.

117. Ibid., p. 20. Gómez later gave a more self-satisfying explanation of his attitude in a letter of September 20, 1895, to Federico Henríquez y Carvajal, Cuba, *BAN* 22 (1923): 215–216.

118. Franco, *Antonio Maceo,* 2:136.

119. For the text of the constitution see Cuba, Secretaría de Gobernación, *Documentos históricos,* pp. 25–28.

120. See Gómez's letter to General Francisco Carrillo, May 29, 1896, Bernabé Boza, *Mi diario de la guerra,* 1:253.

121. The secretary used this expression after the Jimaguayú assembly, Llaverías and Santovenia, *Actas,* 1:5–8.

122. From a note written on the back of a communication from the secretary of the interior (April 26, 1896), quoted by Leopoldo Horrego Estuch, *Máximo Gómez,* p. 178.

123. Maceo to Manuel Sanguily, November 21, 1895, Roig de Leuchsenring, *Ideario cubano,* vol. 3, *Antonio Maceo,* pp. 155–157.

124. Loynaz del Castillo, *La constituyente de Jimaquayú,* p. 23.

125. See, for instance, Eduardo Rosell y Malpica, *Diario del teniente coronel Eduardo Rosell y Malpica, 1895–1897,* vol. 1, p. 28, and Enrique Collazo, *Cuba heroica,* pp. 195–197.

126. The Government Council severely censured Estrada Palma's behavior, Llaverías and Santovenia, *Actas,* 1:104–105.

127. See letter, Maceo to Estrada Palma, September 22, 1895, Roig de Leuchsenring, *Ideario cubano,* vol. 3, *Antonio Maceo,* pp. 71–73.

128. See letter, Gómez to Estrada Palma, Cuba, *BAN* 23 (1924): 317–319.

129. For a sensible and objective treatment of this subject see Philip S. Foner, *The Spanish-Cuban-American War and the Birth of American Imperialism*, 1:21–26, 47–48, 67.

130. Fermoselle, *The Evolution of the Cuban Military*, p. 80.

131. For the Spanish reinforcements shipped to Cuba during the Little War see Pérez Guzmán and Sarracino, *La Guerra Chiquita*, p. 193.

132. Delgado, "The Spanish Army in Cuba," 2:130.

133. Ibid., 131.

134. On the subject of the relative strength of Cubans and Spaniards see Varona Guerrero, *La guerra de independencia*, 2:409; Duarte, *Historiología*, 2:331; José Miró Argenter, *Cuba: crónicas de la guerra*, 1:266–268; Enrique José Varona, *De la colonia a la república*, p. 167.

135. Melchor Fernández Almagro, *Historia política de la España contemporánea* 2:258.

136. Horrego, *Máximo Gómez*, p. 187; Franco, *Antonio Maceo*, 3:363–364.

137. Foner, *The Spanish-Cuban-American War*, 1:208.

138. U.S. Department of State. *Papers Relating to the Foreign Relations of the United States*, 1897, pp. xxix–xxx.

139. Ibid., p. lxxxii.

140. Thomas A. Bailey, *A Diplomatic History of the American People*, p. 496.

141. For García's attitude see his letter to Estrada Palma of January 3, 1897, Cuba, *BAN* 23 (1924): 305–306.

142. Cosme de la Torriente, *La constituyente de La Yaya*, pp. 41–44.

143. Souza, *Máximo Gómez*, p. 246.

144. Llaverías and Santovenia, *Actas*, 2:99–102.

145. Text in Boza, *Mi diario*, 2:14–17; Domingo Méndez Capote, *Trabajos*, 1:31–35.

146. The text of the charter may be found in Cuba, *Documentos históricos*, pp. 28–34.

147. Delgado, "The Spanish Army in Cuba," 2:131; Payne, *Politics and the Military in Modern Spain*, pp. 69–79. To regular Spanish troops it is necessary to add some 60,000 Spanish or pro-Spanish irregulars.

148. Fernández Almagro, *Historia política*, 2:325.

2. The Impact of U.S. Intervention

1. Herminio Portell Vilá, *Historia de Cuba en sus relaciones con los Estados Unidos y España*, 3:465–466.

2. See, for instance, letter, Estrada Palma to Maceo, August 20, 1895, General Antonio Maceo, *Documentos para su vida*, p. 143.

3. There is some evidence that indeed some of the letters that Estrada Palma sent to Cuba at this time never arrived. See Cosme de la Torriente, *Calixto García cooperó con las fuerzas armadas de los Estados Unidos en 1898 cumpliendo órdenes del gobierno cubano*, pp. 36–43.

4. Delgado, "The Spanish Army in Cuba," 2:259.

5. The best source concerning the letter is Horatio S. Rubens, *Liberty: The Story of Cuba*, pp. 287–292.

6. Thomas, *Cuba: The Pursuit of Freedom*, has a good chapter (30) on the *Maine*'s tragedy.

7. See letter, Ricardo Díaz Albertini to Estrada Palma, January 24, 1898. Partido Revolucionario Cubano, *Correspondencia diplomática de la delegación cubana en Nueva York durante la guerra de independencia de 1895 a 1898*, 5:123; also Calixto García to Estrada Palma, March 22, 1898, Cuba, *BAN* 35 (1936): 102–103.

8. Llaverías and Santovenia, *Actas*, 4:7–50; Pérez Landa, *Masó*, pp. 231–35; Enrique Collazo, *Los americanos en Cuba*, 2:104–106, 117–118.

9. Méndez Capote, *Trabajos*, 3:150–151.

10. For a few sarcastic comments on Estrada Palma's silence and the embarrassing situation of the Council see Gómez, *Diario*, p. 409.

11. Blanco met with a rebuff in both cases. Foner, *The Spanish-Cuban-American War*, 1:261; Rubens, *Liberty*, p. 347; Collazo, *Los americanos en Cuba*, 1:129.

12. Llaverías and Santovenia, *Actas*, 4:54–57.

13. Rubens, a New York lawyer who had been Martí's friend and was sympathetic to the Junta, later claimed that Teller wrote the "self-denying ordinance" at his suggestion. See Rubens, *Liberty*, pp. 341–42. Estrada Palma himself attributed it rather to the efforts of a New York financial syndicate to which he promised large amounts of Cuban bonds in return for the evacuation of Cuba and the recognition of its independence by both Spain and the United States. Llaverías and Santovenia, *Actas*, 4:54–57.

14. Quoted by Foner, *The Spanish-Cuban-American War*, 1:277.

15. Rubens, *Liberty*, pp. 326–29; also, the public statement by Gonzalo de Quesada quoted by Foner, *The Spanish-Cuban-American War*, 1:248.

16. Llaverías and Santovenia, *Actas*, 4:54–57.

17. Ibid., 61–66; also Méndez Capote, *Trabajos*, 3:165–170, 174–177, 178–179, 180.

18. See letter, Maceo to Estrada Palma, April 14, 1896, Maceo, *Documentos*, p. 137.

19. Text in Rubens, *Liberty*, p. 347.

20. Gómez to General Jesús Rabí and Méndez Capote, undated but probably written around May 1898, Amalia Rodríguez, *Algunos documentos políticos de Máximo Gómez*, pp. 22–23. See also Gómez, *Diario*, pp. 410, 413–414.

21. Llaverías and Santovenia, *Actas*, 4:51–54. Also Collazo, *Los americanos en Cuba*, 1:129.

22. Llaverías and Santovenia, *Actas*, 4:7–13.

23. The full text of Gómez's plan has been reprinted by Infiesta, *Gómez*, pp. 224–25; further details in Llaverías and Santovenia, *Actas*, 4:51–54.

24. Torriente, *Calixto García cooperó*, p. 33.

25. Ibid.

26. There are indications that García knew of the change in plans but failed to inform his chief. See Rosell Malpica, *Diario*, 2:343.

27. See letter, Gómez to Estrada Palma, June 1898, Cuba, *BAN* 31 (1932): 107–108.

28. Boza, *Mi diario*, 2:268–75; Souza, *Máximo Gómez*, p. 287.

29. Foner, *The Spanish-Cuban-American War*, 2:344–46; see in this connection N. G. González, *In Darkest Cuba*, pp. 89–96.

30. See letter, García to Estrada Palma, August 29, 1896, Cuba, *BAN* 23 (1924): 295–296. García reiterated his offer in a letter to Gómez of May 11, 1898; text in Aníbal Escalante Beatón, *Calixto García, su campaña en el 95*, pp. 413–414.

31. See letter, García to Estrada Palma, May 11, 1897, Cuba, *BAN* 33 (1934): 72–73.

32. See letter, García to Gómez, April 28, 1897; text in Valeriano Weyler, *Mi mando en Cuba*, 5:289–292.

33. Gómez to Méndez Capote, May 4, 1898, Rodríguez, *Algunos documentos*, pp. 26–30.

34. Carlos Manuel de Céspedes y Quesada, *Un instante decisivo de la maravillosa carrera de Máximo Gómez*, p. 29. According to Varona Guerrero, *La guerra de independencia*, 3:1564, García Menocal later stated that he had always been ready to march west, thereby implying that his delay was entirely attributable to Calixto García, his superior. To the commander in chief, however, both officers were equally guilty of insubordination. See Gómez, *Diario*, pp. 358–359.

35. Gómez, *Diario*, p. 363.

36. Llaverías and Santovenia, *Actas*, 4:106–108.

37. Gómez to Ernesto Fonts, July 19, 1898, quoted by Torriente, *Calixto García cooperó*, pp. 58–59.

38. Estrada Palma to Gómez, May 27, 1898, ibid., pp. 36–43.

39. Gómez to Ernesto Fonts, July 31, 1898, Rodríguez, *Algunos documentos*, pp. 39–44.

40. Gómez to Estrada Palma, June 1898, Cuba, *BAN* 31 (1932): 107–108.

41. An allusion to Ulises Hereaux, who tyrannized the Dominican Republic between 1882 and 1899.

42. García to Méndez Capote, May 1, 1898; text in Collazo, *Los americanos en Cuba*, 1:168–174.

43. See, for instance, García to Estrada Palma, March 22, 1898, Cuba, *BAN* 25 (1906): 102–103.

44. See, for example, Fernández Almagro, *Historia política*, 2:309. This historian even suggests that García acquired his sense of discipline while he worked at a bank in Madrid!

45. García to Estrada Palma, July 28, 1896, Cuba, *BAN* 23 (1924): 291–293.

46. García to Estrada Palma, September 24, 1897, Cuba, *BAN* 33 (1934): 86–87.

47. See García's circular of June 7, 1896; text in Juan J. E. Casasús, *Calixto García, el estratega*, p. 60.

48. Costa, *Perfil político*, pp. 23–24.

49. Costa, *Perfil político*, pp. 23–24; also, García to Estrada Palma, June 27, 1898, Cuba, *BAN* 35 (January–December 1936): 108–112.

50. García to Estrada Palma, August 31, 1897, Cuba, *BAN* 26 (1927): 108–112.

51. García to Estrada Palma, August 15, 1897, Cuba, *BAN* 32 (1934): 81–83.

52. García to Estrada Palma, September 24, 1897, Cuba, *BAN* 33 (1934): 86–87.

53. García to Estrada Palma, August 15, 1897, Cuba, *BAN* 32 (1934): 81–83.

54. García to Estrada Palma, May 26, 1897, Cuba, *BAN* 26 (1927): 73–75.

55. See letter, García to Méndez Capote, May 1, 1898, Collazo, *Los americanos en Cuba*, 1:168–174.

56. García to the Government Council, April 18, 1898, ibid., p. 168.

57. García to Estrada Palma, April 26, 1898, Cuba, *BAN* 35 (1936): 104–105.

58. It is Rubens who tells us that Rowan's visit put García in an embarrassing position. Rubens, *Liberty*, p. 386.

59. For the text of García's note and a factual account of Rowan's uneventful journey to Cuba see Escalante Beatón, *Calixto García*, pp. 377–406. Rowan's own account, *How I Carried the Message to García*, is an exercise in self-glorification.

60. Horrego Estuch, *Máximo Gómez*, p. 213. García attempted to justify himself in the communication (May 11) whereby he informed Gómez about Rowan's visit. Text in Escalante Beatón, *Calixto García*, pp. 413–414.

61. The situation in the interior of Oriente was such that García could claim that there was more danger on Broadway than in the territory that he controlled! See letter, García to Estrada Palma, May 26, 1897, Cuba, *BAN* 26 (1927): 73–75.

62. García to Miles, June 6, 1898, Escalante Beatón, *Calixto García*, pp. 429–430.

63. García to Gómez, June 7, 1898, ibid., p. 431; see also, in this connection, Céspedes y Quesada, *Un instante decisivo*, pp. 20–23.

64. See, for example, García's communication of June 7, 1898, to the Cuban secretary of war, Escalante y Beatón, *Calixto García*, p. 430.

65. Estrada Palma to García, June 16, 1898, Torriente, *Calixto García cooperó*, pp. 27–28; for Estrada Palma's suggestion to the Council see Pánfilo D. Camacho, *Estrada Palma, el gobernante honrado*, p. 153.

66. García to Estrada Palma, June 27, 1898, Cuba, *BAN* 35 (1936): 108–112.

67. Masó to José Miró Argenter, June 23, 1898, Pérez Landa, *Masó*, p. 247.

68. For Méndez Capote's opinion see Llaverías and Santovenia, *Actas*, 4:126–128; also Méndez Capote, *Trabajos*, 3:197–215. Estrada Palma set forth his views in a letter to Masó of June 6, 1899, Pérez Landa, *Masó*, p. 301.

69. García to Estrada Palma, June 27, 1890, *Cuba, BAN* 35 (1936): 108–112.

70. Louis A. Pérez, Jr., *Cuba between Empires, 1878–1902*, p. 203.

71. Collazo, *Los americanos en Cuba*, 1:162.

72. Ibid., 2:122–124.

73. David F. Healy, *The United States in Cuba*, p. 59.

74. See, for instance, Collazo, *Los americanos en Cuba*, 2:122–124; also Manuel Piedra Martel, *Campañas de Maceo en la última guerra de independencia*, pp. 340–341, and J. Buttari Gaunard, *Boceto histórico crítico*, pp. 56–65.

75. Horatio S. Rubens, "The Insurgent Government in Cuba," p. 563.

76. García to Silva, May 1, 1898, Cuba, *BAN* 35 (1936), 106–107. García also wrote to Estrada Palma on this matter. See his letter to the head of the New York Junta of April 26, 1898, ibid., pp. 104–105.

77. See letter, García to Estrada Palma, September 30, 1896, Cuba, *BAN* 23 (1924): 297–298. García's threat appears in his letter to Méndez Capote of May 1, 1898, Collazo, *Los americanos en Cuba*, 1:168–174.

78. See García's letter to Estrada Palma of June 27, 1898, Cuba, *BAN* 35 (1936): 108–112.

79. See the text of the circular in Torriente, *Calixto García cooperó*, pp. 75–79; Escalante Beatón, *Calixto García*, pp. 359–342.

80. Gómez's remarks on García's circular were written on the back of the copy that he kept among his papers; quoted by Rodríguez, *Algunos documentos*, p. 37.

81. García to Gómez, August 23, 1898, Cuba, BAN 35 (1936): 119–121.

82. Escalante Beatón, *Calixto García*, pp. 536–537.

83. Ibid., p. 543. It is noteworthy that the general did not bother to send it to the government, from which he had received his post.

84. The introductory paragraphs of García's circular clearly reveal the state of confusion that then prevailed among the Cuban insurgents.

85. By this time García followed a there-is-no-government policy, which is the reason why he no longer reported to the Government Council on his military activities. His reports, as his letter of resignation, were addressed to Gómez. See, for example, Calixto García, *Parte oficial al General en Jefe sobre la campaña de Santiago de Cuba*, passim. It must be noted also that the general used to speak in belittling tones of his position of lieutenant general and had attempted to relinquish it before. See letter, García to Estrada Palma, December 25, 1897, Cuba, *BAN* 26 (1927): 94–95.

86. See letter, García to Estrada Palma, August 22, 1898; also García to Gómez, August 23, 1898, Cuba, *BAN* 35 (1936): 121–123.

87. See García's letter to Estrada Palma of August 1, 1898; Estrada Palma urged García not to give up his command. See Camacho, *Estrada Palma*, p. 166.

88. See García's letter to Estrada Palma of June 27, 1898.

89. Méndez Capote, *Trabajos*, 3:78.

90. Llaverías and Santovenia, *Actas*, 4:119–122.

91. Ibid.

92. Among them, Torriente, *Calixto García cooperó*, p. 35.

93. See Duarte, *Historiología*, 2:307–308.

3. The Liberators As a Political Force

1. See letter, García to Méndez Capote, May 1, 1898, Collazo, *Los americanos en Cuba*, 1:168–174.

2. *New York Herald*, September 25, 1898. García's statement was subsequently reprinted in Spanish in the Havana newspaper *La Lucha*, September 30, 1898.

3. It is known, for example, that Gómez manipulated the election of the delegates to the assembly of La Yaya. See Torriente, *La constituyente de La Yaya*, pp. 16–17. Orestes Ferrara, a young Italian former anarchist who joined the insurgents, has left us a shrewd assessment of their constituencies: "Soldiers do not vote. An army is not free; it is under the control of its commanders. Soldiers simply cannot have an opinion of their own." Orestes Ferrara, *Mis relaciones con Máximo Gómez*, p. 215.

4. Gómez to Méndez Capote, May 14, 1898, Rodríguez, *Algunos documentos*, pp. 31–34.

5. Gómez to Estrada Palma, June 1898, Cuba, *BAN* 31 (1932): 107–108.

6. García to Estrada Palma, August 15, 1897, Cuba, *BAN* 32 (1934): 81–83.

7. U.S. Department of War, *Report on the Census of Cuba, 1899*, p. 72.

8. Thomas, *Cuba: The Pursuit of Freedom*, p. 461.

9. Cuba, Army, Inspección General, *Indice alfabético y defunciones del Ejército Libertador de Cuba*, pp. iv–v.

10. Gómez, *Diario*, pp. 421, 424.

11. See, for example, Souza, *Máximo Gómez*, pp. 210–211.

12. U.S. Department of War, *Civil Report of Major General John R. Brooke*, pp. 15–17; Robert P. Porter, *Report on the Commercial and Industrial Conditions of Cuba*, pp. 204–210.

13. Souza, *Máximo Gómez*, pp. 210–211.

14. See Fernández Almagro, *Historia política*, 2:246–247.

15. Delgado, "The Spanish Army in Cuba," 2:56–57.

16. Ibid., pp. 266–277.

17. Souza, *Máximo Gómez*, pp. 210–211.

18. Delgado, "The Spanish Army in Cuba," 2:271, n. 1.

19. Edwin F. Atkins, *Sixty Years in Cuba*, p. 178.

20. Rafael Fermoselle, *Política y color*, p. 26.

21. Fermoselle, *The Evolution of the Cuban Military*, p. 78.

22. Fermoselle, *Política y color*, p. 26.

23. Mario Riera Hernández, *Ejército Libertador de Cuba, 1895–1898*, pp. 24–25, 46–47.

24. Grover Flint completely misread the situation in *Marching with Gómez*, p. 274.

25. At the time the colored population of Cuba was estimated at slightly over half a million. José R. Alvarez Díaz et al., *Un estudio sobre Cuba*, pp. 11–19.

26. Atkins, *Sixty Years*, p. 186.

27. PRC, *Correspondencia diplomática*, 5:176–177.

28. See John Lynch, *The Spanish-American Revolutions, 1808–1826*, pp. 221–222.

29. Ibid.; see also p. 274.

30. Gómez to Estrada Palma, November 25, 1897, Cuba, *BAN* 33 (1932): 88.

31. U.S. Department of War, *Census of Cuba, 1899*, p. 72.

32. Special Report of General William Ludlow, September 15, 1899, in *Civil Report of Major General John R. Brooke*, p. 360.

33. Ibid., pp. 366–367; see also letter, General Emilio Núñez to Gonzalo de Quesada, January 2, 1899, Gonzalo de Quesada y Miranda, ed., *Archivo de Gonzalo de Quesada, Epistolario*, 2:237–239.

34. U.S. Department of War, *Census of Cuba, 1899*, p. 41; also James H. Hitchman, *Leonard Wood and Cuban Independence*, pp. 60–61.

35. U.S. Department of War, *Census of Cuba, 1899*, pp. 543, 553.

36. Ibid., pp. 512, 540.

37. Alvarez Díaz et al., *Un estudio sobre Cuba*, p. 150.

38. Ibid., p. 156.

39. Atkins, *Sixty Years*, p. 287.

40. The first moratorium was total; the second was partial. Alvarez Díaz et al., *Un estudio sobre Cuba*, pp. 57–58.

41. Alberto Arredondo, *Cuba: Tierra indefensa*, p. 156. For the property mortgage figures see *Census of Cuba, 1899*, p. 41.

42. Pérez, Jr., *Cuba: Between Reform and Revolution*, p. 195.

43. The picture of total destruction presented by traditional Cuban historiography is currently under revision. See Manuel Moreno Fraginals, "Plantations in the Caribbean: Cuba, Puerto Rico, and the Dominican Republic in the Late Nineteenth Century," in Manuel Moreno Fraginals, Frank Moya Pons, and Stanley L. Eugerman, eds., *Between Slavery and Free Labor: The Spanish-speaking Caribbean in the Nineteenth Century*, pp. 20–21. For the conventional view see Alvarez Díaz et al., *Un estudio sobre Cuba*, pp. 96–97; U.S. Department of War, *Census of Cuba, 1899*, pp. 551, 563–564; Heinrich E. Friedländer, *Historia económica de Cuba*, p. 423; Leland H. Jenks, *Our Cuban Colony*, pp. 30–35; Guerra et al., *Historia de la nación cubana*, 9:287–292.

44. Alvarez Díaz et al., *Un estudio sobre Cuba*, pp. 204–205.

45. Moreno Fraginals, "Plantations in the Caribbean," p. 17; also Ramiro Guerra, *Azúcar y población en las Antillas*, p. 89; Guerra et al., *Historia de la nación cubana*, 7:151–244; Alvarez Díaz et al., *Un estudio sobre Cuba*, pp. 116–172.

46. The consequences of the Spanish war policies that deprived 4,424

individuals of their possessions are studied by Joaquín Llaverías, *El consejo administrativo de bienes embargados,* p. 38; also Justo Zaragoza, *Las insurrecciones de Cuba,* 1:508–509. One of the worst cases was that of Francisco Vicente Aguilera, who owned three sugar mills, several coffee estates and stock farms, thirty-five thousand head of cattle, four thousand horses, and five hundred slaves. In various ways most of this empire was swallowed up by the maelstrom of the war. See Eladio Aguilera Rojas, *Francisco Vicente Aguilera,* 1:19–20, 420.

47. On the abolition of slavery the most recent major study is that of Rebecca J. Scott, *Slave Emancipation in Cuba: The Transition to Free Labor, 1860–1899.*

48. According to the Association of Planters and Farmers of the Island of Cuba, the crisis of 1884 was the worst that the industry had encountered in a century. See Círculo de Hacendados y Agricultores de la Isla de Cuba, *Exposición dirigida en julio 8, 1894 por el Círculo de Hacendados y Agricultores de la Isla de Cuba a las Cortes del Reino español en la cual se señalaban las principales causas que por su continuidad producían la excesiva gravedad de la crisis que atravesaba la industria azucarera y las soluciones que había que aplicar entonces con toda urgencia para evitar su inminente ruina,* p. 34. See also Jenks, *Our Cuban Colony,* pp. 30–33; Ramiro Guerra, *La industria azucarera de Cuba,* pp. 98–99.

49. The parvenus acquired most of the farmland lost by the Ten Years' War insurgents and their sympathizers. See Figueras, *Cuba y su evolución colonial,* p. 179; also Elías Entrialgo, *Períoca sociográfica de la cubanidad,* p. 42.

50. The best study of the Cuban sugar aristocracy is Roland T. Ely, *Cuando reinaba Su Majestad El Azúcar.*

51. As pointed out by Entrialgo, *Períoca,* p. 43, the number of truly rich Cubans was rather small in 1895, and it contracted even further as the war progressed. The condition of the Cuban propertied class in 1899 may be gauged by what Atkins wrote to President McKinley on March 7 of that year; see Atkins, *Sixty Years,* pp. 306–307.

52. On the history of the Cuban church as a whole see Gustavo Amigó, S.J., "La Iglesia Católica en Cuba"; Figueras, *Cuba y su evolución colonial,* chap. 8; Ismael Testé, *Historia eclesiástica de Cuba;* Reinerio Lebroc, *Episcopologio;* Fernando Fernández Escobio, *El obispo Compostela y la Iglesia cubana en el siglo XVII;* Miguel Figueroa, *Religión y política en la Cuba del siglo XIX.*

53. For Spanish background materials see Stanley G. Payne, *Spanish Catholicism;* for developments in Cuba see Juan Martín Leiseca, *Apuntes para la histórica eclesiástica de Cuba,* pp. 151–156.

54. See Reinerio Lebroc, *Cuba: Iglesia y sociedad,* pp. 132–140.

55. Manuel P. Maza, S.J., "Between Ideology and Compassion: The Cuban Insurrection of 1895–98 through the Private Correspondence of Cuba's Two Prelates with the Holy See," pp. 66–81.

56. Quoted by Manuel P. Maza, S.J., "Cuba, Iglesia y Máximo Gómez," p. 49; for a study of the active role of masonry in Cuba's independence see

Francisco Ponte Domínguez, *La masonería en la independencia de Cuba;* for a Catholic approach see Richard Pattee and the Inter-American Committee, *Catholic Life in the West Indies,* pp. 18–21.

57. Maza, "Between Ideology and Compassion," pp. 423–438.

58. See Francisco González del Valle y Ramírez, "El clero en la revolución cubana."

59. For the unpopularity of Cuba's prelates at the time see Maza, "Between Ideology and Compassion," chaps. 8 and 9; for the reaction of the insurgents see letter, José A. González Lanuza to Gonzalo de Quesada, August 20, 1899, Quesada y Miranda, *Epistolario,* 2:237–239. A strong indication of Calixto García's feelings appears in Rubens, *Liberty,* p. 389. Máximo Gómez's attitude is studied by Maza, "Cuba, Iglesia y Máximo Gómez," pp. 51–62.

60. See Carlos M. Raggi, "Las estructuras sociales en Cuba en los fines de la etapa colonial."

61. Entrialgo, *Períoca,* p. 31; for an interesting attempt to quantify the various components of the Cuban social classes at this time, see Fe Iglesias, "Población y clases sociales en la segunda mitad del siglo XIX."

62. U.S. Department of War, *Census of Cuba, 1899,* p. 148.

63. Ibid., pp. 96–98.

64. Thomas, *Cuba: The Pursuit of Freedom,* p. 429.

65. U.S. Department of War, *Census of Cuba, 1899,* p. 153.

66. Ibid., pp. 403, 405, 460–465, 544–558.

67. Ibid., p. 137.

68. Even Antonio Maceo himself never discussed what his political future would be once victory over Spain was secured. See Miró Argenter, *Crónicas de la guerra,* 3:265. When he was appointed second in command of the army in 1895 many feared the prospect that one day he might become commander in chief. See Rosell y Malpica, *Diario,* 1:29. Maceo's foremost biographer believes that the racial issue underlay many of the continual difficulties that the general experienced with the civilian leadership. See Franco, *Maceo,* 2:175, 198; 3:176, 199–226, 235, 366.

69. U.S. Department of War, *Census of Cuba, 1899,* p. 69.

70. See, on the Cuban Autonomist party, Antonio Martínez Bello, *Orígen y meta del autonomismo, exégesis de Montoro;* Rafael Montoro, *El ideario autonomista;* Ramón Infiesta, *El autonomismo cubano: su razón y manera;* Antonio Sánchez de Bustamante y Montoro, *La ideología autonomista;* Eliseo Giberga, "Las ideas políticas en Cuba en el siglo XIX." The party's political platform has been published by Pichardo, *Documentos,* 1:419–422.

71. Tomás Estrada Palma was perhaps the most conspicuous example; for a study of the political thought of the emigrés see Gerald E. Poyo, "Evolution of Cuban Separatist Thought in the Emigré Communities of the United States, 1848–1895"; also Gerald E. Poyo, *With All and for the Good of All: The Emergence of Popular Nationalism in the Cuban Communities of the United States, 1848–1898,* passim.

72. See Flint, *Marching with Gómez,* p. 226.

73. The Cuban Revolutionary party underwent a transformation after the war broke out, but it is a mistake to attribute it to Estrada Palma, Martí's successor. The change was basically the consequence of the organization of the insurgent government, and it was carried out at the behest of Martí himself; see Martí's letter to Gonzalo de Quesada and Benjamín Guerra of February 26, 1895, Martí, *Obras*, vol. 1, pt. 2, pp. 237–240. After the Jimaguayú assembly Estrada Palma owed his position as head of the New York Junta to the army delegates, who confirmed him as Delegate Plenipotentiary and foreign representative of the Cuban republic following the recommendation of Máximo Gómez. This is the origin of the subsequent diplomatic orientation of the Junta; see the correspondence on this subject between Cisneros Betancourt and Gómez, on the one hand, and Estrada Palma and Gonzalo de Quesada, on the other, in Cuba, *BAN* 21 (1922), 126–130, 166–168; and Partido Revolucionario Cubano, *La revolución del 95*, 1:41–45; also Rosell Planas, *Las claves de Martí*, pp. 88–91.

74. See, for example, Ferrara, *Mis relaciones con Máximo Gómez*, p. 241.

4. The Disbandment of the Liberating Army

1. Gómez to Ernesto Fonts, July 31, 1898, Rodríguez, *Algunos documentos*, pp. 39–44.

2. Collazo, *Los americanos en Cuba*, 2:221.

3. Lawton to Adjutant General of the Army, August 16, 1898, U.S. Department of War, Adjutant General's Office, *Correspondence Relating to the War with Spain*, 1:230.

4. Shafter to Adjutant General of the Army, August 16, 1898, ibid.

5. Adjutant General of the Army to Lawton, August 16, 1898, ibid., p. 231.

6. Franklin Matthews, *The New-Born Cuba*, pp. 37–38.

7. U.S. Department of War, *Annual Report, 1899*, vol. 1, pt. 1, p. 156.

8. Circular de Casa Azul, Escalante Beatón, *Calixto García*, pp. 342–359.

9. Gómez to Ernesto Fonts, May 28, 1898, Rodríguez, *Algunos documentos*, pp. 35–38.

10. U.S. Department of War, *Civil Report of Major General John R. Brooke*, p. 3.

11. Matthews, *The New-Born Cuba*, pp. 37–38.

12. Gómez to Estrada Palma, June 1898, Cuba, *BAN* 31 (1932): 107–108.

13. García to Estrada Palma, August 22, 1898, Cuba, *BAN* 35 (1936): 121–122.

14. Gómez, *Diario de campaña*, p. 356.

15. García to Estrada Palma, Cuba, *BAN* 35 (1936): 121–122.

16. Gómez to Estrada Palma, Cuba, *BAN* 31 (1932): 107–108.

17. Text in Rodríguez, *Algunos documentos*, pp. 45–46.

18. Gómez to Estrada Palma, Cuba, *BAN* 31 (1932): 107–108.

19. García to Estrada Palma, June 27, 1898, Cuba, *BAN* 35 (1936): 108–112.

20. The manifesto is discussed in chapter 1.

21. Fernández Almagro, *Historia política,* 2:307; for the text of a similar order signed by Gómez in November 1895 see Colonel Ramón M. Barquín, *Las luchas guerrilleras en Cuba: de la colonia a la Sierra Maestra,* 1:23.

22. Public letter to Estrada Palma, August 26, 1898, Cuba, *BAN* 32 (1933): 92–93.

23. Rodríguez, *Algunos documentos,* pp. 45–46.

24. Máximo Gómez, *La independencia de Cuba o el general Máximo Gómez y su política de paz, unión y concordia,* p. 25.

25. Ibid., pp. 28–29.

26. Ibid.

27. "Mayía" Rodríguez, José Miguel Gómez, José de Jesús Monteagudo, Pedro Betancourt, and Quintín Banderas figure among the rebel generals who did so; their views are quoted in ibid., pp. 45–48.

28. See the manifesto addressed by the Council to the inhabitants of areas not occupied by the liberating army; text in Méndez Capote, *Trabajos,* 3:231–45; similar statements by the Council appeared in *Patria,* June 15, 1898, and in the "Exposition to the President of the United States" released on September 1, 1898; for the text of the "Exposition" see also Méndez Capote, *Trabajos,* 3:219–224.

29. That such was not the case is evidenced by Richard B. Gray, *José Martí, Cuban Patriot,* p. 88, and Enrico Santí, "José Martí and the Cuban Revolution."

30. García to Estrada Palma, August 22, 1898, Cuba, *BAN* 35 (1936): 121–122.

31. Gómez to Ernesto Fonts, July 31, 1898, Rodríguez, *Algunos documentos,* pp. 38–44.

32. See, for example, Gómez to Bernabé Boza, August 25, 1900, Boza, *Mi diario,* 2:318–319.

33. Both generals remained involved in public affairs until their deaths. The contradictions that they incurred in this connection were not at all atypical. After telling Estrada Palma one day that it was no longer necessary for him to concern himself with public affairs, for example, García assured his friend on the following day that he was still interested in the lot of the Oriente army; and shortly afterward he had this to say about his dismissal by the Council: "Since I no longer have to answer for my actions as a soldier, I am at liberty to devote my energy to whatever may contribute to the happiness of the fatherland." See his letters to Estrada Palma of August 23 and 24, 1898, Cuba, *BAN* 35 (1936): 124–25. At about the same time, and regardless of his resignation and other statements to the contrary, Gómez publicly stated that he was "quite willing to help to consolidate peace in this land to which I owe so much." See his public letter to Estrada Palma, Cuba, *BAN* 32 (1933): 92–93.

34. García to Estrada Palma, Cuba, *BAN* 35 (1936): 121–122.

35. Gómez to Boza, *Mi diario*, 2:318–319.

36. Ibid.

37. This is how the possible political role of the insurgents was described at the Santa Cruz del Sur assembly; Llaverías and Santovenia, *Actas*, 4:37–46.

38. Most particularly those of Calixto García, as previously discussed.

39. Gómez, *Diario de campaña*, p. 384.

40. Gómez to Ernesto Fonts, Rodríguez, *Algunos documentos*, pp. 39–44.

41. Llaverías and Santovenia, *Actas*, 4:37–46.

42. Fermoselle, *The Evolution of the Cuban Military*, p. 93.

43. "Exposition to the President of the United States," in Méndez Capote, *Trabajos*, 3:219–224.

44. Ibid.

45. Text in Pichardo, *Documentos*, 1:522–535.

46. As, for example, their retirement from public life.

47. Rubens, *Liberty*, p. 378; Collazo, *Los americanos en Cuba*, 2:151; Shafter to Adjutant General of the Army, July 23, 1898, in U.S. Senate, *Report of the Commission Appointed by the President to Investigate the Conduct of the War Department in the War with Spain*, 2:1042.

48. Hermann Hagedorn, *Leonard Wood*, 1:199.

49. See, in this connection, Horacio Ferrer, *Con el rifle al hombro*, pp. 135–137; Collazo, *Los americanos en Cuba*, 2:189–190; Rafael Martínez Ortiz, *Cuba: los primeros años de independencia*, 1:32–33.

50. García to Estrada Palma, August 23, 1898, Cuba, *BAN* 35 (1936): 124–125.

51. García to Estrada Palma, August 22, 1898, ibid., pp. 121–122.

52. Shafter to Adjutant General of the Army, August 17, 1898, U.S. Senate, *Report of the Commission Appointed by the President to Investigate the Conduct of the War Department in the War with Spain*, 2:1102.

53. J. W. Heard to the Adjutant General of the Army, August 21, 1898, U.S. Department of War, *Annual Reports of the War Department: Report of the Major General Commanding the Army, 1898*, p. 376.

54. Jenks, *Our Cuban Colony*, p. 320.

55. García to Estrada Palma, August 22 and August 23, 1898, Cuba, *BAN* 35 (1936): 121–122; ibid., pp. 124–125.

56. Collazo, *Los americanos en Cuba*, 2:178.

57. *The State*, September 24, 1898, quoted by Foner, *The Spanish-Cuban-American War*, 2:400.

58. According to Pérez, Jr., *Cuba between Empires*, p. 245.

59. In an interview that he gave to a U.S. correspondent, as previously discussed.

60. *Washington Post*, November 9, 1898; *The State*, November 22, 1898, quoted by Foner, *The Spanish-Cuban-American War*, 2:401.

61. Hagedorn, *Leonard Wood*, 1:214.

62. García's own reckoning, as previously noted.

63. Llaverías and Santovenia, *Actas,* 4:138; see Masó's message to the Santa Cruz del Sur assembly in Pichardo, *Documentos,* 1:522–535.

64. Leonard Wood, "The Military Government of Cuba."

65. U.S. Department of War, *Civil Report of Major General John R. Brooke,* pp. 16–17.

66. Méndez Capote, *Trabajos,* 3:197–215; Llaverías and Santovenia, *Actas,* 4:126–128.

67. Orestes Ferrara, *Memorias,* p. 100.

68. According to Ferrara, *Mis relaciones con Máximo Gómez,* pp. 223–224.

69. See Masó's message to the Santa Cruz del Sur assembly, Pichardo, *Documentos,* 1:522–535; also General Pedro Betancourt's statement in *Patria,* October 1, 1898, and the letter of Emilio Núñez to Gonzalo de Quesada in Quesada y Miranda, *Epistolario,* 2:123.

70. "We have nothing to eat nor anything to fight with. The blockade has been more real and effective for me and my brave men than for anybody else." Gómez to Estrada Palma, June 1898, Cuba, *BAN* 31 (1932): 107–108; see also, in this connection, Ferrara, *Memorias,* pp. 98–100.

71. One liberator later recalled that suffering "hunger, disease, nakedness, and lack of shoes" was harder and more praiseworthy than facing the enemy on the battlefield. Varona Guerrero, *La guerra de independencia,* 2:854.

72. Avelino Sangenís, *Memorias de la revolución de 1895 para la independencia de Cuba,* p. 143. This is why, on October 27, 1898, General "Mayía" Rodríguez informed the Government Council that peace had deprived the Pinar del Río rebels of their usual means of subsistence. Llaverías and Santovenia, *Actas,* 4:145–152.

73. Gómez to Estrada Palma, October 28, 1898, Cuba, *BAN* 32 (1933): 94–95.

74. Varona Guerrero, *La guerra de independencia,* 3:1706.

75. Letter of José Miguel Gómez, chief of the Sancti Spíritus Brigade, quoted by Rubens, *Liberty,* p. 388; Gerardo Machado, chief of the Villa Clara Brigade, to Gonzalo de Quesada, February 10, 1899, Quesada y Miranda, *Epistolario,* 1:48–50.

76. Ferrara tells us, for example, that four soldiers died from lack of food at the camp of the Sancti Spíritus Brigade; see Ferrara, *Mis relaciones con Máximo Gómez,* p. 220.

77. See letter, Francisco Díaz Silveira to Gualterio García, August 31, 1898, in Gonzalo de Quesada y Miranda, *Archivo de Gonzalo de Quesada, documentos históricos,* p. 486.

78. Sangenís, *Memorias,* p. 144. The local representative of Edwin F. Atkins, in his correspondence, gives us some idea about how some rebel units were helped to survive; see Atkins, *Sixty Years,* pp. 289–290.

79. "The army is going without pay," García wrote to Gonzalo de Quesada on August 24, 1898. "It is naked and starving; the men simply have to go without their daily sustenance" (Quesada y Miranda, *Epistolario,*

2:176–177). To Estrada Palma, García had this to say: "The army, which has received nothing and sees that the remuneration for its services, small though it may be, is not forthcoming, is beginning to run out of patience; anxious to ease up their misery, the men will disband looking for jobs that will permit them to make ends meet" (García to Estrada Palma, August 23, 1898, Cuba, *BAN* 35 [1936]: 124–125).

80. Llaverías and Santovenia, *Actas*, 1:71–73. It has been pointed out that the wages approved by the Council were considerably higher than those paid to members of the U.S. Army; see Healy, *The United States in Cuba*, p. 46.

81. Llaverías and Santovenia, *Actos*, 1:71–73.

82. Ibid., 5:62–63; Pichardo, *Documentos*, 1:522–535.

83. Quesada assured the McKinley administration that the commission would not be antagonistic to U.S. policy; see *The State*, November 3, 1898, quoted by Foner, *The Spanish-Cuban-American War*, 2:400.

84. Albert G. Robinson, "Cuban Self-Government."

85. Llaverías and Santovenia, *Actas*, 5:43–62.

86. Rubens, *Liberty*, pp. 392–393.

87. Sergio Aguirre, "La desaparición del Ejército Libertador," pp. 54–55.

88. Llaverías and Santovenia, *Actas*, 5:152–153.

89. Rubens, *Liberty*, p. 389; "Memoria de la Comisión enviada a Washington, February 25, 1899," in Llaverías and Santovenia, *Actas*, 5:152–54; Robert P. Porter, *Report on the Commercial and Industrial Conditions of Cuba*, pp. 204–210.

90. García to Morgan, undated, in Llaverías and Santovenia, *Actas*, 5:160–165.

91. Ibid., pp. 82–83, 157.

92. Ibid.

93. U.S. Department of State, *Foreign Relations of the United States, 1898*, pp. lxvi–lxviii.

94. *New York Tribune*, December 6, 1898 and *New York World*, December 6, 1898, quoted by Foner, *The Spanish-Cuban-American War*, 2:404.

95. Cuban exiles began to prepare their return to their country as soon as it became clear that Spain would be defeated; see the reports received by Estrada Palma in New York in Partido Revolucionario Cubano, *Correspondencia diplomática*, 2:143–144, 248–249, 251, and in Fanny Azcuy y Alón, *El Partido Revolucionario Cubano y la independencia de Cuba*, p. 125.

96. *Patria*, October 15 and October 19, 1898; Luis A. de Arce, *Emilio Núñez*, pp. 192–194.

97. *Patria*, December 23, 1898.

98. See the correspondence published by Quesada y Miranda, *Epistolario*, 1:179–180, 187.

99. As estimated by Pérez, Jr., *Cuba between Empires*, p. 260; the figure seems somewhat exaggerated.

100. See the so-called Proclamation of Narcisa in Martínez Ortiz, *Cuba: los primeros años de independencia*, 1:33–34.

101. Ibid., pp. 20–27.

102. Atkins, *Sixty Years*, p. 300.

103. McKinley to Brooke, December 22, 1898, copy in William McKinley Papers, Library of Congress.

104. Fitzhugh Lee, "Special Report of Brigadier General Fitzhugh Lee, U.S.V.," September 18, 1899, in U.S. Department of War, *Civil Report of Major General John R. Brooke*, p. 343.

105. James Harrison Wilson to Adjutant General of the Army, U.S. Department of War, *Annual Reports of the War Department: Report of the Major General Commanding the Army, 1899*, p. 156.

106. Leonard Wood, "The Existing Conditions and Needs in Cuba."

107. U.S. Department of War, *Annual Reports of the Secretary of War, 1899–1903*, pp. 121–122.

108. Charles E. Chapman, *A History of the Cuban Republic*, p. 102.

109. Gómez, *Diario*, p. 383.

110. Gómez to Estrada Palma, October 29, 1898, Cuba, *BAN* 32 (1933): 94–95.

111. Gómez to Estrada Palma, August 26, 1898, Cuba, *BAN* 32 (1933): 92–93.

112. "Carta abierta a Bernarda Toro de Gómez y a los dominicanos," n.d., in Emilio Rodríguez Demorizi, *Cartas de Máximo Gómez*, pp. 50–51.

113. Gómez to Francisco Gregorio Billini, November 15, 1898. Emilio Rodríguez Demorizi, ed., *Papeles dominicanos de Máximo Gómez*, p. 76.

114. Gómez to Estrada Palma, December 9, 1898, Cuba, *BAN* 32 (1933): 96–97.

115. Gómez, *Diario*, p. 396.

116. Gómez to General Fernando Freyre de Andrade, January 18, 1899, Rodríguez, *Algunos documentos*, pp. 47–48.

117. Ferrara, *Mis relaciones con Máximo Gómez*, p. 220.

118. Ibid., pp. 193–195, 216.

119. Ibid.

120. Gómez to Executive Committee of the Cuban Assembly, January 6, 1899, Llaverías and Santovenia, *Actas*, 6:34–45.

121. Executive Committee of the Cuban Assembly to Gómez, January 11, 1899, ibid., pp. 35–37.

122. Proclamation of Narcisa, Martínez Ortiz, *Cuba: los primeros años de independencia*, 1:33–34.

123. "According to the agreement between Spain and the United States, the Spaniards will evacuate the island slowly and at their leisure. Afterward, the Americans will occupy it. Meanwhile, it is the unhappy lot of us Cubans to live in the wilds and to endure, in return for our services and sacrifices, hunger and nakedness"(Gómez, *Diario*, p. 386).

124. Ferrara, *Mis relaciones con Máximo Gómez*, pp. 193–194.

125. Gómez, *Diario*, pp. 367–368.

126. Gaspar Carbonell Rivero, ed., *Enrique J. Conill, soldado de la patria*, pp. 22–27.

127. Ferrara, *Mis relaciones con Máximo Gómez*, p. 220.

128. See, for example, Gómez to Gonzalo de Quesada, September 29, 1898, Quesada y Miranda, *Epistolario*, 2:230.

129. Gómez to Estrada Palma, September 16, 1898, Cuba, *BAN* 32 (1933): 94; also, Gómez to Estrada Palma, December 9, 1898, ibid., pp. 96–97.

130. Perhaps the most conspicuous examples that might be mentioned are Domingo Méndez Capote and José Antonio González Lanuza, who resigned from the army assembly to accept posts in Brooke's so-called Cuban cabinet.

131. "If I had been able to count on this people," Gómez sarcastically remarked after the war, "I would have expelled the Spaniards from Cuba long ago" (Varona Guerrero, *La guerra de independencia*, 3:1717–1718).

132. García to Estrada Palma, August 15, 1897, Cuba, *BAN* 32 (1934): 81–83.

133. The full text of García's proclamation appears in Cuba, *BAN* 35 (1936): 107–108. García frequently identified the target of his invectives as "Colonel X" or "Brigadier Z," but on occasion he referred to them by name, as was the case when he put the tag "bon vivant" on General José Lacret Morlot, a veteran of the Ten Years' War. See letter, García to Estrada Palma, March 22, 1898, Cuba, *BAN* 25 (1906): 102–103.

134. Albert G. Robinson, *Cuba and the Intervention*, p. 115.

135. Gómez's appeal to McKinley requesting aid for the army was not what motivated the president's decision; the general's message had been sent two months earlier; see Gómez's letter to Estrada Palma of October 28, 1898, Cuba, *BAN* 32 (1933): 94–95. See on this matter Portell Vilá, *Historia de Cuba*, 3:35.

136. When García and his colleagues were received by McKinley they were received as private citizens and not as representatives of a government; see Healy, *The United States in Cuba*, p. 45.

137. As Foner does, *The Spanish-Cuban-American War*, 2:433–434.

138. See, for instance, Gómez to General Francisco Carrillo, September 2, 1898, Hortensia Pichardo, ed., *Cartas a Francisco Carrillo*, p. 240; also Céspedes y Quesada, *Un instante decisivo*, p. 21.

139. Rubens, *Liberty*, pp. 391–392.

140. Porter's powers were so sweeping that he had no difficulty in getting the governor to sign this letter; see Healy, *The United States in Cuba*, p. 69.

141. Estrada Palma to Gómez, January 26, 1899, Quesada y Miranda, *Documentos históricos*, p. 8.

142. Aguirre, "La desaparición del Ejército Libertador," pp. 63–64, and Raul Roa, *Aventuras, venturas y desventuras de un mambí en la lucha por la independencia de Cuba*, pp. 194–220, attribute Gómez's favorable attitude to his lack of political sagacity, but the complexity of the situation is best reflected by Portell Vilá, *Historia de Cuba*, 3:39–40.

143. This is what Quesada told the Havana newspaper *La Discusión* on the eve of his meeting with the general; see Martínez Ortiz, *Cuba: los primeros años de independencia*, 1:40–41.

144. Robert P. Porter, "Special Report on the Commissioner's visit to

General Gómez and its relation to the payment and disbandment of the Cuban army," included in Robert P. Porter, *Reports on the Commercial and Industrial Conditions of Cuba.*

145. Ibid. According to Chapman, *A History of the Cuban Republic,* p. 101, Gómez suggested that $60 million would be needed to cover the pay of the men as well as the losses they had suffered; Porter later admitted that without Quesada it would have been impossible for him to achieve what he did in a single day's work; see letter, Porter to Rubens, February 7, 1899, Quesada y Miranda, *Documentos históricos,* p. 9.

146. Porter, "Special Report on the Commissioner's visit to General Gómez."

147. Ibid.

148. Quesada proclaimed that the United States would never annex Cuba against its will. Ibid.

149. "Carta abierta a Bernarda Toro de Gómez y a los dominicanos," in Rodríguez Demorizi, *Cartas de Máximo Gómez,* pp. 50–51.

150. Aguirre, "La desaparición del Ejército Libertador," p. 60; Martínez Ortiz, *Cuba: los primeros años de independencia,* 1:43–49.

151. See letter, Domingo Méndez Capote to José Miguel Gómez and others, February 14, 1899, Llaverías and Santovenia, *Actas,* 5:65.

152. See letter, Quesada to Gómez, February 10, 1899, Quesada y Miranda, *Documentos históricos,* pp. 10–11; also Llaverías and Santovenia, *Actas,* 5:75; 6:54–59, 63–64.

153. Portell Vilá, *Historia de Cuba,* 3:44–45.

154. U.S. Department of War, *Civil Report of Major General John R. Brooke,* p. 16.

155. Llaverías and Santovenia, *Actas,* 5:87–103.

156. Aguirre, "La desaparición del Ejército Libertador," pp. 64–65.

157. The text of the manifesto that they issued on March 12, 1899, appears in Martínez Ortiz, *Cuba: los primeros años de independencia,* 1:59–62.

158. Ibid., pp. 54–56.

159. About Sanguily's mixed feelings toward Gómez see José A. Rodríguez, *Manuel Sanguily,* p. 67. Rafael Cepeda, ed., *Manuel Sanguily frente a la dominación yanqui,* pp. 527–562.

160. Llaverías and Santovenia, *Actas,* 5:103–109.

161. Aguirre, "La desaparición del Ejército Libertador," p. 66; Martínez Ortiz, *Cuba: los primeros años de independencia,* 1:59.

162. Text in ibid., pp. 57–58.

163. This was his opinion even before learning about his dismissal; see his letter to Quesada of March 6, 1899, in Quesada y Miranda, *Documentos históricos,* pp. 12–13.

164. U.S. Department of War, *Civil Report of Major General John R. Brooke,* p. 16.

165. Brooke to Alger, March 14, 1899. Copy in William McKinley Papers, Library of Congress.

166. George Cartelyon to Russell Alger, March 15, 1899; Adjutant General of the Army to Brooke, March 17, 1899. Copies in ibid.

167. Llaverías and Santovenia, *Actas*, 5:113–123.

168. The author of the standard Cuban work for the period, for example, neglects to make even a brief reference to the contents of the assembly's manifesto, in his view a document of little historical value; see Martínez Ortíz, *Cuba: los primeros años de independencia*, 1:65.

169. Ibid.

170. Such was the case of General "Mayía" Rodríguez, commander of the rebels who still remained under arms in the west, who said that he preferred to return home "clad in misery and honor, [rather] than stain the last four glorious years by a single act of insubordination, or the acceptance of a reward unauthorized by the assembly which is our supreme authority and to which the army owes obedience because it is the guardian of our interests and honor" (Llaverías and Santovenia, *Actas*, 5:111–112).

171. Ibid., pp. 126–139.

172. Ibid., pp. 113–123.

173. Ibid., pp. 139–145.

174. Ibid., pp. 145–148.

175. U.S. Department of War, *Civil Report of Major General John R. Brooke*, pp. 15–16.

176. For further details on this matter see the manifesto that Gómez addressed to the people and the army on March 18; text in Gómez, *La independencia de Cuba*, pp. 67–74.

177. Later Brooke complained that the amount of labor given to the matter and the time consumed had been out of proportion with the work in hand; U.S. Department of War, *Civil Report of Major General John R. Brooke*, p. 17; see also Healy, *The United States in Cuba*, pp. 78–79.

178. See letters, Gómez to McKinley, October 23, 1899; Quesada to Secretary of War Elihu Root, October 27, 1899; Assistant Secretary of War G. D. Meiklejohn to Quesada, December 12, 1899, in Quesada y Miranda, *Documentos históricos*, pp. 24–32.

179. The full text of the manifesto appears in Gómez, *La independencia de Cuba*, pp. 74–78.

180. *The State*, March 13, 15, 1899. Salvador Cisneros Betancourt also denounced Quesada as "the pliant tool of the military government," charging that the position which the McKinley administration had given him in Washington after his dismissal by the assembly had been "the reward" for his role in convincing Gómez to yield to the terms offered by the U.S.; quoted by Foner, *The Spanish-Cuban-American War*, 2:439.

181. Quoted in ibid., p. 445. The historians who present the army assembly as the ensign bearer of Cuban nationalism at the time conveniently forget that the body as a whole failed miserably to live up to such a role. Even Marxist historians readily admit it. See Aguirre, "La desaparición del Ejército Libertador," p. 54.

182. The purpose of these receptions was to "sweeten" the foreign re-

gime, according to Manuel Márquez Sterling, *Proceso histórico de la enmienda Platt*, p. 62.

183. James H. Wilson, "Special Report of Brigadier General James H. Wilson," September 7, 1899, in U.S. Department of War, *Civil Report of Major General John R. Brooke*, p. 330.

184. One of the most complete lists of rebel officers who occupied positions in the occupation appears in Mario Riera Hernández, *Cuba política, 1899–1955*, pp. 8–16.

185. See, for instance, Tasker H. Bliss, "Annual Report of the Collector of Customs for Cuba, Fiscal Year Ending June 30, 1899," in U.S. Department of War, *Civil Report of Major General John R. Brooke*, pp. 374–375. On the basis of contemporary press releases Pérez, Jr., *Cuba between Empires*, pp. 289, 434, has estimated that by late 1898 50,000 exiles had returned to Cuba, and that 20,000 of them were naturalized U.S. citizens. Given the background and language capabilities of many of them, it is understandable that they should have been considered for office by the occupation authorities. It should also be taken into account that Estrada Palma, Quesada, and other exile leaders became major intermediaries in the dispensation of patronage. See, for instance, William Ludlow, "Report of Brigadier General William Ludlow, Commanding Department of Havana and Military Governor of the City of Havana, Cuba," August 1, 1899, in U.S. Department of War, *Annual Reports of the War Department: Report of the Major General Commanding the Army, 1899*, pp. 231–232; also, the correspondence in Quesada y Miranda, *Epistolario*, 1:52, 65, 186; 2:32, 123, 189.

186. See the discussion above on the disbanding of the liberating army.

187. They aspired to become presidents, congressmen, governors, foreign ministers, and the like, according to Matthews, *The New-Born Cuba*, p. 38; Robinson, *Cuba and the Intervention*, p. 108, astutely observed that after the army assembly passed away, it reappeared "in the persons of some of its members as individual factors in the politics of a later day."

188. This is what he wrote in his memoirs, quoted by Varona Guerrero, *La guerra de independencia*, 3:1032.

189. Ferrara, *Mis relaciones con Máximo Gómez*, p. 225; *Memorias*, pp. 106–107.

190. Lacret Morlot to Gonzalo de Quesada, October 15, 1898, Quesada y Miranda, *Epistolario*, 1:32.

191. Rodríguez to Gonzalo de Quesada, June 13, 1899, ibid., pp. 179–180.

192. Roloff to Quesada, October 23, 1898, ibid., pp. 203–205.

193. Quoted by Landa, *Masó*, p. 287.

194. Text in Quesada y Miranda, *Epistolario*, 2:232.

195. The so-called Quinta de los Molinos, former summer residence of the Spanish captain generals.

196. Robinson, *Cuba and the Intervention*, p. 123. Pérez, Jr., *Cuba between Empires*, p. 301, quotes previously unpublished U.S. sources to the effect that Gómez received $10,000 from Brooke in 1899, and that, in addition, he obtained some $26,000 from the United States over the course of the next two years; these findings run counter to the traditional image of

incorruptibility of the general, which is usually substantiated by such incidents as his refusal to be bribed by Wood when the latter took over the command of the Cuban occupation. See Healy, *The United States in Cuba,* p. 127. Which one is the true Gómez, the one who took money from Brooke or the one who rejected Wood's offer? The subject obviously merits further research.

197. Eliseo Giberga, *Obras,* 3:743–744; Martínez Ortiz, *Cuba: los primeros años de independencia,* 1:41; Gómez, *La independencia de Cuba,* pp. 74–78.

198. Tasker H. Bliss, "Annual Report of the Collector of Customs for Cuba."

199. José María Céspedes, *La intervención,* p. 12, quoted by Foner, *The Spanish-Cuban-American War,* 2:427.

200. See, for instance, William McKinley to the American Evacuation Commission, August 26, 1898, in William McKinley Papers, Library of Congress.

201. Matthews, *The New-Born Cuba,* pp. 42–43; Varona Guerrero, *La guerra de independencia,* 3:1680; Rubens, *Liberty,* p. 384.

202. See letters, Gerardo Machado to Gonzalo de Quesada, February 10, 1899; José Miguel Tarafa to Quesada, February 14, 1899; José de Jesús Monteagudo to Quesada, February 17, 1899, in Quesada y Miranda, *Epistolario,* 2:49–50, 91, 279.

203. The reader should keep in mind the concerns of the liberators about municipal jobs.

204. Ferrara, *Memorias,* p. 107.

205. José A. González Lanuza to Robert P. Porter, n.d., Llaverías and Santovenia, *Actas,* 5:167.

206. Rubens, *Liberty,* p. 397.

207. Rodríguez to Quesada, Quesada y Miranda, *Epistolario,* 1:179–180; also, Escalante Beatón, *Calixto García,* p. 128, and Landa, *Masó,* p. 297.

208. Buttari Gaunard, *Boceto,* p. 75.

209. See, for instance, Lanuza to Porter, n.d., Llaverías and Santovenia, *Actas,* 5:167.

210. *La Lucha,* reprinted in *The State,* February 5, 1899, quoted by Foner, *The Spanish-Cuban-American War,* 2:427.

211. Gómez, *La independencia de Cuba,* pp. 74–78.

212. Foner, *The Spanish-Cuban-American War,* 2:447.

5. The Estrada Palma Interlude

1. U.S. Department of War, *Annual Report of the War Department, 1900: Report of the Military Governor of Cuba on Civil Affairs,* vol. 1, pt. 1, p. 65.

2. Ferrara, *Memorias,* p. 111.

3. Ibid., p. 138.

4. Gómez was also aware of the fact that his candidacy would be somewhat controversial among certain insurgent elements; the text of the state-

ment whereby he declined the nomination appears in Martínez Ortiz, *Cuba: los primeros años de independencia,* 1:360.

5. Estrada Palma's intention of remaining in the United States after the end of the war is explicitly stated in his letter to Gómez of May 27, 1898, quoted by Torriente, *Calixto García cooperó,* pp. 36–43. In addition to Camacho's *Estrada Palma,* biographical sketches of Cuba's first president may be found in Carlos Márquez Sterling, *Don Tomás: biografía de una época;* Hugh Lenox Scott, *Some Memories of a Soldier,* p. 263; Emilio Roig de Leuchsenring, *Historia de la enmienda Platt,* 1:15–23; and Patronato Ramón Guiteras Intercultural Center, *Presidentes de Cuba,* pp. 53–86.

6. See letter, Estrada Palma to Benigno and Plácido Gener, January 13, 1878, in Carlos de Velasco, *Desde el castillo de Figueras: cartas de Estrada Palma (1877–1878),* pp. 72–75.

7. *New York Times,* July 7, 1901, quoted by Pérez, Jr., *Cuba between Empires,* p. 372.

8. Estrada Palma to Teodoro Pérez Tamayo, October 10, 1906, Pichardo, *Documentos,* 2:286–290.

9. See, for example, the blistering criticism of Salvador Cisneros Betancourt, *Appeal to the American People on Behalf of Cuba;* also, General Juan Rius Riveras' public letter to Cosme de la Torriente, April 16, 1900, in Pichardo, *Documentos,* 2:63–66. Because of the publication of this letter Rius Rivera had to resign his position in Wood's cabinet.

10. See the press reports quoted by Foner, *The Spanish-Cuban-American War,* 2:518–519.

11. Martínez Ortiz, *Cuba: los primeros años de independencia,* 1:113–114.

12. By virtue of the amendment, among other things, the United States arrogated to itself the right to intervene in Cuba "for the preservation of Cuban independence, the maintenance of a government adequate for the protection of life, property, and individual liberty, and for discharging the obligations with respect to Cuba imposed by the Treaty of Paris on the United States, now to be assumed and undertaken by the government of Cuba."

13. Text in Pichardo, *Documentos,* 2:138–150.

14. On April 12 the convention voted 18 to 10 to reject the amendment.

15. For Sanguily's position see Manuel Sanguily, "Sobre la génesis de la enmienda Platt"; also Roig de Leuchsenring, *Historia de la enmienda Platt,* 1:217–219.

16. See letter, Gómez to Sotero Figueroa, May 8, 1901, in Rodríguez Demorizi, *Papeles dominicanos de Máximo Gómez,* pp. 396–397.

17. Summarized by Healy, *The United States in Cuba,* pp. 174–175.

18. Ibid.

19. Quoted by Camacho, *Estrada Palma,* pp. 176–177.

20. Souza, *Máximo Gómez,* p. 286.

21. According to U.S. press reports quoted by Foner, *The Spanish-Cuban-American War,* 2:655.

22. Healy, *The United States in Cuba,* pp. 174–175.

23. *The State*, July 8, 1901, quoted by Foner, *The Spanish-Cuban-American War*, 2:655.

24. Ferrara, *Memorias*, p. 121.

25. Mario Riera Hernández, *Cuba Libre, 1895–1958*, p. 37.

26. Text in Martínez Ortiz, *Cuba: los primeros años de independencia*, 2:353–354.

27. Ibid., pp. 350–351.

28. Riera Hernández, *Cuba libre*, pp. 45–46; Mario Riera Hernández, *Cuba republicana, 1899–1958*, pp. 8–9; Duarte, *Historiología*, 2:110–113; Leopoldo Horrego Estuch, *Máximo Gómez*, p. 237.

29. Fermoselle, *The Evolution of the Cuban Military*, p. 99; Pichardo, *Documentos*, 2:203–208.

30. Text in R. Iznaga, *Tres años de república, 1902–1905*, pp. 7–10.

31. Albert G. Robinson, "Some Cuban Opinions," p. 1058.

32. For a vivid description of one of these incidents see Ferrara, *Memorias*, pp. 138–140.

33. Riera Hernández, *Cuba política*, pp. 34–35.

34. See, in this connection, Juan Gualberto Gómez's statement in *Diario de sesiones de la Comisión Consultiva de la República de Cuba bajo la administración provisional de los Estados Unidos, 1907–1909, sesión de 6 de marzo de 1907*, p. 12; also, Miguel Gener's letter to Bishop Sbarreti of March 2, 1902, in Portell Vilá, *Historia de Cuba*, 3:58. Gener was dismissed from the mayoralty of Havana by Leonard Wood presumably because he was a "Masoísta."

35. *New York Evening Post*, January 2, 1902, quoted by Foner, *The Spanish-Cuban-American War*, 2:662.

36. Riera Hernández, *Cuba republicana*, p. 8; not over 30 percent of the qualified voters voted when the constitutional convention was elected; see Healy, *The United States in Cuba*, p. 148–149.

37. Ferrara, *Memorias*, p. 138; also Herminio Portell Vilá, *Nueva historia de la República de Cuba*, p. 62.

38. Duarte, *Historiología*, 2:113.

39. Unrelated to General Máximo Gómez.

40. Duarte, *Historiología*, 2:117.

41. Ibid.

42. Estrada Palma summed up his political creed by saying that Cuba was a republic "without citizens." See the statement quoted by Carlos de Velasco, *Estrada Palma: contribución histórica*, pp. 33–34.

43. Martínez Ortiz, *Cuba: los primeros años de independencia*, 1:371.

44. Riera Hernández, *Cuba libre*, p. 48.

45. Martínez Ortiz, *Cuba: los primeros años de independencia*, 2:407.

46. Ferrara, *Memorias*, p. 152.

47. Portell Vilá, *Historia de Cuba*, 3:348–49; Raul Roa, *Aventuras*, pp. 313–316.

48. José Rivero Muñiz, "La primera huelga general obrera en Cuba republicana"; José Rivero Muñiz, *El movimiento laboral cubano durante el*

período 1906–1911; Instituto de Historia del Movimiento Comunista y de la Revolución Socialista de Cuba, anexo al Comité Central del Partido Comunista de Cuba, *Historia del movimiento obrero cubano, 1865–1958;* Mario Riera Hernández, *Historial obrero cubano,* pp. 33–35; Jorge García Montes and Antonio Alonso Avila, *Historia del Partido Comunista de Cuba,* pp. 14–15.

49. Riera Hernández, *Cuba libre,* pp. 48–51.

50. Martínez Ortiz, *Cuba: los primeros años de independencia,* 2:445–446.

51. Fermoselle, *The Evolution of the Cuban Military,* p. 99; Pichardo, *Documentos,* 2:203–208.

52. Horrego Estuch, *Máximo Gómez,* pp. 242–243.

53. Ferrara, *Memorias,* pp. 148–150.

54. See Portell Vilá, *Nueva historia,* pp. 86–87.

55. Chapman, *A History of the Cuban Republic,* pp. 160–167; Martínez Ortiz, *Cuba: los primeros años de independencia,* 2:443–445.

56. Enrique Barbarrosa, *El proceso de la república,* p. 51.

57. Portell Vilá, *Nueva historia,* pp. 87–88.

58. These orders were issued on May 17 and 21, 1905; see Duarte, *Historiología,* 2:141.

59. Chapman, *A History of the Cuban Republic,* pp. 161–163.

60. Iznaga, *Tres años de república,* pp. 25–35.

61. Quoted by Martínez Ortiz, *Cuba: los primeros años de independencia,* 2:402–403.

62. Ibid., p. 404.

63. "Orígenes de nuestro ejército," p. 41.

64. *New York Times,* August 9, 1901, quoted by Fermoselle, *The Evolution of the Cuban Military,* pp. 95–96.

65. René Reyna Cassio, *Estudios histórico-militares sobre la guerra de independencia de Cuba,* p. 67.

66. Quoted by Allan R. Millett, "The Rise and Fall of the Cuban Rural Guard, 1898–1912," p. 196.

67. Portell Vilá, *Historia de Cuba,* 3:388–389.

68. See the public letter that the general addressed to his son, n.d., Gómez, *La independencia de Cuba,* pp. 79–81.

69. On banditry and its connection with the independence movement see Louis A. Pérez, Jr., "Vagrants, Beggars and Bandits: Social Origins of Cuban Separatism, 1878–1895"; María Poumier-Taquechel, *Contribution a l'etude du banditisme social a Cuba: L'histoire et le mythe de Manuel García, "Rey de los campos de Cuba" (1851–1895);* Louis A. Pérez, Jr., *Lords of the Mountain: Social Banditry and Peasant Protest in Cuba, 1878–1918;* Rosalie Schwartz, *Lawless Liberators: Political Banditry and Cuban Independence.*

70. U.S. Department of War, *Annual Report of the War Department, 1900: Report of the Military Governor of Cuba on Civil Affairs,* vol. 1, pt. 1, p. 63.

71. Colonel L. H. Carpenter, "Report of Colonel L. H. Carpenter, Com-

manding Department of Puerto Príncipe [Camagüey]," July 10, 1899, U.S. Department of War, *Annual Report, 1899*, vol. 1, pt. 1, p. 331.

72. "Orígenes de nuestro ejército," p. 11.

73. Wood and General Fitzhugh Lee, governor of the western end of Cuba, explicitly mentioned this danger. See Hagedorn, *Leonard Wood*, 1:214; also letter, Lee to Joseph Benson Foraker, November 20, 1899, in Joseph B. Foraker, *Notes of a Busy Life* 2:48.

74. Fermoselle, *The Evolution of the Cuban Military*, pp. 94–96.

75. Ibid.; Millett, "The Rise and Fall of the Cuban Rural Guard," p. 193; Hagedorn, *Leonard Wood*, 1:214; Willis F. Johnson, *The History of Cuba*, 5:144–145.

76. The account of the conversation between President McKinley and the Cuban Commission may be found in chapter 4.

77. The Porter-Gómez meeting is also discussed in chapter 4.

78. See Gómez's letter to President McKinley of March 4, 1899, in Infiesta, *Máximo Gómez*, pp. 226–228. This author suggests that possibly this letter was never mailed, although the general himself publicly stated that indeed he did so; see his manifesto to the people and the army in Gómez, *La independencia de Cuba*, pp. 67–74.

79. Healy, *The United States in Cuba*, p. 105.

80. Martínez Ortiz, *Cuba: los primeros años de independencia*, 1:76–77.

81. Healy, *The United States in Cuba*, p. 105.

82. Ibid., p. 186; Portell Vilá, *Historia de Cuba*, 3:9; Millett, "The Rise and Fall of the Rural Guard," p. 194.

83. In addition to the sources cited above, see General Alejandro Rodríguez y Velasco in Cuba, Guardia Rural, *Memoria explicativa de la fundación y reorganización del Cuerpo y de los trabajos realizados por el mismo durante el año fiscal de 1904*.

84. Ibid.; "Orígenes de nuestro ejército"; Captain H. J. Slocum, "Report of Captain H. J. Slocum, 7th U.S. Cavalry, Superintendent of the Rural Guard and Cuerpo de Artillería of the island of Cuba, for the period of January 1st, 1902 to May 20th, 1902," July 2, 1902, in U.S. Department of War, *Civil Report of Brigadier General Leonard Wood, Military Governor of Cuba, for the Period from January 1st to May 20th, 1902*.

85. Cpt. Matthew E. Hanna, "The Necessity of Increasing the Efficiency of the Cuban Army."

86. Fermoselle, *Política y color*, p. 29.

87. Cuba, Guardia Rural, *Memoria explicativa de los trabajos realizados por el Cuerpo durante el año fiscal 1905*, pp. 89–95.

88. Cuba, Camagüey, *Reglamento para el gobierno interior del Cuerpo de Guardia Rural*, p. 4; Slocum, "Report."

89. Matthews, *The New-Born Cuba*, p. 387.

90. Leonard Wood, "The Existing Conditions and Needs in Cuba," p. 600; Slocum, "Report."

91. Slocum, "Report," pp. 3, 26.

92. Ibid.

93. See Millett, "The Rise and Fall of the Cuban Rural Guard," p. 196.
94. Elihu Root, *The Military and Colonial Policy of the United States,* p. 190.
95. Slocum, "Report," pp. 3, 26.
96. U.S. Department of War *Annual Report, 1900,* vol. 1, pt. 1, p. 65.
97. Quoted by Louis A. Pérez, Jr., "The Rise and Fall of Army Preeminence in Cuba, 1898–1908," pp. 23–24.
98. Millet, "The Rise and Fall of the Cuban Rural Guard," pp. 196–197.

6. The Beginnings of Factionalism: The 1906 Uprising

1. See Jenks, *Our Cuban Colony,* p. 96; Johnson, *The History of Cuba,* 4:286.
2. See the anonymous statement quoted by Chapman, *A History of the Cuban Republic,* p. 174.
3. Theodore Roosevelt, *State Papers,* 15:257.
4. Quoted by Martínez Ortiz, *Cuba: los primeros años de independencia,* 2:83.
5. Ferrara, *Memorias,* p. 153.
6. Teresita Yglesia Martínez, *Cuba, primera república, segunda ocupación,* p. 202.
7. Ferrara, *Memorias,* p. 155.
8. Duarte, *Historiología,* 2:147.
9. William H. Taft and Robert Bacon, "Cuban Pacification: Report of . . . What Was Done under the Instructions of the President in Restoring Peace in Cuba," p. 456.
10. Text of Gómez's statement in Duarte, *Historiología,* 2:143–144.
11. Ibid., p. 145.
12. Yglesia Martínez, *Cuba: primera república, segunda ocupación,* pp. 203–204; Duarte, *Historiología,* 2:146; Eduardo Varela Zequeira, *La política en 1905,* pp. 5–60; Mario Guiral Moreno, "El problema de la burocracia en Cuba."
13. Quoted by Martínez Ortiz, *Cuba: los primeros años de independencia,* 2:138.
14. Text in Duarte, *Historiología,* 2:146.
15. Ibid., p. 147.
16. Ibid.
17. For a moving account of the general's death and burial see Tomás Baéz Díaz, *Máximo Gómez, el libertador,* pp. 193–196.
18. Yglesia Martínez, *Cuba: primera república, segunda ocupación,* p. 208.
19. Ibid.
20. Many years later Ferrara gave us a firsthand account of this episode in *Memorias,* pp. 156–158.
21. For a number of examples of the government's interference in municipal politics see Pedro Luis Padrón, *¡Qué república era aquella!* pp. 46–49.

22. Quoted by Yglesia Martínez, *Cuba: primera república, segunda ocupación*, p. 207.

23. Text in Duarte, *Historiología*, 2:150.

24. See Ferrara's account in his *Memorias*, pp. 160–162.

25. *La Lucha*, September 27, 1905.

26. Riera Hernández, *Cuba política*, pp. 83–106.

27. Riera Hernández, *Cuba republicana*, p. 10.

28. Ferrara, *Memorias*, p. 155.

29. Quoted by Duarte, *Historiología*, 2:153.

30. Chapman, *A History of the Cuban Republic*, p. 189.

31. Yglesia Martínez, *Cuba: primera república, segunda ocupación*, pp. 225–228.

32. Ferrara, *Memorias*, pp. 166–178.

33. Guerra et al., *Historia de la nación cubana*, 9:287–288.

34. Taft and Bacon, "Cuban Pacification," p. 457.

35. For a list of the most important veterans involved in the insurrection (which does not include, of course, those who were arrested by the government) see Riera Hernández, *Cuba libre*, p. 54. As to the privates see letter, F. Pedro Griñán and Francisco de P. Valiente to Major E. F. Ladd, October 30, 1906, appended to Taft and Bacon, "Cuban Pacification," pp. 528–529.

36. Cuba, Cámara de Representantes, *Mensajes presidenciales remitidos al Congreso desde el veinte de mayo de mil novecientos dos hasta el primero de abril de mil novecientos diez y siete*, p. 176.

37. Charles E. Magoon, *Report of Provisional Administration: From October 13th, 1906 to December 1st, 1907*, p. 110.

38. Martínez Ortiz, *Cuba: los primeros años de independencia*, 2:404.

39. On this ghastly episode see Tomás Savignón, *Quintín Banderas*, pp. 57–61.

40. David A. Lockmiller, *Magoon in Cuba*, p. 38.

41. Amado Randín, *Cuba reivindicada*, pp. 8–9.

42. Quoted by Yglesia Martínez, *Cuba: primera república, segunda ocupación*, p. 236.

43. Such were at least the conclusions reached in Taft and Bacon, "Cuban Pacification," p. 455.

44. See letters, Sleeper to Secretary of State, August 25 and 28, 1906, U.S. Department of State, *Papers Relating to the Foreign Relations of the United States, 1906*, pp. 456–459.

45. Apparently the Cuban president was unsophisticated enough to have taken ad literam what Secretary of State Elihu Root had stated for public consumption regarding situations such as the one he was facing. See, for example, Root, *The Military and Colonial Policy of the United States*, p. 100.

46. Martínez Ortiz, *Cuba: los primeros años de independencia*, 2:620.

47. Ibid., p. 623.

48. See Sleeper's letters to the Secretary of State, U.S. Department of State, *Foreign Relations, 1906*, pp. 456–459.

49. *La Discusión*, August 31, 1906; *New York Times*, September 1, 1906; Fermoselle, *Política y color*, p. 69.

50. For the sort of incentives offered to the militiamen see Martínez Ortiz, *Cuba: los primeros años de independencia*, 2:620.

51. Ibid., p. 239.

52. Ibid., pp. 238–241.

53. See letter, Estrada Palma to Juan Manuel Galdás, September 1906, Carlos de Velasco, *Estrada Palma*, p. 126.

54. Yglesia Martínez, *Cuba: primera república, segunda ocupación*, pp. 243–244.

55. Martínez Ortiz, *Cuba: los primeros años de independencia*, 2:644–654.

56. What Estrada Palma had in his mind is clearly reflected in his well-known letter of October 10, 1906, to Teodoro Pérez Tamayo, first published by a local newspaper in Sancti Spíritus and subsequently by *Diario de la Marina*, November 6, 1907; Pichardo, *Documentos*, 2:286–290.

57. Steinhart had been in Cuba since the days of Brooke and Wood, under whom he had served as chief clerk; he had been consul general since 1903; Chargé Sleeper was a young man who was temporarily replacing Minister Edwin F. Morgan, who was on vacation; because he frequently bumbled in the discharge of his duties, he has gone down in Cuban history as that "wretched and worthless creature," as President Roosevelt characterized him; see Theodore Roosevelt, *The Letters of Theodore Roosevelt*, 5:402.

58. Taft and Bacon, "Cuban Pacification," pp. 444–447.

59. Ibid.

60. Ibid; also, Portell Vilá, *Historia de Cuba*, 3:458–459.

61. Squiers to Secretary of State, September 30, 1905, quoted by Portell Vilá, *Historia de Cuba*, 3:436.

62. See, for instance, the statement that he gave to the press in New York on October 4, 1905, published by *Diario de la Marina* the same day.

63. *La Discusión*, September 5, 1906.

64. *Diario de la Marina*, October 4, 1905.

65. A face-saving solution of the incident was to send the bluejackets to encamp on the grounds of the U.S. legation; see Portell Vilá, *Nueva historia*, p. 101.

66. Taft and Bacon, "Cuban Pacification," p. 456.

67. Ibid.

68. Roosevelt, *Letters*, 5:411–413.

69. According to Allan Reed Millet, *The Politics of Intervention: The Military Occupation of Cuba, 1906–1909*, pp. 59–119, Roosevelt should bear the historical responsibility for the intervention, which became inevitable only after the president hurriedly dispatched the warships to Cuba; Christopher A. Abel, "Controlling the Big Stick: Theodore Roosevelt and the Cuban Crisis of 1906," also blames Roosevelt for the landing parties put ashore by the *Denver* and the *Marietta*.

70. On the clever use made by the rebels of the property destruction reports see Irene A. Wright, *Cuba*, p. 179.

71. Taft and Bacon, "Cuban Pacification," pp. 475–477.

72. Henry F. Pringle, *The Life and Times of William Howard Taft*, 1:309.

73. Taft and Bacon, "Cuban Pacification," pp. 475–477.

74. Pringle, *Taft*, 1:309.

75. Taft and Bacon, "Cuban Pacification," p. 456.

76. Ibid., pp. 475–477.

77. Quoted by Millet, *The Politics of Intervention*, p. 92.

78. Taft and Bacon, "Cuban Pacification," p. 470.

79. Ibid.

80. Wright, *Cuba*, p. 183.

81. Pringle, *Taft*, 1:305.

82. Wright, *Cuba*, p. 183.

83. Ibid.

84. Pringle, *Taft*, 1:308.

85. Duarte, *Historiología*, 2:175.

86. William Inglis, "The Collapse of the Cuban House of Cards," *Harper's Weekly*, October 20, 1906, p. 1490.

87. Text of Estrada Palma's letter in Taft and Bacon, "Cuban Pacification," p. 512.

88. Roosevelt's letter to Estrada Palma may be found in Roosevelt, *Letters*, 5:422. The text of Estrada Palma's reply appears in Duarte, *Historiología*, 2:177–178.

89. *Diario de la Marina*, September 28, 1906. By this time Taft was acutely aware of the true attitude of both Moderates and Liberals concerning the intervention; see his letter to Roosevelt of the same date, quoted by Millet, *The Politics of Intervention*, p. 101.

90. Text in Taft and Bacon, "Cuban Pacification," p. 486.

91. Duarte, *Historiología*, 2:182–183.

7. "Keeping Cuba Quiet": The Second Intervention

1. Taft and Bacon, "Cuban Pacification," p. 466.

2. Millet, *The Politics of Intervention*, pp. 107, 158.

3. Quoted by Portell Vilá, *Historia de Cuba*, 3:511.

4. Enrique José Varona, "El talón de Aquiles," *El Fígaro* (Havana) 22 (September 30, 1906): 490; subsequently reprinted in Enrique José Varona, *Mirando en torno*, pp. 23–27.

5. Ibid.

6. Taft and Bacon, "Cuban Pacification," pp. 463–464.

7. Ibid., pp. 540–542.

8. Ibid., p. 464. A Cuban historian says that Taft wrote the agreement and then sent it to the committee for signature; see Yglesia Martínez, *Cuba: primera república, segunda ocupación*, p. 292.

9. For the members of the commission, see Martínez Ortiz, *Cuba: los primeros años de independencia*, 2:382.

10. Wright, *Cuba*, p. 184.

11. Taft and Bacon, "Cuban Pacification," pp. 488, 521–522, 533.

12. Ibid., p. 522.

13. See Cuba, *Under the Provisional Government of the United States, Decrees, 1906–1909*, Decree no. 9.

14. Ibid.

15. *Habaneros* were constantly reminded of the affair by the socially prominent young men who later on went prancing around on fine steeds that they had taken from poor farmers who had been neutral or perhaps even voted for the Gómez-Zayas ticket. Martínez Ortiz, *Cuba: los primeros años de independencia*, 2:376; also Wright, *Cuba*, p. 185.

16. Ibid.

17. Quoted by Lockmiller, *Magoon in Cuba*, p. 67.

18. Taft and Bacon, "Cuban Pacification," p. 530.

19. Lockmiller, *Magoon in Cuba*, pp. 81–82.

20. Taft and Bacon, "Cuban Pacification," pp. 488–489, 530–532; Millet, *The Politics of Intervention*, p. 105.

21. Quoted by Millet, *The Politics of Intervention*, p. 105.

22. Ibid., p. 177.

23. Ibid., p. 172.

24. Wright, *Cuba*, pp. 181–182. This is no doubt the reason why Captain John W. Wright, of the Military Information Division, wrote to his friend Wood: "[It was] unfortunate for Cuba that our elections were so near when our policy was dictated. It was the policy to avoid trouble at any price and have everybody satisfied—or at least quiet—by the time our presidential votes were cast. In other words, our policy was directed not by the situation in Cuba, but by the American political status." Quoted by Millet, *The Politics of Intervention*, p. 253.

25. Millet, *The Politics of Intervention*, p. 121.

26. Taft and Bacon, "Cuban Pacification," p. 468.

27. Magoon, *Report, 1906–1907*, pp. 86–87.

28. Taft and Bacon, "Cuban Pacification," p. 487.

29. Millet, *The Politics of Intervention*, pp. 125–133.

30. Taft and Bacon, "Cuban Pacification," p. 487.

31. Magoon, *Report, 1906–1907*, p. 105.

32. Ibid., p. 18.

33. Decree no. 386, September 15, 1906, in Cuba, Cámara de Representantes, *Memoria de los trabajos realizados, tercer período congresional, 1906–1908*, vol. 3. Clearly, Taft did not promote Rodríguez.

34. Yglesia Martínez, *Cuba: primera república, segunda ocupación*, pp. 280, 300, emphasizes that this was the first decree signed by Taft as provisional governor.

35. Magoon, *Report, 1906–1907*, p. 18.

36. Ibid., p. 19.

37. Magoon, *Report, 1906–1907*, pp. 493–551; Cuba, Cámara de Repre-

sentantes, *Mensajes presidenciales, 1902–1917*, p. 262; Cuba, Guardia Rural, *Memoria de los trabajos realizados por el Cuerpo de la Guardia Rural desde el 21 de enero hasta el 30 de junio de 1910 inclusive*, pp. 204–217; Cuba, Presidencia, *Memoria de la administración del presidente de la República de Cuba mayor general José Miguel Gómez durante el período comprendido entre el 1ro de enero y el 31 de diciembre de 1910*, p. 126.

38. Magoon, *Report, 1906–1907*, pp. 493–551.

39. Millet, *The Politics of Intervention*, p. 225.

40. Ibid., p. 266.

41. Magoon, *Report, 1906–1907*, p. 20.

42. Ibid.

43. See Millet, "The Rise and Fall of the Cuban Rural Guard," p. 199.

44. Magoon, *Report, 1906–1907*, pp. 498–500.

45. Millet, *The Politics of Intervention*, pp. 226–27; Millet, "The Rise and Fall of the Cuban Rural Guard," p. 199.

46. Martínez Ortiz, *Cuba: los primeros años de independencia*, 2:384.

47. The provisional government was placed under the supervision of the secretary of war by an executive order issued by Roosevelt on October 3, 1906; see Taft and Bacon, "Cuban Pacification," p. 543.

48. Text in Lockmiller, *Magoon in Cuba*, p. 72.

49. Millet, *The Politics of Intervention*, p. 123. For a biographical sketch of Magoon see Chapman, *A History of the Cuban Republic*, pp. 230–232; also Lockmiller, *Magoon in Cuba*, pp. 70–76.

50. Johnson, *The History of Cuba*, 5:283; for a contemporary Cuban assessment of the motives behind the Liberals' attitude see Enrique Barbarrosa, *El proceso de la república*, p. 65; also, Chapman's account, *A History of the Cuban Republic*, pp. 176, 187.

51. The most important among these was that arising from church property confiscated by the Spanish government in 1842; see, on this matter, Lockmiller, *Magoon in Cuba*, pp. 138–143; also David A. Lockmiller, "The Settlement of the Church Property Question in Cuba." The payment made to the Cuban church was perfectly legal, although no one has ever explained why a "provisional" administration had to settle a claim that had been pending for over half a century; even pro-Magoon writers admit, although not without reluctance, that the price paid for the properties may have been determined with a "too generous sense of fairness"; see Chapman, *A History of the Cuban Republic*, p. 239.

52. Magoon's new roads even helped to suppress some attempts at insurrection; see Wright, *Cuba*, p. 254.

53. See letter, Magoon to General J. F. Bell, July 21, 1907, quoted by Millet, *The Politics of Intervention*, p. 205.

54. Cubans have accused Magoon of dishonesty in the awarding of contracts for public works and question the quality of the roads that he built. According to an anonymous builder quoted by Chapman, *A History of the Cuban Republic*, p. 244, only certain portions of them were "really very good," although it appears that the charges of corruption were unfounded. It seems that the governor was remarkably indiscriminating in giving out

contracts, and so Cuba became a virtual paradise for contractors under his administration according to Jenks, *Our Cuban Colony,* p. 101.

55. Jenks, *Our Cuban Colony,* p. 96.

56. Magoon, *Report, 1906–1907,* pp. 15–16.

57. Martínez Ortiz, *Cuba: los primeros años de independencia,* 2:385.

58. Magoon, *Report, 1906–1907,* pp. 16–17.

59. Martínez Ortiz, *Cuba: los primeros años de independencia,* 2:401.

60. Hudson Strode, *The Pageant of Cuba,* p. 227.

61. Martínez Ortiz, *Cuba: los primeros años de independencia,* 2:385.

62. The charge was made by Carlos M. Trelles, *El progreso (1902 a 1905) y el retroceso (1906 a 1922) de la República de Cuba,* p. 9, who should have known better, since it is obvious that *botellas* existed in Cuba under Spain; he later admitted that his remarks in this connection had been too strong. See Lockmiller, *Magoon in Cuba,* p. 206, n. 31.

63. Chapman, *A History of the Cuban Republic,* p. 253.

64. Lieutenant Colonel Robert L. Bullard was the author of this remark, quoted by Millet, *The Politics of Intervention,* p. 208.

65. Ibid. One Gustavo Escoto, for example, had his mother-in-law on the payroll. Probably because he neglected to keep up appearances, the administration had to discharge him from the department. This is why we know about this case and a few others. Charles E. Magoon, *Report of Provisional Administration: From December 1st, 1907 to December 1st, 1908,* p. 117; Lockmiller, *Magoon in Cuba,* p. 135.

66. Millet, *The Politics of Intervention,* p. 208.

67. Ibid., p. 211.

68. Ibid.

69. Pino Guerra, for example, after being appointed commander in chief of the new Permanent Army, was sent to witness military maneuvers in the United States and France.

70. Martínez Ortiz, *Cuba: los primeros años de independencia,* 2:383.

71. The total number of pardons granted by Magoon amounted to 1,140, according to Trelles, *El progreso y el retroceso,* p. 8; it appears that Estrada Palma granted an average of 6 pardons per month; Magoon, 46; José Miguel Gómez, 30; and Zayas, 33. See Fernando Ortiz, *La decadencia cubana,* p. 15.

72. Magoon, *Report, 1907–1908,* pp. 87, 89–94.

73. Lockmiller, *Magoon in Cuba,* p. 208; Chapman, *A History of the Cuban Republic,* p. 255; Martínez Ortiz, *Cuba: los primeros años de independencia,* 2:383; Manuel Secades and Horacio Díaz Pardo, *La justicia en Cuba; los veteranos y los indultos,* passim.

74. Henry Watterson in the *Havana Post,* January 29, 1909, quoted by Lockmiller, *Magoon in Cuba,* p. 198.

75. Among his detractors figure journalists like Barbarrosa, *El proceso de la república,* pp. 88–89, and Miguel Lozano Casado, *La personalidad del general José Miguel Gómez,* p. 17; others include some of Cuba's leading intellectuals such as Enrique José Varona, *Por Cuba: discursos,* pp. 315–342; Trelles, *El progreso y el retroceso,* and Ortiz, *La decadencia*

cubana; conservative and revisionist historians equally censure Magoon; see, for example, Guerra et al., *Historia de la nación cubana*, 8:36–37; Emilio Roig de Leuchsenring, *El intervencionismo: mal de males de Cuba republicana*, p. 13; and Portell Vilá, *Historia de Cuba*, 3:521 ff. By the same token, this is one point in which exiled Cuban historians such as Jaime Suchlicki, *Cuba: From Columbus to Castro*, p. 90, coincide with their colleagues of Castro's Cuba, among them Oscar Pino Santos, *Historia de Cuba, aspectos fundamentales*, p. 184. Even the usually fair and benevolent Martínez Ortiz, *Cuba: los primeros años de independencia*, 2:856, writes that under Magoon Cuba "returned to the corrupt practices of colonial times."

76. Some do it by implication; a few do it explicitly, like Carlos Márquez Sterling, *Historia de Cuba*, p. 272.

77. Chapman, *A History of the Cuban Republic*, pp. 233–234.

78. Somewhat attenuated, for example, in Suchlicki's *Historical Dictionary of Cuba*, p. 171.

79. Wright, *Cuba*, p. 183.

80. Ibid., p. 184.

81. Taft to Roosevelt, October 10, 1906, quoted by Millet, *The Politics of Intervention*, p. 227.

82. See the correspondence and memorandum quoted by Pérez, Jr., "The Rise and Fall of Army Preeminence in Cuba," pp. 45, 54.

83. Millet, "The Rise and Fall of the Cuban Rural Guard," pp. 200–201.

84. Magoon, *Report, 1907–1908*, p. 108.

85. Magoon to Taft, October 26 and 30 and November 16, 1906, quoted by Millet, *The Politics of Intervention*, p. 227.

86. Magoon to Taft, December 31, 1906, quoted in ibid., pp. 228–229.

87. *La Lucha*, February 4, 1907.

88. Stenographic Report of the Conference, quoted by Pérez, Jr., "The Rise and Fall of Army Preeminence in Cuba," pp. 47–48.

89. Slocum to Magoon, February 26, 1907, quoted in ibid., p. 50.

90. Memorandum, "The Political Aspect of a Cuban Army," Cpt. J. A. Ryan to Maj. H. J. Slocum, February 25, 1907, quoted by Millet, *The Politics of Intervention*, p. 232; see also Millet, "The Rise and Fall of the Cuban Rural Guard," pp. 202–203.

91. H. E. Havens to Taft, February 19, 1907, quoted by Millet, *The Politics of Intervention*, pp. 233–234.

92. Document submitted by the Liberal Committee to the Provisional Governor, March 14, 1907, quoted in ibid., p. 234.

93. Pino Guerra's statement to Magoon of February 19, 1907, quoted by Pérez, Jr., "The Rise and Fall of Army Preeminence in Cuba," pp. 52–53.

94. Millet, *The Politics of Intervention*, p. 234.

95. See *Diario de sesiones de la Comisión Consultiva de la República de Cuba, 1907–1909*, vol. 3, no. 212, January 31, 1908, pp. 141–152.

96. For an ample discussion of the legal reforms introduced by the Magoon administration see Lockmiller, *Magoon in Cuba*, pp. 146–173.

97. Pérez, Jr., "The Rise and Fall of Army Preeminence in Cuba," p. 56.

98. Magoon, *Report, 1907–1908*, p. 22.

99. Magoon to Roosevelt, April 17, 1908, quoted by Pérez, Jr., "The Rise and Fall of Army Preeminence in Cuba," p. 56.

100. Millet, *The Politics of Intervention*, p. 234.

101. Cpt. E. Wittenmeyer to Maj. H. J. Slocum, February 26, 1907, quoted by Pérez, Jr., "The Rise and Fall of Army Preeminence in Cuba," p. 51.

102. Magoon to Taft, April 9, 1908, quoted by Millet, *The Politics of Intervention*, p. 237.

103. Chapman, *A History of the Cuban Republic*, p. 275.

104. Lockmiller, *Magoon in Cuba*, p. 145.

105. Magoon to Taft, April 9, 1908, Millet, *The Politics of Intervention*, p. 237.

106. Martínez Ortiz, *Cuba: los primeros años de independencia*, 2:769; Chapman, *A History of the Cuban Republic*, p. 259.

107. The general expressed this belief in an interview that he granted Lockmiller when Lockmiller was gathering material for his work on the Magoon administration; see Lockmiller, *Magoon in Cuba*, p. 183, n. 36.

108. Millet, *The Politics of Intervention*, p. 161.

109. Martínez Ortiz, *Cuba: los primeros años de independencia*, 2:769; Chapman, *A History of the Cuban Republic*, p. 259.

110. Johnson, *The History of Cuba*, 4:285.

111. For contemporary accounts of Gómez's inauguration see Lockmiller, *Magoon in Cuba*, p. 196, n. 75.

112. Martínez Ortiz, *Cuba: los primeros años de independencia*, 2:469; Duarte, *Historiología*, 2:213; Chapman, *A History of the Cuban Republic*, pp. 256–257. Millet says that it was President Gómez who removed Rodríguez in order to appoint his crony Monteagudo but does not mention his sources; see Millet, *The Politics of Intervention*, p. 238; Millett, "The Rise and Fall of the Cuban Rural Guard," pp. 206–207.

8. The Republic under Its Liberators

1. Zayas never took to the woods or took up arms against any government despite the numerous disturbances engineered by his party in the post-Magoon era.

2. Chapman, *A History of the Cuban Republic*, p. 315.

3. On the national elections of this period see the summary by Riera Hernández, *Cuba republicana*, pp. 11–21.

4. The divorce between Cuban politics and social or economic problems has been emphasized by Jorge Domínguez, *Cuba: Order and Revolution*, pp. 44–46.

5. José Antonio González Lanuza (1865–1917), a university professor and an honest politician: quoted by Emeterio S. Santovenia and Raúl M. Shelton, *Cuba y su historia* 3:217.

6. Quoted by Luis E. Aguilar, *Cuba, 1933: Prologue to Revolution*, p. 33.

7. See the information provided by Louis Pérez, Jr., *Cuba under the Platt Amendment, 1902–1934*, pp. 214–256.

8. Chapman, *A History of the Cuban Republic,* pp. 305–306.

9. Luis de Juan Puñal, *Tirando de la manta,* pp. 147–151; Gerardo Castellanos, *Panorama histórico,* pp. 1368–1369; Portell Vilá, *Nueva historia,* pp. 160–164; Ferrara, *Memorias,* pp. 194–198.

10. Text in Pichardo, *Documentos,* 2:358–361.

11. Rafael Conte and José M. Company, *Guerra de razas;* Serafín Portuondo Linares, *Los independientes de color;* Sergio Aguirre, "El cincuentenario de un gran crimen"; Martín Morúa Delgado, *Integración cubana y otros ensayos;* Martha Verónica Alvarez Mola and Pedro Martínez Pérez, "Algo acerca del problema negro en Cuba hasta 1912"; Rafael Fermoselle, *Política y color,* pp. 87–187; Cathy Duke, "The Idea of Race: The Cultural Impact of American Intervention in Cuba, 1898–1912"; Louis A. Pérez, Jr., "Politics, Peasants, and People of Color: the 1912 'Race War' in Cuba Reconsidered"; René León and Emilio J. León, *La guerra racial de 1912 en Cuba.*

12. See, in this connection, Atkins, *Sixty Years,* p. 312; Esteban Montejo, *The Autobiography of a Runaway Slave,* pp. 216 ff.

13. José Navas, *La convulsión de febrero;* Bernardo Merino and F. de Ibarzábal, *La revolución de febrero;* Waldemar León, "Caicaje: Batalla final de una revuelta"; Herminio Portell Vilá, "La Chambelona en Oriente"; "La Chambelona en Camagüey"; "La Chambelona en Las Villas"; "La Chambelona en Occidente"; Raimundo Cabrera, *Mis malos tiempos;* W. I. Consuegra, *Hechos y comentarios: la revolución de febrero de 1917 en Las Villas.*

14. Ana Cairo Ballester, *El Movimiento de Veteranos y Patriotas.*

15. Alfredo Lima, *La odisea de Río Verde;* Emilio Laurent, "Datos esenciales de la expedición de Gibara."

16. Aguilar, *Cuba, 1933,* pp. 116–127; Jaime Suchlicki, *University Students and Revolution in Cuba, 1920–1968.*

17. Curiously enough, in more than one way Castro's campaign against Batista was a close reproduction, with but few variations, of those old tactics. See Theodore Draper, *Castroism: Theory and Practice,* pp. 21–26.

18. See International Commission of Jurists, *Cuba and the Rule of Law,* p. 47.

19. Ricardo Adam y Silva, *La gran mentira,* p. 11.

20. Fermoselle, *The Evolution of the Cuban Military,* pp. 113, 130, 139.

21. Federico Chang, *El ejército nacional en la república neocolonial,* p. 42.

22. Ibid., p. 45.

23. Ibid., pp. 49–90.

24. Ibid., p. 15.

25. Ibid., pp. 15–16.

26. Ibid., p. 42.

27. Lavastida was ousted in February 1909; charged with plotting against the government he was arrested at Placetas, Las Villas, on the night of March 15 and was shot and killed the following night while allegedly trying to escape; see Chapman, *A History of the Cuban Republic,* pp. 300–302.

28. Adam y Silva, *La gran mentira*, p. 13.

29. Millet, "The Rise and Fall of the Cuban Rural Guard," p. 207.

30. Ibid., p. 210.

31. Pérez, Jr., "The Rise and Fall of Army Preeminence in Cuba," p. 60.

32. On this occasion Menocal sent President Gómez a message offering to back him with 1,000 cavalrymen; the offer was rejected, but the mere fact that it was made further substantiates the militaristic mentality of the Cuban veteran-politicians.

33. Ferrara, *Memorias*, p. 198.

34. Ibid., p. 220.

35. Cuba, Congreso, Cámara de Representantes. *Memoria de los trabajos realizados durante las cuatro legislaturas ordinarias y las dos extraordinarias del octavo período congresional comprendido del dos de abril de mil novecientos diez y siete a siete de abril de mil novecientos diez y nueve*, p. 817; the reason why the official estimate seems too low is that Major Rigoberto Fernández, leader of the Oriente rebels, alone had somewhat less than 1,000 men under his command, and to these forces we would have to add those that declared against Menocal in Camagüey, the province where the uprising was most successful. See Chapman, *A History of the Cuban Republic*, p. 376; Duarte, *Historiología*, 2:268–270.

36. Ferrara, *Memorias*, pp. 201, 220.

37. Trelles, *El progreso y el retroceso*, p. 13.

38. Cuba, *Memoria del octavo período congresional*, p. 816.

39. Germán Wolter del Río, "La hacienda pública en Cuba," in Guerra et al., *Historia de la nación cubana*, 9:143–144; according to this writer, military appropriations increased from 19.6 percent of the national budget in 1914–1915 to 24.1 percent in 1917–1918.

40. Riera Hernández, *Cuba política*, pp. 263–278; León Primelles, *Crónica cubana, 1919–1922*, pp. 26, 159–160; Louis A. Pérez, Jr., "The Military and Electoral Politics: The Cuban Election of 1920."

41. Wolter del Río, "La hacienda pública en Cuba."

42. Duarte, *Historiología*, 2:324; Ricardo Adam y Silva, *Cuba, el fin de la república*, p. 29; "Reloj," October 17, 1973.

43. Adam y Silva, *La gran mentira*, pp. 16–17.

44. Ricardo Adam y Silva, "Reloj," January 23, 1974.

45. Aguilar, *Cuba, 1933*, p. 53.

46. Chapman, *A History of the Cuban Republic*, pp. 488–489.

47. Portell Vilá, *Nueva historia*, p. 315.

48. Ferrara, *Memorias*, p. 275.

49. Wolter del Río, "La hacienda pública en Cuba"; also Ruby H. Phillips, *Cuba: Island of Paradox*, p. 37.

50. Fermoselle, *The Evolution of the Cuban Military*, pp. 138–141.

51. Adam y Silva, *La gran mentira*, pp. 59–60; Edmund A. Chester, *A Sergeant Named Batista*, p. 57.

52. Perez, Jr., "The Rise and Fall of Army Preeminence in Cuba," p. 102.

53. Decree no. 1100, "Organic Law of the Army," Cuba, *Gaceta Oficial de la República* (edición extraordinaria), July 20, 1926, p. 4.

54. Ricardo Adam y Silva, "Las conspiraciones en el ejército durante la dictadura machadista."

55. Adam y Silva, *La gran mentira*, p. 137, *Cuba, el fin de la república*, pp. 7–11, "Reloj," October 19, 1974; see also Phillips, *Cuba: Island of Paradox*, pp. 87–88.

56. Fermoselle, *The Evolution of the Cuban Military*, p. 117.

57. General Francisco Peraza, however, was killed by the army despite his age (seventy-six) together with 27 of his men; see Portell Vilá, *Nueva historia*, p. 374.

58. See Dana G. Munro, *Intervention and Dollar Diplomacy in the Caribbean, 1900–1921.*

59. See, for example, ibid., p. 472.

60. Chapman, *A History of the Cuban Republic*, pp. 306–307, 365–370.

61. Portell Vilá, *Nuestra historia*, pp. 252–284.

62. Chapman, *A History of the Cuban Republic*, pp. 490–491.

63. Fermoselle, *Política y color*, pp. 154–159.

64. Portell Vilá, *Nueva historia*, pp. 206–207.

65. Aguilar, *Cuba: 1933*, p. 88.

66. Since there were at least a score of skirmishes, it is obvious that the army did something to stop the Liberals in 1917; casualties were few, however, and this suggests that neither side fought too hard, or at least not as hard as was maintained by Ricardo Adam y Silva, "Reloj," July 12, 1975; if there was anyone among the Cubans who really contributed to restore order it was Menocal himself, whose resolute attitude apparently convinced Washington that he was able to defend himself. See Ferrara, *Memorias*, p. 220; Ferrara, it must be noted, figured among Menocal's bitterest political enemies at the time.

67. Domínguez, *Cuba: Order and Revolution*, pp. 12–19.

68. Quoted by Millet, *The Politics of Intervention*, p. 259.

69. Sumner Welles, "Is America Imperialistic?" *Atlantic Monthly*, September 1924, pp. 36–44.

70. Domínguez, *Cuba: Order and Revolution*, p. 60.

Bibliography

Unpublished Material

Manuscript Sources

Arnao, Juan and Nicolás. Papers. Miscellaneous Manuscripts Collection. Library of Congress, Washington, D.C.
Cleveland, Grover. Papers. Library of Congress, Washington, D.C.
McKinley, William. Papers. Library of Congress, Washington, D.C.
Olney, Richard B. Papers. Library of Congress, Washington, D.C.
Roosevelt, Theodore. Papers. Library of Congress, Washington, D.C.
Root, Elihu. Papers. Library of Congress, Washington, D.C.
Taft, William Howard. Papers. Library of Congress, Washington, D.C.
Wilson, James Harrison. Papers. Library of Congress, Washington, D.C.
Wood, Leonard. Papers. Library of Congress, Washington, D.C.

Ph.D. Dissertations

Delgado, Octavio A. "The Spanish Army in Cuba, 1868–1898: An Institutional Study." 2 vols. Ph.D. diss., Columbia University, 1980.
Maza, Manuel P., S.J. "Between Ideology and Compassion: The Cuban Insurrection of 1895–98 through the Private Correspondence of Cuba's Two Prelates with the Holy See." Ph.D. diss., Georgetown University, 1986.
Pérez, Jr., Louis A. "The Rise and Fall of Army Preeminence in Cuba, 1898–1958." Ph.D. diss., The University of New Mexico, 1971.

Published Material

Public Documents

Barry, Brigadier General Thomas H. *Annual Report . . . 1907–1908.* Marianao: Headquarters, Army of Cuban Pacification, 1907–1908.
Cuba. Archivo Nacional. *El Archivo Nacional en la conmemoración del centenario del natalicio de José Martí y Pérez, 1853–1953.* Havana: Publicaciones del Archivo Nacional de Cuba, 1953.
———. *Boletín del Archivo Nacional.* 63 vols. Havana: Archivo Nacional, 1901–1963.

————. *Documentos para servir a la historia de la Guerra Chiquita.* 3 vols. Havana: n.p., 1949–50.

Cuba. Army. Inspección General. *Indice alfabético y defunciones del Ejercito Libertador de Cuba* . . . Datos compilados y ordenados por el Inspector General . . . Mayor General Carlos Roloff y Malofsky ayudado del . . . Comandante de Estado Mayor Gerardo Forrest. Havana: Rambla y Bouza, 1901.

Cuba. Camagüey. *Reglamento para el gobierno interior del Cuerpo de Guardia Rural.* Camagüey: Tipografía de Las Dos Repúblicas, 1899.

Cuba. Comisión Consultiva. *Diario de sesiones de la Comisión Consultiva de la República de Cuba bajo la administración provisional de los Estados Unidos, 1907–1909.* 4 vols. Havana: Rambla y Bouza, 1908, 1916.

Cuba. Congreso. Cámara de Representantes. *Memoria de los trabajos realizados, tercer período congresional, 1906–1908.* 3 vols. Havana: Rambla y Bouza, 1911.

————. *Memoria de los trabajos realizados durante las cuatro legislaturas ordinarias y las dos extraordinarias del octavo período congresional comprendido del dos de abril de mil novecientos diez y siete a siete de abril de mil novecientos diez y nueve.* Havana: Rambla y Bouza, 1919.

————. *Mensajes presidenciales remitidos al Congreso, transurridos desde el veinte de mayo de mil novecientos dos hasta el primero de abril de mil novecientos diez y siete.* Havana: n.p., n.d.

Cuba. Congreso. Senado. *Memoria de los trabajos realizados durante las cuatro legislaturas ordinarias y la sesión extraordinaria del primer período congresional, 1902–1904.* Havana: Rambla y Bouza, 1918.

Cuba. Ejército Nacional. Estado Mayor. *Boletín del Ejército.* 1916–1933.

Cuba. Estado Mayor General del Ejército. *Lista, directorio y escalafones.* Havana: Imprenta del Estado Mayor General, 1916.

Cuba. *Gaceta Oficial de la República de Cuba.* 1902–1933.

Cuba. *General Orders, Circulars, and Special Orders, Headquarters, Army of Cuban Pacification, 1906; and General Orders, Circulars and Special Orders, Headquarters, First Expeditionary Brigade, 1906.*

Cuba. *General Orders, Special Orders, and Circulars, Headquarters, Army of Cuban Pacification, 1907–1909.* 5 vols. Havana: n.p., 1908–1909.

Cuba. Guardia Rural. *Memoria explicativa de la fundación y reorganización del Cuerpo y de los trabajos realizados por el mismo durante el año fiscal de 1904.* Havana: Rambla y Bouza, 1905.

————. *Memoria explicativa de los trabajos realizados por el Cuerpo de la Guardia Rural desde el 21 de enero hasta el 30 de junio de 1910 inclusive.* Havana: Rambla y Bouza, 1911.

————. *Memoria explicativa de los trabajos realizados por el Cuerpo durante el año fiscal 1905.* Havana: Rambla y Bouza, 1906.

Cuba. Presidencia. *Memoria de la administración del presidente de la República de Cuba Alfredo Zayas y Alfonso . . . 1921–1924.* Havana: Rambla y Bouza, 1923–1925.

————. *Memoria de la administración del presidente de la República de*

Cuba Gerardo Machado y Morales . . . 1925–1931. Havana: Rambla y Bouza, 1927–1932.

———. *Memoria de la administración del presidente de la República de Cuba Mario G. Menocal . . . 1913–1921.* Havana: Rambla y Bouza, 1915–1923.

———. *Memoria de la administración del presidente de la República de Cuba mayor general José Miguel Gómez . . . 1909–1913.* Havana: Rambla y Bouza, 1910–1913.

———. *Mensaje del presidente Alfredo Zayas y Alfonso al Congreso de la República de Cuba referente a los actos de la administración . . . 1921–1924.* Havana: Rambla y Bouza, 1921–1924.

———. *Mensaje del presidente Gerardo Machado y Morales al Congreso de la República de Cuba referente a los actos de la administración . . . 1925–1931.* Havana: Rambla y Bouza, 1925–1931.

Cuba. Secretaría de Gobernación. *Documentos históricos.* Havana: Rambla y Bouza, 1912.

Cuba. Secretaría de Instrucción Pública y Bellas Artes. *Communicaciones de la Cámara de Representantes desde el día 10 de abril de 1869 hasta el día 10 de junio del mismo año.* Havana: La Universal, 1919.

Cuba. *Under the Provisional Government of the United States, Decrees, 1906–1909.* 9 vols. Havana: Rambla y Bouza, 1907–1909.

Lazcano y Mazón, Andres María. *Las constituciones de Cuba.* Madrid: Ediciones Cultura Hispánica, 1952.

League of Nations. *Armaments Year-Book, 1924–1940.* Geneva: Publications of the League of Nations, 1924–1940.

Lee, Brigadier General Fitzhugh. *Special Report of Brigadier General Fitzhugh Lee on the Industrial, Economic, and Social Conditions Existing in the Provinces of Havana and Pinar del Río.* Quemados, Cuba: Adjutant General's Office, 1899.

Llaverías, Joaquín, and Santovenia, Emeterio S., eds. *Actas de las Asambleas de Representantes y del Consejo de Gobierno durante la Guerra de Independencia.* 5 vols. Havana: El Siglo XX, 1932.

Magoon, Charles E. *Report of the Provisional Administration: From December 1st, 1907 to December 1st, 1908.* Havana: Rambla y Bouza, 1909.

———. *Report on the Law of Civil Government in Territory Subject to Military Occupation by the Military Forces of the United States.* 3d ed. Washington, D.C.: Government Printing Office, 1903.

———. *Supplemental Report, Provisional Governor of Cuba, for the Period December 1, 1908 to January 28, 1909.* 61st Cong., 1st sess., S. Doc. 80, ser. 5572. Washington, D.C.: Government Printing Office, 1909.

Parker, Captain Frank. *Informe anual del instructor de la Guardia Rural sobre la instrucción militar durante el año académico que expiró en 30 junio de 1912.* Havana: Rambla y Bouza, 1912.

Porter, Robert P. *Report on the Commercial and Industrial Conditions of Cuba: Special Report on the Commissioner's Visit to General Gómez and in Relation to the Payment and Disbandment of the Insurgent Army of Cuba.* Washington, D.C.: Government Printing Office, 1899.

————. *Industrial Cuba.* New York: Knickerbocker Press, 1899.

República Dominicana. *Informe que al Secretario de Relaciones Exteriores de la República Dominicana presenta el Encargado de Negocios en La Habana sobre el régimen político en Cuba.* Havana, n.p., 1913.

Richardson, James D., ed. *A Compilation of the Messages and Papers of the Presidents, 1789–1908.* 11 vols. Washington: Government Printing Office, 1908.

Taft, William Howard, and Bacon, Robert. "Cuban Pacification: Report of William H. Taft, Secretary of War, and Robert Bacon, Assistant Secretary of State, of What Was Done under the Instructions of the President in Restoring Peace in Cuba." In Department of War, *Report of the Secretary of War, 1906,* Appendix E. 59th Cong., 2d sess., H. Doc. 2, ser. 5105. Washington, D.C.: Government Printing Office, 1906.

U.S. Bureau of Insular Affairs. *The Establishment of Free Government in Cuba.* 58th Cong., 2d sess., S. Doc. 312. Washington, D.C.: Government Printing Office, 1904.

U.S. Congress. House. *Affairs in Cuba.* 54th Cong., 1st sess., H. Doc. 224, ser. 3425. Washington, D.C.: Government Printing Office, 1896.

U.S. Congress. Senate. *Report of the Commission Appointed by the President to Investigate the Conduct of the War Department in the War with Spain.* 8 vols. 56th Cong., 1st sess., ser. 3859–3866. Washington, D.C.: Government Printing Office, 1900.

————. *Report of the Committee on Foreign Relations: Affairs in Cuba.* 55th Cong., 2d sess., report no. 885, ser. 3624. Washington, D.C.: Government Printing Office, 1898.

U.S. Department of State. *Papers Relating to the Foreign Relations of the United States. 1902–1944.* Washington, D.C.: Government Printing Office, 1902–1967.

U.S. Department of the Navy. *Annual Report of the Colonel Commandant of the United States Marine Corps to the Secretary of the Navy, 1893–1906.* Washington, D.C.: Government Printing Office, 1906.

U.S. Department of War. *Annual Report of the War Department, 1900: Report of the Military Governor of Cuba on Civil Affairs.* 2 vols. 56th Cong., 2d sess., H. Doc. 2, ser. 4080–4087. Washington, D.C.: Government Printing Office, 1901.

————. *Annual Reports, 1899, 1905–1909.* 3 vols. Washington, D.C.: Government Printing Office, 1899, 1906–1909.

————. *Civil Report of Brigadier General Leonard Wood, Military Governor of Cuba, for the Period from December 20, 1899, to December 31, 1900.* 12 vols. Washington, D.C.: Government Printing Office, 1901.

————. *Civil Report of Brigadier General Leonard Wood, Military Governor of Cuba, for the Period from January 1 to December 31, 1901.* 15 vols. Washington, D.C.: Government Printing Office, 1902.

————. *Civil Report of Brigadier General Leonard Wood, Military Governor of Cuba, for the Period from January 1 to May 20, 1902.* 6 vols. Washington, D.C.: Government Printing Office, 1902.

————. *Civil Report of Major General John R. Brooke, Military Governor, Island of Cuba.* 3 vols. Washington, D.C.: Government Printing Office, 1900.

————. *Five Years of the War Department Following the War with Spain, 1898–1903, as Shown in the Annual Reports of the Secretary of War.* Washington, D.C.: Government Printing Office, 1904.

U.S. Department of War. Adjutant General's Office. *Correspondence Relating to the War with Spain, April 15, 1898–July 30, 1902.* Washington, D.C.: Government Printing Office, 1902.

————. Adjutant General's Office. *Official Army Register, 1906–1907.* Washington, D.C.: Government Printing Office, 1905, 1906.

U.S. Department of War. Office of the Chief of Staff. *Military Notes on Cuba, 1909.* Study no. 15, Second Section, General Staff, compiled by Captain John W. Furlong, Military Information Division, Army of Cuban Pacification. Washington, D.C.: Government Printing Office, 1909.

————. *Road Notes, 1909.* Study no. 16, Second Section, General Staff. Washington, D.C.: Government Printing Office, 1909.

U.S. Department of War. Office of the Director of the Census of Cuba. *Report on the Census of Cuba, 1899.* Washington, D.C.: Government Printing Office, 1900.

Memoirs, Diaries, Correspondence, and Other Printed Materials

Agramonte y Loynaz, General Ignacio. *Patria y mujer.* Havana: Publicaciones del Ministerio de Educación, 1942.

Alger, R. A. *The Spanish-American War.* New York and London: Harper & Bros., 1901.

Atkins, Edwin F. *Sixty Years in Cuba.* Cambridge, Mass.: Riverside Press, 1926.

Bacon, Robert, and Scott, James Brown, eds. *Latin America and the United States.* Cambridge, Mass.: Harvard University Press, 1917. (Addresses by Elihu Root)

————. *The Military and Colonial Policy of the United States.* Cambridge, Mass.: Harvard University Press, 1916. (Addresses and reports by Elihu Root)

Boza, Bernabé. *Mi diario de la guerra, desde Baire hasta la intervención americana.* 2 vols. Havana: Ricardo Veloso, 1924.

Cabrales, Gonzalo, ed. *Epistolario de héroes.* Havana: El Siglo XX, 1922.

Cabrera, Raimundo. *Mis buenos tiempos.* Havana: Ricardo Veloso, 1922.

————. *Mis malos tiempos.* Havana: El Siglo XX, 1920.

Carbonell Rivero, Gaspar, ed. *Enrique J. Conill, soldado de la patria.* Havana: P. Fernandez y Cia., 1956.

Castellanos y García, Gerardo. *Motivos de Cayo Hueso.* Havana: n.p., 1935.

Castillo, José Rogelio. *Autobiografía del general José Rogelio Castillo.* Havana: Instituto Cubano del Libro, 1973.

Cepeda, Rafael, ed. *Manuel Sanguily frente a la dominación yanqui.* Havana: Editorial de Ciencias Sociales, 1986.

Céspedes, Carlos Manuel de. *Cartas a su esposa Ana de Quesada.* Havana: Instituto Cubano del Libro, 1964.

Céspedes y Quesada, Carlos Manuel de. *Carlos Manuel de Céspedes.* Paris: P. Dupont, 1895.

———. *Un instante decisivo de la maravillosa carrera de Máximo Gómez.* Havana: El Siglo XX, 1932.

Círculo de Hacendados y Agricultores de la Isla de Cuba. *Exposición dirigida en julio 8, 1894 por el Círculo de Hacendados y Agricultores de la Isla de Cuba a las Cortes del Reino Español en la cual se señalaban las principales causas que por su continuidad producían la excesiva gravedad de la crisis que atravasaba la industria azucarera y las soluciones que había que aplicar entonces con toda urgencia para evitar su inminente ruina.* Havana: Asociación Nacional de Hacendados, 1943.

Cisneros Betancourt, Salvador. *A los cubanos de occidente.* Holguín: n.p., 1873.

———. *Appeal to the American People on Behalf of Cuba.* New York: Evening Post Job Printing House, 1900.

Collazo, Enrique. *Los americanos en Cuba.* 2 vols. Havana: C. Martínez y Cía., 1905–1906.

———. *Cosas de Cuba: cuentas claras.* Havana: La Universal, 1913.

———. *Cuba heroica.* Havana: La Mercantil, 1912.

———. *Cuba independiente.* Havana: La Moderna Poesía, 1900.

———. *Cuba intervenida.* Havana: C. Martínez y Cía., 1910.

———. *Desde Yara hasta el Zanjón, apuntaciones históricas.* Havana: Tipografía de "La Lucha," 1893.

———. *La revolución de agosto de 1906.* Havana: C. Martínez y Cía., 1907.

Consuegra, W. I. *Hechos y comentarios. La revolución de febrero de 1917 en Las Villas.* Havana: La Comercial, 1920.

Dana, Jr., Richard Henry. *To Cuba and Back: A Vacation Voyage.* Boston: Ticknor & Fields, 1859.

Davis, Richard Harding. *Cuba in War Time.* New York: Russell, 1897.

Dolz, Ricardo. *El proceso electoral de 1916.* Havana: n.p., 1917.

Dulce, General Domingo. *Informe al Ministro de Ultramar.* Madrid: Imprenta Nacional, 1867.

Duque, Matías. *Ocios del presidio.* Havana: El Avisador Comercial, 1919.

Escalante Beatón, Aníbal. *Calixto García, su campaña en el 95.* Havana: Editorial Caribe, 1946.

Ferrara, Orestes. *Una mirada sobre tres siglos: memorias.* Madrid: Playor, S.A., 1975.

———. *Mis relaciones con Máximo Gómez.* Havana: Molina y Cía., 1942.

Ferrer, Horacio. *Con el rifle al hombro.* Havana: El Siglo XX, 1950.

Figueredo Socarrás, Fernando. *La revolución de Yara.* Havana: M. Pulido y Cía., 1902.

Flint, Grover. *Marching with Gómez.* Boston: Wolfe & Co., 1898.

Foraker, Joseph Benson. *Notes of a Busy Life.* 3d ed. 2 vols. Cincinnati: Stewart and Kidd Co., 1917.

Funston, Brig. Gen. Frederick. *Memories of Two Wars.* New York: Charles Scribner's Sons, 1911.

Gallego y García, Tesifonte. *La preparación de la guerra.* Vol. 1 of *La insurrección, cubana crónicas de la campaña.* Madrid: Imprenta Central de los Ferrocarriles, 1897.

García, General Calixto. *Parte oficial al General en Jefe sobre la campaña de Santiago de Cuba.* Havana: Academia de la Historia, 1953.

Giberga, Eliseo. *Obras de Eliseo Giberga.* 4 vols. Havana: Rambla y Bouza, 1930–31.

Gómez, Fernando. *La insurrección por dentro, artículos publicados en Diario de la Marina y Diario del Ejército.* Havana: M. Ruiz y Cía., 1897.

Gómez, Juan Gualberto. *La cuestión de Cuba en el 1884.* Madrid: J. Alaria, 1885.

———. *Juan Gualberto Gómez, su labor patriótica y sociológica.* Havana: Rambla y Bouza, 1934.

Gómez, Máximo. *Revoluciones, Cuba y hogar.* Edited by Bernando Gómez Toro. Havana: Rambla y Bouza, 1927.

Gómez y Báez, General Máximo. *Carta del general Máximo Gómez al sr. Tomás Estrada Palma, ex-presidente de la República Cubana.* Santiago de los Caballeros, Dominican Republic: Tipografía de Ulises Francisco Bidó, 1893.

———. *Cartas de Máximo Gómez.* Ciudad Trujillo, Dominican Republic: J.R., Vda. de García, Sucesores, 1936.

———. *Convenio del Zanjón, relato de los últimos sucesos de Cuba.* Kingston, Jamaica: Pedro A. Pomier, 1878.

———. *Diario de campaña.* Havana: Instituto del Libro, 1968.

———. *Horas de tregua.* Havana: Artística Comedia, 1916.

———. *La independencia de Cuba o el general Máximo Gómez y su política de paz, unión y concordia.* Havana: Tipografía de Los Niños Huérfanos, 1899.

———. *La insurrección de Cuba pintada por sí misma.* Trinidad de Cuba: El Imparcial, 1884.

———. *Recuerdos y previsiones.* Havana: Publicaciones de la Secretaría de Educación, Dirección de Cultura, 1935.

González, N. G. *In Darkest Cuba.* Columbia, S.C.: The State Company, 1922.

Gutiérrez de la Concha e Irigoyen, José. *Memoria sobre el estado político, gobierno y administración de las isla de Cuba.* Madrid: J. Trujillo, 1853.

———. *Memoria sobre la guerra de la isla de Cuba y sobre su estado político y económico desde . . . 1871 . . . a . . . 1874.* Madrid: R. Labajos, 1875.

Hazard, Samuel. *Cuba with Pen and Pencil.* Hartford, Conn.: Hartford Publishing Co., 1871.

Hernández, General Eusebio. *Maceo: dos conferencias históricas.* Havana: Instituto del Libro, 1968.

———. *El período revolucionario de 1879 a 1895.* Havana: El Siglo XX, 1914.

Hevia, Aurelio. *Colección de artículos y documentos referentes a la condición actual de Cuba.* Havana: Rambla y Bouza, 1909.

Kelly, James J. *The Mambí-land, or Adventures of a Herald Correspondent in Cuba.* Philadelphia: J. R. Lippincott & Co., 1874.

Kennan, George. *Campaigning in Cuba.* New York: Century Co., 1899.

Lanuza, José A. González. *Discursos y trabajos.* Havana: Rambla y Bouza, 1921.

Laurent, Emilio A. *De oficial a revolucionario.* Havana: Ucar, García y Cía., 1941.

Lima, Alfredo. *La odisea de Río Verde.* Havana: Cultural, S.A., 1934.

Lodge, Henry Cabot. *Selections from the Correspondence of Theodore Roosevelt and Henry Cabot Lodge.* 2 vols. New York: Charles Scribner's Sons, 1925.

———. *The War with Spain.* London: Harper & Brothers, 1899.

Lorenzo, General Manuel. *Manifiesto del general Manuel Lorenzo a la nación española sobre los acontecimientos de Santiago de Cuba.* Cádiz: Campes, 1837.

Loynaz del Castillo, Enrique. *La constituyente de Jimaguayú.* Havana: El Siglo XX, 1952.

Maceo, General Antonio. *Antonio Maceo: ideología política, cartas y otros documentos.* Havana: Sociedad Cubana de Estudios Históricos e Internacionales, 1950.

———. *Documentos para su vida.* Havana: Publicaciones del Archivo Nacional, 1945.

———. *Papeles.* Havana: A. Muñiz y Hno., 1938.

———. *Papeles de Maceo.* Havana: Academia de la Historia de Cuba, 1948.

———. *El pensamiento vivo de Maceo: cartas, proclamas, artículos y documentos.* Havana: Organización Continental de los Festivales del Libro, 1960.

Manzano, Juan Francisco. *Autobiografía de un esclavo.* Edited by Ivan A. Schulman. Madrid: Ediciones Guadarrama, 1975.

María, Jacinto. *Los voluntarios de Cuba y el obispo de la Habana.* Madrid: Pérez Dubrull, 1871.

Martí, José. *Obras completas.* 4 vols. Caracas: Litho-tip, 1964.

———. *Páginas escogidas.* Buenos Aires: Espasa-Calpe Argentina, 1953.

Maza, Gomez de la. *Máximo Gómez y la Asamblea.* Havana: n.p., 1899.

Méndez Capote, Domingo. *Trabajos.* 3 vols. Havana: Molina y Cía., 1930.

Miró Argenter, General José. *Cuba: crónicas de la guerra, las campañas de la invasión y de Occidente, 1895–1896.* 3 vols. Havana: Editorial Lex, 1945.

Montejo, Esteban. *The Autobiography of a Runaway Slave.* Edited by Miguel Barnet and translated by Jocasta Innes. New York: World Publishing Co., 1969.

Montero, Tomás. *Grandezas y miserias, el libro de un reporter.* Havana: Editorial Alfa, 1944.

Morison, E. E., ed. *The Letters of Theodore Roosevelt.* 8 vols. Cambridge, Mass.: Harvard University Press, 1952.

Morúa Delgado, Martín. *Integración cubana y otros ensayos.* Havana: Comisión Nacional del Centenario de . . . , 1957.

Ochando, T. *El general Martínez Campos en Cuba: reseña político-militar de la última campaña.* Madrid: Imprenta de Fortanet, 1878.

Otero Pimentel, Luis. *Memoria sobre los Voluntarios de la Isla de Cuba: consideraciones relativas a su pasado, su presente y su porvenir.* Havana: La Propaganda Literaria, 1878.

Partido Revolucionario Cubano. *Correspondencia diplomática de la delegación cubana en Nueva York durante la guerra de independencia de 1895 a 1898.* 5 vols. Havana: El Siglo XX, 1943–1946.

————. *La revolución del 95 según la correspondencia de la delegación cubana en New York.* 5 vols. Havana: Editorial Habanera, 1932–1937.

Pérez, Luis Marino, comp. *Newspaper Clippings Relative to the Period of the Administration of Cuba by the United States, September, 1906, to January, 1909.* 15 vols. Available in the Library of Congress, Washington, D.C.

Phillips, Ruby Hart. *Cuba: Island of Paradox.* New York: McDowell, Oblonsky, 1959.

————. *Cuban Sideshow.* Havana: Cuban Press, 1935.

Pichardo, Hortensia. *Cartas de Máximo Gómez a Francisco Carrillo.* Havana: Instituto Cubano del Libro, 1971.

————. *Documentos para la historia de Cuba.* 2 vols. Havana: Editorial de Ciencias Sociales, 1976, 1977.

Piedra Martel, General Manuel. *Compañas de Maceo en la última guerra de independencia.* Havana: Editorial Lex, 1946.

————. *Mis primeros treinta años.* Havana: Minerva, 1944.

Piñeyro, Enrique. *Como acabó la dominación de España en América.* Paris: Garnier Hnos., 1908.

Polavieja y del Castillo, Camilo García. *Relación documentada de mi política en Cuba.* Madrid: Minuesa, 1898.

Post, Charles Johnson. *The Little War of Private Post.* New York: Little, Brown, 1961.

Puri, Manuel C., ed. *La revolución de agosto: historia de un corresponsal por Arturo Sáinz de la Peña.* Havana: La Prueba, 1908.

Quesada y Miranda, Gonzalo de. *Archivo de Gonzalo de Quesada, documentos históricos.* Havana: Editorial de la Universidad de La Habana, 1965.

————. *Archivo de Gonzalo de Quesada, epistolario.* 2 vols. Havana: El Siglo XX, 1948, 1951.

La República de Cuba en 1909, Septiembre. Havana: Rambla y Bouza, 1909. (Articles from *El Mundo* in Spanish and English)

Rhodes, Charles D. *The Santiago Campaign.* Military Information Division. Washington, D.C.: Government Printing Office, 1898.

Ribó, José Joaquín. *Historia de los voluntarios cubanos.* 2 vols. Madrid: Imprenta y Librería de N. González, 1872–1876.

Roa, Ramón. *Con la pluma y el machete.* 3 vols. Havana: Ministerio de Educación, 1950.

Roa, Raúl. *Aventuras, venturas y desventuras de un mambí en la lucha por la independencia de Cuba.* México: Siglo XXI Editores, S.A., 1970.

Rodríguez, Amalia, ed. *Algunos documentos políticos de Máximo Gómez.* Havana: Biblioteca Nacional Jose Martí, 1962.

Rodríguez Demorizi, Emilio. *Cartas de Máximo Gómez.* Ciudad Trujillo: J.R. Vda. de Garcia, 1936.

———. *Papeles dominicanos de Máximo Gómez.* Ciudad Trujillo: Editora Montalvo, 1954.

Roig de Leuchsenring, Emilio, ed. *Ideario cubano.* 3 vols. Havana: Municipio de La Habana, 1936.

Roosevelt, Theodore. *Autobiography.* Vol. 22 of *The Works of Theodore Roosevelt,* edited by Hermann Hagedorn. New York: Charles Scribner's Sons, 1926.

———. *The Rough Riders.* Vol. 13 of *The Works of Theodore Roosevelt,* edited by Hermann Hagedorn. New York: Charles Scribner's Sons, 1924.

———. *State Papers.* Vol. 15 of *The Works of Theodore Roosevelt,* edited by Hermann Hagedorn. New York: Charles Scribner's Sons, 1926.

Rosell y Malpica, Eduardo. *Diario del teniente coronel Eduardo Rosell y Malpica, 1895–1897.* 2 vols. Havana: Academia de la Historia de Cuba, 1949–1950.

Rowan, Andrew. *How I Carried the Message to Garcia.* San Francisco: Walter D. Harney Publishers, n.d.

Rubens, Horatio S. *Liberty: The Story of Cuba.* New York: Brewer, Warren & Putnam, 1932.

Sanguily y Garritte, Manuel. *Obras de Manuel Sanguily.* 10 vols. Havana: A. Dorrbecker, 1919.

Sanjenís, Avelino. *Memorias de la revolución de 1895 por la independencia de Cuba.* Havana: Rambla y Bouza, 1913.

———. *Mis cartas: memorias de la revolución de 1895 por la independencia de Cuba.* Sagua la Grande: El Comercio, 1900.

Scott, Maj. Gen. Hugh Lenox. *Some Memories of a Soldier.* New York and London: Century Co., 1928.

Secades y Japón, Manuel, and Díaz Pardo, Horacio, eds. *La justicia en Cuba: los veteranos y los indultos.* Havana: La Prueba, 1908.

———. *La justicia en Cuba: patriotas y traidores.* 2 vols. Havana: P. Fernández y Cía., 1912, 1914.

Solano Alvarez, Luis. *Mi actuación militar o apuntes para la historia de la revolución de febrero de 1917.* Havana: El Siglo XX, 1920.

Tacón y Rosique, General Miguel. *Correspondencia reservada, 1834–1836.* Edited by Juan Pérez de la Riva. Havana, 1963.

———. *Memoria del general Miguel Tacón y Rosique.* Havana: Imprenta del Gobierno, 1838.

———. *Relación del gobierno superior . . .* Havana: Imprenta del Gobierno, 1838.

Torriente, Cosme de la. *Calixto García cooperó con las fuerzas armadas de los Estados Unidos en 1898 cumpliendo órdenes del gobierno cubano.* Havana: El Siglo XX, 1952.

———. *La Constituyente de La Yaya.* Havana: El Siglo XX, 1952.

———. *Cuarenta años de mi vida, 1898–1938.* Havana: El Siglo XX, 1939.

Trujillo, Enrique. *Apuntes históricos, propaganda y movimientos revolucionarios cubanos en los Estados Unidos, desde enero de 1880 hasta febrero de 1895.* New York: Tipografía de "El Porvenir," 1896.

Valdes Domínguez, Fermín. *Diario de un soldado.* 4 vols. Havana: Universidad de la Habana, 1972–1974.

Vandama Calderón, Eugenio. *Colección de artículos sobre el Instituto de los Voluntarios de la isla de Cuba.* Madrid, n.p., 1896–1897.

Varela Zequeira, Eduardo. *La política en 1905 o episodios de una lucha electoral.* Havana: Rambla y Bouza, 1905.

Varona, Enrique José. *De la colonia a la república: selección de trabajos políticos, ordenada por su autor.* Havana: Cuba Contemporánea, 1919.

———. *Mirando en torno.* Havana: Rambla y Bouza, 1910.

———. *Por Cuba: discursos.* Havana: Rambla y Bouza, 1918.

Varona Guerrero, Miguel. *La guerra de independencia de Cuba.* 3 vols. Havana: Editorial Lex, 1946.

Velasco, Carlos de. *Desde el Castillo de Figueras: cartas de Estrada Palma (1877–1878).* Havana: Cuba Contemporánea, 1918.

Villaverde, Cirilo. *Cecilia Valdés o La Loma del ángel.* New York: Las Américas Publishing Co., 1964.

Weyler, Valeriano. *Mi mando en Cuba.* 5 vols. Madrid: F. González Rojas, 1910–1911.

Wilson, James Harrison. *Under the Old Flag.* 2 vols. New York and London: D. Appleton & Co., 1912.

Wright, Irene. *Cuba.* New York: Macmillan Co., 1910.

Zambrana, Antonio. *La república de Cuba.* New York: N. Ponce de León, 1873.

Zarazoga, Justo. *Las insurrecciones de Cuba.* 2 vols. Madrid: Imprenta de M. G. Hernández, 1872–1873.

Newspapers and Magazines

Bohemia (Havana)
Carteles (Havana)
Diario de la Marina (Havana)
La Discusíon (Havana)
Harper's Weekly
Havana Post
Heraldo de Cuba (Havana)
Journal of the Military Service Institution
La Lucha (Havana)
El Mundo (Havana)
Nation
New York Herald Tribune

The New York Times
North American Review
Outlook
El País (Havana)
Patria (New York)
Review of Reviews
State
Times (London)
Washington Evening Star
Washington Post
World (New York)

Books

Abel, Christopher, and Torrents, Nissa, eds. *José Martí, Revolutionary Democrat*. Durham, N.C.: Duke University Press, 1986.
Adam y Silva, Ricardo. *Cuba, el fin de la república*. Miami: A.I.P. Publications Center, 1973.
———. *La gran mentira: 4 de septiembre de 1933*. Havana: Editorial Lex, 1947.
Aguilar León, Luis. *Cuba, 1933: Prologue to Revolution*. Ithaca and London: Cornell University Press, 1972.
Aguilera Rojas, Eladio. *Francisco Vicente Aguilera y la revolución cubana*. 2 vols. Havana: La Moderna Poesía, 1909.
Alvarez Díaz, José, et al. *Cuba: geopolítica y pensamiento económico*. Miami: Colegio de Economistas de Cuba en el Exilio, 1964.
———. *Un estudio sobre Cuba*. Miami: University of Miami Press, 1963.
Alvarez Estévez, Rolando. *La emigración cubana en Estados Unidos, 1868–1878*. Havana: Editorial de Ciencias Sociales, 1986.
———. *General José Lacret Morlot, ensayo biográfico*. Havana: Editorial de Ciencias Sociales, 1983.
Alvarez Tabío, Pedro, ed. *Antimperialismo y república: Juan Gualberto Gómez, Enrique José Varona, S. Cisneros Betancourt, Manuel Sanguily*. Havana: Ediciones Políticas, 1975.
Arce, Luis A. de. *Emilio Núñez (1875–1922): historiografía*. Havana: Editorial Niños, 1943.
Armiñán y Perez, Luis de. *Weyler, el gran capitán*. Madrid: Editorial "El Gran Capitán," 1946.
Arredondo, Alberto. *Cuba: Tierra indefensa*. Havana: Editorial Lex, 1945.
———. *El negro en Cuba*. Havana: Editorial Alfa, 1939.
Averhoff Purón, Mario. *Los primeros partidos políticos*. Havana: Instituto Cubano del Libro, 1971.
Azcuy y Alón, Fanny. *El Partido Revolucionario Cubano y la independencia de Cuba*. Havana: Molina y Cía., 1930.
Baeza Flores, Alberto. *Vida de José Martí*. Santo Domingo, Dominican Republic: Biblioteca Nacional, [c. 1986].

Báez Díaz, Tomás. *Máximo Gómez, el libertador*. Santo Domingo, Dominican Republic: Publicaciones América, 1986.

Bailey, Thomas A. *A Diplomatic History of the American People*. New York: F. S. Croft and Co., 1947.

Barbarrosa, Enrique. *El proceso de la república: análisis de la situación política y económica de Cuba bajo el gobierno presidencial de Tomás Estrada Palma y José Miguel Gómez*. Havana: Imprenta Militar de A. Pérez Sierra, 1911.

Barquín, Ramón M. *Las luchas guerrilleras en Cuba: de la colonia a la Sierra Maestra*. 2 vols. Madrid: Playor, S.A., 1975.

Beale, Howard K. *Theodore Roosevelt and the Rise of America to World Power*. Baltimore, Md.: Johns Hopkins Press, 1956.

Benjamin, Jules R. *The United States and Cuba: Hegemony and Dependent Development, 1880–1934*; Pittsburgh, Pa.: University of Pittsburgh Press, 1974.

———. *The United States and the Origins of the Cuban Revolution: The Empire of Liberty in an Age of National Liberation*. Princeton, N.J.: Princeton University Press, 1990.

Brown Castillo, Gerardo. *Cuba colonial. Ensayo histórico social de la integración de la sociedad cubana*. Havana: Jesús Montero, 1952.

Buttari y Gaunard, J. *Boceto crítico-histórico: obra escrita en cuatro etapas*. Havana: Editorial Lex, 1954.

Cabrera, Raimundo. *Cuba and the Cubans*. Philadelphia: Levytype Co., 1896.

Cairo Ballester, Ana. *El Grupo Minorista y su tiempo*. Havana: Editorial de Ciencias Sociales, 1978.

———. *El Movimiento de Veteranos y Patriotas*. Havana: Instituto Cubano del Libro, 1976.

Callcott, Wilfrid. *The Caribbean Policy of the United States*. Baltimore, Md.: Johns Hopkins Press, 1942.

Camacho, Pánfilo D. *Aguilera, el precursor sin gloria*. Havana: Publicaciones del Ministerio de Educación, 1951.

———. *Biografía de la Cámara de la Guerra Grande*. Havana: El Siglo XX, 1945.

———. *Estrada Palma, el gobernante honrado*. Havana: Editorial Trópico, 1938.

———. *Martí y el Partido Revolucionario Cubano*. Havana: El Siglo XX, 1953.

Carballal, Rodolfo Z. *El general José Miguel Gómez*. Havana: Rambla y Bouza, 1913.

Carbonell, José M. *Cuba Independiente*. Vol. 11 of *Historia de América*. Edited by Ricardo Levene. 14 vols. Buenos Aires: Imprenta López, 1941.

Carbonell, Miguel Angel. *Antonio Maceo*. Havana: Editorial Guáimaro, 1935.

———. *Eusebio Hernández*. 2 vols. Havana: Editorial Guáimaro, 1939.

———. *Juan Gualberto Gómez*. Havana: Editorial Guáimaro, 1938.

————. *Sanguily*. Havana: Editorial Guáimaro, 1938.

Carbonell, Néstor. *Martí, sus últimos días*. Havana: El Siglo XX, 1950.

Carbonell, Néstor, and Santovenia, Emeterio. *Guáimaro: 10 de abril, 1869–10 de abril, 1959: reseña histórica de la primera Asamblea Constituyente y la primera Cámara de Representantes de Cuba*. Havana: Seoane y Fernández, 1919.

Carricarte, Arturo R. *Lo que dice y lo que no dice el Manifiesto de Montecristi*. Havana: El Sol, 1940.

Casasús, Juan J. E. *Calixto García, el estratega*. Havana: Cultural, S.A., 1942.

————. *La emigración cubana y la independencia de la patria*. Havana: Editorial Lex, 1953.

————. *La invasión: sus antecedentes, sus factores, su finalidad. Estudio crítico-militar*. Havana: n.p., 1950.

————. *Vida de Ignacio Agramonte*. Camagüey, Cuba: Imprenta Ramentol, 1937.

Castellanos, Gerardo. *Legado mambí: formación, odisea y agonía del archivo del general Máximo Gómez*. Havana: Ucar, García y Cía., 1940.

————. *Un paladín (Serafín Sánchez)*. Havana: Editorial Hermes, 1926.

————. *Panorama histórico: ensayo de cronología cubana desde 1492 hasta 1933*. Havana: Ucar, García y Cía., 1934.

————. *Pensando en Agramonte*. Havana: Ucar, García y Cía., 1939.

————. *Raíces del 10 Octubre de 1868: Aguilera y Céspedes*. Havana: El Siglo XX, 1937.

————. *Sondeo histórico: Máximo Gómez y su diario de campaña*. Havana: Ucar, García y Cía., 1941.

————. *Tierras y glorias de Oriente, Calixto García*. Havana: Editorial Hermes, 1927.

————. *Los últimos días de Martí*. Havana: Ucar, García y Cía., 1937.

Cepero Bonilla, Raúl. *Azúcar y abolición: apuntes para una historia crítica del abolicionismo*. Havana: Editorial Echevarría, 1960.

Céspedes y Quesada, Carlos Manuel de. *Manuel de Quesada y Loynaz*. Havana: El Siglo XX, 1925.

Chadwick, French E. *The Relations of the United States and Spain. The Spanish-American War*. 2 vols. New York: Charles Scribner's Sons, 1911.

Chang, Federico. *El ejército nacional en la república neocolonial*. Havana: Escuela de Ciencias Sociales, 1981.

Chapman, Charles E. *A History of the Cuban Republic: A Study in Hispanic American Politics*. New York: Macmillan Co., 1927.

Chester, Edmund A. *A Sergeant Named Batista*. New York: Henry Holt and Co., 1954.

Conte, Rafael, and Company, José M. *Guerra de razas*. Havana: Imprenta Militar, 1912.

Corbitt, Duvon C. *The Colonial Government of Cuba*. Chapel Hill: University of North Carolina Press, 1938.

Córdova, Federico. *Manuel Sanguily*. Havana: Seoane, Fernández y Cía., 1942.

Costa, Octavio R. *Antonio Maceo, el héroe*. Havana: Academia de la Historia, 1947.

———. *Estudios históricos*. Havana and Madrid: Aldus, S.A., 1926.

———. *Juan Gualberto Gómez, una vida sin sombra*. Havana: El Siglo XX, 1950.

———. *Manuel Sanguily, historia de un ciudadano*. Havana: Editorial Unidad, 1948.

———. *Perfil político de Calixto García*. Havana: El Siglo XX, 1948.

Cuba bajo la administración del mayor general José Miguel Gómez. Havana: Rambla y Bouza, 1911.

Cuesta, Leonel Antonio de la. *Constituciones cubanas: desde 1812 hasta nuestros días*. Recopilación bibliográfica de Rolando Alum Linera. Madrid: Ediciones Exilio, 1974.

Dihigo y Mestre, Juan Miguel. *El mayor general Pedro E. Betancourt y Dávalos en la lucha por la independencia de Cuba*. Havana: El Siglo XX, 1934.

Domínguez, Jorge I. *Cuba: Order and Revolution*. Cambridge, Mass.: Harvard University Press, 1978.

Draper, Theodore. *Castroism: Theory and Practice*. New York: Praeger, 1965.

Duarte Oropesa, José A. *Historiología cubana*. 4 vols. Miami: Ediciones Universal, 1974–1989.

Duffy, Herbert S. *William Howard Taft*. New York: Minton, Balch & Co., 1930.

Duplessis, Gustavo. *Un hombre, sus ideas y un paraguas: evocación de Juan Gualberto Gómez y su ideario*. Havana: Universidad de La Habana, 1959.

Ely, Roland T. *Cuando reinaba Su Majestad El Azúcar*. Buenos Aires: Editorial Sudamericana, 1963.

Entrialgo, Elías. *La insurrección de los diez años: una interpretación social de este fenómeno histórico*. Havana: Departamento de Intercambio Cultural de la Universidad de la Habana, 1950.

———. *La liberación étnica cubana*. Havana: Universidad de la Habana, 1953.

———. *Períoca sociográfica de la cubanidad*. Havana: Jesús Montero, 1947.

Estévez y Romero, Luis. *Desde el Zanjón hasta Baire, datos para la historia política de Cuba*. Havana: La Propaganda Literaria, 1908.

Estrade, Paul. *José Martí, militante y estratega*. Havana: Editorial de Ciencias Sociales, 1983.

———. *José Martí, 1853–1895: des fondements de la democratie en Amérique latine*. 2 vols. Paris: Editions Caribéenes, 1987.

Fermoselle, Rafael. *The Evolution of the Cuban Military, 1492–1986*. Miami: Ediciones Universal, 1987.

———. *Política y color: la guerrita de 1912*. Montevideo: Ediciones Géminis, 1974.

Fernández Almagro, Melchor. *Historia política de la España contemporánea*. 2 vols. Madrid: Ediciones Pégaso, 1956.

Fernández Escobio, Fernando. *El obisp. Compostela y La Iglesia cubana en el siglo XVII*. Miami: Rapid Printing, n.d.

Fernández Pellicer, Juan A. *Juan Gualberto Gómez, un hombre, una actitud, un símbolo.* Havana: Editorial Lex, 1957.

Figueras, Francisco. *Cuba y su evolución colonial.* Havana: El Avisador Comercial, 1907.

———. *La intervención y su política.* Havana: El Avisador Comercial, 1906.

Figueroa y Miranda, Miguel. *Religión y política en la Cuba del siglo XIX: el Obispo Espada visto a la luz de los Archivos Romanos, 1802–1832.* Miami: Ediciones Universal, 1975.

Fitzgibbon, Russell H. *Cuba and the United States, 1900–1935.* New York: Russell and Russell, 1964.

Foner, Philip S. *A History of Cuba and Its Relations with the United States.* 2 vols. New York: International Publishers, 1962, 1964.

———. *The Spanish-Cuban-American War and the Birth of American Imperialism.* 2 vols. New York and London: Monthly Review Press, 1972.

Franco, José L. *Antonio Maceo, apuntes para una historia de su vida.* 3 vols. Havana: Publicaciones de la Sociedad de Estudios Históricos e Internacionales, 1951–1957.

———. *Apuntes para una historia de la legislación y administración colonial.* Havana: Editorial de Ciencias Sociales, 1985.

———. *La reacción española contra la libertad.* Havana: Oficina del Historiador de la Ciudad de la Habana, 1961.

———. *La revolución de Yara y la constituyente de Guáimaro.* Havana: Ayón, Impresor, n.d.

Freidel, Frank. *The Splendid Little War.* Boston: Little, Brown, 1958.

Freidlander, Heinrich E. *Historia económica de Cuba.* Havana: Jesús Montero, 1944.

Fuerzas Armadas Revolucionarias, Centro de Estudios de Historia Militar. *Mayor general Máximo Gómez Báez: sus campañas militares.* 2 vols. Havana: Editora Política, 1986.

García Cisneros, Florencio. *El león de Santa Rita, el general Vicente García y la Guerra de los Diez Años.* Miami, Fla.: Ediciones Universal, 1989.

———. *Máximo Gómez, ¿caudillo o dictador?* New York: Ediciones Universal, 1986.

García Montes, Jorge, and Alonso Avila, Antonio. *Historia del Partido Comunista de Cuba.* Miami: Ediciones Universal, 1970.

Garrigó, Roque E. *La convulsión cubana.* Havana: La Razón, 1906.

———. *Historia documentada de la conspiración de los Soles y Rayos de Bolívar.* 2 vols. Havana: Academia de la Historia de Cuba, 1939.

González, Diego. *Historia documentada de los movimientos revolucionarios por la independencia de Cuba, 1852–1867.* 2 vols. Havana: Academia de la Historia de Cuba, 1939.

González, Edelmira. *La revolución en Cuba: Memorias del coronel Rosendo Collazo.* Havana: Hermes, 1934.

González y Rodríguez de la Peña, Hipólito. *Weyler, el hombre de hierro.* Madrid: Espasa Calpe, 1934.

Granda, Manuel J. *La paz del manganeso*. Havana: Academia de la Historia de Cuba, 1939.

Gray, Richard B. *José Martí, Cuban Patriot*. Gainesville: University of Florida Press, 1962.

Griñán Peralta, Leonardo. *Maceo, análisis caracteriológico*. Havana: Editorial Trópico, 1936.

Guerra Alemán, José. *¡Juro, pero no prometo! Biografía del general José Braulio Alemán y otros relatos de la guerra y de la paz*. México, D.F.: Costa-Amic Editores, S.A., 1989.

Guerra y Sánchez, Ramiro. *Azúcar y población en las Antillas*. 2d ed. Havana: Cultural, S.A., 1935.

———. *Un cuarto de siglo de evolución cubana*. Havana: Librería Cervantes de R. Veloso, 1924.

———. *Guerra de los Diez Años, 1868–1878*. 2 vols. Havana: Cultural, S.A., 1950–1952.

———. *La industria azucarera de Cuba*. Havana: Cultural, S.A., 1940.

———. *Manual de historia de Cuba desde su descubrimiento hasta 1860: económica, política y social*. 2d ed. Havana: Consejo Nacional de Universidades, 1964.

Guerra y Sánchez, Ramiro, et al. *Historia de la nación cubana*. 10 vols. Havana: Editorial Historia de la nación cubana, 1952.

Guggenheim, Harry F. *The United States and Cuba: A Study in International Relations*. New York: Macmillan Co., 1934.

Hagedorn, Hermann. *Leonard Wood: A Biography*. 2 vols. New York and London: Harper and Bros., 1931.

Harbaugh, William H. *Power and Responsibility: The Life and Times of Theodore Roosevelt*. New York: Farrar, Straus and Cudahy, 1961.

Healy, David F. *The United States in Cuba, 1898–1902*. Madison: University of Wisconsin Press, 1963.

Hernández Corujo, Enrique. *Organización civil y política de las revoluciones cubanas de 1868 y 1895*. Havana: Rambla y Bouza, 1929.

Hitchman, James H. *Leonard Wood and Cuban Independence, 1898–1902*. The Hague: Martinus Nijhoff, 1971.

Horrego Estuch, Leopoldo. *Antonio Maceo, estudio político y patriótico*. Havana: Academia de la Historia, 1947.

———. *Juan Gualberto Gómez, un gran inconforme*. Havana: Editorial Mecenas, 1949.

———. *Maceo, héroe y carácter*. Havana: La Milagrosa, 1952.

———. *Martín Morúa Delgado, vida y mensaje*. Havana, 1954.

———. *Máximo Gómez*. Havana: P. Fernández y Cía., 1945.

———. *El sentido revolucionario del 68, historia de un proceso ideológico*. Havana: Jesús Montero, 1945.

Hubbard, Elbert. *A Message to García*. East Aurora, N.Y.: Roycroft Shop, 1899.

Ibarra, Jorge. *José Martí, dirigente e ideólogo revolucionario*. Mexico, D.F.: Editorial Nuestro Tiempo, 1981.

Ibarra Martínez, Francisco. *Cronología de la Guerra de los Diez Años.* Santiago de Cuba: Instituto Cubano del Libro, 1976.

Infiesta, Ramón. *El autonomismo cubano: su razón y manera.* Havana: Jesús Montero, 1939.

———. *Historia constitucional de Cuba.* Havana: Editorial Selecta, 1942.

———. *Máximo Gómez.* Havana: El Siglo XX, 1937.

Instituto de Historia del Movimiento Comunista y de la Revolución Socialista de Cuba, anexo al Comité Central del Partido Comunista de Cuba. *Historia del movimiento obrero cubano, 1865–1958.* Vol. 1: *1865–1935.* Havana: Editoria Política, 1985–.

International Commission of Jurists. *Cuba and the Rule of Law.* Geneva: n.p., 1962.

Iznaga, R. *Tres años de república, 1902–1905.* Havana: Rambla y Bouza, 1905.

Jenks, Leland H. *Our Cuban Colony.* New York: Vanguard Press, 1928.

Jensen, Larry R. *Children of Colonial Despotism: Press, Politics and Culture in Cuba, 1790–1840.* Tampa: University of South Florida Press, 1988.

Jessup, Philip C. *Elihu Root.* 2 vols. New York: Dodd, Mead & Co., 1938.

Johnson, John J. *The Military and Society in Latin America.* Stanford, Calif.: Stanford University Press, 1964.

Johnson, Willis F. *The History of Cuba.* 5 vols. New York: B. F. Buck and Co., 1920.

Kirk, John M. *Between God and the Party: Religion and Politics in Revolutionary Cuba.* Tampa: University of South Florida Press, 1989.

———. *José Martí, Mentor of the Cuban Nation.* Gainesville: University of Florida Press, 1983.

Kuethe, Allan J. *Cuba, 1753–1815: Crown, Military, and Society.* Knoxville: University of Tennessee Press, 1986.

La Feber, Walter. *The New Empire.* Ithaca: Cornell University Press, 1963.

Lamore, Jean. *José Martí, La Guerre de Cuba et le destin de l'Amerique latine.* Paris: Ed. Aubier-Montaigne, 1973.

Langley, Lester D. *The Cuban Policy of the United States.* New York: John Wiley & Sons, 1968.

———. *The United States and the Caribbean, 1900–1970.* Athens: University of Georgia Press, 1980.

La Riverend, Julio. *La Habana (biografía de una provincia).* Havana: El Siglo XX, 1960.

———. *Historia económica de Cuba.* Havana: Consejo Nacional de Universidades, 1965.

Lebroc, Reinero. *Cuba: Iglesia y sociedad, 1830–1860.* Madrid: Lit. Barrero, S.L., 1977.

———. *Episcopologio.* Miami, Fla.: Hispamerican Books, 1985.

Lee, Fitzhugh, and Wheeler, Joseph. *Cuba's Struggle against Spain, with the Causes of American Intervention and a Full Account of the Spanish-American War, Including the Peace Negotiations.* New York: American Historical Press, 1899.

Leech, Margaret. *In the Days of McKinley.* New York: Harper and Brothers, 1959.

Leiseca, Juan M. *Apuntes para la historia eclesiástica de Cuba.* Havana: Talleres Tipográficos de Carasa y Cía., 1938.

———. *Historia de Cuba.* Havana: Cervantes, 1925.

León, René, and León, Emilio J. *La guerra racial de 1912 en Cuba.* Library of Congress Catalog no. TX2-416-562.

Llaverías, Joaquín. *La Comisión Militar Ejecutiva y Permanente.* Havana: Academia de la Historia, 1929.

———. *El consejo administrativo de bienes embargados.* Havana: El Siglo XX, 1941.

———. *Los periódicos de Martí.* Havana: Pérez Sierra y Cía., 1929.

Lockmiller, David A. *Enoch H. Crowder: Soldier, Lawyer, Statesman.* University of Missouri Studies, no. 27. Columbia: University of Missouri Press, 1955.

———. *Magoon in Cuba: A History of the Second Intervention, 1906–1909.* Chapel Hill: University of North Carolina Press, 1938.

Lozano Casado, Miguel. *La personalidad del general José Miguel Gómez.* Havana: n.p., 1913.

Lubián y Arias, Rafael. *Martí en los campos de Cuba libre.* 2d ed. Miami: Ediciones Universal, 1982.

Lynch, John. *The Spanish-American Revolution, 1808–1826.* New York: W. W. Norton, 1973.

MacGaffey, Wyatt, and Barnett, Clifford R. *Twentieth-Century Cuba: The Background of the Castro Revolution.* Garden City: Doubleday & Co., 1962.

Mañach, Jorge. *El militarismo en Cuba.* Havana: Seone, Fernández y Cía., 1939.

———. *Martí, el apóstol.* New York: Las Américas Publishing Co., 1963.

———. *El pensamiento político y social de Martí.* Havana: Edición Oficial del Senado, 1941.

Márquez Sterling, Carlos. *Don Tomás: biografía de una época.* Havana: Editorial Lex, 1953.

———. *Historia de Cuba.* New York: Las Américas Publishing Co., 1963.

———. *Ignacio Agramonte, el bayardo de la revolución cubana.* Havana: Seoane, Fernández y Cía., 1936.

Márquez Sterling, Manuel. *Proceso histórico de la Enmienda Platt, 1897–1934.* Havana: El Siglo XX, 1941.

Marrero, Levi. *Cuba: economía y sociedad.* 12 vols. Madrid: Editorial Playor, 1972–.

———. *Historia económica de Cuba: guía de estudio y documentación.* 2 vols. Havana: Universidad de la Habana, 1956.

Martínez Bello, Antonio. *Orígen y meta del autonomismo, exégesis de Montoro.* Havana: P. Fernández y Cía., 1952.

Martínez Fraga, Pedro. *El general Menocal: apuntes para su biografía.* Havana: Talleres de la Editorial "Tiempo," 1941.

Martínez Ortiz, Rafael. *Cuba: los primeros años de independencia.* 2 vols. 3d ed. Paris: Editorial Le Livre Libre, 1929.

————. *General Leonard Wood's Government in Cuba.* Paris: Imprimere Dubois et Bauer, 1920.

Matthews, Franklin. *The New-Born Cuba.* New York and London: Harper and Brothers, 1899.

May, Ernest. *Imperial Democracy: The Emergence of America as a Great Power.* New York: Harcourt, Brace & World, 1961.

Mazarr, Michael J. *Semper Fidel: America & Cuba, 1776–1988.* Baltimore, Md.: Nautical and Aviation Publishing Co., 1988.

Mendez, Manuel Isidro. *Acerca de la Mejorana y Dos Ríos.* Havana: Oficina del Historiador de la Ciudad, 1954.

Merchán, Rafael María. *Cuba, justificación de sus guerras de independencia.* Havana: Imprenta Nacional de Cuba, 1961.

Merino, Bernardo, and Ibarzábal, Federico de. *La revolución de febrero: datos para la historia.* 2d ed. Havana: Librería Cervantes, 1918.

Millet, Allan Reed. *The Politics of Intervention: The Military Occupation of Cuba, 1906–1909.* Columbus: Ohio State University Press, 1968.

Millis, Walter. *The Martial Spirit: A Study of Our War with Spain.* Boston: Houghton Mifflin, 1931.

Mínguez, Bernardino Martín. *Política y militarismo: defensa del general Weyler, cuestión palpitante y transcendental.* Madrid: Imprenta de los Hijos de M. G. Hernández, 1897.

Mora, Flora. *Biografía de Perucho Figuerdo.* Miami, Fla.: n.p., 1974.

Morales y Morales, Vidal. *Hombres del 68: Rafael Morales y González.* Havana: Rambla y Bouza, 1904.

————. *Iniciadores y primeros mártires de la revolución cubana.* 3 vols. Havana: Cultural, S.A., 1931.

Morgan, H. Wayne. *William McKinley and His America.* Syracuse, N.Y.: Syracuse University Press, 1963.

Mowry, George E. *The Era of Theodore Roosevelt and the Birth of Modern America.* New York: Harper & Row, 1958.

Munro, Dana G. *Intervention and Dollar Diplomacy in the Caribbean, 1900–1921.* Princeton: Princeton University Press, 1964.

————. *The United States and the Caribbean Area.* Boston: World Peace Foundation, 1934.

Navas, José. *La convulsión de febrero.* Matanzas, Cuba: Imprenta y Monotipo El Escritorio, 1917.

————. *Cuba y los Estados Unidos: boceto histórico sobre el eco de la causa cubana en la gran nación vecina.* Havana: P. Fernández y Cía., 1916.

Nearing, Scott, and Freeman, Joseph. *Dollar Diplomacy: A Study in American Imperialism.* New York: Viking Press, 1925.

Oliva Pulgarón, Luis. *Apuntes históricos sobre la masonería cubana.* Havana: n.p., 1934.

Ortiz, Fernando. *La crisis política cubana (sus causas y remedios).* Havana: La Universal, 1919.

—————. *La decadencia cubana*. Havana: La Universal, 1924.

Padrón, Pedro Luis. *¡Qué república era aquella!* Havana: Editorial de Ciencias Sociales, 1986.

Pardo Suárez, Vicente. *La elección presidencial en Cuba*. Havana: Rambla y Bouza, 1923.

Patronato Ramón Guiteras Intercultural Center. *Presidentes de Cuba (1868–1933)*. Miami, Fla.: Editorial Cubana, 1987.

Pattee, Richard. *Catholic Life in the West Indies*. Washington, D.C.: Catholic Association for International Peace, 1946.

Payne, Stanley G. *Politics and the Military in Modern Spain*. Stanford: Stanford University Press, 1967.

—————. *Spanish Catholicism: A Historical Overview*. Madison: The University of Wisconsin Press, 1984.

Peralta, Víctor M. de. *Commonitorio de intervención a intervención*. Havana: La Prueba, 1907.

Pérez, Jr., Louis A. *Army Politics in Cuba, 1898–1958*. Pittsburgh, Pa.: University of Pittsburgh Press, 1978.

—————. *Cuba between Empires, 1878–1902*. Pittsburgh, Pa.: University of Pittsburgh Press, 1983.

—————. *Cuba: Between Reform and Revolution*. New York and Oxford: Oxford University Press, 1988.

—————. *Cuba under the Platt Amendment, 1902–1934*. Pittsburgh, Pa.: University of Pittsburgh Press, 1986.

—————. *Intervention, Revolution, and Politics in Cuba, 1913–1921*. Pittsburgh, Pa.: University of Pittsburgh Press, 1978.

—————. *Lords of the Mountain: Social Banditry and Peasant Protest in Cuba, 1878–1918*. Pittsburgh, Pa.: Pittsburgh University Press, 1989.

Pérez, Luis Marino. *Miguel Jerónimo Gutiérrez*. 2d ed. Havana: Editorial Hércules, 1958.

Pérez Cabrera, José M. *El cincuentenario del Partido Revolucionario Cubano*. Havana: El Siglo XX, 1942.

—————. *Estrada Palma y el alba de la república*. Havana: Cuadernos de la Universidad del Aire, 1952.

—————. *Los primeros esbozos biográficos de Céspedes*. Havana: El Siglo XX, 1947.

Pérez de la Riva, Juan, et al. *La república neocolonial*. 2 vols. Havana: Editorial de Ciencias Sociales, 1975–1978.

Pérez de la Riva y Pons, Francisco. *El café: historia de su cultivo y explotación en Cuba*. Havana: Jesús Montero, 1944.

Pérez Guzmán, Francisco, and Sarracino, Rodolfo. *La Guerra Chiquita: una experiencia necessaria*. Havana: Editorial Letras Cubanas, 1982.

Pérez Landa, Rufino. *Bartolomé Masó y Márquez, estudio biográfico documentado*. Havana: El Siglo XX, 1947.

Perkins, Dexter. *The United States and the Caribbean*. Cambridge, Mass.: Harvard University Press, 1947.

Pezuela, Jacobo de la. *Diccionario geográfico, estadístico e histórico de la isla de Cuba*. 4 vols. Madrid: Mellado, 1863–1866.

————. *Historia de la isla de Cuba.* 4 vols. Madrid: Bailliere y Hnos., 1868–1878.

Pina y Estrada, Rogelio. *Los presupuestos del estado. Análisis de los presupuestos del estado desde el establecimiento de la república.* Havana, 1936.

Pino Santos, Oscar. *Historia de Cuba, aspectos fundamentales.* Havana: Editorial Universitaria, 1964.

Pirala, Antonio. *Anales de la guerra de Cuba.* 4 vols. Madrid: F. González Rojas, 1895–1898.

Plasencia, Aleida, ed. *Recuerdos de las guerras de Cuba, 1868–1871.* Havana, 1963.

Ponte Domínguez, Francisco. *Historia de la Guerra de los Diez Años.* 2 vols. Havana: El Siglo XX, 1944.

————. *La idea invasora y su desarrollo histórico.* Havana: Cultural, S.A., 1930.

————. *La masonería en la independencia de Cuba.* Havana: Editorial Modes Magazine, 1954.

Portell Vilá, Herminio. *Céspedes, el padre de la patria cubana.* Madrid: Espasa Calpe, 1931.

————. *Historia de Cuba en sus relaciones con los Estados Unidos y España.* 3 vols. Havana: Jesús Montero, 1939.

————. *Narciso López y su época, 1848–1950.* 3 vols. Havana: Cultural, S.A., 1930–1958.

————. *Nueva historia de la República de Cuba.* Miami, Fla.: La Moderna Poesía, 1986.

Portuondo, Fernando. *Historia de Cuba.* Havana: Editorial Minerva, 1950.

Portuondo, Fernando, and Pichardo, Hortensia, eds. *Carlos Manuel de Céspedes: escritos.* 3 vols. Havana: Editorial de Ciencias Sociales, 1982.

Portuondo Linares, Serafín. *Los independientes de color.* 2d. ed. Havana: Librería Selecta, 1950.

Poumier-Taquechel, María. *Contribution a l'etude du banditisme social a Cuba: L'histoire et le mythe de Manuel García, "Rey de los Campos de Cuba" (1851–1895).* Paris: Editions L'Harmattan, 1986.

Poyo, Gerald E. *"With All and for the Good of All": The Emergence of Popular Nationalism in the Cuban Communities of the United States, 1848–1898.* Durham and London: Duke University Press, 1989.

Pratt, Julius. *America's Colonial Experiment.* New York: Prentice-Hall, 1950.

Primelles, León. *Crónica cubana, 1915–1918, 1919–1922.* 2 vols. Havana: Editorial Lex, 1955, 1957.

Pringle, Henry F. *The Life and Times of William Howard Taft.* 2 vols. New York and Toronto: Farrar and Rinehart, 1939.

————. *Theodore Roosevelt.* New York: Harcourt, Brace & Co., 1931.

Puñal, Luis de Juan. *Tirando de la manta.* Havana: Arroyo, Fernández y Cía., n.d.

Quesada, Gonsalo de. *Ignacio Mora.* New York: Imprenta América, 1894.

Raggi Ageo, Carlos M. *Condiciones económicas y sociales de la República de Cuba.* Havana: Editorial Lex, 1944.

Randín, Amado. *Cuba reivindicada.* Havana: Imprenta Bolívar, 1907.

Rea, George Bronson. *Facts and Fakes about Cuba.* New York: George Munro's Sons, 1897.

Regan, Maj. Carl J. *The Cuban Armed Forces: 1933–1952.* Gainesville: University of Florida Press, 1970.

Reyna Cossío, René E. *Estudios histórico-militares sobre la guerra de independencia de Cuba.* Havana: Impresora Modelo, S.A., 1954.

Rhodes, James Ford. *The McKinley and Roosevelt Administrations, 1897–1909.* New York: Macmillan Co., 1922.

Riera Hernández, Mario. *Bayamo política, 1898–1956.* Havana: Impresora Modelo, S.A., 1957.

———. *Cincuenta y dos años de política, Oriente, 1900–1952.* Havana: Llinás esq. a Belascoaín, 1953.

———. *Cuba libre, 1895–1958.* Miami: Colonial Press of Miami, 1968.

———. *Cuba política, 1899–1955.* Havana: Impresora Modelo, S.A., 1955.

———. *Cuba republicana, 1899–1958.* Miami: Editorial AIP, 1974.

———. *Ejército Libertador de Cuba, 1895–1898.* Miami: n.p., 1985.

———. *Historial obrero cubano, 1574–1965.* Miami: Rema Press, 1965.

Ripoll, Carlos. *José Martí: letras y huellas desconocidas.* New York: Eliseo Torres & Sons, 1976.

Rivero Muniz, José. *El movimiento laboral cubano durante el período 1906–1911.* Santa Clara, Las Villas, Cuba: Dirección de Publicaciones de la Universidad Central de Las Villas, 1962.

Robinson, Albert G. *Cuba and the Intervention.* London and Bombay: Longmans, Green and Co., 1905.

———. *Cuba Old and New.* New York: Longmans, Green and Co., 1915.

Rodríguez Altunaga, Rafael. *El general Emilio Núñez.* Havana: Sociedad Colombista Panamericana, 1958.

Rodríguez Demorizi, Emilio. *Maceo en Santo Domingo.* Barcelona: Gráficas M. Pareja, 1978.

———. *Martí en Santo Domingo.* Havana: Ucar, García, S.A., 1953.

Rodríguez García, José A. *Manuel Sanguily.* Havana: Imprenta Cuba Intelectual, 1927.

Rodríguez Morejón, Gerardo. *Menocal.* Havana: Cardenas y Cía., 1941.

Roig de Leuchsenring, Emilio. *La colonia superviva: Cuba a los veintidos años de república.* Havana: El Siglo XX, 1925.

———. *Cuba no debe su independencia a los Estados Unidos.* Havana: Sociedad Cubana de Estudios Históricos, 1950.

———. *Cuba y los Estados Unidos, 1805–1898.* Havana: Sociedad de Estudios Históricos e Internacionales, 1949.

———. *La Enmienda Platt: su interpretación primitiva y sus aplicaciones posteriores.* Havana: El Siglo XX, 1922. (1922 yearbook, Sociedad Cubana de Derecho Internacional)

———. *Los Estados Unidos vs. Cuba republicana.* 2 vols. Havana: Consejo Nacional de Cultura, 1964.

————. *La guerra cubana-hispanoamericana fué ganada por el lugarteniente general del Ejército Libertador Calixto García Iñiguez.* Havana: Oficina del Historiador de la Ciudad, 1955.

————. *La guerra hispano-cubano-americana.* Havana: Oficina del Historiador de la Ciudad, 1955.

————. *La guerra libertadora cubana de los treinta años, 1868–1898.* Havana: Oficina del Historiador de la Ciudad, 1952.

————. *Historia de la Enmienda Platt.* 2 vols. Havana: Cultural, S.A., 1935.

————. *El intervencionismo, mal de males de Cuba republicana.* San José de Costa Rica: Repertorio Americano, 1931.

————. *Juan Gualberto Gómez, paladín de la independencia y la libertad de Cuba.* Havana: Oficina del Historiador de la Ciudad, 1954.

————. *La lucha cubana por la república, contra la anexión y la enmienda Platt.* Havana: Oficina del Historiador de la Ciudad, 1952.

————. *Males y vicios de Cuba republicana, sus causas y sus remedios.* Havana: Oficina del Historiador de la Ciudad, 1959.

————. *Martí anti-imperialista.* Havana: Instituto Cubano del Libro, 1967.

————. *Máximo Gómez, el libertador de Cuba.* Havana: Oficina del Historiador de la Ciudad, 1959.

————. *1895 y 1898, dos guerras cubanas: ensayo de revaloración.* Havana: Cultural, S.A., 1945.

————. *Revolución y república en Maceo.* Havana: P. Fernández y Cía., 1945.

————. *Weyler en Cuba, un precursor de la barbarie fascista.* Havana: Editorial Páginas, 1947.

Romano, Julio. *Weyler, el hombre de hierro.* Madrid: Espasa-Calpe, 1934.

Ronning, C. Neale. *Jose Martí and the Emigré Colony in Key West: Leadership and State Formation.* New York: Praeger, 1990.

Rosell Planas, Rebeca. *Factores económicos, políticos y sociales de la Guerra Chiquita.* Havana: El Siglo XX, 1955.

————. *Las claves de Martí y el plan de alzamiento para Cuba.* Havana: Publicaciones del Archivo Nacional, 1948.

Sáinz de la Peña, Arturo F. *La revolución de agosto.* Havana: La Prueba, 1909.

Sánchez de Bustamante y Montoro, Antonio. *La ideología autonomista.* Havana: Molina y Cía., 1933.

Sanjenís, Avelino. *Tiburón.* Havana: Librería Hispanoamericana, 1915.

Santovenia, Emeterio. *Armonías y conflictos en torno a Cuba.* Mexico: Fondo de Cultura Económica, 1956.

————. *Estudios, biografías y ensayos.* Havana: Comisión Organizadora del Homenaje al Dr. Emeterio S. Santovenia, 1957.

————. *Gómez, el Máximo.* Havana: El Siglo XX, 1936.

————. *José Miguel Gómez. Contribución histórica a la conmemoración del primer centenario de su nacimiento.* Havana: Academia de la Historia de Cuba, 1958.

————. *El mayor general Bartolomé Masó, presidente de la república en armas y su influencia en la organizacion y desarrollo de la revolución por la independencia.* Havana: Cuadernos de Divulgación Histórica de la Asociación de Veteranos de la Independencia de Cuba, 1957.

————. *Los presidentes de Cuba libre.* Havana: Seoane y Fernández, 1930.

————. *Theodore Roosevelt y la soberanía de Cuba.* Havana: Academia de la Historia de Cuba, 1958.

Santovenia, Emeterio S., and Shelton, Raúl. *Cuba y su historia.* 3 vols. Miami: Rema Press, 1965.

Santovenia, Emeterio S., Llaverias, Joaquín, and Valverde, Antonio. *Las constituciones cubanas de Guáimaro (1869), Jimaguayú (1895) y La Yaya (1897).* Havana: La Universal, 1926.

Savignon, Tomás. *Quintín Banderas: El mambí sacrificado y escarnecido.* Havana: P. Fernández y Cía., 1948.

Schwartz, Rosalie. *Lawless Liberators: Political Banditry and Cuban Liberation.* Durham and London: Duke University Press, 1989.

Scott, James Brown. *Robert Bacon: Life and Letters.* New York: Doubleday, Page and Co., 1923.

Scott, Rebecca J. *Slave Emancipation in Cuba: The Transition to Free Labor, 1860–1899.* Princeton, N.J.: Princeton University Press, 1985.

Smith, Robert F. *The United States and Cuba: Business and Diplomacy, 1917–1960.* New Haven, Conn.: College and University Press, 1960.

————, ed. *Background to Revolution: The Development of Modern Cuba.* New York: Knopf, 1966.

Sosa de Quesada, Aristides. *Militarismo, anti-militarismo, pseudo-militarismo.* Havana: Instituto Cívico-Militar, 1939.

Souza, Benigno. *Ensayo histórico sobre la invasión.* Havana: Imprenta del Ejército, 1948.

————. *Máximo Gómez, el generalísimo.* Havana: Editorial Trópico, 1936.

————. *Máximo Gómez y las invasiones del 75 y del 95.* Havana: Editorial Minerva, 1932.

Strode, Hudson. *The Pageant of Cuba.* New York: Random House, 1936.

Suárez Vera, Luis. *General Emilio Núñez: su historia revolucionaria y su actuación en la vida pública.* Havana: Imprenta Pí y Margall, 1915.

Suchliki, Jaime. *Cuba: From Columbus to Castro.* New York: Charles Scribner's Sons, 1974.

————. *Historical Dictionary of Cuba.* Metuchen, N.J.: Scarecrow Press, 1988.

————. *University Students and Revolution in Cuba, 1920–1968.* Coral Gables, Fla.: University of Miami Press, 1969.

Testé, Ismael. *Historia eclesiástica de Cuba.* 5 vols. Barcelona: Artes Gráficas Medinacelli, S.A., 1969–1975.

Thomas, Hugh. *Cuba: The Pursuit of Freedom.* New York: Harper & Row, 1971.

Torres-Cuevas, Eduardo; Mencía, Mario; and Benítez, Augusto E. *El alma visible de Cuba: José Martí y el Partido Revolucionario Cubano.* Havana: Editorial de Ciencias Sociales, 1985.

Torriente, Cosme de la. *Fin de la dominación de España en Cuba (12 de agosto de 1898.)* Havana: El Siglo XX, 1948.

Trelles, Carlos M. *El progreso (1902 a 1905) y el retroceso (1906 a 1922) de la República de Cuba.* Havana: El Score, 1923.
Turton, Peter. *Jose Martí, Architect of Cuba's Freedom.* London: Zed Books, 1986.
Ubieta, Enrique. *Efemérides de la revolución cubana.* 4 vols. Havana: Molina y Cía., 1910.
Varios. *Apuntes biográficos del mayor general Serafín Sánchez.* Havana: Ediciones Unión, 1986.
Vázquez, Eduardo I. *Cuba independiente. Primer período presidencial: 1902–1906.* Havana: Editorial Acosta, 1906.
Velasco, Carlos de. *Aspectos nacionales.* Havana: Librería Studium, 1915.
———. *Estrada Palma: contribución histórica.* Havana: La Universal, 1911.
Yglesia Martínez, Teresita. *Cuba: primera república, segunda ocupación.* Havana: Editorial de Ciencias Sociales, 1976.
———. *El segundo ensayo de república.* Havana: Editorial de Ciencias Sociales, 1980.
Zarragoitia Ledesma, Leopoldo. *Biografía de Antonio Maceo.* Havana: Editorial Lex, 1945.

Articles

Abad, Diana. "Documentos del Partido Revolucionario Cubano." Parts 1–2. *Universidad de La Habana* 233 (1988): 155–162; 234 (1989): 103–111.
———. "Para un estudio del Partido Liberal (Autonomista)." *Universidad de La Habana* 233 (1988): 105–124.
Abel, Christopher A. "Controlling the Big Stick: Theodore Roosevelt and the Cuban Crisis of 1906." *Naval War College Review* 40: 3/319 (Summer 1987): 88–98.
Adam y Silva, Ricardo. "Las conspiraciones durante la tiranía en el ejército." *Bohemia* (Havana), October 14, 1934, pp. 14–15, 51–53.
———. "Reloj." *Diario Las Américas* (Miami), January 23, 1974, pp. 4, 17; October 17, 1974, pp. 4, 15; October 19, 1974, pp. 4, 17; July 12, 1975, pp. 4, 13.
Aguilar León, Luis E. "Cuba c. 1860–1934." In *The Cambridge History of Latin America,* edited by Leslie Bethel, vol. 5, pp. 229–263. Cambridge: Cambridge University Press, 1984–1986.
Aguirre, Sergio. "El cincuentenario de un gran crimen." *Cuba Socialista* (December 1962): 33–51.
———. "La desaparición del Ejército Libertador." *Cuba Socialista* 28, no. 3 (December 1963): 51–58.
Alea Lastra, Carmen. "Martí y el Partido Revolucionario Cubano." In Universidad de la Habana, Seminario Martiano, *Homenaje al maestro en el centenario de su nacimiento.* Havana: Imprenta Universitaria, 1953.
Alvarez Mola, Martha Verónica, and Martínez Pérez, Pedro. "Algo acerca del problema negro en Cuba hasta 1912." *Universidad de La Habana* 179 (May 1966): 79–93.

Amigó, Gustavo. "La Iglesia Católica en Cuba." *Revista Javeriana* (Bogotá), nos. 138 and 140, (September 1947): 166–175, 329–335.

Armas, Ramón de. "Apuntes acerca de la estrategia continental de José Martí: papel de Cuba y Puerto Rico." *Universidad Central de Las Villas* (Cuba) 1, 80 (January–April 1988): 9–34.

———. "La revolución pospuesta: destino de la revolución martiana de 1895." *Pensamiento crítico* (Havana) 49–50 (February–March 1971): 9–118.

Brooks, Sydney. "Cuba." *Fortnightly Review* 88 (November 1910): 796–806.

Brownell, Atherton. "The Cuban Republic on Trial." *Review of Reviews* 34 (October 1906): 424–425.

Bryce, James. "Some Reflections on the State of Cuba." *North American Review* 174 (March 1902): 449–456.

Bullard, Lt. Col. Robert L. "Education in Cuba." *Educational Review* 39 (April 1910): 378–384.

———. "The Army in Cuba." *Journal of the Military Service Institution* 41 (September 1907): 152–157.

Cabrera Cuello, Migdalia. "Presencia de Máximo Gómez en Villa Clara." *Islas* (Cuba) 85 (September–December 1986): 168–178.

Cárdenas, Raúl de. "Los gobiernos de Cuba: Estrada Palma, 1902–1906." *Bohemia* (Havana), June 5, 1938, pp. 26–27, 122–123, 126–127.

Carrera Jústiz, Francisco. "Los gobiernos de Cuba: Charles E. Magoon." *Bohemia* (Havana), June 5, 1938, pp. 20–21, 106, 118.

Carrillo Aldama, M. "The Cuban Government's Side." *Independent*, September 20, 1906, p. 664.

Carrión, Miguel de. "El desenvolvimiento social de Cuba en los últimos veinte años." *Cuba Contemporánea* 27 (September 1921): 5–27.

Castellanos, Jorge. "El pensamiento social de Máximo Gómez." *América* (Havana) (February–March 1946): 22–28.

Collazo Pérez, Enrique. "La Liga Patriótica Cubana y el Partido Revolucionario Cubano." *Revista de la Biblioteca Nacional José Martí* 31:2 (May–August 1989): 109–120.

Cortina, José Manuel. "Los gobiernos de Cuba: Alfredo Zayas, 1921–1925." *Bohemia* (Havana), June 5, 1938, pp. 46–49, 116–117, 121, 124–125, 128–129.

Coyula, Miguel. "Los gobiernos de Cuba: Mario G. Menocal, 1913–1921." *Bohemia* (Havana), June 5, 1938, pp. 44–45, 110–114.

Cronon, E. David. "Interpreting the New Good Neighbor Policy: The Cuban Crisis of 1933." *Hispanic American Historical Review* 39 (November 1959): 538–567.

Crowder, Enoch Herbert. "El memorándum no. 13" (in Spanish). *Heraldo de Cuba*, August 5, 1922.

DeBekker, Leander J. "Cuba and Her President." *Nation* 110 (February 21, 1920): 230–231.

Díaz de Acevedo, Roberto. "Más en torno al Manifiesto de Montecristi." *Bohemia* (Havana), January 29, 1930, pp. 4–5, 55–68.

Diez Acosta, Tomás. "Espíritu y voluntad de lucha: la Protesta de Baraguá." *Universidad de La Habana* 233 (1988): 125–131.

Duke, Cathy. "The Idea of Race: The Cultural Impact of American Intervention in Cuba, 1898–1912." In *Politics, Society, and Culture in the Caribbean*, edited by Blanca G. Silvestrini, 87–109. San Juan: Universidad de Puerto Rico, 1983.

Dupuy, William A. "Road Building by the United States in Cuba." *Scientific American*, February 13, 1909, pp. 136–138.

Estrada Palma, Tomás. "The Future of Cuba." *Independent*, April 3, 1902, p. 54.

Estrade, Paul. "Cuba en 1895: las tres vías de la burguesía insular." *Casa de las Américas* (Havana) 13 (September–October, 1972): 55–65.

Forbes-Lindsay, C. H. "Cuba: The Land of Promise." *World Today* 14 (February 1908): 141–50.

Foster, John W. "The Annexation of Cuba." *Independent*, October 25, 1906, pp. 965–968.

García y Azcuy, Angel A. "La Guardia Rural, su función, sus obligaciones y su espíritu." *Boletín del Ejército* (Cuba) 1 (September–October 1950): 56–57.

Giberga, Eliseo. "Las ideas políticas en Cuba en el siglo XIX." *Cuba Contemporánea* 10 (April 1916): 347–381.

González del Valle y Ramírez, Francisco. "El clero en la revolución cubana." *Cuba contemporánea* 18 (1918): 140–205.

González Valdés, José. "La Guardia Rural." *Boletín del Ejército* (Cuba) 6 (February 1919): 783–785.

Guas Inclán, Rafael. "Los gobiernos de Cuba: Gerardo Machado, 1925–1933." *Bohemia* (Havana), June 5, 1938, pp. 54–55, 100–101, 105.

Guerra Puente, Faustino. "Causes of the Cuban Insurrection." *North American Review* 599 (September 1906): 538–540.

Guiral Moreno, Mario. "El problema de la burocracia en Cuba." *Cuba Contemporánea* 2 (August 1913): 260.

———. "Nuestros problemas políticos, económicos y sociales." *Cuba Contemporánea* 5 (August 1914): 401–424.

Hanna, Capt. Matthew E. "The Necessity of Increasing the Efficiency of the Cuban Army." *Journal of the Military Service Institution* 35 (July 1904): 28–36.

Hernández y Hernández, Heriberto. "Origen del ejército cubano." *Boletín del Ejército* (Cuba) 27 (June 1929): 459–460.

Hershey, Amos S. "Intervention and the Recognition of Cuban Independence." *Annals of the American Academy of Political and Social Science* 9 (May 1898).

Hitchman, James H. "The American Touch in Colonial Administration: Leonard Wood in Cuba, 1898–1902." *Americas* 24, no. 4 (April 1968): 394–403.

Horrego Estuch, Leopoldo. "La Mejorana: lo que allí ocurrió." *Bohemia* (Havana), May 8, 1949, pp. 3, 117.

Iglesias, Fe. "Población y clases sociales en la segunda mitad del siglo XIX."

Revista de la Biblioteca Nacional José Martí 24, no. 3 (September–December 1982): 100–103.

Inglis, William. "The Armed Struggle for Control of Cuba." *Harper's Weekly*, September 29, 1906, pp. 1344–1347, 1363.

———. "The Collapse of the Cuban House of Cards." *Harper's Weekly*, October 20, 1906, pp. 1488–1491, 1505.

———. "The Disappointed Rebels in Wait about Havana." *Harper's Weekly*, October 13, 1906, pp. 1454–1456.

———. "How Cubans Fight Cubans." *Harper's Weekly*, October 6, 1906, pp. 1416–18, 1434–1435.

———. "How the Warlike Cubans Gave Up Their Arms." *Harper's Weekly*, November 3, 1906, pp. 1564–1566.

———. "The Last Act of Cuba's Tragi-Comedy of Insurrection." *Harper's Weekly*, October 27, 1906, pp. 1524–1526, 1541.

———. "The Rain-Coat of Rodríguez." *Harper's Weekly*, July 27, 1907, pp. 1092–1093.

———. "With the Rebel Leader in the Cuban Hills." *Harper's Weekly*, September 29, 1906, pp. 1380–1383.

Kuethe, Allan J. "The Development of the Cuban Military as a Socio-Political Elite, 1763–83." *Hispanic American Historical Review* 61, no. 4 (November 1981): 695–704.

———. "Guns, Subsidies, and Commercial Privilege: Some Historical Factors in the Emergence of the Cuban National Character, 1763–1815." In University of Pittsburgh, Center for Latin American Studies, *Cuban Studies*. Pittsburgh, Pa.: University of Pittsburgh Press, 1986, pp. 123–138.

"Las relaciones Gómez-Carrillo." *Islas* (Cuba) 85 (September–December 1986): 179–199.

Laurent, Emilio. "Datos esenciales de la expedición de Gibara." *Bohemia* (Havana), August 20, 1934, pp. 24–50.

Leon, Waldemar. "Caicaje: batalla final de una revuelta." *Bohemia* (Havana), May 22, 1960, pp. 100–102, 113.

Le Riverend Brusone, Julio. "Cuba: la revolución de 1868 como transición ideológica." *Casa de las Américas* (Havana) 14 (May–June 1974): 3–18.

———. "Raíces del 24 de febrero: la economía y la sociedad cubana de 1878 a 1895." *Cuba Socialista* 5 (February 1965): 1–17.

———. "Sobre la industria azucarera de Cuba durante el siglo XIX." *El Trimestre Económico* (Cuba) 9 (1944): 52–70.

Llaverías, Joaquín. "El Manifiesto de Montecristi." *Patria y Libertad* (Havana) 1, no. 1 (May 1943): 8–9.

Lockmiller, David A. "The Advisory Law Commission of Cuba." *Hispanic American Historical Review* 17 (February 1937): 2–29.

———. "La base legal de la intervención de los Estados Unidos en Cuba en 1906." *Revista bimestre cubana* 38 (September–December 1936): 268–281.

———. "The Settlement of the Church Property Question in Cuba." *Hispanic American Historical Review* 17 (November 1937): 488–498.

MacGaffey, Wyatt. "Social Structure and Mobility in Cuba." *Anthropological Quarterly* 35, no. 2 (April 1961): 94–109.

Márquez Sterling, Carlos. "Alfredo Zayas, el abogado de la revolución de 1906." *Bohemia* (Havana), March 19, 1950, pp. 62–63, 92–93.

Martínez Ortiz, Rafael. "Juicio acerca de los sucesos políticos de Cuba en 1906." *Cuba Contemporánea* 15 (October 1917): 118–130.

Maza, Manuel P., S.J. "Cuba, Iglesia y Máximo Gómez." *Estudios Sociales* (Dominican Republic), no. 67 (January–March 1987): 40–54.

Meyer, Leo J. "The United States and the Cuban Revolution of 1917." *Hispanic American Historical Review* 10 (May 1930): 138–166.

Millet, Allan R. "The General Staff and the Cuban Intervention of 1906." *Military Affairs* 31 (Fall 1967): 113–119.

———. "The Rise and Fall of the Cuban Rural Guard, 1898–1912." *Americas* 29 (October 1972): 191–213.

Minger, Ralph Eldin. "William H. Taft and the United States Intervention in Cuba in 1906." *Hispanic American Historical Review* 41 (February 1961): 75–89.

Moore, John Basset. "Cuban Belligerency." *Forum* 21 (May 1896): 288–295.

Moreno Fraginals, Manuel. "Plantations in the Caribbean: Cuba, Puerto Rico and the Dominican Republic in the Late Nineteenth Century." In *Between Slavery and Free Labor: The Spanish-speaking Caribbean in the Nineteenth Century*, edited by Manuel Moreno Fraginals, Frank Moya Pons, and Stanley L. Eugerman, pp. 13–14. Baltimore and London: Johns Hopkins University Press, 1985.

"Orígenes de nuestro ejército." *Boletín del Ejército* (Cuba) 3 (July–August 1952): 35–46.

Ortiz, Fernando. "La crisis política cubana, sus causas y remedios." *Revista bimestre cubana* 14 (January–February 1919): 5–22.

———. "La reforma electoral de Crowder en Cuba." *Reforma Social* (Cuba) 20 (July 1921): 214–225.

Osa, Enrique de la. "Una interpretación materialista de la Guerra de los Diez Años." *Bohemia*, October 8, 1961, pp. 54 ff.

Paradela, Francisco de. "La paga del Ejército Libertador y la economía cubana." *Revista Bimestre Cubana* 47 (May–June 1941): 431–444.

Pasalodos, Dámaso. "El gobierno del General Gómez." *Bohemia* (Havana), June 12, 1938, pp. 8–9, 57.

Perdomo y Granela, Bernardo. "La Guardia Rural en la conservación del orden público." *Boletín del Ejército* 7 (May–June 1956): 40–44.

Pérez, Jr., Louis A. "The First Cuban Revolution, 1895–1898: An Unfinished Agenda." *Revista Interamericana* 14, no. 4 (Winter–Spring 1984): 133–153.

———. "The Imperial Design: Politics and Pedagogy in Occupied Cuba, 1899–1902." In University of Pittsburgh, Center for Latin American Studies, *Cuban Studies 12*. Pittsburgh, Pa.: University of Pittsburgh Press, 1982, pp. 1–19.

———. "In Defense of Hegemony: Summer Welles and the Cuban Revolution of 1933." In *Ambassadors in Foreign Policy: The Influence of Individuals on U.S.–Latin American Policy*, edited by C. Neale Ronning and Albert P. Vannucci, pp. 28–48. New York: Praeger, 1987.

————. "The Military and Electoral Politics: The Cuban Election of 1920." *Military Affairs* 37 (February 1973): 5–8.

————. "Politics, Peasants, and People of Color: The 1912 'Race War' in Cuba Reconsidered." *Hispanic American Historical Review* 66, no. 3 (August 1986): 509–539.

————. "The Pursuit of Pacification: Banditry and the United States Occupation of Cuba, 1889–1902." *Journal of Latin American Studies* 18, no. 2 (November 1986): 313–332.

————. "Vagrants, Beggars, and Bandits: Social Origins of Cuban Separatism, 1878–1895." *American Historical Review* 90 (December 1985): 109–121.

Pérez, Luis Marino. "Cuba and the United States." *Inter-America* (English ed.) 5 (August 1922): 358–361.

Pérez Vega, Oscar. "El frente interior y la Guardia Rural." *Boletín del Ejército* 6 (May–June 1955): 83–91.

Platt, Orville, H. "Cuba's Claim upon the United States." *North American Review* 170 (August 1902): 145–151.

————. "The Pacification of Cuba." *Independent*, June 27, 1901.

————. "The Solution of the Cuban Problem." *World's Work* 2 (May 1901): 729–735.

Poey Baró, Dionisio. "Apuntes sobre la participación de José Martí en el movimiento revolucionario cubano durante los años 1882 y 1883." *Anuario del Centro de Estudios Martianos* (Cuba) 9 (1988): 269–283.

Portell Vilá, Herminio. "La Chambelona en Camagüey." *Bohemia* (Havana), May 8, 1960, pp. 12–13, 119.

————. "La Chambelona en Las Villas." *Bohemia* (Havana), May 15, 1960, pp. 36–37, 98.

————. "La Chambelona en Occidente." *Bohemia* (Havana), May 22, 1960, pp. 36–37, 82.

————. "La Chambelona en Oriente." *Bohemia* (Havana), April 24, 1960, pp. 36–37.

————. "La intervención militar norteamericana." *El Mundo* (Havana), May 20, 1952, pp. 34–36.

Portuondo, Fernando. "Martí y el Partido Revolucionario Cubano." *Islas* (Cuba) 11 (October–December 1968): 171–174.

Portuondo, José Antonio. "Ideología del Partido Revolucionario Cubano." *Cuadernos de Historia Habanera* 22 (1942): 63–70.

Poyo, Gerald E. "Evolution of Cuban Separatist Thought in the Emigré Communities of the United States, 1848–1895." *Hispanic American Historical Review* 66, no. 3 (August 1986): 485–507.

Poyo, Raúl A. "Génesis del Partido Revolucionario Cubano." *El Mundo* (Havana), May 20, 1934, p. 5.

Prieto, Enrique. "The Organization of the Cuban Army." *Military Engineer* 20 (September–October 1928): 386–389.

Raggi, Carlos M. "Las estructuras sociales en Cuba en los fines de la etapa colonial." *Exilio, Revista de Humanidades* (Miami) (Spring–Fall 1970): 63–80.

Ripoll, Carlos. "Grandezas y miserias de La Mejorana." *Diario Las Américas* (Miami), May 20, 1987, pp. 10C–11C.

Rivero Muniz, José. "La primera huelga general obrera en Cuba republicana." *Islas* (Cuba) (May–August 1961): 4–13.

Robinson, Albert G. "Cuban Self Government." *Independent*, December 13, 1900, pp. 2968–2971.

———. "Our Legacy to the Cuban Republic." *Forum* 33 (June 1902): 450–458.

———. "Some Cuban Opinions." *Independent*, May 9, 1901, p. 1058.

Roig de Leuchsenring, Emilio. "La guerra de independencia de 1895: el Manifiesto de Montecristi." *Carteles* (Havana), May 9, 1948, p. 12.

———. "La guerra de independencia de 1895: el Partido Revolucionario Cubano y el general en jefe del Ejército Libertador." *Carteles* (Havana), May 2, 1948.

———. "La guerra de independencia de 1895: el plan de alzamiento de Fernandina." *Boletín del Archivo Nacional* (Cuba) 47 (January–December 1948): 16–25.

Rowe, Leo Stanton. "The Reorganization of Local Government in Cuba." *Annals of the American Academy of Political and Social Science* 25 (March 1905): 311–321.

Rubens, Horatio S. "The Insurgent Government in Cuba." *North American Review* 498 (May 1898): 560–569.

Runcie, James. "American Misgovernment of Cuba." *North American Review* 170 (February 1900).

Sanguily, Manuel. "Sobre la génesis de la Enmienda Platt." *Cuba Contemporánea* 30, no. 118 (October 1922): 117–125.

Santí, Enrico M. "José Martí and the Cuban Revolution." In *Proceedings of a Conference Held at UCLA, March 1–2, 1985*. Los Angeles: UCLA Latin American Center Publications, 1986, pp. 13–23.

Scott, James Brown. "The Attitude of the United States toward Political Disturbances in Cuba." *American Journal of International Law* 11 (April 1917): 419–423.

Smith, Robert F. "Cuba: Laboratory for Dollar Diplomacy, 1898–1917." *Historian* 28 (August 1966): 586–609.

Sosa de Quesada, Aristides. "El militarismo." *Ultra* (Havana) 7 (September 1939): 276–278.

Spinden, Herbert J. "Elecciones espurias en Cuba." *Reforma Social* (New York and Havana) 19 (April 1921): 353–367.

———. "Shall the United States Intervene in Cuba?" *World's Work* 41 (March 1921): 465–483.

Stokes, William S. "National and Local Violence in Cuban Politics." *Southwestern Social Science Quarterly* 34 (September 1953): 57–63.

Suchliki, Jaime. "Stirrings of Cuban Nationalism: The Student Generation of 1930." *Journal of Inter-American Studies* 10 (July 1968): 350–368.

Thomas, Hugh. "Cuba from the Middle of the Eighteenth to circa 1870." *The Cambridge History of Latin America*, edited by Leslie Bethel, vol. 3, pp. 277–296. Cambridge: Cambridge University Press, 1984–1986.

Toledo Sande, Luis. "José Martí y Máximo Gómez: en el camino de la hermandad." *Casa de las Américas* (Havana) 27: 158 (September–October 1986): 13–29.

Velasco, Carlos de. "Estrada Palma y la formación de ciudadanos." *Cuba Contemporánea* 18 (November 1918): 261–273.

Weightman, Richard C. "Cuba's American Governor." *Review of Reviews* 34 (November 1906): 556–559.

Welles, Summer. "Is America Imperialistic?" *Atlantic Monthly*, September 1924, pp. 412–423.

Williams, Talcott. "The Causes of the Cuban Insurrection." *Outlook*, September 15, 1906, pp. 111–114.

Wood, Leonard. "The Existing Conditions and Needs in Cuba." *North American Review* 168 (May 1899): 593–601.

———. "The Military Government of Cuba." *Annals of the American Academy of Political and Social Science* 31 (March 1903): 153–182.

Wright, Irene A. "The Cart-Roads of Mister Magoon." *World Today* 16 (June 1909): 641–648.

Yeste y Cabrera, Adolfo. "Génesis y transformaciones del ejército de Cuba." *El Ejército Constitucional, Revista Oficial* 6 (September–October 1941): 284–285.

Index